European B

F R A M E W O R K S

Each book in the Frameworks series is a
comprehensive and concise introduction to
the subject. The books are well structured
and provide a step-by-step guide to essential
principles. They develop a basic framework
of understanding to underpin further study
of core business, financial and legal subjects
in the higher education curriculum.

FRAMEWORKS

European Business

Roger Bennett
BA, MSc(Econ), DPhil
London Guildhall University

FINANCIAL TIMES

Prentice Hall

An imprint of **Pearson Education**

Harlow, England · London · New York · Reading, Massachusetts · San Francisco
Toronto · Don Mills, Ontario · Sydney · Tokyo · Singapore · Hong Kong · Seoul
Taipei · Cape Town · Madrid · Mexico City · Amsterdam · Munich · Paris · Milan

Pearson Education Limited
Edinburgh Gate
Harlow
Essex CM20 2JE
England

and Associated Companies throughout the world

Visit us on the World Wide Web at:
http://www.pearsoneduc.com

First published in Great Britain 1997

The right of Roger Bennett to be identified as Author of
this Work has been asserted by him in accordance with
the Copyright, Designs and Patents Act 1988.

© Pearson Professional Limited 1997

ISBN 0 273 63438 0

British Library Cataloguing in Publication Data
A CIP catalogue record for this book can be obtained from the British Library.

10 9 8 7 6 5 4 3
05 04 03 02 01

Printed and bound in Great Britain by Antony Rowe Ltd, Eastbourne

CONTENTS

PREFACE

European business is changing faster and more radically than at any time in its history, and coping with the new situation is perhaps the dominant issue currently facing European firms. Laws and practices that regulated commercial activity for generations have altered fundamentally; national company laws now have to conform with EU Directives; new technical product standards and industrial health and safety requirements apply; fresh rules on intellectual property, advertising, marketing and sales promotion, agency, consumer protection and public procurement have come into operation. A European single currency is on the horizon, and an expanded EU role in labour relations and employee protection is seemingly assured. Enlargement of the European Union, moreover, creates the second largest association of industrially developed countries (after NAFTA) in the entire world, generating enormous opportunities for innovative companies.

Clearly, all students of business, management, economics and other social sciences require at least a working knowledge of the European Union, of EU laws and regulations, management systems and practices in other European countries, the problems confronted by the European Union, and the nature and extent of Western Europe's business relationships with the rest of the world. This book covers all the major subject areas connected with European business and trade, seeking to present the material concisely and in a straightforward, informative and readable way. It assumes that readers are not familiar with EU affairs or with continental European business practices. EU institutions and common policies are covered as well as commercial issues. The text contains chapters on European business environments, EU business laws, the organisation of European companies, marketing, and the management of human resources. Logistics, distribution and other aspects of cross-border European operations are also discussed. The book is intended for use by undergraduates undertaking degrees in management and business studies, economics, law, politics and other social services, and by students of the main professional bodies who require up-to-date information on the European business scene. It should be especially valuable to students preparing for the LCCI Diploma in European Business Administration, the European Business unit of the IAM, and as supplementary reading for students of international marketing, human resources management and international accounting and finance.

My thanks are due to Rosalind Bailey who word-processed the text, to Adrienne Crossley for research assistance, and to Pitman Publishing for efficiently expediting the production of the book.

1

THE EUROPEAN UNION

EU ORIGINS

1. Origins and development of European unification

In 1951 six countries (Belgium, France, West Germany, Italy, Luxembourg and the Netherlands) signed the Treaty of Paris establishing the European Coal and Steel Community (ECSC); an arrangement involving the abolition of import duties on cross-border movements of coal and steel within the six countries, while imposing a common external tariff on supplies of these products from the rest of the world. Also, the six member states agreed to co-ordinate their national policies relating to the payment of government subsidies to domestic coal and steel industries, to remove restrictions on the free movement of coal and steel within the ECSC, and to outlaw discriminatory practices that impeded free competition in relation to these goods. The European Economic Community (EEC) was a common market of the same six countries set up in 1957 via the Treaty of Rome. A 'common market' is a trading group with tariff-free trade among member states in conjunction with the application of a common external tariff to imports from outside the group. In a common market, quotas and other non-tariff barriers are determined by and for the entire common market, not by individual members. Business laws, rules on competition, etc., are harmonised among member nations and there is free movement within the market of capital and labour as well as goods. Commercial laws drafted by the authorities of the common market override domestic national legislation. This differs from a 'free trade area', which is a grouping of nations which remove trade barriers against each other, but with each member country continuing to determine and apply its own unique set of barriers (tariffs, quotas, etc.) to the entry of imports from other nations that do not belong to the free trade area.

EURATOM (the European Atomic Energy Community) was also constituted in 1957 as a means for developing the peaceful use of nuclear and atomic energy within the six states. Initially, EURATOM, the EEC and ECSC were managed by separate administrative institutions. From 1967 onwards, however, these institutions were merged and the resulting bodies used to manage EURATOM, the ECSC and the EEC, which collectively became known as the European Community (EC). Denmark, the UK and Ireland joined the EC in 1973, followed by Greece in 1981, Spain and Portugal in 1986, and Austria, Finland and Sweden in 1995. Other countries are scheduled to enter in the near future, and many nations have either applied for membership or expressed their wish to accede to the Community (now known as the European Union, see below).

The desire for European unification

At least 40 million Europeans (east and west) died in consequence of the two World Wars 1914-18 and 1939-45 (Hartmann 1983). Europe in 1945 was devastated. Mass bombing, occupation by foreign armies, the use of industrial capacity for armaments production rather than for the supply of civilian goods, destruction of the housing stock, disruption of international trade and the collapse of agriculture in many regions had impoverished European nations and left the continent disunited and heavily dependent on US foreign aid. It seemed, moreover, that no West European country had actually gained anything from the war. Much of Germany had been reduced to rubble; France, Benelux and Denmark experienced nearly five years of military occupation; while the United Kingdom (the dominant power of pre-War Western Europe) was in a perilous economic state. Food rationing applied throughout Western Europe until well into the 1950s.

It was obvious to many influential politicians and other important decision makers that the best long-term prospects for peace, economic development and political stability lay in West European integration. Foremost among the advocates of closer economic and political ties between European states was Jean Monnet, the Minister of Planning in the immediate post-Second World War French government of Charles De Gaulle. Monnet had been closely involved in the negotiations for a political union between Britain and France proposed following the invasion of France by Germany in 1940. This union would have entailed common defence and foreign policies as well as the harmonisation of financial and economic activities. The fall of France in June 1940 prevented the union from going ahead although Monnet was able to develop his ideas in subsequent years, culminating in his drafting of the 'Schuman Plan' (named after Robert Schuman, the French Foreign Minister) through which coal and steel production in France and West Germany were to be pooled. Hence neither France nor Germany could dominate the control of these (then) strategically important resources.

2. The Treaty of Paris and the Treaty of Rome

Under the Paris Treaty the production of coal and steel within the ECSC was to be supervised by a Council of Ministers drawn from the six member nations and assisted by a secretariat based in Luxembourg. A Court of Justice to interpret and enforce the Treaty was also established. From the outset the ECSC had its own 'legal personality' to which member countries transferred some of their sovereign rights. The High Authority of the ECSC (of which Monnet was appointed President) was empowered to adopt legally binding Decisions. There was also a Common Assembly to represent the peoples of member states, though it only had an advisory role.

The Treaty of Rome

The Treaty of Rome demanded the free movement of goods, labour, services and capital within the six founding countries; the establishment of common external tariffs on all imported products; the harmonisation of business laws in member countries; and common policies for agriculture, transport and business competition. It is important to note that the precise forms of the common policies were not specified, only that they be devised and implemented. Thus for example, the way the common agricultural policy developed was not determined by the Treaty of Rome. As with the ECSC the Treaty gave the EEC a distinct legal personality and set up institutions to administer the system: an Assembly (subsequently renamed the European Parliament), a Council of Ministers with the power to legislate, a Court of Justice, and a European Commission (akin to the High Authority of the ECSC). The EURATOM Treaty was signed in Paris on the same day (25 March 1957). EURATOM also had its own autonomous institutions prior to the Merger Treaty effective from 1967. Thereafter the same institutions governed the ECSC, EEC and EURATOM, but derived their powers and functions from whichever Treaty they were acting under at a particular moment in time. Hence the European Commission was technically the Commission of the European Communities (plural) rather than just the Commission of the EEC.

Other key events

A number of other events had a bearing on Europe's progress towards economic and political unification. The Benelux customs union of Belgium, Luxembourg and the Netherlands was formed in 1948, with tariff-free internal trade and a common external tariff. Lessons learned from the Benelux experiment proved invaluable when setting up the European common market. In 1952, Monnet suggested the formation of a European Defence Community and a European Political Community, neither of which were implemented, although a wide-ranging Franco-German Co-operation Agreement was signed in 1963.

Dislike of the idea of European political integration was a major factor contributing to the formation in 1958 of the European Free Trade Area (EFTA) by Austria, Denmark, Norway, Portugal, Sweden, Switzerland and the UK. EFTA emerged as a response to the EEC from European countries which wanted free trade, but without further economic unification. All these states subsequently defected to the EU, except for Norway and Switzerland. EFTA now comprises the latter two nations plus Iceland and Liechtenstein (Finland was also a member for a time, prior to it joining the EU in 1995). In 1970 the central banks of the six EC countries agreed a monetary support mechanism, and in 1981 the European Currency Unit was introduced.

3. The Single European Act

All internal import tariffs within the EC had been abolished by 1968, but a number of non-tariff barriers to intra-Community trade persisted, notably national differences in technical standards, rules on public procurement, and the provision of work permits to foreign EC nationals. In 1985, therefore, EC heads of state agreed to accelerate the development of a single European market. This resulted in each EC country implementing in 1986/87 the Single European Act (SEA) via their domestic legislatures. The SEA transformed the EC from being little more than a customs union into a genuine single market with complete freedom for Community businesses to set up anywhere in the EC and to engage in cross-border intra-Community trade *as if* they were doing business within a single country. Under the revised terms of operation of the Economic Community the following were to apply:

(a) Free movement of labour, with workers from member nations able (i) to obtain employment and live in any Community state, (ii) to receive unemployment benefit in their chosen country of residence, and (iii) to have equal access to public housing and to education for their children in the adopted nation. Individuals could then retire and continue to live in that country.

(b) Free movement of capital, so that firms and individuals could obtain finance and/or deposit funds anywhere in the Community. All intra-Community exchange controls have now been abolished.

(c) Freedom of establishment for businesses, enabling any EC resident to commence operations (or purchase an existing firm) in any Community state and to compete on equal terms with local enterprises.

(d) Open access to public sector contracts (i.e. supply contracts for national and local government agencies and publicly owned organisations) for all EC firms.

The Single European Market was to be completed by January 1993. Accordingly, hundreds of measures were initiated in order to dismantle trade barriers between EC nations; remove obstacles to free competition; harmonise technical standards and business procedures; and generally promote European economic integration. Also a number of social initiatives (such as aid for regional development and/or for the retraining of unemployed workers) accompanied the programme with a view to improving living standards and stimulating growth. Qualified majority voting (*see* 16) was introduced for matters relating to the harmonisation of technical standards and business practices; the free movement of goods, services and capital; freedom of establishment for firms; and the common recognition of the qualifications of workers.

4. The Maastricht Treaty 1992

This agreement (formally known as the Treaty on European Union) concerned economic and political union. The majority of EC members committed themselves to the introduction of a single European currency by the end of the decade. Britain (and subsequently Denmark) negotiated the right not to adopt the common currency if they so wish, and the UK further refused to accept the European Social Charter (*see* 16:31). The Maastricht Treaty also included agreements on common foreign policy and defence, and established a Cohesion Fund to promote economic development in the EC's poorer regions. The EC changed its name to the European Union following ratification of the Treaty by member states in 1993.

4

The Maastricht Protocol

A version of the European Social Charter was included as a separate chapter of the proposed Maastricht Agreement. Britain used its veto to prevent acceptance of this Social Chapter, but the (then) other eleven countries wished to go ahead. Accordingly, all 12 countries agreed that the EU eleven excluding the UK could use EU procedures and institutions to implement the Social Chapter, with the UK 'dropping out' of deliberations and discussions on these matters and not being obliged to apply decisions arrived at by the other eleven states.

5. How the EU is financed

The annual budget of the European Union averages about one per cent of its aggregate gross domestic product and around three per cent of EU member countries' combined budgetary expenditure. Each year's budget has to be approved by the Council of Ministers (*see* 7) and the European Parliament (*see* 9). Collection of EU budget revenues is based on the 'principle of own resources', the money coming from:

- customs duties collected by each member country from the common external tariff
- agricultural levies
- up to one per cent of a country's VAT receipts on certain goods and services.

The above funds are deemed to belong to the EU, not national governments – which in effect act as tax collectors for the Union.

Agricultural support and the common fisheries policy absorb the bulk of the EU budget. Otherwise the money is spent on regional development (accounting for about 12 per cent of total budgetary expenditure), the European Social Fund (two per cent), the Social Cohesion Fund (two per cent), plus a variety of lesser Funds and support programmes (e.g. for research and technical development). The Social Fund is intended to help reduce youth unemployment and encourage vocational training; the Cohesion Fund was set up in 1992 to improve the economic and industrial infrastructures of less-developed EU nations, especially in relation to transport systems and the physical environment.

The budgetary process

The budgetary process is as follows:

(a) By May of each year the European Commission calculates the percentage rate by which 'compulsory' expenditure (*see* 10) needs to be increased.

(b) By July the main EU institutions (Parliament, the Commission, the ECJ, the Court of Auditors and ECOSOC – *see* below) submit estimates of their expenditures for the following year.

(c) In September the Commission prepares a preliminary draft budget and places this before the Council of Ministers, which has to adopt it (by qualified majority voting if appropriate) by early October.

(d) The draft budget must be handed over to the European Parliament within 45 days, and changes may be recommended. These suggestions have to be considered by the Council of Ministers within 15 days. The draft now returns to Parliament, where it is accepted or rejected. If the budget is thrown out a fresh draft needs to be submitted.

Criticisms of the EU budget

Critics of EU budgetary systems allege that far too much money is spent on the common agricultural policy (CAP) and not enough on regional and industrial development; that there is little budgetary discipline (spending seems constantly to expand); that costs will soar as poorer countries from Eastern Europe and the Mediterranean join the Union (all requiring big subsidies from the rest of the EU); and that the national distribution of contributions to the budget is grossly unfair. For example, the UK is one of the less well off members of the EU, yet is one of its largest financial contributors. This is because the country's agricultural sector is small and efficient and hence receives relatively little from the CAP, and because Britain is a major international trader so that it imports large amounts of goods from non-EU sources (a significant part of the duties on these imports have to be turned over to the EU). The counter-argument to complaints about the extent of the UK contribution is that such duties actually 'belong' to the EU and not the United Kingdom, i.e. that they are the EU's *own resources*.

EU INSTITUTIONS

The principal EU institutions are the European Commission, the Council of Ministers, the European Court of Justice, and the European Parliament. Additionally there are three major EU committees (the Economic and Social Committee, the Consumer Consultative Council, and the Committee of the Regions) plus two support organisations: the Court of Auditors and the European Investment Bank.

6. The European Commission

Located in Brussels the European Commission is effectively the civil service of the EU. There are 20 Commissioners. Germany, Spain, France, Italy and the United Kingdom each contribute two Commissioners; other countries contribute one. National governments select their countries' Commissioners, in 'common accord' with other member countries and with the approval of the European Parliament. Appointments are for (renewable) five-year terms. Most Commissioners are ex-politicians, although former trade union leaders and business people sometimes serve. The President of the Commission has to be agreed by the governments of all EU states. Once appointed, Commissioners are obliged to adopt pan-EU rather than nationalistic perspectives.

Each Commissioner has a specific area of responsibility and is advised and assisted by around half a dozen personal appointees. The distribution of responsibilities is determined by the Commission itself, by majority vote if necessary.

Commissioners meet on a weekly basis in a College of Commissioners at which important decisions are taken. Staff reporting to the Commission (of which there are nearly 14,000) are organised into Directorates-General, which are then placed into groups for allocation to the responsibility of particular commissioners. Examples of Directorates-General are DG II (Economic and Financial Affairs), DG VI (Agriculture), DG XII (Science and Research and Development), and DG XVII (Energy).

The Commission's role is threefold:

1 To plan policies arising from the Treaty of Rome, the Single European Act, the Maastricht Agreement and other relevant Treaties and hence to initiate proposals to the Council of Ministers (*see* 7) for new Directives and Regulations.

2 To implement decisions taken by the Council of Ministers. Accordingly, the Commission drafts the annual EU budget (which it then places before the Council of Ministers and the European Parliament), administers the various funds established by the EU (the social and regional funds for example), and negotiates international agreements on behalf of the Union.

3 To act as the guardian of EU Treaties. In this capacity the Commission is empowered to take member states to the European Court of Justice (*see* 9) if they fail to comply with EU legislation, and will mediate disputes between member states' governments. The Commission has a limited power to legislate in its own right in the field of competition policy, and may impose fines on companies that violate EU competition regulations. Decisions within the Commission are taken via simple majority voting.

The Commission is advised by a network of committees, of which there are two sorts:

1 *Expert committees* comprising specialists and technical experts nominated by national governments. Some of these committees meet on a periodic basis, others are essentially *ad hoc*. Examples of expert committees are the Advisory Committee on Restrictive Practices and Dominant Positions and the Advisory Committee on Action for the Elderly.

2 *Consultative committees* made up of representatives of interest groups. These are organised, chaired, and funded by the Commission itself without reference to national governments. UNICE and ETUC are examples of organisations that contribute members to consultative committees.

Criticisms of the Commission are that:

- It has too much power (possibly because other EU institutions have failed to provide firm leadership).
- Although nominally independent, Commissioners do in fact possess national and political allegiances which might influence their judgement.
- At the time they are appointed Commissioners are typically drawn from the ranks of the political parties that currently form the governments of member states. Governments change, however, so that the political complexion of the Commission at any given moment might not reflect political opinion in member nations.

7. The Council of Ministers

This is the major decision-making body of the European Union and consists of representatives of the governments of each EU country. Membership of the Council is constantly changing according to the subject being discussed. Thus, for example, the Council will comprise Ministers of Transport when transport matters are under consideration; Ministers of Agriculture when agricultural topics are being discussed, and so on. Ministers from Austria and Sweden have four votes each. Luxembourg has two votes; Denmark, Finland and Ireland three; Austria and Sweden four; Belgium, Greece, the Netherlands and Portugal five; Spain eight; and France, Germany, Italy and the UK ten. The Council has a rotating presidency with member nations taking turns, in alphabetical order, to assume this role for six month periods.

Holding the Presidency is a serious matter, since it involves, *inter alia*:

- seeking consensus among member nations on recent EU initiatives
- arranging, setting agendas for and chairing all Council meetings
- proposing compromises when disputes arise
- representing the Council in dealings with non-member countries and non-EU institutions
- ensuring consistency in the development of EU policies. This is facilitated by a 'Troika' arrangement involving meetings between representatives of the current, preceding and immediately forthcoming Presidencies.
- advancing the interests of the European Union.

Council meets normally between 90 and 100 times a year. It has its own Secretariat and a staff of around 2000 people.

Support and administrative work for the Council of Ministers is provided by COREPER (the Committee of Permanent Representatives) comprising the Ambassadors to the EU of the member countries, assisted by their advisers and national civil servants. The role of the Council of Ministers is to create Directives and Regulations (which are legally binding on all member states), according to the procedure outlined in **16**.

8. The European Council

This is not to be confused with the Council of Ministers, as the European Council is in fact the name given to the summit meetings of EU heads of state that occur twice each year. The President of the European Commission and the Ministers for Foreign Affairs of all member states assist at these meetings, which aim to establish an overall strategic direction for the European Union.

The requirement for the European Council to meet at least twice-yearly is embodied within Article 2 of the Single European Act, although no specific powers or functions are mentioned. In practice, however, meetings of the European Council are *extremely* important for the determination of EU policy.

Council itself is chaired by the head of government of the state currently holding the Presidency of the Council of Ministers. Representatives of this country are responsible for preparing European Council meetings. Hence the chair can influence the composition of agendas and the degree of vigour with which certain items are discussed. Apart from matters raised by the chair, agenda items normally include:

- the current state of the European economy
- proposals put forward by the European Commission
- matters that the Council of Ministers has been unable to resolve
- urgent issues in the field of international relations, e.g. emergency famine relief, breakdowns in multilateral trade negotiations, military assistance to the United Nations, and so on.

Periodically, agenda items concerning the enlargement of the European Union and/or institutional and constitutional reform also require attention.

The advantage the European Council enjoys over the European Commission and the Council of Ministers is its ability to determine for itself what it will do and how it will develop. Decisions are taken at the highest possible level and, once finalised, they are sure to be implemented. Disadvantages include lack of formal procedures, and possible domination of meetings by political posturing more concerned with impressing national electorates than with advancing the interests of the EU. Arguably, moreover, the Council has undermined the European Commission's authority in relation to the initiation of policies, and is making it difficult for the European Parliament to extend its role.

9. The European Court of Justice (ECJ)

This comprises one judge from each member state. Additionally Germany, France, Italy, Spain and the UK each supply one Advocate-General: the other states collectively rotate three Advocates-General. As the European Union is enlarged, then whenever there is an even number of member countries the larger countries will participate in a system involving the rotation of an extra judge. Appointments are for (renewable) six-year terms, with partial replacement every three years. An important difference between the ECJ and English legal system is that whereas in the latter judges are selected from barristers, the ECJ contains judges appointed from a much wider field, including university academics.

Advocates-General have the same status as judges. Their role is specified by Article 166 of the Treaty of Rome as that of 'making impartially and independently, reasoned submissions in open court on cases brought before the ECJ in order to assist the Court in the performance of its duties'. The post is derived from the French legal tradition and has no counterpart in English law. An Advocate-General will digest all the facts of a case as would a judge, and then states his or her opinion prior to the judges hearing the case reaching their decision. A single judgement is given by the ECJ, without any statement of dissenting views.

The working language of the ECJ is French, reflecting the heavy influence of the French legal system on the Court's administrative procedures. The Court sits in Luxembourg.

ECJ procedures

These are intended to be as informal and straightforward as possible. Much of the Court's work is conducted through written communications rather than requiring the attendance of large numbers of people at the Court's premises. An action begins with an application by the plaintiff stating the subject matter of the dispute, the grounds of the action and the remedy sought. The Court's Registry translates this into appropriate languages and notifies the defendant and other interested parties. Defendants must lodge their defences within a month of the date of service of the application. Cases are conducted in the language chosen by the applicant. There are no Court fees.

One of the judges hearing the case is appointed the *Juge-Rapporteur*. This person prepares a preliminary report suggesting how the case should be handled. Expert witnesses may now offer opinions; documents relevant to the case are examined. The Juge-Rapporteur then presents to the Court a summary of the facts and of the parties' arguments. Next, each party presents its written pleadings, which are translated into French plus any other necessary language and distributed to Court members. There is a brief oral hearing, followed by a statement of opinion by an Advocate-General. The Court now deliberates on the case and delivers a judgement.

Prior to the enlargement of the European Union in 1995 full Court sittings required an odd number of judges, with a quorum of seven (or three for lesser cases heard in Chambers) although this is due to alter according to the number of countries actually joining the Union. Decisions are by majority vote. The Court's jurisdiction extends to disputes between member states; between the European Union and member states; between individuals and corporate bodies; appeals against decisions by the highest Courts of member countries, plus matters arising from the interpretation of EU Treaties. Much of the work of the ECJ concerns allegations of non-compliance with EU legislation, especially in the field of business competition. Since 1995 the Court has had the power to fine member nations for not respecting its judgements. There is no appeal against an ECJ ruling, which is legally binding in all member countries (possibly overriding national Court decisions or government legislation). Cases may be referred to the European Court by individuals, national Courts or governments, by the European Commission, or by the Council of Ministers. The Court is also willing to act as an independent arbitrator. Legal aid is available to persons or organisations wishing to use the Court, at the latter's discretion.

The Court of First Instance

So heavy was the workload of the ECJ that a Court of First Instance was established in 1989 to hear cases mainly involving competition law, damages actions brought by individuals, and actions initiated by officials of the European Commission. Each member country contributes one member to the Court, the decisions of which are subject to appeal to the ECJ on (only) points of law.

Advantages and problems of the ECJ

The ECJ provides the individual with an extra possibility for appeal against potentially biased judgements in national legal systems. Its rulings are final and the Court has been generally effective in ensuring that EU Treaties and legislation are actually applied. Increasingly, however, litigants in test cases in national Courts assume they will have to go to the EJC for the ultimate decision on an issue. Arguably this undermines and makes irrelevant the work of national legal systems in relation to important matters of legal principle. The ECJ has been criticised, moreover, for the long periods that elapse prior to cases reaching Court, and for not having a sufficient range of sanctions.

10. The European Parliament

The original European Parliament (known as the European Assembly) was not democratically elected at all. Rather, its membership was nominated by the governments of EEC member countries with a remit of exercising an advisory and overall supervisory role. This was justified by the EEC's founding fathers on the grounds that during the Community's early years it was essential to have strong central control by the Council of Ministers; otherwise little would ever get done. Another argument for restricting the European Parliament's role is that democratic decision making already occurs through national Parliaments and hence through the Council of Ministers. Nevertheless, it was recognised that the EEC would eventually need a democratic governing body, so the powers of the European Parliament have been increased systematically over time.

Today the European Parliament is directly elected by the people of the European Union although it is not (at the time of writing) a law-making body as such. Rather, it acts as a forum for discussion and gives its opinions on proposals referred to it (compulsorily) by the European Commission. Also, Parliament has the powers:

- To dismiss the European Commission via a vote of censure that obtains at least a two-thirds majority of the votes cast (the larger EU countries have more members of the European Parliament than the smaller nations).
- To change or reject the annual draft budget of the EU. Note however that Parliament's ability to change the budget only applies to 'non-compulsory' expenditure, i.e. that which is not the consequence of EU legislation. This includes social, regional and industrial policies and covers about 40 per cent of the total EU budget. 'Compulsory' expenditure, conversely, is that committed under the Treaty of Rome or as a result of EU legislation, e.g. spending on the common agricultural policy. The Parliament may only propose alterations to this type of expenditure: final decisions are taken by the Council of Ministers. However the Parliament may reject the budget *outright* on a two-thirds majority vote. This has never happened: a 'conciliation committee' comprising representatives from the European Parliament and the Council of Ministers exists to try to resolve disagreements before they reach crisis proportions.
- To veto the appointments of new European Commissioners.
- To put questions to the European Commission and Council of Ministers and have them answered (the answers are given by Ministers from the country currently holding the presidency of the Commission).

- To advise the European Council, although this advice may be ignored in most subject areas.
- To reject major international agreements negotiated by the Commission.

There are 624 MEPs. Luxembourg contributes six members; Ireland 15; Denmark and Finland 16; Austria 20; Sweden 21; Belgium, Greece and Portugal 25; Netherlands 31; Spain 64; France, Italy and the UK 87; Germany 99. MEPs enjoy the (important) right to be informed about the European Commission's activities. In particular, the Commission is obliged to reply to Parliamentary questions within a specified period. Answers to questions may be written or oral, but all are published in the *Official Journal* of the EU. If a question is put orally then a supplementary question may be asked.

Parliament has numerous standing committees including, *inter alia*, committees on the environment, women's rights, political affairs, and the reform of EU institutions. There are in addition temporary and special committees set up on an *ad hoc* basis. Members of the European Commission can be summoned to attend these committees to explain the Commission's position on particular issues. Reports of committees serve as the foundation for the majority of Parliamentary debates. Such reports may be initiated by individual MEPs or by the Council of Ministers.

Criticisms of the European Parliament are that:

- It is subject to intense lobbying by outside commercial interests, much of this being done in secret.
- As it is an advisory rather than law-making body, all its substantive recommendations have to be considered by other EU institutions. This imposes an enormous administrative strain on these other institutions. For example, the Council of Ministers will typically be considering around 450 EP opinions at any particular moment in time.
- Parliament does not have to be consulted by the Council of Ministers on all intended legislation (notably that involving external relations, including trade treaties [Nugent 1994]).

Petitions to the European Parliament

Every EU citizen has the right, individually or collectively, to file a petition with the European Parliament. This commonly occurs in relation to VAT matters, barriers to the free movement of capital, and questions relating to EU law. Parliament has a 'petitions committee' comprising representatives of member countries and political parties selected on a proportional basis. This committee decides whether a petition is admissable and, if so, whether an EU law has been violated. Admissible petitions are then heard by a Parliamentary committee, to which the European Commission may be invited to express an opinion. A Parliamentary 'Resolution' of the petition is then drafted. If the petitioner is not satisfied with the Resolution the matter may be referred to the European Court of Justice.

11. The Economic and Social Committee (ECOSOC)

Also known as The Other Assembly (after its original formal title The Economic and Social Consultative Assembly), ECOSOC is a Brussels-based advisory body comprising representatives of trade unions, professional bodies and other interest groups and which expresses opinions on Commission proposals. ECOSOC emerged from the negotiations preceding the Treaty of Rome. It was a logical development considering that five of the EEC's six founder members (West Germany being the odd country out) already had comparable organisations within their own national systems. Specific reasons for the formation of ECOSOC included:

- recognition of the need for an influential forum in which sectional interests could express their views
- fears that the European Assembly (subsequently the European Parliament) would not be adequate as a vehicle for discussing social issues
- acceptance of the fact that European economic integration implies social change.

Luxembourg contributes six members; Denmark, Ireland and Finland nine; Austria and Sweden eleven; Belgium, Greece, Portugal and The Netherlands 12; Spain 21; and the remaining countries 24 each. Members are split into three groups representing employers, employees, and 'various other interests'. National governments nominate individuals to serve on ECOSOC, although the Council of Ministers makes the final selection. Members serve on a part-time basis for renewable four-year periods. The chair of ECOSOC rotates between the three groups for two years at a time.

According to the European Commission, ECOSOC exists to 'represent groups of people active in economic and social life'. It scrutinises Commission proposals and suggests amendments. Members of ECOSOC are in close touch with officials of the Commission and with key people in their own countries. The Committee may issue Own-Initiative Opinions on any subject of relevance to the European Union. As well as expressing opinions, ECOSOC publishes information and reports on issues of contemporary concern, liaises with various international bodies, and organises conferences.

ECOSOC is important because (i) it represents directly the interests of important business groups, (ii) by statute it must be consulted on any proposal made by the European Commission that has a social aspect, and (iii) its opinions have to be expressed before the proposal goes to the Council of Ministers. Many European Commission proposals have been amended, or even abandoned, in consequence of referral to ECOSOC.

The Committee meets in plenary session on a monthly basis. Its detailed work is completed by specialist committees. The organisation has nine sections, as shown in Figure 1.1. Sometimes, outside experts are engaged to comment on Commission proposals.

Figure 1.1 ECOSOC

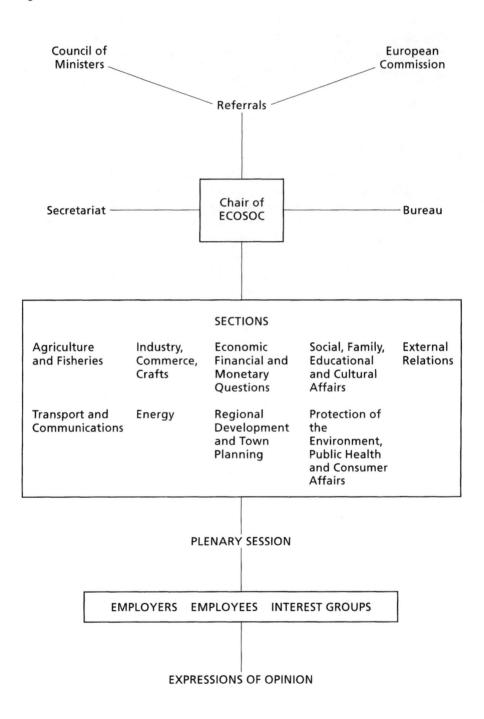

Source: Economic and Social Committee

12. The Consumer Consultative Council and the Committee of the Regions

The Consumer Consultative Council has a membership made up of representatives from the EU's major consumer organisations. It serves as a forum for discussion, a medium for conducting research into consumer affairs, and a vehicle for initiating new proposals concerning consumer interests for consideration by the European Commission. The Committee of the Regions is an advisory committee which first met in 1994 and aims to promote regional development and the representation of the interests of the EU's regions. (Prior to enlargement in 1995 the Union had 237 distinct regions.) The national composition of the membership of the Committee is the same as for ECOSOC (*see* 11), with which it shares administrative services.

A number of factors led to the formation of this Committee, in particular:

- The very large sums of money being paid to regions in the forms of investment grants, research and development incentives, etc., and hence the need to have regional representation within the organisations responsible for distributing these funds.
- The huge variations in wealth and income that occur between the regions of EU member countries. The Union's ten most prosperous regions have three times the level of per capita income of the ten poorest (all of which are in Greece and Portugal).
- The possibility of mutually destructive competition between regions as they attempt to attract new business investment.
- The reality that regional politicians already lobby EU institutions in a high-powered manner.

Members are appointed by national governments for four-year terms. Although the terms of reference of the Committee of Regions are still evolving, it has to date:

- advised the European Commission on how the EU's Cohesion Fund should be spent (the Cohesion Fund finances economic development in the Union's poorer countries)
- expressed opinions on pan-European transport systems and on education and training programmes
- established links with the European Parliament and with industrial and employers' associations.

13. The Court of Auditors

Established in 1977, the Court of Auditors comprises one auditor from each member state and has the following functions:

- Examination of the accounts of the EU and all its organisations.
- Monitoring the EU's general budget and all EU borrowing and lending.
- Ensuring the legality and accuracy of EU financial transactions.
- Production of reports on financial misconduct and/or the waste of EU money.

Auditors are appointed by the Council of Ministers for renewable six-year periods.

Each auditor must be professionally qualified in the audit field, and promise to act in the EU's interest independent of national considerations. Members of the Court elect a President who holds the office for a (renewable) three-year term. The Court is situated in Luxembourg and has fewer than 450 employees – a small number considering the extent and importance of its role.

14. The European Investment Bank (EIB)

Based in Luxembourg, the EIB was set up in 1958 to finance capital investment projects intended to develop the economies of the (then) EEC member countries. Today it is one of the largest lending and borrowing institutions in the world. It borrows on the international capital markets and on-lends for projects mainly in the EU's less prosperous regions. The Bank does not seek to make a profit and thus can offer low rates of interest on loans. A maximum of half the cost of a project may be funded. Projects themselves usually involve infrastructure improvement (e.g. telecommunications systems, energy conservation, transport, or environmental protection). The Bank also finances projects in economically underdeveloped countries with which the EU has co-operation agreements, and lends money to East European nations to assist them in their transition to market economies. Its shareholders are the member states of the EU, and its board of governors comprises the Finance Ministers of the EU countries. Executive control lies with the Bank's President and six vice-Presidents, all appointed for renewable six-year terms by the board of governors on the recommendation of a separate part-time board of directors. The latter consists of 21 banking experts: 20 nominated by member states and one by the European Commission.

The Bank is managed according to commercial principles: it is not in the business of dispensing aid. However, because it is non-profit making and itself enjoys a very high credit rating (so that it is able to borrow cheaply) the EIB can lend at extremely attractive rates. Repayments may be deferred for the first couple of years; repayment periods vary from five to 20 years. Normally the Bank is only interested in lending sums of at least 10 million ECU. To qualify for funding, projects must:

- improve economic and social cohesion (typically by contributing to the economic development of underdeveloped regions); *or*
- facilitate the modernisation and hence increased competitiveness of EU industry; *or*
- provide benefits to several EU countries (in the fields of transport or telecommunications for example).

Projects must be technically sound and financially viable (evidenced by adequate security against EIB loans).

15. Criticisms of the European Union

Critics of West European economic and political integration (or the 'Eurosceptics' as they are sometimes called) allege that the EU is inadequate in some or all of the following respects.

(a) The EU is fundamentally undemocratic. Decisions are made and implemented without the debate and the checks and balances characteristic of national political systems.

(b) There is too much bureaucracy and red tape.

(c) National governments lose their sovereignty over basic issues affecting the lives of the citizens they were elected to represent.

(d) No pan-European policy can benefit every EU country to an equal extent. In reality there already exists a 'two-speed' Europe. Certain nations, regions and groups of citizens are bound to lose from the application of pan-European policies.

(e) Too much money is spent on the Common Agricultural Policy, which continues to absorb the bulk of EU expenditures. The CAP is allegedly unfair, inefficient, and encourages waste.

(f) EU Committees, it has been argued, are in reality toothless tigers. The Economic and Social Committee has been particularly criticised for being over-large, bureaucratic, ineffective, and concerned more with uttering patronising statements than with genuinely influencing EU affairs.

(g) Member states differ in relation to how vigorously they enforce EU Directives. Note that the European Commission only employs around 13,000 staff (a third of whom are concerned with translation and interpreting) compared with perhaps 20,000 civil servants employed by a single UK Ministry. Thus the Commission itself has been criticised for being excessively bureaucratic and too powerful (it exerts strong influence at all stages in the legislative procedure). Note the enormous complexity of the Commission's role, the need to integrate the activities of people from all the EU member countries, and having to work in (currently) nine different languages. Also the Commission depends heavily on national governments for the supply of information and for investigating allegations of infringements or non-implementation of EU law.

Advocates of greater European integration reply that, in reality, there can be no such thing as absolute national sovereignty in the modern world. International trade is extensive and affects the economic performances of all advanced nations. Every West European country is locked into defence treaties and depends heavily on partners for military assistance. Genuine democracy within the EU can be achieved immediately through giving the European Parliament proper legislative powers. The European Commission, moreover, is in fact the servant of the Union, not its master. Its role is simply to suggest, not to approve, new legislation. All major EU decisions require the consent of the Council of Ministers.

Reform of EU institutions

The main overall criticism of EU institutions is perhaps that (apart from the European Parliament) they have remained largely unchanged since they were set up in the 1950s; yet the size of the EU has grown, as have the levels of importance of the decisions taken by various institutions. A number of enquiries have been conducted into how the EU institutions could be reformed (Archer 1994), but few actions have been taken. This is due perhaps to:

- a general reluctance to interfere with systems and procedures that seem to be working reasonably effectively
- fears on the part of national governments that proposed reforms (which would have to be ratified by national Parliaments) might be turned down at the national level amid much political controversy
- resistance to change within the institutions themselves.

LAW-MAKING IN THE EU

16. Forms of EU legislation

There are three types of EU legislative measure:

(a) *Regulations,* i.e. laws that apply immediately and equally in all member states.

(b) *Directives*, which specify a necessary outcome (e.g. to achieve equal pay for work of equal value done by men and women) but then allow the government of each member country to introduce its own particular legislation to achieve the desired objective. Every Directive states a time period (usually two years but sometimes longer) within which member states must attain the result required by the Directive. If this does not occur within the designated period an individual may seek to enforce the Directive through his or her national Courts.

(c) *Decisions* of the European Court of Justice, which have the same effect as Regulations.

Additionally, the European Commission issues Recommendations which are not legally binding, but express the Commission's considered opinions about how certain matters should be dealt with. Commission Notices are also important, especially in relation to competition law. These are pronouncements of the European Commission on various matters, such as:

- the legality or otherwise of exclusive dealing contracts with commercial agents
- co-operative joint ventures
- the activities of motor vehicle intermediaries
- exclusive purchasing and distribution agreements.

Although a notice can be withdrawn, and despite the fact that the Commission is not legally bound by the terms of a Notice it has issued, it is unlikely that the

Commission could fine a company in relation to a restrictive agreement covered by a Notice.

Today, EU Directives, Regulations, etc., affect most aspects of European business. There are Directives on consumer protection, advertising and cross-border broadcasting, company administration, intellectual property, agency and distribution arrangements, business mergers and acquisitions, working conditions, health and safety, gender equal opportunities in employment, and on numerous other facets of personnel and general business management.

Voting procedures

Unanimity is required for decisions concerning taxation, employment and social protection, social security, employee participation in management decision making, the employment conditions of third country nationals legally working in the EU, and financial measures for job creation. Otherwise, 'qualified majority voting' applies, i.e. each nation casts a number of votes according to the size of its population but, in order to ensure that small countries do not have to surrender vital national interests, a certain threshold number of votes must be exceeded before a proposal can be accepted (this was 54 out of 76 before the enlargement of the Union in 1995).

17. The legislative process

The procedure whereby Directives and Regulations become legally binding on member countries is as follows:

Stage 1 Staff of the European Commission originate a proposal. The idea might have come from a national government, a national or EU level interest group, or from a particular member of the European Commission. The Commission organises a study of the issue, in consultation with national governments and relevant interest groups. ECOSOC and specialist committees of the European Parliament might also be approached on an informal basis. A draft proposal is then put before the Council of Ministers and published in the *Official Journal* (OJ) of the European Union.

Stage 2 The Council of Ministers initiates the 'consultation procedure', i.e. it formally requests the opinions of ECOSOC and the European Parliament. Comments received are published in the OJ, and suggested amendments are referred back to the Commission. A revised proposal may emerge which again goes to ECOSOC and the European Parliament. National governments and interest groups will express opinions on the proposal. COREPER (*see* **6**) will arrange a working party to discuss the text of the proposal and make appropriate comments, liaising with the Commission where necessary.

Stage 3 The Council of Ministers adopts a common position on the proposal. This might mean rejection of the proposal, unanimous approval or approval by qualified majority voting if this is permitted for the issue concerned. The proposal now goes before the European Parliament and the 'co-operation procedure' is implemented, as shown in Figure 1.2. Final legislation is published in

Figure 1.2 The co-operation procedure

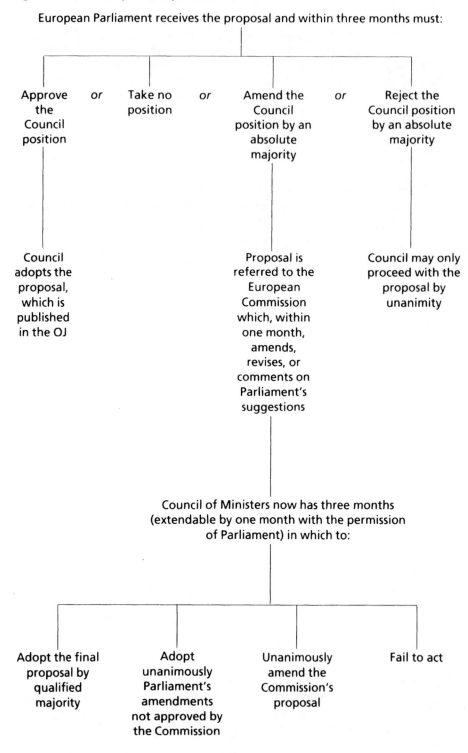

European Parliament receives the proposal and within three months must:

| Approve the Council position | *or* | Take no position | *or* | Amend the Council position by an absolute majority | *or* | Reject the Council position by an absolute majority |

Council adopts the proposal, which is published in the OJ

Proposal is referred to the European Commission which, within one month, amends, revises, or comments on Parliament's suggestions

Council may only proceed with the proposal by unanimity

Council of Ministers now has three months (extendable by one month with the permission of Parliament) in which to:

| Adopt the final proposal by qualified majority | Adopt unanimously Parliament's amendments not approved by the Commission | Unanimously amend the Commission's proposal | Fail to act |

the OJ. If the Council of Ministers fails to act the proposal lapses, is dropped, or started again from the beginning.

The procedure has been criticised for being slow and cumbersome. It takes years before proposals become law, and the need to appease so many disparate national interests arguably results in compromises that satisfy no specific member country.

Subsidiarity

In 1992 the (then) 12 member countries of the EU agreed that the 'principle of subsidiarity' should be applied to EU legislation, i.e. action should not be taken at the Union level if the desired objective could be better achieved through separate government policies implemented by each member state. Thus, the Commission should only initiate proposals for EU legislation where transnational considerations have to be taken into account, where EU Treaties demand pan-Union legislation, where the scale of pan-EU action would facilitate the solution of a problem, or where the harmonization of national laws or practices is essential to achieve agreed EU objectives. It was further decided in 1992 that:

- Local difficulties should be resolved by local action, not by EU legislation.
- Laws should not be imposed if voluntary co-operation among member countries could achieve similar outcomes.
- The actions required by EU laws should be as simple as possible.
- Only minimum standards should be set at EU level, leaving each nation to apply more stringent requirements if it so wishes.
- The benefits of intended EU laws should be measured against the costs they are likely to impose on EU citizens and local and national governments.

18. Problems with EU legislation

A number of difficulties have been encountered when attempting to devise and implement pan-European Union laws:

(a) Most Union level laws will be detrimental to at least one EU member, either because it conflicts with national policy or represents such a break with existing practice that it will be more expensive to apply than in nations where it is already embodied (wholly or in part) in domestic legislation. For example, a law compelling employers to grant full holiday pay to part-time workers would be expensive to implement in a country where there is no requirement to pay part timers during holidays, yet costless in a nation in which this is compulsory.

(b) The need to negotiate compromises results in long delays (lasting many years in certain cases) in the law-making process.

(c) Unanimity is still required for legislation concerning certain matters.

(d) Some proposed EU legislation has domestic political implications for the governments of a number of member nations.

(e) In general, penalties for breaking EU laws are determined by member states rather than at the Union level. Thus the fine or term of imprisonment for violating a law resulting from an EU Directive (on equal opportunities or insider dealing for example) might vary substantially from country to country.

19. Lobbying

In view of the enormous importance of EU activities and decisions it is hardly surprising that numerous organisations wish to exert influence on EU affairs. The major lobbyists are businesses (especially multinational companies); political representatives of the EU's poorer regions; and environmental, consumer protection and other interest groups. Of particular importance has been the rise of the 'Euro-group', i.e. a group with members sharing a common interest in several EU countries. The majority of Euro-groups represent various industrial and agricultural sectors (Greenwood 1992). Lobbying can be highly effective. Note that apart from the bundle of measures necessary to implement the Single European Market, less than half the proposals put forward by the European Commission have actually passed into law. Lobbying can occur via;

- Members of the European Parliament (MEPs). An MEP will sit on various Parliamentary committees and have many contacts with Commission staff. Committees of the EP hear about proposed legislation at a very early stage. Parliament has an information office that will advise which MEPs have interests in particular areas. MEPs may be seen in their constituencies, in Brussels or in Strasbourg.
- Trade associations, interest groups or MPs in national Parliaments.
- Representations to members of ECOSOC.
- Civil servants in appropriate national Ministries.
- COREPER (at the time that working parties are being formed).
- Professional lobbyists (a sizeable lobbying industry has arisen in Brussels).
- The European Commission itself. Industry associations sometimes arrange meetings between groups of heads of large businesses and European Commissioners and their staff (Mazey and Richardson 1993).

The Commission does not object to lobbying *per se*, because the Commission itself can benefit from the process. Lobbyists might be able to provide useful information which the Commission would otherwise have to gather, possibly at very high cost. Also the Commission needs to 'keep its finger on the pulse' of current events in particular areas, and generally wishes to gain the support of powerful pressure groups when formulating proposals. If the Commission drafts proposals opposed by influential groups then the process of gaining their acceptance by the Council of Ministers could be difficult.

Disadvantages to lobbying are that the better organised and more powerful pressure groups (especially those financed by big business) are bound to exert greater influence than poorly co-ordinated (but equally worthy) lobbyists, that the process is undemocratic, and that it is open to corruption.

UNICE and ETUC

Founded in 1973, ETUC is a confederation of 35 trade union organisations of 20 West European (not just EU) countries. It seeks to influence EU policies on work and employment matters, and has direct representation on the Consumer Consultative Council (*see* **12**). UNICE is a confederation of employers' associations in 22 West European nations. It co-ordinates the views of its members on business and employment issues and lobbies the Commission and other EU institutions. UNICE has a number of policy committees and working groups, a substantial permanent staff, and has been quite successful in influencing EU legislation.

Meetings between ETUC and UNICE have occurred since 1985, promoted by the European Commission via the so called *Val Duchesse* dialogue. To date however no tangible outcomes have emerged from these discussions. UNICE has refused to allow itself to become a *de facto* bargaining body responsible in part for determining the direction of EU social policy. ETUC similarly has no desire (or constitutional authority) to negotiate agreements. Hence the social dialogue initiated by the *Val Duchesse* talks have remained purely consultative, and arguably inconsequential (Rhodes 1992).

20. The Inter-Governmental Conference 1996/97

This was convened in March 1996 to consider the progress achieved towards the implementation of the Maastricht Treaty (including the single European currency) and, importantly, to revise the institutional structure of the EU. Any member nation could submit items for discussion at the IGC. At the time of writing the following issues appear most likely to appear on the agenda:

(a) A strengthening of the powers of the European Parliament.

(b) Streamlining of the European Commission. A number of (somewhat contentious) issues have been identified here, notably whether:

(*i*) The President of the Commission should be empowered to dismiss individual Commissioners (e.g. for breaching their oath of impartiality). At present the European Parliament can dismiss the entire Commission, but not specific people.

(*ii*) The selection of the President of the Commission should remain the sole prerogative of member states, rather than the Commission itself having some input to the selection process.

(*iii*) The President should have some say in the choice of other Commissioners (who at present are appointed by national governments).

(*iv*) The number of Commissioners should be reduced.

(*v*) The right of the Commission to initiate legislation should be curbed.

(c) A change in voting procedures and the balance of votes between member states in the Council of Ministers (*see* **7**). Two proposals have been advanced in this regard. The first is to extend the principle of majority voting to the majority of the remaining 50 or so areas (including social policy and taxation) which still require unanimity in decision making. This is because it will be extremely difficult to achieve unanimity in an enlarged EU possibly comprising more than 20 members. Also the behaviour of the UK government in 1996 whereby it vetoed all proposals requiring unanimity (in retaliation for the EU decision to ban the sale of British beef outside the UK) is likely to increase the pressure for an extensive enlargement of the issues to which majority voting applies. The second proposition is to change the weighting of votes in the Council of Ministers. Currently a minority of 29 per cent of votes in the Council can block acceptance of any proposal to which qualified majority voting (*see* **16**) applies. Yet the countries holding this 29 per cent of votes might represent less than ten per cent of the total population of an enlarged European Union. Accordingly, the European Commission has suggested a new system that would relate the percentage of votes needed to block legislation to the combined population of the countries voting against the proposal concerned. If the combined population of these nations is very small relative to the total for the entire EU then a high percentage of Council votes will be needed to block legislation.

(d) Establishment of a timetable for the enlargement of the EU. This will be undertaken in conjunction with a reconsideration of the rules for allocating Structural Funds (*see* **6:23**) for training and regional development, as the cost of extending existing benefits to new entrants would be impossibly high. One suggestion is to create a ceiling on the amount of assistance given to any one country. This ceiling might be computed as some percentage (e.g. four per cent) of its Gross Domestic Product.

(e) Creation of independent agencies to regulate utilities (the gas and electricity generating industries for example) at the pan-European level.

(f) Setting up a 'cartel authority' to take over the European Commission's present supervision and enforcement functions in relation to competition law.

(g) Formulation of a 'Bill of Rights' listing all the rights of citizens of the EU, including the right not to be unfairly discriminated against on the grounds of sex, race or national origin. The latter provision would apply to *all* forms of unfair sexual, racial or xenophobic discrimination, not just to pay and conditions of employment as is presently the situation.

(h) Revision of the structure and jurisdiction of the European Court of Justice (*see* **9**). Although no major changes are predicted there might be an alteration in the basis upon which judges are appointed to the Court (their numbers could exceed 60 in an enlarged EU), plus a reorganisation of the Court of First Instance intended to improve its efficiency. The Court might also be given a wider range of powers for enforcing its judgements.

(i) Development of a pan-European strategy for employment. This suggestion (originally put forward by Sweden) would require the surveillance and co-ordination of all EU national employment policies, in the same manner as currently applies to national economic policies.

Background to the IGC

The requirement that the IGC begin in 1996 was laid down in the Treaty of European Union (Maastricht Treaty). Its importance has been intensified, however, in consequence of the desire of many EU member nations to see a substantial deepening and widening of the European Union over the next few years. Further West European economic and political integration ought in principle to ensure that Germany (the dominant economic power of the European Union) remains fully committed to Western (rather than Central and Eastern) Europe and that German power is constrained. Additionally it should create a solid foundation upon which enlargement of the EU can be based. Also the institutional structure of the EU (designed originally to co-ordinate the activities of just six countries) requires urgent adaptation to enable it to cope with perhaps 20 or 25 nations. A more practical purpose of the Conference is to rewrite and perhaps combine the various Treaties pertaining to European integration (the Treaty of Rome, the Treaty of Union, the ECSC Treaty, etc.) as the constant amendment of these has led to certain (important) sections becoming so confused as to be almost unreadable. Note that the future financing of the European Union will *not* be discussed at the IGC, as this matter will be dealt with separately in negotiations scheduled to commence in 1998.

BUSINESS IMPLICATIONS OF WEST EUROPEAN INTEGRATION

21. Economic factors

As competition within the EU intensifies firms are compelled to use their resources more efficiently, leading inevitably to unemployment in some industries and regions. EU nations have become much more dependent on other member countries for imports and exports than before, and their businesses have a greatly enlarged market. Increased competition should eliminate incompetent managements, reduce consumer prices and stimulate cross-border trade (with consequent improvements in rates of economic growth). Business rationalisations should help European firms compete more effectively in the rest of the world. The pursuit of competitive advantage may lead to more research and technical development and hence to product innovation. A wider choice of products is now available to West European consumers, who may purchase items supplied tariff-free from other EU countries.

Benefits and problems for the individual business

Benefits of European integration for the individual firm include larger markets leading to economies of scale and hence the possibility of developing a business capable of competing with US and Pacific Rim rivals; lower input costs; faster cross-border transmission of new business practices and ideas; and easier access to joint venture partners in other EU countries. No foreign trade documentation is needed for intra-EU transactions, and the cross-border EU transport infrastructure is improving year by year.

Threats to the individual business arising from European economic integration include:

- reduced market shares for many companies

- a higher level of uncertainty making it difficult to take long-term investment decisions
- increased possibilities for hostile takeover attempts as competing firms seek to position themselves in the most advantageous market locations
- entry to existing markets of powerful Japanese and US companies which manufacture locally in order to avoid paying the EU common external tariff
- potential for price wars, especially as large firms enter new markets previously served only by smaller companies.

22. Further implications for business of West European economic integration

Completion of the European Single Market has numerous implications for EU businesses, including:

(a) The need to monitor EU legislation in order to assess whether, and if so to what extent, new Directives or Regulations will affect the firm.

(b) Increased competition in consequence of any EU firm being able to sell its products freely in all EU states.

(c) Access to tariff-free inputs from other EU countries.

(d) Opportunities for the sale of a standardised product across Europe following the introduction of a harmonised technical standard.

(e) The need to conduct market research to establish the nature of consumer tastes and preferences in other EU nations.

(f) The ability to tender for public sector contracts anywhere in the EU.

(g) Mergers and takeovers as firms sell and buy over a wider area and thus seek local subsidiaries to handle their foreign EU activities.

(h) Possibly the need to redesign products to make them suitable for foreign EU markets.

(i) Increases in employee benefits and remunerations as the European Social Charter is implemented.

(j) The need to adopt pan-European perspectives when formulating business strategies.

(k) Fresh training requirements, especially in languages and the business conditions and practices of other EU nations.

(l) The ability to commence or expand operations at will in the lowest cost and most profitable locations in the Union.

(m) Opportunities for the cross-border recruitment of skilled workers.

(n) The need to translate and perhaps redraft sales and purchasing contracts and promotional literature to make them suitable for foreign EU countries.

23. Strategic aspects

European business is dynamic, sophisticated, complex, and altering faster and more extensively than in any other international trading area. Markets are fragmenting into many more sub-units than in the past and there is intense rivalry for domination of markets from efficient low price and aggressive foreign European firms. To succeed in this environment a business must be adaptable, immediately aware of fresh opportunities, able to manage change and, importantly, able to learn from and quickly rectify its mistakes. Volatility and the numerous uncertainties connected with the current situation establishes the need for strategies, management styles and organisational systems that are flexible and easily altered to suit the needs of changing conditions. Examples of flexibility include the following:

(a) Alignment of internal business systems (organisational, procurement, staffing, budgeting, marketing, quality control, etc.) to satisfy pan-European operational requirements (Jacquemin and Wright 1993).

(b) Action-orientated strategies rather than fixed quantitative objectives. Strategies should be seen as sort of route map for guiding the enterprise towards the attainment of its mission, not as a collection of rigid rules. For further information on strategic management see *Corporate Strategy and Business Planning*, published in this series.

(c) Linking strategy with operational management (Brown 1994).

(d) Ensuring that the company's core businesses can cope with environmental turbulence.

(e) Organisational design and development strategies involving the selection and implementation of the administrative arrangements best suited to obtain maximum benefit from an enterprise engaged in pan-European trade.

(f) Human resources strategies, incorporating decisions on such matters as:

- The types of managerial recruit best equipped to handle the demands imposed by open pan-European competition, and where to find the best people.
- Training expenditures on the management skills required for doing business in European markets. Examples of relevant competencies include language skills; export marketing; logistics and documentation; trading in foreign currencies; familiarity with EU advertising media; knowledge of the contents and implications of relevant EU Directives; and familiarity with EU market structures and business methods.

A combination of offensive and defensive strategies is required. The former for assaulting new markets; for improving, altering and developing products; obtaining EU public sector contracts; entering strategic alliances with foreign European firms; and so on. Defensive measures might be necessary in order to retain domestic market share, cut costs and maintain the keenest local prices, and to avoid being taken over by a foreign EU company. Mergers and/or collaborative ventures with other domestic businesses may be essential to de-velop a critical mass sufficient to fight off increased competition from EU rivals or to operate joint procurement, research or distribution services.

24. Nature of the West European market

The West European market is dominated by a 'golden triangle' (roughly within the area enclosed by Liverpool, Cologne and Paris) that contains more than half the entire EU population, but with a land mass smaller than the UK. The Union itself represents one of the largest and most affluent integrated trading groups in the developed world. It has four really large markets: Germany, France, Italy and the UK. Germany has West Europe's highest population, and is the domi-nant economic power. Other West European nations have smaller populations but many are, nevertheless, extremely affluent and represent lucrative markets for foreign firms, and even the poorer EU members are experiencing steady long-run economic growth. The outstanding demographic fact pertaining to Western Europe is the low (or zero) rates of growth of population in most nations. This has caused a significant increase in the average age of the West European population and (in consequence) changing attitudes and spending patterns among European consumers. At the same time, younger Europeans are increasingly well educated, with nearly a quarter of the West European popula-tion now in some kind of full-time education. Virtually all EU households possess a television set and telephone, and nearly 95 per cent have a refrigerator. Rates of ownership of other key consumer durables are high. An important consequence of West European prosperity is the low number of people per average household in EU countries compared to other states. Typical household size varies between 2.1 and three for all member nations except Ireland, where the average is 3.8. There are 60 United Nations member countries with average household sizes of five or more.

Even before the accession of Sweden, Austria and Finland in 1995, the combined national income of the then 12 EU countries exceeded that of the United States by more than ten per cent and was more than double that of Japan. Germany has Western Europe's highest level of industrial production, followed by France, Italy and the UK. Spain's industrial production is 42 per cent that of France. The Netherlands and Belgium have industrial outputs of 26 per cent and 16 per cent respectively of the French figure. Today Germany accounts for nearly 20 per cent of all European consumer spending (including non-EU and Eastern block countries). France accounts for 13 per cent, and Italy and Britain for 12 per cent each. The European Union is the largest single international trader in the world, accounting for more than a fifth of global imports and exports (compared with about 15 per cent for the USA and ten per cent for Japan).

Post-Second World War Western Europe has seen the emergence of compa-rable fashions, music, television programmes, and (importantly) a broadly similar youth culture in all industrially developed nations. The fact that more Europeans visit other countries than at any time in history has greatly contrib-uted to this trend, as have the activities of large multinational corporations that offer near identical products in all European states. Note however that European economic integration does not mean that Germans will cease to be German, that the Dutch will no longer be Dutch, or that the French will not be French. The Single Market has not created 'grey uniformity' among national consumer populations; indeed, regional cultures appear if anything to have been reinforced, with the consequence that small but significant niche markets are flourishing throughout the EU.

Progress test 1

1. List the member countries of the EU.

2. Explain the difference between a common market and a free trade area.

3. What was the purpose of the Treaty of Paris.

4. Why was the Single European Act considered necessary?

5. What is the Maastricht Protocol?

6. How is the European Union financed?

7. Explain the role of the European Commission.

8. List the main functions of the President of the Council of Ministers.

9. What is the role of the Court of First Instance?

10. State three criticisms of the European Parliament.

11. Why is ECOSOC sometimes referred to as 'the Other Assembly'?

12. Outline the reasons behind the formation of the Committee of the Regions.

13. Explain the difference between an EU Directive and an EU Regulation.

2

THE MEMBER COUNTRIES OF THE EUROPEAN UNION

THE FIFTEEN NATION STATES

1. Austria

Austria's accession to the European Union in 1995 fortuitously coincided with the nation's recovery from recession and a significant improvement in its rate of economic growth. This is a landlocked German-speaking country situated in central Europe which has strong links with both East and West European states. A fifth of the nation's population lives in Vienna, the capital city. Other major population centres are Graz and Linz, each with populations of around 220,000. Six per cent of the population are non-Austrian, mainly immigrants from the former Yugoslavia, Turks and Germans.

AUSTRIA – KEY FACTS

Population: 8 million

Area: 83,850 sq.km.

Currency: Schilling = 100 Groschen

Per capita GDP (1994): $US 23,600

Capital: Vienna

Main language: German

Minority languages: Slovene (16%)
Croat (1%)

Main religions: Roman Catholic
Protestant (6%)

Austria is a Federal Republic with nine Provinces. The country has 3.3 million households, with an average household size of 2.5 persons. Austria's national statistical authorities employ a social grading system based on the UK ABC1C2DE system. The population is relatively evenly divided among the social classes, with about ten per cent of all Austrians in each of categories A and E, and around 20 per cent in each of the other classes.

Manufacturing accounts for 25 per cent of GDP; services for 55 per cent. Traditionally, mining and mineral extraction and metal processing formed the base of the economy. Since the 1950s, however, government policy has encouraged widespread diversification into all sectors of manufacturing. The strength of the Austrian economy lies in its thriving small business sector. Forty per cent of all Austrian manufacturing firms employ fewer than five workers; less than 200 of the country's manufacturing businesses have more than 500 employees. Thirty per cent of the labour force is employed in manufacturing, 18 per cent in wholesale and retail distribution (including restaurants and hotels), 24 per cent in social and personal services, and 8 per cent in agriculture. Transport and financial services each absorb around six per cent of the workforce.

Germany is the country's dominant trading partner, accounting for 45 per cent of its imports. Seventy per cent of Austrian imports originate in the EU; only seven per cent in other West European countries. Food, drink and tobacco take about 20 per cent of the typical Austrian household's monthly income. Clothing and footwear account for ten per cent; leisure and education for approximately the same amount. Personal care items and household equipment each take around eight per cent of the average household spend.

2. Belgium

It is frequently stated that if a firm can succeed in Belgium it should be able to do well anywhere else in the EU because Belgium reproduces in miniature many of the differences in culture, religion, lifestyles, etc., that divide the north of Europe from the south. Importantly moreover, Belgian patterns of consumption, average age and family size, age distribution and levels of spending on various commodity groups match pan-European averages very closely indeed, making Belgium an ideal country for test-marketing.

BELGIUM – KEY FACTS

Population: 10 million

Area: 30,519 sq. km.

Currency: Belgian Franc
= 100 centimes

Per capita GDP (1994): $US 20,000

Capital: Brussels

Main languages: Dutch, French, German

Main religions: Roman Catholic (85%)
Protestant (8%)

The Belgian union was created in 1830 from three linguistic communities. Dutch is the first language of the people in the north, French is spoken in the south, and German in a small part of the east of the nation. Brussels, the nation's capital and the home of the administrative headquarters of the EU, is predominantly French speaking even though it is situated within northern (Flemish) territory. The latter has an efficient industrial infrastructure, ready access to sea ports and excellent inland communications. Belgium is a highly industrialised state with substantial engineering, textiles, paper, footwear and agricultural

31

equipment industries. The country is a major provider of European horticultural products, which in turn has generated a number of service and supply industries specifically geared to the horticultural trade.

French-speaking Belgians are referred to as Walloons. Both the Flemish and the Walloonian communities take their culture, customs and language seriously, with linguistic differences having caused many social and political crises in previous times. The state divides into regions. Main Dutch-speaking provinces are Eastern Flanders (which has a population of around one million), Antwerp (1.5 million) and Limbourg (0.75 million). French is the majority language in the southern regions of Hainut (1.2 million), Liege (one million) and Namur (0.5 million). The Brababt area (2.2 million) straddles the two communities – Dutch is spoken in the north; French in the south. Brussels itself has a population of about 0.75 million. Other major urban population centres include the cities (as opposed to the administrative regions they represent) of Antwerp (0.4 million), Liege, Ghent and Charleroi (about 0.2 million each). Three per cent of the population are Italian, 1.5 per cent French and one per cent Moroccan.

The service sector accounts for about 68 per cent of employment, industry for around 30 per cent and agriculture for two per cent. Approximately one in five Belgian workers are engaged in manufacturing, slightly fewer in commerce. Credit and insurance absorbs about eight per cent of the workforce, transport seven per cent and construction five per cent. The rest are engaged in a miscellaneous assortment of Belgium's highly diversified industries. Belgium is ideally located for the European Single Market, facing Britain across the North Sea to the west, The Netherlands to the north, Germany and Luxembourg to the east, and France to the south. Not surprisingly, Belgians have an internationalist European perspective, with the majority speaking foreign languages as a matter of course. English is a widely used second language throughout Belgium (all the national English daily and Sunday newspapers are available in main Belgian towns), and many Belgians occasionally watch British TV. Goods from other EU countries are easily transported to the country. Belgium is a hereditary monarchy with (currently) a centre right coalition government. All Belgian political parties have two wings, each catering for one of the two main languages.

According to the Belgian state statistical service, two thirds of the population are waged industrial operatives or clerical workers; ten per cent middle managers; and 12 per cent senior managers, professional employees or self-employed. The country has approximately 3.8 million households, with an average household size of about 2.5.

3. Denmark

Denmark consists of that part of the Jutland peninsula which does not belong to Germany, plus about 500 islands between the Danish mainland and the south of Sweden. Two of the islands, Funen and Zealand, are more important economically than the rest. Greenland and the Faroe islands used to be administered by and from Denmark; today both enjoy home rule. There is minimal government intervention in industrial affairs. Hence there are hardly any centralised state

DENMARK – KEY FACTS

Population: 5.2 million

Area: 43,077 sq. km..

Currency: Danish Krona = 100 Ore

Per capita GDP (1994): $US 27,500

Capital: Copenhagen

Main language: Danish

Main religion: Protestant

purchasing units. Small to medium-sized enterprises dominate the economy: over half the industrial workforce is employed in firms with fewer than 200 employees.

The Danish economy is extremely diverse. Manufacturing is the largest single source of employment (accounting for around 20 per cent of the workforce), followed by financial and other business services (nine per cent), transport (seven per cent), construction (six per cent) and wholesaling and retailing (about six per cent each). However, miscellaneous activities not covered by the above continue to account for 40 per cent of all workers.

One in five Danes is aged 60 or above. Half are between 25 and 59; eight per cent are between 20 and 24; nine per cent between 14 and 19. The remaining 13 per cent of the population is aged 13 or below. Denmark has, therefore, an ageing population – which is predicted to shrink in the early years of the next century (the OECD forecasts a Danish population of only 4.8 million by the year 2020, six per cent lower than today). OECD further estimates that by the end of the century 45 per cent of Danes will be over 45 years of age. Denmark is a Protestant (Lutheran) country with few foreign residents; only 2.5 per cent of the population are not Danish (small by EU standards – the corresponding figure for Belgium is nine per cent; for The Netherlands, six per cent; for Germany, seven per cent). Many Danes can speak English. The country's national statistical authorities classify the workforce into categories for (a) skilled workers (accounting for about eleven per cent of all employees), (b) unskilled workers (12 per cent), (c) executives (nine per cent), and (d) general 'employees' such as retail workers, clerks, etc. (about 20 per cent). Six per cent of the population is self-employed, 15 per cent are students, 21 per cent are pensioners. An important characteristic of the Danish population is its heavy concentration in just a few areas, notably around Copenhagen, Aarhus and the larger Zealand cities. This creates a basic homogeneity within the Danish market, with little need to alter marketing methods or messages from one region to the next.

4. Finland

Originally a part of Sweden, Finland became an autonomous protectorate of Russia in 1809, declaring itself independent in 1917. Russian influence remained strong, however, and Finland was (and is) heavily involved in trade with Russia and other East European countries. Hence the Finnish economy suffered extremely badly following the disruptions consequent to the collapse of communism in those nations. Unemployment rose to nearly ten per cent of the

33

FINLAND – KEY FACTS

Population: 5 million	Capital: Helsinki
Area: 338,140 sq.km.	Main languages: Finnish (93%)
Currency: Markkas = 100 Pennia	Swedish (6%)
Per capita GDP (1994): $US 21,700	Main religion: Protestant (88%)

---

workforce in 1992, and the country's GDP actually fell by five per cent in the previous year. Positive growth returned in 1993 however and since then the economy has continued to improve.

Finland is a Parliamentary Republic with two official languages: Finnish (spoken by 93 per cent of the population) and Swedish which is the first language of the other 7 per cent. A fifth of all Finns are under 15 years of age; 13 per cent are over 65. Twenty per cent of the population live in Helsinki, the nation's capital. Other important cities are Turku (population 260,000) and Tampere (250,000). There are 2.1 million households, with an average of 2.3 persons per household. Finland's statistical authorities categorise the population as managerial/supervisory (15 per cent of the total), blue-collar workers (29 per cent), self-employed (eight per cent), other employees (16 per cent) and non-workers (32 per cent). Manufacturing accounts for about 25 per cent of GDP, services for 60 per cent. Forestry – once the dominant factor within the Finnish economy – today contributes less than three per cent of GDP. Finland has experienced much new investment during recent years.

5. France

France experienced an 'economic miracle' during the 1950s and 60s, giving the country the second largest economy in Europe and transforming it into a major high technology based industrial power. This is a large country in terms both of population and geographical size. Seventy-six French cities have populations exceeding 75,000, although no single French conurbation outside Paris has a population exceeding 1.5 million. Paris itself has around 8.5 million residents, though there is today an annual net migration out of the city – notably towards

---

FRANCE – KEY FACTS

Population: 57 million	Capital: Paris
Area: 543,965 sq.km.	Main language: French
Currency: Franc = 100 Centimes	Main religion: Roman Catholic
Per capita GDP (1994): $US 23,000	(80%)

---

the south (especially Toulouse and Montpellier), where many of France's newer microtechnology industries are situated.

France has a large public sector and a long history of state intervention in industrial affairs, focusing on the provision of assistance to selected industries to encourage them to rationalise (via mergers and acquisitions), and the introduction of advanced technology into large manufacturing firms. Conventionally, French industrial policy involved the identification and support of a handful of 'national champions' (i.e. large companies dominating certain markets) which received the great majority of public subsidies. This approach resulted from the assumption that excellence within these national champions would trickle down to smaller firms by the example they provided and through the sub-contracting of tasks. More recently, however, the concept of national champion subsidy has been attacked. A major criticism has been that it has led to the concentration of power in the hands of a small clique of industrialists, civil servants and politicians. Arguably, moreover, generous state provision of research and development funding to large companies has held back the private financing of research and development in smaller firms. (Private R&D is a much lower percentage of the total funding than in the United States, Germany or Japan.) Also the economy has been encouraged to become overdependent on the contributions of a handful of giant enterprises.

One third of France's GDP emanates from the industrial sector. Services account for about 60 per cent of GDP; agriculture for four per cent. A fifth of the country's workforce is employed in manufacturing; 18 per cent in wholesale and retail distribution, restaurants and hotels; ten per cent are in financial and business services; and seven per cent in construction. Only six per cent of the working population is engaged in agriculture, despite the high profile that French agriculture commands. France has an ageing population; two-thirds of all French citizens are aged 24 or more. Twenty per cent are between 35 and 49 and 30 per cent are over 50. Of France's younger generation, 20 per cent are under 15, and 14 per cent between 15 and 24. There are around 21 million households with an average household size of about 2.5 persons. A quarter of the population lives in single-person households, 31 per cent in households with two people, 19 per cent with three, the remaining quarter with four or more. The country's national statistical service, INSEE, categorises 22 per cent of French workers as 'blue collar', eleven per cent as 'white collar', eight per cent as 'middle managers', 15 per cent as 'professional', and six per cent as senior management or self-employed.

6. Germany

Germany is the economic powerhouse of the European Union. For administrative purposes the country is divided into 16 regions (Laender) the most economically important of which are North Rhine Westphalia (population sixteen million), Bavaria (eleven million), Baden-Württemburg (nine million), and Lower Saxony (seven million). Banking, finance and financial services (including a rapidly expanding insurance industry) are centred on Frankfurt. Heavy

```
GERMANY – KEY FACTS

Population:  81 million

Area:  357,046 sq.km.              Capital:  Berlin

Currency:  Deutschemark            Main language:  German
            = 100 Pfennig          Main religions:  Protestant (55%)

Per capita GDP (1994):                              Roman Catholic
            $US 7,400 (East)                            (40%)
            $US 27,000 (West)
```

industry is found mainly in the Ruhr; electronics and information technology businesses tend to be located in Baden-Württemburg. Germany is a country that manufactures goods rather than provides services and, while its services sector has expanded, the rate of growth of service industries has been lower than the corresponding rate in other EU nations.

Overall, Germany appears to have been the EU's most productive country since the 1950s; its output per person in manufacturing industry averaging about 150% that of the UK (the least productive advanced industrial EU economy) over the last four decades, according to United Nations figures. Germany's economic miracle from the mid-1950s onwards was engineered largely by three government ministries: Economic Affairs, Research and Technology, and Regional and Urban Affairs. The former was responsible for co-ordinating programmes for assisting small businesses, for competition policy, and for state subsidisation of industry as a whole. Intervention policy was based on the following general principles:

(a) Subsidies were to be used only to reinforce, not subvert, free markets. According to government documents, subsidies were to be used only where there was a genuine public interest, they were to be temporary, and to help enterprises help themselves.

(b) There was little state intervention in declining industries, but extensive support in thriving sectors.

(c) Interventions proceeded on an industry-wide basis, rather than the promotion of specific firms.

(d) Policies were invariably designed to modernise industries and make them more flexible, rather than to protect employment

Eastern and Western Germany

About 80 per cent of East Germans are nominally Protestant, the rest mainly Catholic. In the West there is an even division between Catholics and Protestants. Nearly 2.5 per cent of the West German population is of Turkish origin, one per cent is from the former Yugoslavia and one per cent is Italian. West Germany's economy outperformed the East throughout the post Second World

War period, with many social consequences. At the time of writing, living standards are lower and unemployment significantly higher in the East than in the West. Infant mortality is worse in the East (8.5 per thousand live births, compared with 7.5 in Western Germany) and life expectancy is lower (73 as opposed to 75). However, the Eastern Laender have higher birth rates than the Western (13.6 per thousand head of population in the East against 11 per thousand in the West), which will ease the problems created by an ageing West German population. Twenty per cent of the people of the East are under 15 years of age (14 per cent in the West). At present there is much unemployment in the East German manufacturing sector as surplus labour is shaken out, and the service sector is set to expand. Around 40 per cent of the West German workforce is engaged in manufacturing (an extremely high percentage by European standards), 55 per cent work in miscellaneous services, and the remainder in agriculture.

7. Greece

Greece adopted a democratic constitution in 1975, and joined the EU in 1981. It is one of the poorer EU members, and the only nation not to share a border with another EU state. The country covers a geographical area similar in extent to that of England, yet has a population of just ten and half million. Forty per cent of the population live in Athens or Salonika. About 20 per cent of Greece consists of islands. Over half of all Greek industry is concentrated around Athens (population three million), which has steelworks, refineries, shipyards, electrical industries, and textile and chemical plants. Major population centres outside Athens are Macedonia (population approximately 2.2 million) and Peloponnese (one million). Greece has a less severe ageing problem with its population than most other EU states. There are around 3.4 million households with an average of three people per household (high by EU standards). Greece's largest ethnic minorities are Macedonian (1.5 per cent of the population), Turkish (one per cent) and Albanian (0.5 per cent).

A quarter of the country's population is employed in agriculture; 20 per cent in manufacturing; 16 per cent in wholesale and retail distribution, hotels and restaurants; and 18 per cent in the provision of other personal services. The extent of the socio-economic data available on Greek consumers is not as extensive as for most other EU countries. Information on the socio-economic

---

GREECE – KEY FACTS

Population: 10.5 million

Area: 131,950 sq.km.

Currency: Drachmae = 100 Leptae

Per capita GDP (1994): $US 6,800

Capital: Athens

Main language: Greek

Main religion: Greek Orthodox

(95%)

---

status of various consumer groups is particularly difficult to obtain. Until recently the country's statistical authorities simply divided the population into categories for 'urban' dwellers (about 60 per cent of the total population), semi-urban (around 12 per cent) and 'rural' (28 per cent); rather than into classes based on income and/or other socio-economically meaningful criteria.

8. Ireland

Ireland is one of the poorer EU countries, although rates of economic growth have been considerably higher than the EU average over recent years. Twenty-six counties of Ireland became independent of Britain in 1921, with the six northern counties remaining within the UK. The island of Ireland faces the Atlantic Ocean on one side and the UK on the other. Ireland has a younger population than the rest of the EU. About 30 per cent of the nation's residents are under 15 years of age; approximately 17 per cent are between 16 and 24; around a quarter of the population is in the 25 to 44 age category; 16 per cent are

---

IRELAND – KEY FACTS

Population: 3.5 million	Capital: Dublin
Area: 70,280 sq.km.	Main languages: English, Irish
Currency: Punt = 100 Pence	Main religion: Roman Catholic
Per capita GDP (1994): $US 12,000	(95%)

---

between 45 and 64. The remaining 12 per cent are over 65. According to the Irish Central Statistical office, 25 per cent of Irish people are professional workers (ten per cent 'higher professional', 15 per cent 'lower professional'); 18 per cent are 'other non-manual'. Thirty-eight per cent are skilled or semi-skilled manual workers, and ten per cent are unskilled (the remainder are not classified). Ninety-five per cent of the Republic's population is Roman Catholic, and the influence of the Catholic Church is felt throughout society.

The country is heavily dependent on agriculture, especially on barley and potatoes, cattle and dairy products. An industrialisation programme is under way, but as yet has failed to provide the domestic jobs needed to halt large-scale emigration. The UK remains Ireland's major trading partner. Without doubt, the Republic's accession to the EU in 1973 boosted the country's economy, since it created for the Republic a large market for agricultural products. Also, the EU has provided financial assistance with a range of important projects intended to encourage industrial expansion. About 15 per cent of the Republic's labour force continues to be employed in agriculture. Only 18 per cent of workers are engaged in the manufacture of goods. A quarter of all workers are involved with the provision of community and social services, about 20 per cent work in the wholesale and retail distribution industries, restaurants and hotels.

ITALY – KEY FACTS

Population: 57 million

Area: 301,280 sq.km.

Currency: Lire

Per capita GDP (1994): $US 21,000

Capital: Rome

Main language: Italian

Main religion: Roman Catholic (90%)

---

9. Italy

Italy is a large country with a highly industrialised north and an economically underdeveloped south. The south of the peninsula, Sardinia and Sicily are collectively known as the Mezzogiorno. Italy's major cities are Milan (population four million), Turin and Piedmont in the north, Venice in the north east, Rome and Florence. Genoa and Naples are also important centres of population and industrial/commercial activity. Nearly a third of Italy's industry and a fifth of the country's banking services are to be found around Milan and Lombardy. A wide range of industries is located in this region, particularly steel, machine tools, footwear, chemicals and automotive products.

The country is predominantly Italian speaking, but with small French, German, Albanian and Catalan minorities in certain regions. The country is a Republic with a president as head of state and a prime minister in charge of the government. Italy is not renowned for its political stability. Italian society is noted for the strength of influence exerted by the family, due partly to the country's relatively high average household size. The country's population is predicted to fall slightly by the end of the century, but dramatically for the following 25 years (possibly to as low as 51 million by the year 2025). Currently, about 18 per cent of the population are between 15 and 34; a quarter are between 35 and 54; and about 20 per cent are 55 or more. Women outnumber men in all age categories beyond 45. The Italian statistical authorities divide the population into five socioeconomic categories, A to E. About 12 per cent of the people lie in the top grade A; around a third in category B; 18 per cent in C; 30 per cent in D; and the remaining seven per cent in class E.

Italy remains an important agricultural country, with around 10 per cent of the labour force working on the land. About 22 per cent of the labour force is engaged in manufacturing, the same as for wholesale and retail distribution including restaurants and hotels. Thirty-one per cent of all Italian workers are employed in the provision of financial, business and personal services.

10. Luxembourg

This is a tiny country bordered by France, Germany and Belgium. A quarter of Luxembourg's 370,000 residents are of foreign nationality: eight per cent are Portuguese, six per cent Italian and four per cent French. The main town is Luxembourg-Ville which is situated on the main railway lines running from

---

LUXEMBOURG – KEY FACTS

Population: 0.37 million	Capital: Luxembourg-Ville
Area: 2,580 sq.km.	Main languages: Letzeburgish
Currency: Luxembourg Franc	French
= 100 Centimes	(administrative
(the Belgian Franc is	language)
also legal tender)	German
Per capita GDP (1994): $US 24,000	Main religion: Roman Catholic (95%)

Ostend and Amsterdam to Strasburg and Basle. The country has three official languages: French, German and the indigenous language of Letzeburgish. French is normally used for commercial correspondence. There are four industries: steel, agriculture, banking and financial services, plus recently introduced computing technology and software development. Luxembourg is a constitutional monarchy, with a grand duke as head of state.

Most Luxembourgians are Catholics, and extremely affluent. The country's statistical authorities divide residents of the country into five income classes. Half the population is in the bottom two categories, and six per cent in the top group. Fifteen per cent of Luxembourgians are in the next to top category; a quarter in the middle class. Considering the high per capita income of the country this distribution means there are some *extremely* affluent Luxembourgians. Eighty per cent of the quarter of the country's population that is of foreign nationality occupy managerial positions.

Decline in the European steel and agricultural industries in the 1960s and 1970s hit the Luxembourg economy hard. In consequence, the country's government encouraged firms to diversify away from heavy industry towards services, particularly banking and finance. Nevertheless, manufacturing still accounts for 30 per cent of both the gross domestic product and the employed labour force (the rest are employed in finance, business and insurance services, apart from the three per cent that continue to work in agriculture and forestry). A notable feature of the Luxembourg economy is the low representation (less than 30 per cent) of women in the labour force – far less than in most other European states.

11. The Netherlands

The Netherlands has borders with Germany to the east and Belgium to the south and west. More that 50 per cent of the country lies below sea level. Half the Dutch population live in the west of the country where the principal cities, Amsterdam (the nation's capital, population one million), Rotterdam (population one million) and the Hague (650,000), are situated. Rotterdam is the world's largest port. Amsterdam also handles a large volume of sea traffic. The country is ideally located for trade with other EU nations, facing Britain on one side and having borders with Germany and Belgium on the other.

NETHERLANDS – KEY FACTS

Population: 15 million

Area: 40,850 sq.km.

Currency: Florin or Guilder
   = 100 Cents

Per capita GDP (1994): $US 21,000

Capital: Amsterdam

Main language: Dutch

Main religions: Roman Catholic
   (40%)
   Protestant (30%)

Manufacturing accounts for 18 per cent of the total labour force. Most Dutch workers today work in service industries (35 per cent in community, social and personal services; ten per cent in finance, insurance and business services: and 18 per cent in wholesale and retail outlets, restaurants and hotels). Eighteen per cent of the population are under 15 years of age; 16 per cent are between 15 and 24. About a third of all Dutch people are between 25 and 44; 20 per cent between 45 and 64. The country's national statistical authorities define four major social classes: higher management (40 per cent); clerical and skilled manual workers (36 per cent); and semi and unskilled employees, pensioners and widows (nine per cent).

The Dutch economy is extremely diverse, supplying an enormous range of manufactured products and services, especially financial services. A notable feature of the Netherlands is how economic activity is concentrated into a single industrialised area (the Randstrad) encompassing Rotterdam, Amsterdam, The Hague and Utrecht. The rest of the country is largely agricultural, although Dutch agriculture is itself highly mechanised. The Netherlands has been described as the distribution centre of Europe and, as such, has highly sophisticated warehousing (including bonded warehousing) and physical distribution systems. There are no freeports or free zones in the Netherlands, but arrangements for bonded warehousing are extremely liberal – goods can be labelled, repacked, repaired, blended and processed while under bond. Moreover, bonded goods can be moved around the country and kept for several years without paying duty.

12. Portugal

Portugal became a democracy in 1975, following 40 years of military dictatorship. A new constitution was introduced in 1982, committed to the liberalisation of

---

PORTUGAL – KEY FACTS

Population: 10.5 million

Area: 92,390 sq.km.

Currency: Escudo
   = 100 Centavos

Per capita GDP (1994): $US 7,700

Capital: Lisbon

Main language: Portuguese

Main religion: Roman Catholic

---

society and the promotion of business. Portugal joined the EU in 1986, and since then conditions have dramatically improved. There has been much new investment, and consumers' incomes and expenditures have increased. The capital city is Lisbon (population one million) in the south of the country. Oporto (population 750,000) is the dominant northern city. Otherwise, the population is thinly spread across the country: none of Portugal's 21 administrative regions outside Lisbon or Oporto account for more than seven per cent of the total population. Many Portuguese citizens continue to reside in remote rural areas.

Manufacturing accounts for about 35 per cent of the country's working population. Services contribute half of aggregate GDP and absorb around 44 per cent of the labour force. Within the service sector, personal and community services employ 22 per cent of all workers; wholesaling, retailing, restaurants and hotels accounts for 15 per cent; transport and communications for four per cent; and financial services for three per cent. Agriculture contributes just six per cent of GDP, yet employs 20 per cent of all Portuguese workers. Twenty-two per cent of the population is under 15 years of age. Seventeen per cent is between 15 and 24; 28 per cent between 25 and 44; and 22 per cent between 45 and 64. The country's national statistical office categorises Portuguese people into classes distinguished by occupation and household income. Three per cent of the population is estimated to be 'upper class'; 13 per cent middle class; 20 per cent lower middle; 27 per cent skilled workers; and the remaining 37 per cent 'working class'.

13. Spain

Spain's first free elections for 40 years were held in 1977, followed by the introduction of a new constitution in 1978. The dictatorship years were characterised by industrial inefficiency and low economic growth, and the transition to a deregulated market economy has not been easy. However, growth in real GDP has been extremely rapid over the last decade. Unfortunately, unemployment is a major problem. It exceeded 20 per cent in the mid-1980s and is still around the 14 to 15 per cent level. Spain acceded to the EU in 1986.

Spanish economic policy during the 1970s and early 1980s focused on easing structural change from the country's dependence on labour-intensive heavy industries towards the introduction of new technologies. Most schemes con-

---

SPAIN – KEY FACTS

Population: 39 million	Capital: Madrid
Area: 504,780 sq.km.	Main languages: Castilian Spanish
Currency: Peseta	Catalan
= 100 Centimos	Galician
Per capita GDP (1994): $US 13,700	Basque
	Main religion: Roman Catholic

cerned export industries and devices for attracting incoming foreign investment (so as to maintain domestic employment), rather than for technical development *per se*. The emphasis altered from 1984 onwards, however, and support for traditional industries was greatly reduced. Early retirement and improved unemployment benefits were introduced for people made redundant by restructuring. Current policy is to encourage high technology manufacturing, electronics, and software engineering, telecommunications and other technically advanced industries.

The country divides into 50 provinces which are in turn split into municipalities. Central government is based in Madrid (population about 1.3 million), the nation's capital. Spain is a constitutional monarchy, with a bicameral national assembly plus regional Parliaments for 17 'autonomous communities' (Cataluna and the Basque country, for example). Branches of the various government ministries are located in the provinces. Cataluna in the north-east is Spain's most prosperous region, with extensive trading, cultural and transport connections with the south of France. The regional capital is the port of Barcelona (population 1.7 million), which has a freeport zone and supports a wide range of industries. Tarragona is the second biggest port in the region and itself supports an industrial hinterland. Valencia (in the south of the country) is another important centre for banking, insurance and general financial services. Spain controls the Balearic Islands and the Canaries. The Balearics comprise Majorca, Minorca, Ibiza, Formentera and Cabrera, plus six smaller islands. The Canaries consist of seven islands, of which Tenerife and Grand Canary are the most important. EU firms can now do business in the Spanish Canary Islands on equal terms with Spanish companies.

About a quarter of the country's population is under 15 years of age. Approximately 30 per cent is between 15 and 34; 20 per cent between 35 and 54; and a quarter are 55 or over. The Spanish national statistical authorities divide the population into social classes: 'upper' (containing around 14 per cent of all Spanish households); 'middle' (22 per cent); 'lower middle' (25 per cent); and 'working' (39 per cent). The Spanish population is overwhelmingly Roman Catholic. Twenty-two per cent of the workforce is engaged in the provision of social and personal services. Financial services account for five per cent of all employees. Twenty-one per cent of the labour force works in manufacturing; 20 per cent in the wholesale and retail industries, restaurants and hotels. Agriculture remains important, employing around 15 per cent of the workforce.

14. Sweden

Swedish living standards are among the highest in the world. The country's economy is strong and diversified, based as it is on a mixture of manufacturing and the exploitation of an abundant stock of natural resources. Main industries include automotive products, light engineering, computer technology, textiles and clothing, forestry, pulp and paper, and mineral extraction and processing. Manufacturing accounts for nearly a third of Sweden's GDP; services for 53 per cent; agriculture for five per cent. Eighteen per cent of the population live in Stockholm, the nation's capital. Other important cities are Göteborg (population

---

SWEDEN – KEY FACTS

Population: 8.8 million

Area: 450,000 sq.km.

Currency: Krona = 100 Ore

Per capita GDP (1994): $US 28,400

Capital: Stockholm

Main languages: Swedish

Finn

Lapp

Main religion: Protestant (90%)

750,000), Malmo (450,000) and Helsingborg (220,000). Several Swedish cities have populations of around 175,000. Most Swedes live in the southern part of the country, as weather conditions in northern Sweden are extremely harsh. The dominant religion is Lutheran Protestant. Nearly two per cent of the resident population have Finnish nationality.

About half the country is forested, and there are many thousands of lakes. The north of Sweden is mountainous and extends far into the Arctic Circle. Wood products (timber, pulp, paper, etc.) account for ten per cent of all Sweden's exports. Manufacturing accounts for nearly a third of Sweden's GDP, services for 53 per cent, agriculture for five per cent. Inflation and unemployment have been low by international standards. Most Swedish workers are employed in service industries. Social and personnel services account for 37 per cent of the labour force; wholesale and retail distribution (including restaurants and hotels) for 14 per cent; financial services for eight per cent. Manufacturing accounts for 22 per cent of the workforce. Sweden moved into recession in the early 1990s. The budget deficit and rate of inflation rose, and the country's ability to finance its extensive state welfare programmes has been threatened.

15. United Kingdom

'Britain' comprises three countries: England, Scotland and Wales, under a single government. The United Kingdom consists of Britain *plus* Northern Ireland, the Isle of Man, the Channel Islands, the Orkneys and various other offshore islands. Technically, therefore, the UK is not the same as 'Britain', though in practice the two names are used interchangeably. English is used throughout the UK. The Celtic language of Welsh is also commonly spoken in parts of Wales. The latter has a population of about three million; Scotland has five million; and Northern Ireland 1.5 million. England's 48 million inhabitants are spread unevenly around the country. A third live in seven major conurbations: London, Merseyside, Tyneside, Clydeside, the west Midlands, west Yorkshire and south Lancashire. London (the capital city) has a population of about 6.8 million (substantially more if immediately surrounding areas are also considered).

The UK population is large and expanding: there will be about three million extra Britons by the end of the century. Approximately 20 per cent of the population is under 15 years of age; fifteen per cent is between 15 and 24; 29 per

---

UNITED KINGDOM – KEY FACTS

Population: 58 million	Capital: London
Area: 244,100 sq.km.	Main languages: English
Currency: Pound = 100 Pence	Welsh
Per capita GDP (1994): $US 18,100	Main religions: Mostly Church of
	England and
	other Protestant
	denominations
	Roman Catholic (8%)
	Islam

---

cent between 24 and 44; 21 per cent between 45 and 64. Statistical and marketing organisations conventionally divide the UK population into six social classes: A, B, C1, C2, D and E. Category A consists of the wealthy, upper-middle class and contains about three per cent of all Britons. Class B (the managerial middle class) has around 14 per cent; C1 (the lower middle class – supervisors, clerks, etc.) has 27 per cent; C2 (the skilled working class) about 25 per cent. Categories D and E represent the poorest elements of British society. Class D is the unskilled working class and accounts for 19 per cent of all people; class E, i.e. people living at or near subsistence level (the unemployed or the poor elderly for example) has 12 per cent. Social class is a key determinant of attitudes, beliefs, consumption habits and lifestyle among British people.

Compared to the majority of Continental EU nations British economic performance during the post-Second World War period has been poor. From 1950 to 1980 the country's real per capita GDP grew by an average of less than two per cent per annum. This should be compared with a 3.5 per cent annual growth rate in France over the same period, and 4.5 per cent in Germany. In 1950 the UK had the world's sixth highest GDP per head of population; by 1994 it had the 23rd.

The causes of the UK's long-term economic decline are many and varied. The UK was the world's first major industrial power and, arguably, its unchallenged position during the last century has led to the absence of the dynamism necessary to succeed in the post-Second World War years. Manifestations of decline have included the loss of world markets, low productivity, low investment, inadequate training and technical education, high inflation, chronic balance of payments problems, high unemployment, overmanning and poor industrial relations, and insufficient research and development (UK spending on R&D per employee in the 1980s was only two-thirds that of West Germany and 80 per cent that of France). However, the effects of these problems have been felt unevenly – certain sections of UK society are extremely affluent, while others are among the poorest in the EU. It should be noted that living standards in some parts of the south-east of England are *extremely* high, matching those of the most affluent regions of Western Europe.

The majority of the workforce is employed in the service sector. Community, social and personal services account for 30 per cent of employment; financial services for eleven per cent; and wholesale and retail distribution (including restaurants and hotels) for 20 per cent. Manufacturing absorbs barely 21 per cent of the workforce. Women now constitute more than half the working population, but are concentrated into a small number of industries and occupations (particularly retailing, health care and administration). A notable feature of the UK market is the presence within it of sizeable ethnic minority segments, living predominantly within inner cities. The ethnic minorities are significantly poorer on average than the rest of the population and experience far higher rates of unemployment. Their spending habits and consumer goods ownership patterns are also different to the majority of the people.

ENLARGEMENT OF THE EUROPEAN UNION

16. Implications of enlargement

Proposals to enlarge the EU have political as well as economic dimensions. The governments of applicant countries want access to the developed world's largest and most affluent market, and wish to anchor their political systems against the democratic institutions and stable political environments of West European nations. Note how applicant countries with poorly developed commercial legal systems and regulatory institutions can acquire tried and tested systems and institutions 'off-the-shelf' simply by adopting those already in place within the European Union. Enlargement is also desired by the leaders of certain existing EU members, who see the entry of particular newcomers as a means for supporting their positions on key issues in internal EU negotiations. For the individual country, the economic consequences of entry are uncertain, and may be split into short-term and long-term categories (Haack 1972).

Short-term effects include the impact on the domestic economy of the country's financial contribution to the EU budget, changes in state agricultural support arrangements following implementation of the Common Agricultural Policy, and an improvement or deterioration in the nation's balance of payments. The direction of the movement in the balance of payments is virtually impossible to predict, as it will result from the complex interactions of two forces: trade *creation* as fresh trade arises with EU partners; and trade *diversion* consequent to the replacement of existing trading links with non-EU countries by new arrangements with Union members. Outcomes will depend on:

- The country's tariff levels at the moment of entry. If these are significantly higher than those operated by the EU then, as tariffs are lowered to EU levels, imports from EU members might rise sharply – whereas exports will maintain their prices in EU markets.

- The extent of preferential *ad hoc* bilateral trade agreements that the country previously enjoyed with non-EU nations but which will have to be abandoned following EU entry.
- The underlying strength of the country's domestic economy.

Further short-term effects will be determined by the consequences of (i) the introduction of value added tax, (ii) the implementation of EU competition law (which might necessitate the privatisation of state-owned industries), and (iii) receipts of EU regional investment grants and subsidies.

The hoped-for long-term effects of a country's entry to the European Union include economies of scale in production and distribution that become available to domestic firms as they begin to operate in the wider European market; increased investment in industry (especially inward foreign investment); an intensification of business competition (with resultant benefits for consumers); greater business efficiency and faster economic growth. Domestic companies are likely to become larger (possibly via mergers and acquisitions) and then perhaps to engage in more technical research. These benefits might not be realised, however, if the managements of domestic companies fail to rise to the challenge; do not modernise business methods to match EU levels; or if the country's labour force does not possess the necessary skills or if industrial relations are poor.

Arguments against further enlargement of the EU are as follows:

(a) Enlargement might detract from the pressing need to 'deepen' the EU, i.e. move towards further economic and political integration.

(b) The Single Market needs to be fully completed, with the complete removal of *all* barriers to the free movement of goods, capital and labour, prior to taking in new members.

(c) Most applicant countries are considerably less well off than the majority of EU nations. Hence the entry of these poorer states will place severe burdens on the EU's regional assistance and other support programmes.

Progress test 2

1. Why is Belgium an ideal country for the test marketing of pan-European campaigns?

2. Why did the Finnish economy decline so sharply in the early 1990s?

3. What are the criticisms of the French practice of subsidising 'national champions'?

4. State the currencies of (i) Portugal, (ii) The Netherlands, (iii) Greece, (iv) Finland.

5. What are the capital cities of (i) Finland, (ii) Sweden, (iii) Luxembourg, (iv) Denmark, (v) Portugal?

6. In which year did Spain accede to the European Union?

7. Which three EU countries have (i) the highest living standards, and (ii) the lowest living standards?

8. Why do certain non-EU countries wish to join the EU?

9. What are the likely short-term effects on a country's economy of it becoming a member of the European Union?

10. List the major arguments against further enlargement of the EU.

3

EAST EUROPE

THE DYNAMICS OF TRANSITION

1. Introduction

Business in East Europe is characterised by enormous commercial energy, high aspirations and escalating demands for imported goods, but also by economic disruption, extremely low living standards in many regions, acute shortages of foreign exchange, managerial inefficiency, mass unemployment and inability to pay for imports. The area has a population of 400 million (including the former USSR) and there is excess demand for nearly every type of product. Consumers are well educated and as such are responsive to advertising and other promotional campaigns. Literacy levels are among the highest in the world, and many workers possess top class industrial skills. At least 85 per cent of all workers in Poland and Hungary have completed some form of industrial training, a higher percentage than for any European Union country.

Most East European nations have extensive engineering industries capable of manufacturing virtually all categories of item (over a quarter of all output in Hungary, Poland, Russia and the Czech and Slovak Republics consists of manufactured goods), and the local availability of such items greatly enhances the possibilities for barter trade. Note how the combination of low wages with highly skilled industrial workforces could lead to Western manufacturers locating just inside the Western borders of East European nations, in order to serve West European markets. Also, the existence of well-educated and highly trained workforces raises the possibility of technological leapfrogging by East European states, provided their commercial infrastructures are satisfactory.

2. Nature of the East European market

Important consumer import markets have arisen for food items (consequent to the removal of price controls and hence the uncompetitiveness of certain locally produced items); house and home improvement goods (resulting from the pressing need to make good dilapidated housing); clothing and footwear; and computer hardware and software of all kinds. Other areas of increasing demand include automotive products, electronic equipment (especially videos), toys and health care items. Equipment for business and industrial modernisation is in particularly heavy demand. Opportunities for industrial exports to East Europe focus on building materials, office equipment, textile and food processing equipment, medical supplies, machinery of all kinds, items connected with environmental improvement, telecommunications, distribution and transport equipment, and computers. Openings have arisen for the export from West to East Europe of agricultural equipment (as former state-run and inefficient collective farms are modernised), white goods and pharmaceuticals. The sale of automotive products is sure to increase sharply as road systems improve.

The majority of East Europeans live in cities and have lifestyles essentially similar to urban dwellers in the West, although rates of ownership of consumer goods and other household items are well below those for advanced Western States. East European consumers are familiar with Western products, advertisements and selling methods and wish to purchase Western exports. However, wages are low (on average barely ten per cent of West European and US levels) so that consumers do not have the cash to satisfy their demands. The populations of East European nations are generally younger than in the West. A crucial feature of East Europe is its ethnic diversity. There are substantial numbers of people of German descent living in Poland, Romania and Russia. Bulgaria has a large Turkish minority; there are Russians and Hungarians in Romania, Croats in Hungary, Poles in Russia, Ukrainians in the Slovak Republic, and so on. Often, diverse local cultures and languages co-exist within the same national frontiers. This gives rise to the need for extensive research into national markets. Unfortunately, market research data and facilities are extremely limited in these countries.

3. Economic liberalisation

Transition to a market economy has several dimensions: privatisation, removal of price controls, abolition of state subsidies to industry, the opening up of foreign trade and investment, making the local currency internally and externally convertible, and the establishment of business services and institutions (banks, insurance companies, stock exchanges, etc.). Each of these requires an enormous amount of effort, and progress has varied from nation to nation. Some East European countries (notably Poland, Hungary and the Czech Republic) adopted 'big bang' approaches to liberalisation. Others have proceeded more cautiously. In Russia the transition to a Western-style economy was supposed to occur via the Shatalin Plan of 1989, although not all of its objectives have been achieved. The plan itself involved a 500-day programme for installing capitalism in the Russian Republic, requiring:

- removal of all price controls
- elimination of state subsidies on food and rents
- establishment of a stock exchange
- recognition of trade unions
- offer for sale of state-owned factories to their employees through share issues
- sale of collective farms to peasants
- privatisation of 40 per cent of all Russian industry (60 per cent of the food industry and 50 per cent of construction) by the 400th day

- reduction of the size of the state budget deficit to five per cent of its initial figure within 100 days.

It is important to note that the economic and political situations of many East European countries are in a state of turmoil and liable to sudden and unexpected change. All remain nominally committed to market reforms, though the pace, pattern and detail of reform frequently alters in consequence of political factors.

4. Privatisation of enterprises

Privatisation of industry lies at the heart of the liberalisation process, but is proving extremely difficult. Many of the firms offered for sale are simply unviable (Frydman and Ropaczynski 1993). They are overmanned, technically backward, burdened with debt, and not worth buying at any price. Others require drastic reorganisation and labour redundancies to bring them up to international standards. And even when an enterprise is profitable there are few local residents with sufficient cash to finance the purchase.

East European governments have privatised state-run enterprises in order to improve their efficiency, to enable market forces to determine which should succeed and which fail, and in consequence of pressures exerted by the World Bank, International Monetary Fund and other financial institutions which have lent money to these nations (Schwartz and Lopes 1993). Other hoped-for benefits of privatisation include a reduction in the state bureaucracy needed to administer industrial affairs, cuts in budget deficits, lower taxes, and the creation of an internationally competitive economy capable of sustaining long run growth. It is important to realise, moreover, that the word 'privatisation' in East Europe has a different meaning to how it is used in the West. In a technical sense, an East European enterprise is 'privatised' when at least 51 per cent of its ownership is transferred into private hands. However, East European governments continue to give direct and indirect assistance to 'private' firms. In particular, labour costs to enterprises are far lower than in the West because of the extensive social welfare and income support mechanisms that apply in East European states. Enterprises frequently receive cheap loans from state-owned banks, and market their outputs through collective distribution systems. Arguably, therefore, East European privatisation is as much a *political* as an economic phenomenon, intended to underscore a government's commitment to individualistic values and the encouragement of personal initiative in the accumulation of private wealth.

5. Privatisation methods

Various approaches to privatisation have been adopted, including mass sales, sector by sector disposals, and conversion of individual operations into private companies. For example, in 1991 the former Czechoslovakia denationalised many state-run enterprises via a voucher system intended to convert a mass of state firms into private businesses very quickly and at minimal cost. Importantly, the government did not attempt to restructure firms and/or industries prior to their privatisation.

Residents were able to purchase books of vouchers at a very low price, these vouchers then being exchangeable for shares in companies of their choice as they were put up for auction. If people were not prepared to take shares in certain enterprises, the firms involved simply went into liquidation. Foreigners were not allowed to purchase vouchers, but 100 per cent ownership of enterprises was allowed. The currency became internally convertible at the same time. A Stock Exchange was established to create a marketplace for shares. Around eight million people participated in the scheme. Privatisation has been severely hindered by disputes over the ownership of land and property nationalised in 1948.

Russia too initiated a voucher system. Books of vouchers were issued free of charge to any resident over 18 years of age wishing to participate. Around 100 million people took vouchers. Poland, Hungary and Bulgaria privatised a number of particular industrial sectors, one at a time. The idea was to retain key sectors intact and prevent investors taking only the very best companies within them. Privatisation of individual enterprises occurred concurrently in these (and all other East European) states. The Hungarian authorities, for example, converted a number of state firms into private companies which were then offered to the highest bidder. Private shareholding has been encouraged via the provision of interest-free five-year loans to finance share purchases. As in other East European nations, numerous disputes are arising over who exactly owns the land on which shops, factories and offices are built. In Poland management buy-outs have been a common device for shifting enterprise ownership into private hands. Otherwise businesses were handed over to local authorities and National Investment Funds which then became responsible for their privatisation. A Stock Exchange has been established, which will offer for sale shares in particular enterprises. Bulgaria and Romania have been more cautious in privatising their economies than most other East European states, preferring to encourage new start-ups of private businesses rather than the wholesale selling off of state-owned firms. Romania is privatising many of its industries by transferring their ownership to five investment trusts, which in turn will administer enterprises as joint stock companies. The remainder are available to international investors.

The case for rapid privatisation is that if privatisation is slow then existing inefficiencies are preserved. Fast privatisation means however that very many enterprises will not survive competition, leading to high unemployment (Aylen 1987; Asah 1990). Further difficulties are that:

- Many enterprises are sure to fail immediately following their entry to free markets, leaving shareholders with worthless investments.
- The price reductions and special inducements needed to unload certain firms may be so costly to the national authorities as to make the programme uneconomic.
- The administrative systems established to organise privatisations are themselves bureaucratic and frequently inefficient.
- The task involved is so enormous that there may be little prospect of success. Arguably a much longer-term perspective should be adopted.

- The financial infrastructure needed to facilitate privatisation did not exist at the time enterprises were put up for sale. There were no merchant banking, underwriting or pre-existing share transfer systems; no accounting standards, financial information or credit rating companies, no investor relations consultants to assist with the preparation of prospectuses, etc. Privatisation has proven problematic even in countries that have extensive financial services industries (the UK and France for example).
- The speed at which privatisation proceeded gave it a high profile and perhaps generated unrealistic expectations among the population, which was encouraged to believe that privatisation would, at a stroke, solve all a country's economic problems.
- Although much East European industry is worthless, parts of it have great potential and it is arguable that these sectors have been sold off far too cheaply.

PROBLEMS AND CHALLENGES

6. Economic problems in East Europe

Privatisation only makes sense in the context of an economy in which prices are determined by the forces of supply and demand, otherwise there are no fundamental criteria against which to assess a newly privatised business's capacity to survive. Yet allowing prices to rise has caused great hardship for the populations of East European states. It is likely to be the case, however, that prices will only stabilise once they are determined entirely by market forces. Also the price system itself might not direct resources in the most profitable ways. Even the most optimistic forecasts suggest that only a minority of East European enterprises can compete internationally, and that many have no hope of survival in the long term. Others might continue but only after drastic restructuring. The situation is made worse by the fact that in the past central planners encouraged the creation of very large production units, as they were easier to control and their outputs could be dovetailed into national and regional planning frameworks. As they collapse these huge combines are creating mass unemployment in particular areas. High rates of inflation have occurred as cheap sources of raw materials disappeared.

Conversion of East European economies from centrally planned to private enterprise systems has been traumatic. National incomes tumbled, although the few figures that are currently available suggest that Hungary, Poland and the Czech (but not the Slovak) Republic have experienced positive growth since 1993. Other East European economies continue to experience acute difficulties, though note that published information relates primarily to the (rapidly declining) public sectors of these countries and that their expanding private sectors may in practice partially offset the observed reductions in official national incomes. Economic austerity measures imposed in attempts to curb inflation and increase earnings of foreign exchange have had an enormous social cost. Income distributions within East European states are increasingly uneven, and the unemployed face grave poverty.

Foreign trade

An important feature of East European economies is their relative lack of involvement with international trade, resulting from decades of government policies aimed at economic self-sufficiency and Eastern bloc political isolation. East European import tariffs are generally high, and many East European nations apply protectionist foreign trade policies. However, tariffs are beginning to fall in consequence of the conclusion in December 1993 of the Uruguay Round of GATT and through bilateral trade agreements between individual countries and the US, Japan, and (in particular) the European Union. Tariff rates vary enormously between East European nations and among product groups, and rates themselves are subject to sudden and unpredictable alteration. Quota and import licensing systems are common. Free ports and free trade zones now exist in Bulgaria, Hungary, the Czech Republic, Russia, Romania, Belarus, Estonia and the Ukraine.

Exports to Western Markets are relatively low, leading to chronic shortages of foreign exchange. Currency devaluations are common, leading to increased import prices, including imports of much needed capital goods.

7. Operational difficulties

Among the many operational problems confronting foreign companies wishing to do business in East Europe the following are worthy of particular mention:

- The impossibility of preparing accurate business forecasts in fast changing and uncertain economic, political and legal environments.
- Foreign firms having to compete against state-owned local enterprises that continue to receive government subsidies.
- Having to rely on payment by cheque or post office transfers for consumer purchases (in consequence of the underdevelopment of commercial banking systems).
- Sparcity of market information.
- Delays and frustrations arising from having to deal with numerous (well-meaning) state officials who do not possess the authority to take significant decisions.
- Labour problems for firms wishing to establish a permanent presence resulting from employees not being culturally attuned to the cut and thrust of free labour markets. In Russia, for example, school leavers prior to liberalisation were assigned to jobs for three-year periods during which they could not be dismissed. Working methods in many industries are so out-of-date that employees' attitudes may have been adversely affected, leading perhaps to an unwillingness to accept the latest technologies. In Poland and Romania, foreign companies may dismiss workers in manners analogous to those used in the West. Elsewhere however local rules on labour lay-offs apply, and can make dismissal procedures extremely problematic and protracted.

- Lack of formal business procedures. These countries have yet to develop proper legal frameworks for consumer and employee protection, contract, business insolvency, etc., within a private enterprise system.

All East European countries now have internally convertible currencies, meaning that local currency (roubles for example) can be freely exchanged into foreign currencies (such as US dollars) at a local market price set by supply and demand. However, not all East European states allow the unfettered transmission of 'hard' foreign currencies (i.e. those which are internationally acceptable as a means for financing transactions) to other countries. Hence, although domestic currency can be exchanged for foreign currency and the latter used to purchase items *within* the country concerned, the export of hard currency might be restricted. A common condition is that foreign firms can only repatriate locally earned profits in the form of hard currency to the extent that these companies *earn* foreign exchange through selling their outputs to third party nations. Note however that such limitations are systematically being removed.

Foreign investment

Foreign ownership of local enterprises is permitted in all East European nations, although some states impose restrictions on foreigners' abilities to purchase land. The latter results from the fact that in most East European countries the state at some time or other confiscated all land and buildings so that, on privatisation of these assets, there is much confusion regarding who owns specific properties; the families from whom they were initially confiscated; past or present occupants; or recent purchasers. There are no local content requirements in any East European country. All East European nations now have laws guaranteeing foreigners that their investments will not be expropriated, or that full (hard currency) compensation at current market value will be paid if expropriation occurs. In most East European countries the taxes on the profits earned by foreign enterprises are low relative to international standards (and lower than for domestic firms), and all East European states provide extensive grants and subsidies for new job creation, location in depressed areas, inward technology transfer, and for research and technical development.

8. Management of East European enterprises

Prior to economic reform, enterprise management in East European countries was regarded as a technical resource whose role was to plan, organise and deploy resources to achieve targets set by central state administrators who, in effect, held a government monopoly over business affairs. This had the following consequences:

(a) Managers' performances were appraised not in terms of their ability to improve profitability, but rather of their contributions to national, local and industry economic plans.

(b) Decisions did not have to be based on the comparative prices of inputs and final products. Instead, decisions related to general economic, political and/or technical considerations.

(c) Managers did not need to concern themselves with marketing, or even with making goods appear attractive to consumers.

(d) Firms were instructed where to obtain supplies and where to deliver final outputs.

(e) Arguably, lack of commercial accountability meant that managers could take reckless decisions without fear of consequences.

For decades managements were told who would supply their inputs and how they were to price their outputs. Goods were distributed by the state, which also determined how labour was to be treated and how much the individual worker was to be paid. Output levels were decided centrally according to the requirements of national and regional economic plans. Foreign trade was conducted (with the exception of Hungary) through foreign trade organisations (FTOs) operated on product lines. FTOs would buy and sell on their own accounts, find foreign customers for specific deals, research international price levels for various products and determine foreign technical standards requirements.

These circumstances led to an acute lack of commercial management skills among enterprise managers. The absence of managerial know-how is particularly severe in the following areas:

(a) Quality management and quality assurance standards (ISO 9000 for instance).

(b) Cost and management accounting. Concepts of profit, loss, overheads absorption, marginal cost pricing, etc., had little meaning in a centrally planned socialist economic system. Not knowing how much it costs to produce a particular item results in arbitrary pricing decisions with consequent detrimental effects on profits.

(c) All aspects of marketing.

(d) Organisation design and development.

Managements need to learn how to structure their internal organisations in manners that will equip them for international competition, with new departments to deal with advertising and marketing, personnel management, information technology, and so on.

STRUCTURES FOR SUCCESS

9. Long-term prospects for East Europe

Once their transition to well-organised mixed economies is complete the East European states will constitute one of the world's most attractive environments for international business. Communications between East European and other nations are straightforward, and it is easy to investigate East European markets first hand. Business laws, rules and practices in East European countries will soon be identical with those of the West, while improvements in industrial infrastructures will themselves increase employment, output and hence consumer demand.

East European consumers may be characterised as having the capacity to become sophisticated and discerning buyers, but at present lacking the cash to satisfy their requirements. They are familiar with Western products, advertisements and selling methods and, critically, they want to purchase imported goods. Entrepreneurs in East Europe are desperately anxious to establish contacts with Western partners, and fresh possibilities for profitable business constantly emerge. The region is a seller's market: everything is in demand, the only missing factor is the hard currency needed to pay for imports.

It is not generally feasible to do business in East Europe opportunistically and without taking a long-term view. Many years will elapse before these countries are able to fully transform their legal, accounting and business education systems to Western standards and have stable economies with modern industrial infrastructures and convertible currencies. Accordingly, firms must be prepared to wait for a number of years prior to obtaining a significant return, and have to accept a high level of risk in the interim period. The pace of economic progress in East European nations will depend substantially on the nature of their relations with the EU. Several East European countries have stated their desire to join the Union, although a number of factors militate against this eventuality in the short to medium term. Disruptions in the East led to large-scale immigration from East European countries into France, Italy, Benelux and (especially) Germany. This in turn caused political problems for West European governments and, it seems, disinterest in the prospect of opening the Single Market's borders to workers from East European states (as would happen automatically if these countries joined the EU). Another difficulty is that since many East European nations are heavily dependent on agriculture they would immediately qualify for huge amounts of EU agricultural subsidies and support. The Common Agricultural Policy in its present form could not cope with the resulting drain on its resources. Also the fact that East European countries are poor by Western standards means that they would absorb most of the EU's regional development budget.

The low wage costs of East European enterprises could give them a competitive advantage against EU firms. Average per capita income of Bulgaria, Hungary, Poland, Romania and the Czech and Slovak Republics is about 12 per cent of the average for the European Union, and just 60 per cent of the per capita GDP of Portugal, the poorest member state.

10. The Visegrad group and EU Association Agreements

In 1995 Hungary, Poland and the Czech and Slovak Republics decided to begin dismantling tariffs against each other (aiming to create a free trade area within a decade) and to co-ordinate their effects to join the European Union. Advantages enjoyed by these countries (which came to be known as the Visegrad group) include their geographical nearness to affluent West European markets, their trained and generally well-educated workforces, low labour costs, and reasonable industrial infrastructures. The Visegrad nations were the first to establish Association Agreements (also known as Europe Agreements in order to distinguish them from similar agreements between the EU and certain other non-East European nations) with the European Union, providing for reciprocal trade concessions between the EU and these states plus the setting up of a legal framework for political dialogue among the parties. EU Association Agreements with other East European nations followed. The main provisions of Association Agreements were as follows:

(a) All quotas on entry to EU markets of products other than those listed in (c) below have been abolished, and EU import tariffs are being reduced systematically. The East European countries will themselves remove quotas and tariffs by the year 2002. Only goods with at least 60 per cent East European local content will qualify for duty-free EU entry.

(b) Workers from these countries who already live in the EU may continue to reside in the Union and (importantly) will receive social security benefits equal to those available to EU residents. However, further labour migration to the EU will not be permitted.

(c) The Union has committed itself to allow open entry to East European food, coal, steel and textiles, but only in the long run.

(d) Association Agreement countries can continue giving state aid to backward industries. However they had to begin applying EU rules on business competition from 1995.

Consequent to the signing of Association Agreements about 60 per cent of EU imports from these countries now enter the Union free of duty, and the introduction of new trade restrictions on exports to and from signatory countries is prohibited. In 1992 the EU concluded ten-year Trade and Co-operation Agreements with Albania, Latvia, Estonia and Lithuania. These are bilateral trade agreements offering improved (but not preferential) access to EU markets.

Problems with Association and Trade and Co-operation Agreements

Critics of Association and Trade and Co-operation Agreements allege that they are too partial and are to be implemented over too long a period to be effective. What is really needed, they argue, is a 'big bang' to link East and West Europe immediately and inextricably and genuinely boost economic development in Eastern nations. In principle, Association and Trade and Co-operation Agreements provide beneficiaries with lower tariffs and more favourable export opportunities than other states, plus an assortment of financial credits and direct assistance schemes. In reality, however, the hoped-for benefits have not been fully realised. Fears of cheap agricultural and other products from East Europe have led to the imposition of *de facto* protective measures in several EU countries, and the European Commission has not intervened to outlaw violations of the original agreements. The agreements themselves leave many opportunities for the imposition of restrictions on their implementation. Recession in Western Europe, moreover, has depressed West European firms' sales within EU nations hence increasing the latter's reluctance to allow low-cost East European products free access to their markets. The fact that so many East European enterprises continue to enjoy state subsidy is another reason advanced for not opening up West European markets to Eastern businesses. Trade between East and West Europe has grown rapidly since the collapse of communism, although it still represents only a small percentage of total EU external transactions. Imports to the EU from the Visegrad countries, for example, never accounted for more than six per cent of aggregate EU imports prior to 1995.

11. The European Bank for Reconstruction and Development (EBRD)

Established in 1991 the London-based EBRD has 53 member countries plus the European Union and the European Investment Bank (*see* 1:**14**). Its purpose is to facilitate the transition to market economies of East European nations through fostering private enterprise and entrepreneurial initiative. This it does by providing loans, direct financial investments and technical assistance to East European states that have demonstrated their commitment to multiparty democracy and the maintenance of human rights. Under the Bank's internal rules at least 60 per cent of its funding must go to existing private companies or state-owned enterprises undergoing privatisation or to the creation of new companies (including joint ventures with foreign investors). The remaining 40 per cent is directed towards infrastructure and other public sector projects. Further EBRD activities include the analysis of specific industry sectors and particular issues relating to privatisation and economic restructuring, and the publication of research studies.

The Bank receives its money from Western governments, supplemented by borrowing on the international money markets, and uses its resources to fund projects intended to:

- implement privatisation
- encourage direct foreign investment
- restructure industries and develop industrial infrastructures
- create and strengthen financial institutions
- improve the physical environment.

Typically the Bank will contribute up to 35 per cent of the cost of a project, the rest coming from local banks and project sponsors. The criteria applied when evaluating proposals submitted by private companies or enterprises about to be privatised include commercial viability (evidenced by the clear existence of sound market prospects), significant contributions of permanent risk capital by sponsors, the extent to which the enterprise's competitiveness will be improved, the quality of management and the dependability of the technology involved. Loans are denominated in convertible currencies and must be repaid in those currencies. Normally the projects to be funded must have a value of ECU 5 million or above. The bank does not *itself* provide technical assistance, financial advice or training to funded projects, relying instead on member governments and/or consulting firms to supply these services. Fees for such purposes are regarded as a permissible use of EBRD funding.

COUNTERTRADE

Although countertrade is used throughout the world as a device for settling cross-border transactions it is particularly common for trade between East European and Western countries. The following discussion applies to countertrade activities in all other regions.

12. Nature of countertrade

Countertrade encompasses barter, compensation trading (*see* below), and other forms of direct or indirect exchange of goods for goods across national frontiers. Typically it occurs in situations where one or more of the parties is unable to pay for imports using foreign currency, either because its central bank has insufficient stocks of foreign exchange or in consequence of government restrictions on the availability of foreign exchange imposed for political reasons (Kotabe 1989). According to the OECD, countertrade may account for anything up to five per cent of total world trade; ten per cent for trade involving developing nations, and 35 per cent for trade between the latter and East European states.

13. Advantages and disadvantages of countertrade

Countertrade enables international trade to take place without the need to exchange hard currency. Developing countries are able to import high-technology products and pay for them using items they might not otherwise have been able to market internationally. Exporters can sell their outputs in a wider range of countries, including many large and fast-growing markets. Countertrade can assist technology transfer from advanced to developing countries and facilitate economic growth in the latter. Importantly, it can be used to circumvent protectionist government policies in certain nations (Jacobs and Palia 1986). Note how the individual exporter can use countertrade to offer what is in effect an extremely favourable price to a potential customer in a country where there is fierce local competition. It may even be more convenient for a customer to pay in goods rather than in cash, as a countertrade deal can provide an immediate market for a firm's output, without any need for advertising or other forms of promotion.

Problems with countertrade

Critics of countertrade allege that it distorts the normal competitive process whereby prices are determined by the interplay of supply and demand in free markets. Only a minority of companies have the knowledge or capacity to engage in countertrade (so the number of firms competing within certain countries is diminished), and there is little empirical evidence that countertrade actually improves the foreign exchange positions of the countries in which it is common. A problem confronting the national tax authorities of a country involved in extensive countertrade is that the 'dumping' of a foreign product at below its cost of production may be occurring without the fact being evident (because the price at which the item is imported is not stated in monetary units). Accordingly, national tax authorities which suspect that countertrade deals are in reality a form of disguised dumping might impose *ad hoc* import duties on the transaction. To avoid such accusations and to ensure that all local anti-dumping rules are complied with, the exporter might record all details of the intended deal in a separate document (known as an evidence account) which is formally deposited with the appropriate government department of the import-ers country. Specific difficulties faced by the individual firm involved in a countertrade deal are:

- its administrative cost and complexity
- the possibility of a sudden collapse in the world market price of the goods received as payment, and the scarcity of potential third party buyers for certain types of item
- that foreign customers might be more interested in having their suppliers act as unpaid distributors for their outputs in foreign markets than in the imported goods themselves
- the possibility of disputes arising over the acceptability of the level of quality of the barter goods actually delivered, especially if no precise quality specification for the goods has been agreed. An exporter could be landed with poor quality goods which are difficult to sell. This imposes warehousing costs on the firm receiving them and causes a deterioration in its liquidity position.
- delays in the delivery of barter items, due perhaps to production hold-ups, transportation or documentation difficulties, the need to obtain an export licence, etc.
- absence of clearcut procedures for resolving disputes (in contrast with deals involving the exchange of goods for money).

14. Techniques of countertrade

Firms engaging in countertrade involving product categories with which they are already familiar might decide to organise and administer their own counter-trade transactions. If the company has little knowledge of the items it will receive in payment for exports, however, then the services of an expert intermediary will probably be necessary (Vergariv 1985; Welt 1990). Countertrade intermedi-aries will store and process goods and advertise and otherwise promote the items on offer. The intermediary will act either as an agent or a principal and normally charge between three and 15 per cent commission for its services.

Barter, i.e. the straightforward exchange of item for item (so many barrels of oil for so many units of machinery for example), is the simplest form of countertrade. Deals are usually transacted at the prevailing world market prices of the products involved. Barter arrangements are also known as 'contra-trading' or 'reciprocal trading'. Barter transactions are easy to set up, and unavoidable in situations where hard currency to pay for imports is unobtainable. In risky situations the exporter might insist on receiving the barter goods before despatching the export consignment. The exporter sells the_____ goods, the money received being paid to an independent third party (usually a bank) which holds it 'in escrow' (meaning that the money is held in trust until certain conditions have been fulfilled). As soon as sales revenues are sufficient to finance the deal the exporter sends off the goods and the third party releases the money.

Switch deals occur where the exporter (or an intermediary) arranges for the disposal of the barter goods to a third party, which receives the goods direct from the importer and assumes responsibility for selling them – often in foreign countries. Switch trading via intermediaries originally developed in Austria, where banks have traditionally been prepared to advance cash to exporters prior to finding third party customers for the goods. Many Austrian banks have subsidiaries which directly engage in international trade, and so may actually buy the products offered by importers (enabling importers to make cash payments to suppliers). *Compensation dealing*, as opposed to straight barter, is where the exporting firm receives part payment in its own currency and the remainder in goods. *Buyback* occurs when a firm supplies plant and equipment to a foreign importer under a contract requiring the exporter to accept output produced by the plant and equipment supplied as whole or part payment for the transaction. If wages and other non-capital production costs are lower in the importing country then the plant and equipment supplier can obtain finished output at highly competitive prices. The problem is finding buyers for the output received. Note how this could lead to the exporter entering into competition with its own domestic customers (to whom the firm might have supplied similar plant and equipment to produce the same type of item). Buyback contracts need to specify very carefully the quality level and delivery schedule of the buyback product. It is sometimes the case that a government will sanction the import of major capital goods only on condition that they contain a specified proportion of local inputs or that the exporter agrees to purchase locally produced items of at least a certain value. This is known as an 'offset' arrangement, and might include a buyback element.

The term *counterpurchase* is sometimes used to denote the situation whereby the exporting firm receives part payment in its own currency or a hard foreign currency and the balance in the currency of the importer's country. The exporter then uses the latter currency to purchase whatever products in the importer's country happen to be available.

Progress test 3

1. What are Association Agreements? Which countries have Association Agreements with the EU?

2. Which countries belong to the Visegrad group?

3. List the main elements of the Shatalin Plan of 1989.

4. What benefits did East European countries hope to obtain from the privatisation of state-owned enterprises?

5. Explain the voucher method of privatisation.

6. List five operational difficulties confronting Western companies wishing to do business in East Europe.

7. Why do many East European nations impose constraints on foreign companies' abilities to purchase land?

8. Why is it necessary to take a long-term view when doing business in Eastern Europe?

9. What is a Trade and Co-operation Agreement?

10. Outline the role and functions of the EBRD.

11. What is a buyback agreement?

12. List the main advantages to countertrade.

4

THE WEST EUROPEAN ECONOMIC ENVIRONMENT

THE PRESENT SITUATION

1. Importance of the economic environment

European businesses exist and trade within national economic systems possessing unique characteristics, prospects and difficulties, and within a pan-European economic environment with features that transcend national frontiers. Managements of companies wishing to do business in multiple European markets need to take an interest in national economic environments in order to:

- establish the sizes and characteristics of various markets
- assess the degree of risk attached to operating in specific nations
- identify high growth sectors
- make investment decisions
- deploy company resources in the most effective way.

National economic policies

All governments would claim to aspire to attaining four basic economic objectives:

- full employment
- a high rate of economic growth
- a low rate of inflation
- absence of a deficit in the country's balance of payments.

Certain governments would also include such targets as equality in the distribution of the nation's wealth, an even pattern of regional economic development, or making the country attractive to foreign investors – according to the political objectives of the government concerned. In relation to the four primary objectives, however, the essential problem is that economic policies which help achieve the first pair of aims (full employment and a high rate of growth) are usually damaging for the second pair. Expansionary measures such as low interest rates, tax cuts and increases in public spending stimulate the economy and create jobs, but also encourage (a) firms to raise their prices and (b) workers to demand higher wages (using the threat of industrial action in a labour shortage situation). Also, increased consumer expenditure leads to higher imports and a worsening of the country's balance of trade!

The policy-making problem, therefore, is how best to balance the effects of the policies needed to achieve the four objectives. Of course, the difficulty would be overcome if it were possible to have a separate and *independent* policy to deal with *each* objective in isolation. For example, interest rates could be varied to control inflation; public spending and/or tax rates could be altered to secure economic growth; export promotion programmes could be applied to improve the balance of payments; and government make-work programmes and perhaps military conscription could be used to secure full employment. In the real world, however, democracies cannot impose draconian legislative controls (and it is by no means certain that the laws would be obeyed if they did), and international agreements (plus the threat of foreign retaliation) prohibit interference with the flow of foreign trade.

Effects of European economic integration

West European integration has enormous implications for the management of European enterprises. Most EU members are committed to the creation and use of a common currency (*see* **10**) and, independent of EU institutions, to the adoption of key elements of the European Social Charter (*see* 16:**31**). Laws and practices that regulated European commercial activity for generations have altered within just a few years: company law in EU nations has had to be changed to comply with EU Directives, as have technical product standards; industrial health and safety requirements; the law on intellectual property; public procurement arrangements; laws on advertising; marketing and sales promotion; agency law; consumer protection regulations; the law on business competition; and rules concerning company mergers, acquisitions and financial control.

2. Overview of the EU economy

The fifteen countries of the European Union have a combined population of around 370 million people and an aggregate national income which exceeds that of the USA by about 14 per cent and is more than double that of Japan. According to EUROSTAT, the aggregate GDP of the 15 EU countries accounts for over one third of World GDP: exports from the EU to other regions represent nearly a quarter of World exports, while imports into the EU account for nearly a fifth of total World imports. Germany has West Europe's highest level of industrial production, followed by France, Italy and the UK. Spain's industrial production is 42 per cent of that of France. The Netherlands and Belgium have industrial outputs of 26 per cent and 16 per cent respectively of the French figure. Germany accounts for nearly 20 per cent of European consumer spending (including East European nations as well as the EU); France accounts for 13 per cent, and Italy and Britain for 12 per cent each.

Unemployment has been a major problem, averaging nearly ten per cent of the EU workforce from 1980 onwards (compared to seven per cent for the USA and three per cent for Japan). It has been especially severe in Spain, in Ireland, the north of England, parts of Scotland and Wales, and southern Italy. Job shortages affecting young people have been particularly acute. EU countries' inflationary records have been mixed. Inflation has been higher in the south of Europe than in the north. Germany and the Netherlands have had the lowest long-term rates of inflation; Greece and Portugal the highest.

National economies within the EU have become increasingly interconnected and interdependent. Intra-EU trade accounts for more than 70 per cent of total EU trade, and each individual EU member state does at least 55 per cent of its aggregate trade with other EU members (and the figure is rising). The 'openness' of an economy can be measured by the ratio of exports to GDP. According to the *Annual Economic Reports* of the European Commission this ratio ranged in the mid-1990s from 19 per cent in Spain to 89 per cent in Luxembourg. The Netherlands, Ireland and Belgium had ratios in excess of 50 per cent; all EU nations except Spain and Italy (21 per cent) had ratios between 25 and 50 per cent. About twenty per cent of both imports into and exports from the EU involved the USA. Ten per cent of the Union's imports came from Japan, which took five per cent of exports. Developing countries accounted for 32 per cent of both imports and exports.

3. Economic performance

The six founding member countries of the EEC experienced very high rates of economic growth (typically five or six per cent per annum) in the years immediately following the formation of the Community. Growth rates declined throughout Western Europe in the mid-1970s, falling to an average of just 1.4 per cent per annum for the (then) EC twelve during 1980–85. Thereafter significant differences in national growth rates began to emerge, depending on how badly particular countries were affected by the economic recessions occurring over the next ten years. Nevertheless, overall EU economic performance has been generally satisfactory compared to most regions of the world, and living standards have continued to rise. The average EU growth rate has been lower than in Japan, but at least equal to that achieved in the USA over the last two decades.

Factors contributing to the slowdown in European economic growth in the 1990s included:

- The depth and persistence of the UK recession, which meant reduced demand in Europe's third largest consumer market and thus affected consumer goods suppliers throughout the EU.
- The high cost of German reunification. It turned out that reunification of East and West Germany caused balance of payments problems for the entire country, accompanied by unprecedented rates of inflation. Hence, the German authorities raised domestic interest rates, causing parallel upward interest rate movements in all other EU states.
- The poor performance of the US economy (a major market for European goods).
- Large exchange rate variations between the US dollar, Japanese Yen and European currencies.
- Loss of important export markets resulting from economic disruptions in Eastern Europe.

- A downturn in the normal investment cycle. Capital investment had increased at the extraordinarily high rate of seven per cent per annum on average during the last 1980s so there was a sharp fall in capital spending when new investment ceased.

Industrial and consumer goods outputs

Growth rates of industrial output (i.e. items sold to other firms as inputs to their own products) have been highest for plastics, aerospace products, machine tools, printing and publishing and textiles. Highest growth rates for consumer goods industries occurred for consumer electronics, motor cars, and domestic appliances and furniture. European industries with the poorest growth records include clothing and footwear, steel tubing, farming machinery, railway equipment, and shipbuilding (CEC 1996). Above-average growth in the future is predicted for electrical engineering, telecommunications, data processing and office equipment, rubber and plastics, furniture and carpets, household furnishings, and anything concerned with environmental protection (exhausts and filters, energy conservation, waste treatment, etc.). Low future growth rates are forecast for domestic appliances, vehicles, clothing and footwear, metal products, and transport equipment and vehicles. It seems, moreover, that more European industries are vulnerable to foreign competition than ever before. Heavy industry has of course been in decline for many years. Today, electronics and data processing firms and office equipment manufacturers are also having to struggle to remain competitive with foreign (particularly Japanese) rivals. Generally, the highest forecast growth rates are in fields where (i) some EU countries lag behind others (in telecommunications for instance), (ii) there have been recent deregulations, or (iii) extensive investments in economic infrastructure are taking place (e.g. in consequence of the replacement of outdated technologies).

Business competitiveness

Measures of the competitiveness of various EU industrial sectors are published biennially in the *Panorama of EU Industries*. Two criteria are used to assess 'competitiveness': the ratio of exports to imports in a given industry sector; and the share of exports in the total output of that sector. These variables supposedly indicate how well a European industry's products are doing relative to goods produced in the rest of the world. According to these yardsticks the European Commission estimates that the EU's *least* competitive industries are consumer electronics, computers, office equipment, children's toys, electronic components, and clothing. Note how these are precisely the industries for which demand is increasing most rapidly throughout the world. The EU's most competitive industries on the criteria mentioned are textiles, rubber, materials-manufacturing machinery, precision instruments, machine tools, medical equipment, and the production of measuring and monitoring instruments. Productivity (measured in terms of output per person employed) has increased most in those sectors in which international competition is least severe, notably electricals and electronics, data processing, precision instruments, chemicals and transport equipment. European industries with the worst productivity records in recent years are construction, agricultural equipment, industrial machinery, and the majority of services.

Prospects for the European economy

EU industry faces a number of serious challenges. The Union does not have enough high technology firms offering the new products for which worldwide demand is increasing most rapidly, and there are many mature industries supplying items for which there is limited market potential. A major drawback is the fragmentation of markets caused by continuing differences in national product standards and the lack of a common European currency – difficulties not experienced by competitors in the USA and Japan. Nevertheless, Europe excels in several important industrial sectors; there is much new investment compared to the United States and Japan; the opening up of Eastern Europe will eventually cause a major boost to East / West European trade; and the industrial, commercial and transport infrastructures of the core European nations are continually improving. Continental European firms have, on the whole, sounder financial bases than many of their US and Japanese rivals, and Continental public sector investments (in highways, water and waste disposal systems, tunnels, etc.) are proceeding at an unprecedented rate. Note in particular that by the year 2000, high-speed trains (capable of travelling at speeds of up to 250 miles per hour) will link all the EU's large markets (apart from the UK), while avoiding the delays and inconveniences of air travel. Passengers and goods will be able to move from one Continental EU city centre railway station to another in about half the journey time currently required.

4. The EU market

The European Union has four really large markets; Germany has West Europe's highest population, and is the dominant economic power of the EU. Other member states have smaller populations but many are, nevertheless, extremely affluent and represent lucrative markets for foreign firms. The dominant demographic fact relating to the EU is the low (or zero) rates of growth of population in most nations. This has caused a significant increase in the average age of the West European population and (in consequence) changing attitudes and spending patterns among European consumers. At the same time, younger Europeans are increasingly well educated, with nearly a quarter of the West European population now in some kind of full-time education. Other important trends are (i) the steady reduction in average household size that has occurred in all EU nations except Portugal, and (ii) an increase in the number of working women. The latter has had a major impact on certain consumer markets (convenience foods for example).

Market characteristics

The countries of the European Union can be categorised into three groups according to their per capita gross domestic products. There are the rich countries, Austria, Sweden, Denmark, Germany, Luxembourg and France; the middling countries, Finland, the Netherlands, Belgium, Italy and the UK; and the less prosperous states of Spain, Ireland, Portugal and Greece (although the recent economic development of Spain has been extremely rapid). All EU countries, however, contain substantial groups of consumers whose tastes, living standards and lifestyles are virtually identical to those of equivalent consumers in the richer EU states.

Virtually all EU households have a television set and telephone, more than 90 per cent possess a refrigerator, and ownership rates for dishwashers, video recorders, microwaves and other consumer durables are extremely high. As well as being prosperous in comparison with the overwhelming majority of the rest of the world's nations, Europeans have long life expectancies. Males can expect to live 74 years in The Netherlands, Sweden, Greece and Spain, and about 72 in other EU states. French, Spanish and Dutch females can anticipate living until they are 80; or around 78 years in the rest of the EU. Note, however, that the increasing affluence of modern Europeans has brought with it a number of health and social problems. Death rates from heart attacks, cancer and strokes in EU nations are among the world's highest. No less than seven of the top ten places in the international league table for the percentage of a country's deaths attributable to cancer are occupied by EU states, and three others are in the top twenty! Portugal leads the world in the population of its citizens dying from strokes; Greece, Spain, Luxembourg and Italy also appear in the top ten for this category.

Another less salubrious aspect of European affluence is the fact that six of the world's ten biggest alcohol drinking countries (measured in terms of annual average number of litres of alcohol consumed per head of population) are from the EU, with two more EU states figuring in the top 20 drinking nations. Also, four EU countries are among the world's top 20 tobacco smoking countries. Greece heads the tobacco smoking list (with the average Greek consuming around 3300 cigarettes annually), followed by Spain (2000 per annum), and Germany and Belgium (about 1800 each) (Eurostat 1995).

Western Europe's declining birth rate is affecting the culture of European society. A sharp decline in the number of people in their late teens and early 20s has occurred, with corresponding falls in their societal influence and the consumption of goods that the young typically purchase. Today, nearly two-thirds of all EU households do not include children under 15 years of age. Several factors explain the trend, all of which have interest for advertisers. Foremost is the general rise in living standards that has taken place, to greater or lesser degrees, in all EU countries over the post-Second World War period. Further reasons include:

- changing lifestyles and attitudes towards family size, with a greater preference for the acquisition of material possessions than for having larger families
- large rises in the number of single-person households, and in two-person households in which both partners have full-time jobs
- higher divorce rates
- housing shortages in urban areas (critical in some countries, especially in the South of England and in Western Germany)

- increases in the numbers of working women in most EU nations.

Another major trend has been the sharp rise in the number of children born out of wedlock. In 1960 less than five percent of children in the pre-1995 EU twelve countries had unmarried parents; by 1990 the figure exceeded 17 per cent. Half of all live births in Denmark and more than a quarter in France and Britain are now out of wedlock. Conversely, only one birth in 50 in Greece is in this category; one in 17 in Italy; and one in 10 in Germany and the Netherlands.

Europe's population is becoming increasingly middle aged, particularly in the Netherlands (which the OECD predicts will experience a 45 per cent increase in the number of people aged 65 or over and a 20 per cent decline in the 15–44 age group by the year 2020). Further EU countries expecting large increases in the proportions of their populations aged more than 65 years are France, Ireland, Denmark and Germany. EU nations other than The Netherlands likely to see drastic falls in the numbers of 15 to 44 year olds are Germany, Italy, Belgium and Denmark. Population growth is highest in Ireland (the population of which is predicted to increase by a quarter by 2020), Portugal and Greece (where six per cent population increases are anticipated). The total populations of the UK, the Netherlands, Spain and France are forecast to increase by 2020, while the populations of Denmark, Belgium, Italy and Germany are expected to fall.

THE SINGLE EUROPEAN CURRENCY

5. The European Currency Unit

The ECU is the official monetary unit of the European Union, used already for many business purposes, although (at the time of writing) it is not available for consumer transactions. Its value is defined in terms of a 'basket' of the currencies of all 15 EU countries, weighted according to each nation's economic importance measured in relation to its gross national product and the extent of its intra-EU trade. Weightings are reviewed periodically (normally once every five years), or whenever the exchange rate of a member country changes by a large amount. Through the 1980s the Deutschmark carried a weight of about 30 per cent, the French franc around 20 per cent, and the UK pound approximately 15 per cent. These percentage weightings are then converted into corresponding values of the national currencies that make up the ECU. Since it is based on a mixture of currencies the value of the ECU against any particular EU currency does not alter much over time. This inherent stability makes the ECU an attractive currency to hold.

ECUs have for some years been used to value European Union countries' central bank reserves and to denominate debts and credit transfers between EU financial institutions. The major EU banks (plus banks in the USA and Japan) have since 1986 operated an extensive and efficient ECU clearing and settlement system, based in Paris and enabling the rapid transfer of ECU balances among transactors throughout the world without any need to convert currencies or assume exchange rate risk. ECU bank deposits reached ECU 6 trillion in 1996 (double the value of dollar bank deposits in the United States), and the ECU bond market has expanded dramatically in recent years. Note how a new generation of financial institutions and instruments is emerging to deal with this vast and lucrative market.

The ECU's stability makes it ideal for the repurchase transaction market (commonly referred to as the 'repo' market) whereby the seller of a financial security simultaneously agrees to buy it back at a specified future date and price. And it is indeed the case that the volume of ECU repo deals is expanding enormously. Parties to ECU-based repo transactions are reasonably assured that fluctuations in exchange rates will not significantly affect the foreign currency values of repayments.

ECU valuation of commercial transactions

Increasingly, ECU valuations are applied to private commercial transactions and to the pricing and the invoicing of goods. Quoting a price in ECUs removes many of the trading risks connected with currency fluctuations, since a fairly predictable amount of money will eventually be collected from foreign customers, even if the exchange rate between the exporting and the importing countries changes substantially. This can obviate the need to take forward cover (*see* 11:8) on credit sales invoiced in foreign currencies. Consider, for example, the fact that the ECU has never fluctuated against the Deutschemark by more than five percent during any one year, whereas annual sterling/Deutschemark fluctuations of 15 percent are not uncommon. Furthermore, ECUs may be used (a) to denominate the bank loans and deposits of private businesses; (b) for forward exchange transactions; (c) to value travellers' cheques, credit cards and similar personal financial instruments; and (d) to value mortgages.

ECU debenture issues are possible and there are French unit trusts that invest exclusively in ECU denominated bonds. Some Continental companies now publish their annual balance sheets in ECU units. It is important to note, however, that ECUs are used more extensively in some EU countries than others. Italy, for example, recognises the ECU as a proper currency in its own right with a status equal to that of (say) US dollars or Japanese Yen. Germany, in contrast, has in the past prohibited private German residents from holding ECU denominated assets and, in consequence, ECU valuations are (currently) used far less widely in Germany than in other European states.

The ECU has proven invaluable for certain international industries where direct, instant and meaningful price comparisons are necessary. The European railway companies, which must price transactions across national borders as a matter of course, are a good example. ECU valuations are also gaining ground as a means for invoice settlement in Portugal and Greece (the national currencies of which are not widely acceptable abroad) and in Eastern Europe, as an alternative to the US dollar.

6. The proposed single European currency

The most dramatic event likely to affect European business over the next decade was, perhaps, the decision by the majority of EU nations in 1991 to commit themselves to the creation and use of a single European currency by the end of 1999. Under the formula originally agreed at the Maastricht negotiations the single currency could have been introduced by 1997, provided the economies of a majority of EU countries had converged to a sufficient degree. This was not the case, however, so 1999 became the target year for the implementation of the common currency scheme. At the time of writing it is unclear whether the United Kingdom and Denmark will participate in the system. It appears certain however that the EU's core countries of France, Germany and Benelux *will* have a common currency within the next few years.

The main macroeconomic implications of a common European currency relate to the needs for a European Central Bank and common monetary policies applicable throughout the European Union; and to the effects of common monetary policies on regional development within particular countries. If one common currency area (CCA) nation is prosperous and experiencing inflation while another has price stability but is economically depressed then a decision by a pan-European Union Central Bank to raise interest rates in order to cure inflation in the prosperous country will, because the interest rate rises will apply throughout the CCA, increase unemployment in the depressed country and hence make its overall economic situation significantly worse. For a common European currency to succeed, therefore, labour and capital must be able and willing to move from poor to wealthy areas, thus equalising unemployment and economic growth rates in various regions. With a European common currency, any pan-European Central Bank decision is bound to make some regions better off while harming others, so that wages and prices in disadvantaged areas must fall relative to those in prosperous regions in order to attract new business start-ups and to encourage additional capital investments by existing firms. Otherwise mass unemployment and low living standards will occur in those parts of the CCA whose economic interests have not been prioritised by the pan-European Central Bank (Crawford 1993). Note moreover that national attitudes towards what represents an appropriate inflation/unemployment trade-off differ considerably from state to state. Some national governments prefer a higher rate of inflation but with more jobs; others have price stability as the dominant policy objective. Counter-arguments to these objections are that:

- The benefits to industry and commerce of a single European currency will be so enormous that economic growth is bound to be stimulated *through-out* the CCA in the longer term.
- Governments of all nation states face dilemmas *vis-à-vis* the regional effects of central economic policy decisions. All that differs in relation to a pan-European common currency is the magnitude of the results. Losers must be compensated by gainers and helped to mitigate adverse effects. Within any common currency area (such as the present United Kingdom of England, Scotland, Northern Ireland and Wales) the central government may tax its citizens and then channel resources – in the form of grants, subsidies, preferential interest rate arrangements and other forms of regional development aid – towards those areas badly affected by central monetary and other economic policies. Hence it will simply be

necessary for a central CCA governmental authority to tax CCA residents (possibly via national governments) in order to raise the funds necessary to assist depressed regions.

7. Implementation of the common currency system

In 1994 the European Commission set up the European Monetary Institute (EMI) to oversee the initial stages of the introduction of the common currency. The EMI's work will be taken over by the European Central Bank as soon as this has been established. Under the Maastricht agreement, all intra-EU exchange rate fluctuations were to be removed and there was to be EU-level economic policy co-ordination, equalisation of inflation rates and other key economic indicators, convergence of budgetary policies and synchronisation of national budgetary procedures prior to the introduction of the single currency. According to the original formula the single currency was to have been introduced any time between 1 January 1997 and December 1998, *provided* the economies of a majority of Union countries had by then converged to a sufficient degree. Otherwise the common currency system would commence on 1 January 1999. Prospects for an early introduction of the single currency were disrupted by turbulence within the foreign exchange markets during 1993 and the consequent *de facto* floating of most EU currencies. Nevertheless, the core Continental European economies of France, Germany and Benelux affirmed their desire to have a common currency in place by the end of the decade. And the remaining EU countries (other than Britain and Denmark) avowed their intention to join the common currency area at the earliest possible time.

At the time of writing the plan is to launch the single currency in 1999 and to include in the CCA any country that satisfies the criteria, even if these countries only represent a minority of the Union states party to the original agreement. Thereafter, countries that initially fail to meet the convergence criteria will be able to join the system at subsequent entry points prescribed once every two years, as long as the convergence conditions are fulfilled. The problem, of course, is the continuing divergence of national inflation and interest rates, sizes of government financial deficits, and ratios of national incomes to national debt, especially for Greece, Portugal and Italy. Advocates of the single currency assert, however, that convergence is *not* essential for the success of the proposed scheme, because:

- Periodic balance of payments deficits, increases in unemployment and destabilising currency speculation necessarily cause governments to alter interest rates, levels of national debt, taxes and other instruments of economic policy that lead to divergences of national economies. Such events are natural and unavoidable and should not be a cause of concern.
- Fluctuations in the currency exchange rates of CCA member nations will *automatically* cease the moment the common currency is created.

In other words, divergences in the key economic variables are the *consequence* of having a plethora of national currencies: the implementation of a single European currency will itself help *cure* member countries' economic ills. Inflation rates for example should equalise once the CCA is formed, because high inflation in some regions will result in CCA residents purchasing (in the common currency) comparable goods and services from low price areas, hence causing cash flow from the former to the latter and making the high rate of inflation unsustainable in the longer term. Money supply falls in the high inflation region; local credit becomes tighter and generates numerous deflationary effects.

8. Objections to the single European currency

Britain and Denmark negotiated the right to opt-out from the common currency scheme, largely in consequence of fears concerning loss of national sovereignty. In 1991 the British government suggested that a common European currency circulate alongside the (then) twelve EU national currencies, so that individuals and businesses could choose to use the European currency if they so desired. This proposal was rejected by the other EU states, on the following grounds:

(a) The additional currency would have to be valued separately against every existing EU currency. Conversion costs would be incurred; speculation against particular currencies would continue, and individual nations might devalue their exchange rates against the new currency.

(b) Uncertainty over future exchange rates and hence the need for firms to hedge against possible currency deprecations would not be eliminated. (Hedging involves the purchase, at additional cost, of foreign currency to be delivered at a specified date in the future at a predetermined fixed rate of exchange.)

(c) The proposed scheme would do nothing to help combat inflation.

(d) Conflicts between national central banks might arise.

(e) National monetary policy would become extremely complicated.

A two-speed Europe

In view of the widely disparate economic situations currently existing among EU nations, it is extremely likely that at first just a few countries will form the common currency area, with others coming in at later dates. It seems, therefore that a 'two-speed Europe' is inevitable where the common currency is concerned, quite apart from the special positions of Denmark and the UK. The problem here is that EU countries outside the CCA might be able to devalue their currencies to such an extent that they gain an unfair price advantage when exporting to CCA states. Arguably, therefore, special tariffs should be imposed on imports from non-CCA nations to offset these effects.

9. Doing business in a single European currency

Regardless of how many countries eventually participate, the use of a single common currency by the European Union's core nations will alter fundamentally and forever the volume and characteristics of Continental European trade. It will require firms to quote prices in a common unit, and enable consumers readily to compare the prices of similar items sold in various EU countries. It means pan-European price labelling and packaging, easier product positioning in national markets, and the absence of currency conversion costs for businesses in nations that are members of the scheme. Companies outside the common currency area, conversely, will need separate prices, packaging and labelling for domestic and European markets, and must incur the (substantial) expense of currency conversion. A common currency removes entirely the currency exchange risk associated with international transactions. However, such risks – and the consequent need to hedge against them via the forward currency exchange markets – will continue to apply to non-CCA firms. Share prices in European companies will be quoted in the same currency units everywhere, facilitating pan-European share trading and the access to all European Stock Exchanges by investors and companies throughout the Union, a major advantage to businesses seeking external finance. Also a common currency will expedite intra-EU cash transfers, leading perhaps to far wider pan-European ownership of company shares than has previously been the case. Common currency company reports, share price quotations and flotations will enable investors to compare directly the financial performances of enterprises throughout the EU. Firms will have to pay great attention, therefore, to the ways in which they present financial information to the outside world, making this appear attractive and understandable to the pan-European investor.

Consequences for labour

Wages, national insurance contributions and social security benefits will be payable in the same currency throughout the CCA, enabling instant and meaningful comparison of reward packages in different CCA countries. This might encourage pan-EU management/union collective bargaining and a harmonisation of wages across national frontiers. A bank clerk (say) in London will clearly see a difference between his or her salary (paid in the single currency) and the single currency salary of a bank clerk in Düsseldorf or Amsterdam. Employees doing identical work in firms using the same level of technology in various EU regions will be able to compare their earnings and living costs against a standard and easily understandable yardstick. This could encourage the migration of labour from less prosperous to more affluent areas. Equally, the transparency of labour could lead to firms relocating in low wage regions.

10. Advantages of a single European currency

The following advantages to businesses should result from the use of a single European currency:

(a) Lower costs of cross-border transactions in consequence of not having to convert currencies. The story of the EU official who in 1991 set out from Brussels with 1,000 Belgian Francs, converted them into Deutschemarks, then into Spanish Pesetas, Irish Punts, etc., for all 12 Community states and found that he had less than half the value of his money at the end of the exercise than at the beginning (the rest being taken by currency conversion costs) is well documented. Indeed, in 1994 the European Commission estimated that the aggregate cost of converting EU currencies totalled about 0.5 per cent of the combined GDP of the European Union.

These transaction costs hurt small firms and small countries especially severely: the latter because their currencies are not generally accepted as payment for foreign transactions (so that large numbers of expensive conversions are necessary); the former through their inability to obtain bulk-business discounts from banks for their foreign currency trade (large companies often have in-house treasuries able to complete foreign currency administrative work cheaply).

(b) Less book-keeping for firms with transactions in several CCA states, since no foreign exchange calculations will be required. Businesses will be able to record and compare all accounting values in one unit, making for easy identification of the most costly and the most profitable activities in various markets.

(c) Faster execution of cross-border cash transactions.

(d) Lower levels of cash balance held within firms engaged in cross-border EU trade in consequence of the disappearance of the need to accumulate temporary foreign exchange balances. A common currency will enable cash received from several different countries to be lumped together instantly and without conversion and deposited in the highest interest earning country.

(e) Clearer and better information on input costs and competitors' prices and on potential customers' creditworthiness.

(f) Increased competition between larger and smaller businesses, since the competitive advantages enjoyed by larger firms with expertise and economies of scale in handling foreign currencies will be removed.

(g) Improved long-term planning and strategy formulation, as there will be less uncertainty concerning prospective returns on foreign EU activities. The risk of currency depreciation is a deterrent to cross-border long-term investment because both the capital value of an investment and the flow of income generated are likely to fall in terms of domestic currency.

(h) A stable monetary environment within the CCA. Once in place, the single currency is to be managed by a pan-European Central Bank with a board comprising a politically independent President plus the Governors of the national central banks of CCA member nations. National central banks themselves will act as local operating arms of the European Central Bank (ECB). It has already been agreed that price stability is to be the ECB's key objective. Decisions on national taxes, public spending and borrowing will remain with national governments, subject to co-ordination and guidance from the ECB, which is to have a mixture of powers and rights to be consulted in relation to the formulation of national monetary policies. No government will be able to spend or borrow beyond limits prescribed by formulae applied equally to all participants. Hence, interest rates should fall throughout the common currency area and fluctuations within them diminish.

Note moreover that the common European currency is sure to be widely used for financing international trade outside the European union. Many non-EU exporters (especially in Eastern Europe) will be prepared to accept the new currency in payment of invoices, so that firms within the currency area will be saved the expense of raising foreign exchange for non-EU transactions.

11. Implementation problems

At the time of writing it is unclear whether the single currency will be introduced in a 'big bang', or whether implementation will be preceded by a period during which there will be free interchange of existing EU currencies at immutably fixed rates of exchange. Much confusion and disruption of commercial life is likely to accompany either alternative. For retailers, the major practical problem with the introduction of a common currency will be the cost of re-equipping with new cash tills, slot machines, money handling systems, etc. Note moreover how the main precedent for the mass conversion of a nation's currency system (namely the 1969 decimalisation of the British Pound) was highly inflationary in its effects, with retailers generally 'rounding up' to the nearest whole unit when converting values in order to cover their implementation costs. Special difficulties will be experienced within countries initially outside the common currency area but which then adopt the common currency later on, after equipment has already been installed and is fully operational in other nations. By then, procedures will have been established and industry standards devised for the benefit and convenience of those countries' businesses. Latecomers will also experience cost disadvantages in relation to re-labelling, redrafting documentation (contracts, price lists, etc.), changing internal financial appraisal systems, reorganisation of sourcing arrangements, and so on. Companies in fast track countries, moreover, will possess staff fully conversant with common currency trading well before the common currency is adopted elsewhere, with consequent efficiency advantages.

Further costs and transitional problems that will probably be experienced while introducing the single European currency are as follows:

(a) The need for staff training to familiarise employees with new cash tills, money handling arrangements, etc.

(b) Culture shock among CCA consumers when they confront retail prices expressed in single currency terms, and among employees as they begin to receive single currency wages. Note moreover that in the longer term the trans-national use of the same currency should bring national cultures closer together – creating a shared understanding of monetary worth and common perspectives on what represents, in single currency terms, good value for money.

(c) Industrial relations difficulties as employees compare their single currency remunerations with those of workers in comparable firms in other CCA states.

Progress test 4

1. Managers of businesses engaged in cross-border European trade need to take an interest in the European economic environment for a number of reasons. What are these reasons?

2. List the main factors that contributed to the slowdown in European economic growth that occurred in the early 1990s.

3. How does the European Commission measure business competitiveness?

4. The European Union has four very large markets. What are they?

5. How is the decline in the West European birthrate affecting European business?

6. What is the European Currency Unit and how is it valued?

7. What are the major macroeconomic implications of the introduction of a single European currency?

8. List the main objections to a single European currency.

9. List six examples of how businesses will benefit from using a single European currency.

10. Why might the introduction of a single European currency create problems for employee relations?

5
COMMON POLICIES OF THE EUROPEAN UNION

ENERGY POLICY

1. Origins of EU energy policy

The EEC (as it then was) showed little interest in developing an energy policy until the 1973 oil crisis, which dramatically exposed Western Europe's overdependence on external energy supplies and hence the needs to conserve energy and exploit alternative energy sources. Key elements of the energy policy that emerged from subsequent discussions were as follows:

(a) Establishment of an integrated energy market, including the exchange of electricity (via linkages between national grids) and gas between member countries. It was hoped that increased competition would lower energy prices and help increase the overall international competitiveness of European industry.

(b) Improvements in the security of supply of energy through encouraging domestic production (including regional development grants and/or specific funding programmes).

(c) Protection of the physical environment in relation to energy production.

(d) Promotion of research and development concerning energy efficiency, the discovery of fresh and renewable sources of energy, new technologies and nuclear power.

(e) Encouragement of the substitution of oil by other fuels.

(f) The circulation of guidelines to national governments regarding the principles upon which energy pricing should be based, namely that:

- consumer prices should be closely related to world market prices
- the costs of replacing and developing energy resources should be incorporated into consumer prices
- the maximum degree of price transparency should apply to energy pricing; thus, comparative energy prices should be published and made available to actual and potential consumers so as to enable them to choose wisely between fuels and energy suppliers

- consumers should be made aware of the costs of the energy used by various appliances and installations.

2. Rational use of energy

A number of specific programmes have sought to encourage reductions in energy consumption through the 'rational use of energy'. Energy saving in the home was to occur through raising compulsory minimum performance requirements for new housing and heating systems; individual metering and control of heating in multi-occupied residential buildings; provision of financial assistance for necessary improvements to existing houses; and through publicity campaigns regarding the need for economy in domestic fuel consumption. Measures recommended to promote energy savings in non-domestic uses included the following:

(a) *Industry*. Computerised control and metering of energy; energy auditing; grants and tax reliefs to small businesses wishing to improve their energy systems.

(b) *Building*. Development of energy-related Codes of Practice for use within the construction industry; specification of minimum operating standards for heating systems, boilers, and ventilation and air-conditioning systems.

(c) *Transport*. Implementation of a standard method of measuring the fuel consumption of vehicles; establishment of targets for lower fuel consumption for new vehicles sold within the European Union; encouragement of public transport.

ENVIRONMENT POLICY

3. Environment policy of the European Union

The need for a pan-European environment policy was first recognised by EC heads of government at a summit meeting held in 1972 which affirmed the objective of 'improving the setting, the quality of life, the surroundings and living conditions of the peoples of the European Community'. Specific programmes on the physical environment were initiated via the Single European Act of 1986. Three objectives were established:

1. Greater economy in the use of natural resources

2. Protection of human health and physical safety

3. Protection, preservation and improvement of the quality of the environment.

Attainment of these aims was to be based on the following principles:

(a) Environmental problems should be rectified at source.

(b) The polluter should pay for the consequences of environmental pollution.

(c) Environmental protection requirements should be incorporated into the (then) EC's other policies.

(d) Legislation on the environment should be largely determined by qualified majority voting.

(e) Prevention is better than cure.

(f) Policies implemented at the EU level should not inhibit progress on environmental protection within particular nations.

(g) The environmental consequences of policy decisions should be considered at the earliest possible stage in the decision making process.

(h) Scientific research should be undertaken to improve knowledge about environmental matters.

(i) Economic and other policies implemented in one member state should not cause environmental problems in others.

(j) Actions should be taken at the appropriate level (EU, national or regional) depending on the type of pollution involved.

EU environmental policy covers the protection of land, sea, inland waters, flora and fauna, and air quality. Regulations have been introduced regarding the cross-border shipment of dangerous waste, prevention of the dumping of dangerous substances on land and at sea, and the storage of radioactive waste. Standards have been set for the quality of drinking water, beaches, and for pollutants discharged into rivers (Lefferink 1993). Between 1978 and 1981 a number of Directives were introduced designed to reduce the level of substances in the atmosphere.

Problems with EU environment policy include the potentially enormous cost of attaining policy targets, difficulties in reaching consensus on minimum standards, and basic conflicts of interest between the EU's industrially advanced and less industrially developed countries. Europe's poorer nations are more interested in stimulating economic growth than in environmental protection.

Future priorities

The European Commission has stated its intention to give priority to the following environmental issues over the next decade:

(a) Legislation to extend companies' civil liability for the pollution they cause.

(b) Establishment of 'no fault' compensation schemes for particular industry sectors, financed by the industry sectors themselves.

(c) Integration of pollution prevention and control, involving common licensing rules intended to prevent companies from gravitating towards countries where licenses to set up environmentally harmful production processes are easiest to obtain. Under this proposal licenses could only be awarded by a nationally appointed authority obliged to apply criteria determined at the EU level. Firms would have to use the best available techniques for pollution control, and be subject to regular inspection. Also they would have to provide detailed information on their inputs (including sources of energy) and operational processes.

Certain industry sectors likely to be affected by these proposals have opposed them vehemently, on the grounds both of cost and the possible extent of liability. Also the government of the United Kingdom has voiced its disapproval of the Commission's position, alleging that the suggested schemes would violate the principle of subsidiarity (*see* 1:**17**).

The European Environment Agency

This was established in 1990 to collect data on environmental matters and to monitor member states' compliance with EU environmental Regulations and Directives. The Agency is based in Copenhagen and administered by a management board comprising one representative from each EU member state, plus two appointees of the European Parliament and two of the European Commission. As well as gathering information the Agency liaises with non-EU countries in relation to environmental matters, and publishes reports on its activities.

4. The EU eco-management and auditing scheme

In 1992 the European Commission introduced a *voluntary* Regulation on environmental management and auditing, to be followed by any company wishing to do so. Businesses conforming to the guidelines specified in the Regulation may display a special logo on their promotional literature, and have their names published by the Commission on a Registered Members List. Each EU member country has established an accreditation authority (either in the form of an environmental protection agency or through an existing government ministry) with the remit to:

- develop knowledge of the criteria, principles and methodologies relevant to the conduct of environmental audits
- prepare guidelines and user guides for firms to follow
- launch publicity campaigns to raise the level of awareness of the scheme among businesses.

In the UK the British Standards Institution (BSI) has developed an environmental management standard, BS 7750, adherence to which satisfies the requirements of the EU scheme (*see* below).

Requirements of the eco-scheme

These apply to a *specific* production or operational site (rather than to an entire company) and necessitate the systematic and periodic evaluation of the site's environmental performance. An independent audit must be conducted and the report of findings made available to the public. The firm must establish an environment protection system, and have this regularly monitored by an outside expert. Audits need to cover, *inter alia*: air emissions; use of energy, waste, materials and packaging; discharges to water; noise and other nuisances; health and safety of employees and members of the public; and the protection of trees and wildlife. Additionally they should:

- verify the adequacy of the company's environmental management systems
- ensure that the firm is complying with all relevant legislation
- identify the risks of possible environmental failure
- seek to discover new ways of minimising the consumption of materials and energy.

Firms should benefit from such measures through experiencing lower operating costs and an improved public image. Also the audit might uncover inefficiencies and defects in other fields of activity (Rothery 1993).

Following the first audit the company is obliged to set targets for improving its environmental performance within a certain time. Progress towards the achievement of these targets has to be monitored and the results made known to the public. Reports must be verified by an independent third party, and fresh targets established once the initial targets have been attained.

The eco-labelling Regulation 1991

The purpose of this Regulation was to provide a means for the identification of products with minimal adverse effects on the physical environment and to help consumers obtain better information on the environmental impacts of various brands of products. Brands with the lowest environmental consequences within a particular product group are entitled to use a special label attesting their approval by the EU authorities. In order to qualify for an eco-label the supplier must provide detailed information about input components and materials as well as its own production processes. Hence *suppliers of inputs* need to be environmentally friendly, not just the firm selling the final good. Eco-labels may only be attached to specific products, so that multi-product firms have to make separate applications for each item for which they desire an eco-label. Assessments are based on the criteria of consumption of energy and natural resources; amount of waste; air and water contamination; soil pollution; noise; and effects on ecological systems. The entire life-cycle of the product is considered during the evaluation, including pre-production, the production process itself, distribution, untilisation and disposal. Decisions to award eco-labels are taken at the national level by bodies comprising representatives from industry, government, and environmental and consumer groups.

The Draft Directive on integrated prevention and control of environmental damage

This is a proposed framework Directive scheduled for implementation in 2005. If adopted it will require firms engaging in environmentally sensitive activities to obtain a permit prior to commencing operations (or continuing to operate an established plant) and to use the 'best available techniques' to prevent or minimise pollution.

THE COMMON AGRICULTURAL POLICY

The purposes of the Common Agricultural Policy were set out in the Treaty of Rome; namely, to raise farmers' living standards, increase agricultural productivity, stabilise markets, guarantee security of food supplies, and ensure reasonable prices for EEC consumers. Attempts at achieving these aims occurred via the creation of a single market for agricultural products, imposition of a common external tariff on imported agricultural goods, and through the Common Agricultural Policy. It is important to note that all West European countries were anxious to support agriculture in the years immediately following the Second World War. Food rationing operated in most European nations, and a number of foodstuffs were not available at all. Agriculture, moreover, employed large numbers of workers.

At the time the EEC was formed, a fifth of its working population was engaged in agriculture. Agricultural incomes, moreover, were less than half the average level of employees in other sectors.

5. Operation of the CAP

'Target' prices are set for agricultural commodities by the Council of Ministers, acting on the advice of the European Commission. These targets represent the prices that decision makers predict the items will sell for on the open market. 'Intervention' prices are then determined as fixed percentages of target prices. The percentage varies from commodity to commodity, ranging for example from 40 to 50 per cent for fruits and vegetables, to 90 to 95 per cent for certain other items. Whenever the market price of a particular item falls below the specified intervention price the EU authorities enter the market and buy the item at the intervention price, either destroying the food purchased or putting it into storage – hence creating so-called 'food mountains'. 'Threshold' prices are the minimum prices at which agricultural produce can be imported to the EU. Thus the threshold price of a particular item is its world market price plus the EU import duty levied on the commodity. If world market prices are below EU target prices then EU exporters of certain approved items receive a subsidy to bring their export incomes up to the internal EU level. In addition to the price support, numerous cash grants are available to farmers, including monetary inducements *not* to produce specific agricultural outputs. The latter is known as *set aside*. Money for agricultural support is channelled through the European Agricultural Guidance and Guarantee Fund (EAGGF). This body finances food purchases by intervention authorities, pays storage costs, provides direct financial assistance to small farmers, offers cash grants for farm modernisation and the retraining and redeployment of redundant farmers, and finances export refunds. The latter arise when EU farmers sell their outputs outside the Union at prices below those available internally (the EAGGF makes up the difference).

Green currencies

When EU farmers turn over their surplus produce to the CAP authorities they receive payment in their own currencies. All calculations to determine the amounts payable are completed in ECUs. Then the appropriate number of ECUs is converted into national currency *not* at the prevailing spot rate of exchange, but at a special fixed rate of exchange, known as the 'green currency' rate. Green rates sometimes differ from spot rates by substantial margins, so that the actual levels of support received by farmers in various countries also differ. Prior to 1992, compensation to nations 'losing out' in consequence of large adverse disparities between spot and green rates was given via Monetary Compensation Amounts (MCAs). These were phased out in 1992/93 in anticipation of European Monetary Union which, of course, will remove all currency exchange rates including those pertaining to green currencies.

In past years agricultural support has accounted for up to 80 per cent of the EU's budget (today the figure is around 60 per cent), despite so few people being employed in farming. This is partly attributable, perhaps, to the high level of social and political influence exerted by European farmers and rural landowners relative to their numerical strength. Farming is associated with the ownership of land, which itself has connections with wealth and social power. Farmers' associations are well organised, have extensive resources and many full time employees.

Food mountains

Overproduction of foodstuffs is encouraged in consequence of farmers being guaranteed minimum returns when selling their outputs. Food mountains have been huge at times, and are condemned by critics of the CAP on the grounds that it is inappropriate to destroy or hoard food while so many people in the world are starving! In 1978, for example, it would have taken five years to consume the skimmed milk mountain at the then annual rate of consumption, and the EEC's 'wine lake' exceeded 7000 million litres. The financial cost of storing surplus produce (often in refrigerated conditions) is considerable. Possible solutions to the food mountain problem include:

- reducing intervention prices
- giving food away to underdeveloped countries as foreign aid
- selling surplus stock at low prices to certain social groups such as senior citizens or families in receipt of social security
- increasing taxes on items that compete with surplus products, e.g. putting an extra tax on the sale of lamb in order to reduce the beef mountain.

Concerns over constantly rising food mountains and the consequent bad publicity surrounding them led to the imposition of production quotas on certain items, beginning with milk in 1988. Set-aside payments were also introduced in that year.

6. Advantages of the CAP

Advocates of the CAP assert that it has led to an abundance of food within the European Union. There have been no famines or even food shortages within the European Union since the CAP started. West Europe's shops and supermarkets are overflowing with food; in sharp contrast to East Europe and other parts of the world with different agricultural support systems. As to the question of the propriety of maintaining food mountains while residents of poor countries are starving, CAP-enthusiasts point out that poverty in the Third World is mainly due to political factors: civil war, repressive dictatorial governments, bribery and corruption, lack of effective public administration, etc. Many of the world's poorest nations are rich in natural resources; simply handing out free food from the European Union will *not* solve these countries' economic problems. Also the transport, storage and logistics problems associated with distributing the food would be immense, and the collapse in local food prices would discourage local farm production.

Specific arguments in favour of the CAP are:

(a) The availability of artificially high prices for agricultural produce may stimulate new investment in agricultural industries.

(b) In the absence of EU intervention, food prices are liable to fluctuate dramatically. Food expenditures account for a fifth of all EU household spending. Hence, upward fluctuations in food prices can be highly inflationary.

(c) Large-scale imports of food create balance of payments problems. Domestic food production saves foreign exchange as well as jobs.

(d) Farmers are the 'guardians' of the countryside, so that support for agriculture facilitates environmental protection.

Another important benefit claimed for the CAP is the prevention of any single EU member state from gaining a competitive edge over others through directly subsidising agriculture and hence lowering food prices (and in consequence wage levels) in that country.

7. Criticisms of the CAP

The main consequences of the CAP have been higher food prices for European consumers; increased agricultural production (some of which is unwanted by consumers) relative to what would have occurred if food prices were determined by international market forces; and a shift in food production away from low-cost non-EU countries towards the (high-cost) EU. In order to understand the force of the criticisms that have been levelled against the CAP it is instructive to compare it with the British system of agricultural support that operated prior to the UK joining the European Common Market. The UK approach had two aspects:

(*i*) Grants payable for investments in building, fixed machinery, land drainage, etc., and for the purchase of certain fertilizers

(*ii*) 'Deficiency payments' whereby food produced in the UK was sold at the same (low) world market prices as it was imported. The difference between the world market price and the cost of UK production was paid to the farmer.

Alleged benefits of this system were that consumers paid low world market prices for food; domestic agriculture was safeguarded (through the maintenance of farmers' incomes); economically underdeveloped countries (many of which are heavily dependent on the export of agricultural products) had open access to lucrative markets; and the forces of supply and demand supposedly directed resources to their most efficient uses. With the CAP, conversely, consumers pay artificially high, administratively determined prices set at levels that ensure profitable internal food production. High food prices hit poor families particularly severely. Further criticisms of the CAP are that it is protectionist (denying markets to underdeveloped countries), wasteful, creates unwanted food surpluses, and that it is extremely expensive. The CAP absorbs most of the EU budget, yet agriculture accounts for less than five per cent of the Union's workforce. A major problem is finding appropriate common target prices for particular agricultural products in view of the large differences in agricultural productivity and costs between various EU countries. Note moreover that the Treaty of Rome did not specify that any particular method of agricultural support be adopted by the European Economic Community. The CAP emerged from political negotiations, and there is no constitutional reason why it should not be abandoned. Specific criticisms of the CAP are as follows:

(a) Although certain agricultural products may enter the EU from economically underdeveloped countries free of tariffs, these items are typically ones that are not produced within the EU, so that the EU would have encouraged importation anyhow and hence there is really no net gain to the poorer countries.

(b) Although it is undoubtedly true that agricultural productivity increased enormously in the 1960s and 70s (output per head grew by an average 6.5 per cent per annum between 1965 and 1974), this was arguably due mainly to cash grants and other modernisation incentives rather than to the CAP price support system, which enabled low productivity farms to continue in production.

(c) Improvements in agricultural productivity have led to excessive profits for farmers because, until the early 1990s, intervention prices were hardly ever lowered. Note nevertheless that the incomes of agricultural employees did *not* rise in proportion to the increased profits received by farmers.

(d) Periodically the European Commission exports foodstuffs to East Europe and elsewhere at very low prices in order to reduce food mountains (see above). This is unfair to EU consumers who themselves are paying grossly inflated prices for exactly the same items.

8. The Common Fisheries Policy (CFP)

This was introduced in 1971 and from the outset was the subject of great controversy, especially in the United Kingdom since, although 60 per cent of total EU fish stocks lie in British waters, British fishing vessels take only one per cent of their catch from the waters of other EU countries. Britain, Ireland and Denmark were in the process of applying for membership of the (then) EEC in 1971, but were not invited to take part in the negotiations leading up to the CFP's establishment. Rather they were required to accept the CFP as part of the entry package. As with the CAP, the CFP provides minimum guaranteed prices for fish. Intervention occurs, but there is no fish mountain because surpluses are easily converted and sold as fishmeal products.

Under the CFP foreign EU vessels have access to the territorial waters of any EU country except for close coastal areas. Quotas restricting total catches are allocated among EU members by agreement. Overfishing is further discouraged via regulations concerning minimum mesh sizes for nets, the sizes of fish that may be caught, and the maximum period a vessel may remain at sea. Grants are paid to boat owners who lay up or destroy their vessels.

Progress test 5

1. What was the key event leading to the formulation of a common EEC policy on energy?

2. Explain the term 'rational use of energy.'

3. What are the objectives of EU environment policy? What are the basic principles underlying EU environment policy?

4. List the main problems associated with the implementation of EU environment policy.

5. How does the EU eco-management and auditing scheme operate?

6. What is BS 7750?

7. State the purpose of the EU eco-labelling Regulation 1991.

8. All West European countries were anxious to support agriculture in the years immediately following World War II. Why was this the case?

9. Explain the difference between target, threshold and intervention prices.

10. How does the EAGGF operate?

11. What are the possible solutions to the problem of the 'food mountains' resulting from the CAP.

12. Why has the Common Fisheries Policy been a subject of great controversy?

6

COMPETITION AND INDUSTRIAL POLICY

COMPETITION LAW

1. EU competition policy

The founding fathers of the European Common Market envisaged the creation of an integrated European economy based on the principles of private enterprise and free competition among businesses. This, it was believed, would lead to a wider choice of products for consumers, lower prices, better customer service, and greater industrial efficiency (Jacquemin 1993). It was recognised from the outset, however, that the motivation to maximise profits in a competitive market environment might equally cause firms to ensure their prosperity through deliberately distorting and/or undermining market mechanisms. Monopolies naturally arise in uncontrolled private enterprise situations as companies merge and as the more efficient firms force less successful rivals out of business. Companies might collude to fix prices, restrict output, carve up markets, and so on. Unfettered competition, moreover, can lead to waste and inefficiency as certain industries fragment into small units of production. Potential economies of scale are sacrificed and the business environment becomes uncertain and unpredictable hence discouraging new investment in high-risk sectors. Indeed, some goods and services might not be produced at all within a volatile *laisser-faire* competitive system.

It is not surprising, therefore, that the European Commission has a somewhat ambivalent attitude towards competition between firms and the growth of business organisations. On the one hand, the Treaty of Rome expressly forbids restrictive trade practices and/or monopolies likely to interfere with trade within or between countries. Simultaneously however the Commission recognises the need for Europe to possess large economic units able to achieve economies of scale and compete effectively in world markets. Thus, in recent years new regulations have been introduced which allow cross-frontier amalgamations and for large firms to organise themselves on a Europe-wide basis. Taxes which discriminate against cross-frontier mergers (compared to mergers within a single country) have been largely abolished, and many legal barriers to international amalgamations of EU firms have been removed. In general, the Commission now seems to favour larger European firms. Nevertheless, EU regulation of competitive practice is wide, covering both horizontal and vertical integration, market sharing agreements, retailing arrangements (exclusive dealerships are not allowed), joint ventures, patents and trademarks, and franchise agreements. And the community regulations apply to services as well as goods.

Specific reasons for the EU possessing a competition policy are:

- to ensure the free movement of goods across the Union by preventing firms from setting up 'invisible frontiers' via cartels and market sharing agreements
- to clarify what exactly companies may and may not do in relation to restrictive trade practices
- to improve the competitiveness of EU industry relative to Japanese and US companies
- to encourage large firms to rationalise their production and distribution systems and apply the latest management techniques
- to help small businesses develop and to allow them to enter collaborative arrangements with other enterprises according to an orderly and well-defined set of rules.

2. Articles 85 and 86 of the Treaty of Rome

Article 85 of the Rome Treaty prohibits trade practices which prevent, restrict or distort competition. Agreements by firms to carve up the European market among themselves are void and thus unenforceable in the Courts of member states. Article 85 has a wide scope of application. It covers all forms of undertaking including companies, partnerships, individuals or any other type of business organisation and extends to unwritten agreements and informal understandings. Note moreover that EU (rather than national) competition law can apply when all the parties to an anti-competitive agreement are in the same member state or where one or more of the businesses are outside the Union – *provided* trade between EU member states is affected by the agreement. Article 86 prohibits firms which already occupy a dominant position in an EU market from abusing that position. A dominant position is defined as a position of economic strength which enables an enterprise to prevent effective competition by being able to operate independently of its competitors and customers. There have been cases in the European Court where abuse has occurred through firms increasing their market shares by taking over competitors, or through gaining control over the supply of raw materials and then cutting off supplies to competing firms. Additionally, the Treaty of Rome defines the following business practices as abuses of a dominant position:

Imposition of unfair prices for the purchase of raw materials or sale of final goods.
Restrictions on production.
Restrictions on distribution.
Holding back technological development.
Charging different prices to different consumers.

Role of the European Commission

The Commission can act independently when seeking to enforce EU competition law: it does not require the permission of the Council of Ministers. Actions are initiated either on the Commission's own initiative or following a complaint by an individual, member state or business. First the Commission will approach the company accused of anti-competitive practices and ask it to change its policies. Very often the company agrees and this is the end of the matter. Otherwise the Commission conducts an investigation and reaches a decision which, if the case against the company is proved, may result in the Commission ordering the firm to alter its practices and/or imposing a fine of up to ten per cent of the value of the sales affected by the anti-competitive behaviour. Commission staff are legally empowered to visit companies without warning, inspect documents and take photocopies. Fines may be imposed on companies for:

- Failing to allow Commission officials to enter their land, premises and vehicles for the purposes of examining company books and records. A daily penalty of between 50 and 1000 ECU can be imposed (in addition to a lump sum fine) if the commission deems it is appropriate.
- Intentional infringements of Articles 85 and 86 or infringements due to negligence. These fines may range from 1000 to one million ECU or ten per cent of the undertaking's turnover, whichever is the larger.
- Refusing to supply information, intentionally or negligently, that has been demanded by the Commission. Daily fines of between 100 and 5000 ECU can be levied in these circumstances.

The factors considered by the Commission when calculating the levels of fines include the nature of the offence and whether it was deliberate, the behaviour of the parties, the sizes and economic importance of the firms involved, and the duration and gravity of the infringement. If a company violates both EU and national competition law it can be fined twice: once by the Commission and once by the national government.

Fines might be reduced or cancelled by the European Commission in consequence of:

- recession in the industry in which the offending company operates
- the guilty parties demonstrating their willingness to alter their behaviour
- offending firms establishing definite programmes for ensuring that they will never again violate EU competition law.

Firms can appeal against Commission rulings to the European Court of Justice (*see* 1:9) – either against the conviction itself or the size of the fine.

3. Enforcement by the individual firm

Articles 85 and 86 are directly enforceable in each EU member country. Aggrieved businesses (or individuals) may pursue the following courses of action:

(a) Seek whatever remedies are available for breaches of Articles 85 and 86 as are available for similar violations of national law. In most countries it is possible to sue for damages. It is always the case that an injunction to prevent the anti-competitive practice can be requested from a national Court. Rulings of national Courts remain valid until a negative clearance or exemption (*see* 5) is granted by the European Commission.

(b) Complain to the national competition authorities of the home country (in the UK this is the Competition Policy Division of DTI) which then passes the matter to the European Commission. Typically complaints involve allegations that other businesses are imposing unfair materials input prices or other unfair trading conditions, threatening retailers with withdrawal of supplies if they take a certain firm's products, or applying exceptionally onerous obligations on contracts. The complainant is not required to prove that an infringement has occurred; it is up to the Commission to investigate the issue and reach a conclusion. Nevertheless, the complainant is expected to provide extensive background information on the details of the complaint, including a precise statement of why and how the infringement prevents fair competition.

Additionally it is possible for businesses to take action against the EU itself if they believe the Commission has acted unlawfully and/or unfairly victimised particular firms. The measures available are as follows:

(a) Ask a domestic court to seek a preliminary ruling from the European Court of Justice (ECJ) on a question concerning EU law. This enables firms to challenge indirectly the validity of EU Regulations, Directives and Decisions without having to bring an action in the ECJ. Note that businesses are entitled to complain if larger EU firms unfairly prevent them from competing in a particular market, e.g. by imposing unfair materials input prices or other unfair trading conditions, threatening retailers with withdrawal of supplies if they take a certain firm's products, or applying exceptionally onerous obligations on con- tracts. The complainant is not required to prove that an infringement has occurred; it is up to the Commission to investigate the issue and reach a conclusion. Nevertheless, the complainant is expected to provide extensive background information on the details of the complaint, including a precise statement of why and how the infringement prevents fair competition.

(b) Approach the ECJ directly and request that it annul the EU Directive, Regulation or Decision that created the problem in the first instance. This is possible only if the firm has a direct and immediate interest in the situation. Such actions are extremely important in cases of alleged restrictive practices, since the European Commission prohibits perceived restrictive practices via Decisions that are served on the parties to the agreements. Often the latter will ask the ECJ to annul the original Decision. This request must be registered within two months of the Decision's publication.

(c) Sue the European Union for damages. Here the firm must prove that the EU acted unlawfully and that, in direct consequence, this unlawful behaviour caused actual financial harm. Ultimately, all complaints are heard by the Euro- pean Court of Justice. The workload of this Court is extremely heavy and it can take two or three years before a case is heard. Thus there is now a Court of First Instance attached to the ECJ empowered to deal with minor cases.

4. Definition of the relevant market

Articles 85 and 86 apply to situations where anti-competitive practices may affect trade *between member states*. Otherwise national competition law applies. Hence it is crucially important to define precisely the natures and extents of the markets covered by an agreement. Test cases in the European Court of Justice have established the following general principles:

(a) Identification of the appropriate product market requires the identification of products that are substitutable for each other. If products are not reasonably interchangeable they are not part of the same product group. Whether items are substitutable depends on how customers use them, their prices and characteristics. For example, the relevant market for motor tyres was held to be the market for replacement tyres (excluding tyres supplied as part of new vehicles) and not retreads, industrial tyres for heavy equipment, etc.

(b) EU competition rules are only violated if a 'substantial part' of the Single Market is affected. This could involve several countries or just one, depending on circumstances.

(c) Several factors affect whether an undertaking has a dominant position, including:

- market share relative to that of the nearest competitor (large market shares represent *de facto* evidence of the existence of dominant market positions)
- technological superiority
- well-developed sales networks
- negligible potential competition.

(d) 'Abuse' of a dominant position occurs when the structure of the market is weakened in such a way as to hinder competition.

5. Exemptions from Articles 85 and 86

The European Commission is anxious to encourage co-operation among businesses and thus will not regard as violations of Articles 85 or 86 any agreement for the following purposes:

(a) Exchanges of opinion

(b) Joint market research

(c) Joint collection of trade and market statistics

(d) Co-operation on the preparation of accounts or on matters relating to tax

(e) Provision of trade credit

(f) Joint-debt collecting.

Position of small firms

A wide range of practices common among small firms could be caught by EU competition law, notably:

(a) Exclusive dealership arrangements

(b) Joint ventures with other businesses

(c) Licensing of intellectual property rights

(d) Franchising.

Additionally EU law extends to any 'concerted practice' that prevents, restricts or distorts competition. A concerted practice is a situation where businesses do not enter a formal agreement but where their collective actions imply collusion. In recognition of the fact that co-operation between small firms will not distort competition appreciably, the Commission has issued a 'Notice on Minor Agreements' exempting from Articles 85 and 86 all situations where:

(a) the goods or services covered by an agreement represent less than 5 per cent of the total market for these goods or services; and (additionally)

(b) the aggregate turnover of the parties to the agreement is less than a certain threshold (currently 200 million ECU).

6. The block exemptions

Even if the criteria outlined in **5** are not satisfied the Commission may exempt agreements that:

(a) contribute to improving the methods of producing or distributing goods or to the promotion of technical or economic progress; *and*

(b) give consumers a fair share of resulting benefits; *and*

(c) will not significantly reduce competition across the entire Single European Market.

Applications for exemption must be submitted to the Commission *unless* the following are involved, in which case an automatic 'block exemption' applies and no formal application is needed (provided of course that points **(a)** to **(c)** immediately above are met):

(a) Specialisation agreements

Here the companies party to the agreement deliberately restrict their product ranges in order to develop expertise in particular fields. Justification for this exemption lies in the increased efficiency and lower production costs made possible by these arrangements, although competition must continue to prevail in the market concerned. The exemption only applies to agreements with a combined turnover of less than ECU 500 million and a maximum 20 per cent market share. Also the contract must be fair to all signatories and not cover prices or the production levels (rather than product ranges) of individual firms.

(b) Exclusive distribution arrangements

The European Commission has issued a block exemption releasing virtually all small to medium sized business from EU legislation in the exclusive distribution field. Under the exemption, agreements between pairs of undertakings whereby one agrees to supply exclusively to the other pre-specified goods for resale in a certain area and which require the distributor to obtain goods only from the other party, are legal provided:

- there is an alternative local source of supply of the type of product involved in the agreement
- the supplying firm's output is available from at least one other source than the distributor, e.g. from a distributor in another territory or direct from at least one other source than the distributor, e.g. from a distributor in another territory or direct from the supplier's own premises
- one of the parties to the deal has an annual turnover of less than 100 million ECU
- the goods supplied under the agreement have a market share of less than five per cent.

Also, manufacturers of the same type of product cannot appoint each other as exclusive distributors in order to carve up the total European market, e.g. if a British manufacturing firm has its French counterpart as its exclusive distributor in France, and vice versa, so that consumers only have one source of supply in either country.

Sales to selected distributors (dealers) whereby the supplier is prepared to sell only to particular dealers who then promise not to resell to anyone other end users, are not generally covered by the distribution block exemption because of the control over prices they might allow. However, the Commission has agreed not to take action against suppliers so long as:

- the agreement is 'reasonably necessary', e.g. by virtue of the needs for special facilities for selling the product, for after-sales service, or for technical expertise among distributors
- quantitative limits are not placed on the number of approved dealers within a specific area (a city for instance)
- selection criteria are objective and applied uniformly; examples of suitable yardsticks are the dealer's technical knowledge, calibre of premises or extent of facilities
- competition within the market is not adversely affected.

(c) Exclusive purchasing agreements

These are contracts whereby the purchaser agrees to buy only from a specific supplier. All the provisions applicable to the block exemption for exclusive distribution arrangements apply to such deals, plus a limit of five years on the duration of the agreement and a proviso that the contract may only apply to goods that are connected with each other.

(d) Patent licensing contracts

Typically a licensee is given exclusive rights to work a patent within a specified territory. This is legal provided:

- licensees are free to sell in other licensees' territories in response to unsolicited orders
- intra EU trade in the patented product is not impeded
- continuing R & D is encouraged and a favourable environment for technology transfer created.

Rules relating to the exemption of patent licensing agreements from EU competition law are now embodied within the 1996 Technology Transfer Regulation (*see* 12:**2**).

(e) Collaborative research and technical development agreements

These are permissible provided there are no adverse effects on competition in the final consumer market for the goods and the parties to the contract collectively do not hold more than a 20 per cent share of the market for the product that is being researched. All the parties to the agreement must have right of access to the results of the R & D and freedom of distribution.

(f) Franchising

The franchising block exemption only applies to distribution and service activities. At the time of writing there is no exemption in relation to industrial or manufacturing franchises. Under the block exemption it is permissible for distribution franchise agreements to restrict franchisees' abilities to:

- disclose to outsiders the know-how gained during the period of the agreement
- decline to sell the entire range of the franchiser's products
- sell or use competing products during or up to one year after the termination of the contract
- seek custom outside the designated territory
- engage in independent advertising
- scale down the extent of the operations of their outlets.

(g) Know-how licencing

Know-how is confidential non-patented technical knowledge, and it can be licensed. Arguably, know-how (and patent) licensing is a barrier to free competition and could be used to sustain a monopoly. Equally, however, licensing is a major vehicle for the fast and efficient transfer of new technologies across national frontiers. Hence it is permissible for know-how licence agreements to restrain licensees from exploiting the licensor's know-how in territories not covered by the contract. The rules relating to lawful know-how licensing are set out in the EU Technology Transfer Regulation 1996 (*see* 12:**2**). It is possible under the exemption to impose contractual obligations on the licensee to maintain the secrecy of the know-how following the termination of the agreement and to divulge any new discoveries resulting from the use of the know-how.

Since 1992 the exemptions covering patent and know-how licensing, specialisation agreements, and collaborative research and development have applied to all co-operative joint ventures.

The need for all these exemptions arises from the fact that under EU competition law *all* agreements which restrict competition are illegal. Hence it has been necessary to introduce a plethora of block exemptions and procedures for securing individual exemptions simply to prevent the Commission having to prosecute vast numbers of businesses that, through their normal day-to-day operations, routinely break the law. This leads to the criticisms that the selection of companies for prosecution becomes somewhat arbitrary and that the determination of whether particular businesses do or do not fall within specific exemption criteria becomes extremely confused. Another major problem with EU competition policy is that whereas it recognises the impropriety of companies gaining competitive advantage via restrictive trade practices, it ignores the fact that equally unfair competitive advantages are enjoyed by firms that operate in the EU nations with the fewest regulations in relation to minimum wages, safety standards, working conditions and hours of work, etc. This problem is referred to as 'social dumping' and is discussed in Chapter 16.

MERGERS AND ACQUISITIONS

7. Amalgamation of businesses

A merger (or 'amalgamation') is a voluntary and permanent combination of businesses whereby one or more firms integrate their operations and identities with those of another, and henceforth work under a common name and in the interests of the newly formed amalgamation (Hamill 1992).

Typically, the companies which combine jointly issue new shares in the freshly created organisation to replace existing shares in the merging organisations. This differs from a hostile 'takeover' situation whereby one business buys a majority shareholding in another company, against the wishes of the latter's management. Reasons for mergers and takeovers include:

- economies of scale possibly made available through more extensive operations
- the desire to acquire businesses already trading in certain markets and/or possessing certain specialist employees and equipment
- removal of competitors
- acquisition of land, buildings, and other fixed assets that can be profitably sold off
- the ability to control supplies of raw materials
- expert use of resources, e.g. if one firm possesses large amounts of land and buildings and the other is exceptionally skilled in property management

- reduction of the likelihood of company failure through spreading risks over a wider range of activities
- full use of production capacity and idle cash, and an increase in the ability to borrow funds
- additional financial and other resources, including greater capacity to undertake research
- tax considerations, e.g. the carry-over of past trading losses into the merged business
- the potential ability of a larger organisation to influence local and national governments
- desire to become involved with new technologies and management methods, particularly in high-risk industries.

8. Avoiding a takeover

Managements of enterprises subject to takeover bids but which do not wish to be taken over may resort to a number of devices to thwart the predator company, including the following.

(a) Making the company unattractive to predators

Although it is easy to make a business unattractive to potential buyers, the actions taken will themselves damage the company in the longer term. Nevertheless, desperate managements do sometimes resort to this tactic. Specific devices are as follows:

(a) Selling land, buildings and other fixed assets and using the proceeds to pay higher dividends to existing shareholders. Increased dividends might temporarily raise the market price of the company's shares, thus making it more expensive for a predator to buy a majority interest. The method is particularly appropriate if the motivation behind the attempted acquisition is the predator's desire to obtain the fixed assets of the target firm.

(b) Locking the firm into long-term supply and customer contracts which the target knows will not appeal to the predator's business.

(c) Making large issues of new shares free of charge to existing shareholders in order to increase for the predator the cost and effort involved in acquiring a majority shareholding.

(d) Borrowing extensively and then rearranging the company's finances so as to be able, in effect, to use the money to pay higher dividends to current shareholders. Share prices will rise temporarily, and if the takeover goes through the predator will be left with a large burden of high-interest debt.

(b) Direct action

Directors of the target company might circularise shareholders and advise them not to accept the outsider's bid. If the predator has offered to pay for the target company's shares using shares in the predator's company the target's circular may argue that acceptance would be against shareholder's interests, because dividends on the predator's shares could deteriorate following the acquisition.

The existing management will enumerate its achievements – especially the company's long-run growth, its commanding positions in various markets, its success in developing new products and so on – and will explain future prospects under the existing management in an attractive manner. Other direct measures to prevent a takeover include:

(a) Encouraging a friendly outside business – quite unconnected with the predator – to purchase a large number of shares in the target company, thus making it more difficult for the predator to acquire a controlling interest. Such friendly outsiders are sometimes referred to as White Knight companies.

The deal may involve an exchange of shares in the White Knight for shares in the target, or a straight cash offer to the target's shareholders, vigorously endorsed by the existing management. Equally the target might issue a large block of freshly created shares direct to the White Knight, provided this is permissable under the target's articles of association. Inevitably, however, share dilution will result in the latter situation, and current shareholders might object to this occurring.

(b) Merging with another company which is more acceptable to the existing management. Of course, the predator might then attempt to take over the entire newly merged conglomeration, but this will be more difficult in consequence of the increased expenditure needed to buy a majority stake in the larger business. This practice is referred to as 'defensive merger'.

(c) Financing equity expansion through the issue of non-voting shares. The problem here is that non-voting shares are unattractive to investors (since their prices do not rise during takeover attempts) and thus can only be issued cheaply – and even then there could be few purchasers.

9. Extent of EU takeover activity

Reliable statistics on the extent of cross-border acquisitions are few and far between, since there are no laws requiring that they be reported. Thus, press cuttings and *ad-hoc* industry surveys have to be used to assess the current situation. However, the European Commission conducts surveys into cross-border EU takeovers, the results of which are published in the Commission's *Annual Report on Competition Policy*. It seems that a very substantial increase in trans-national EU takeovers has taken place, with about 1200 to 1500 significant EU companies being purchased each year by investors outside the home countries of the acquired firms. Also about 1000 major EU companies are involved in corporate joint ventures and/or strategic cross-shareholdings annually. According to the Commission, the volume of cross-border mergers and acquisitions (M&As) has equalled that of domestic EU M&As since the formation of the Single Market. Also the average real value of acquisitions is rising sharply, indicating that larger firms are being acquired. Residents of the United Kingdom have made the highest number of acquisitions in other EU nations (on average between 300 and 500 per annum), followed by France (around 200 each year). European merger and acquisition activity has been highest in the fields of food and food retailing; automotive products; banking and financial services (including insurance); electronics, electrical engineering and computers; paper and printing; chemicals and plastics; and building materials. Much of the food industry's M&A effort has concerned brand ownership, especially in relation to snack foods, confectionery and dairy products.

The Commission's annual surveys have revealed that the main motivations for cross-border M&As have been the wish to improve market share, desires to expand and obtain economies of scale, complementarity of the activities of the businesses involved in a takeover, and the need to reorganise and restructure enterprises. Further reasons for acquisitions and mergers, the Commission suggests, include the opening up of national capital markets to foreign EU businesses, acceptance by banks and other finance providers of higher ratios of borrowing to fixed assets within client companies, the fact that a growing number of European companies are being forced to adopt cross-border trading perspectives, and the increased willingness of large conglomerates to discard subsidiaries in order to concentrate on core business.

10. Barriers to takeover activity

It is more difficult to acquire firms in certain EU countries than in others. Note for example how Germany, despite its attraction as the economic powerhouse of the EU, typically has less than 200 of its significant companies taken over by foreigners each year. This is attributable no doubt to the technical problems associated with acquiring German firms (*see* Chapter 11). Equally the annual aggregate value of takeovers of British firms by foreign EU companies frequently exceeds that of British takeovers of other EU firms by four hundred per cent, indicating the ease with which UK businesses can be acquired. Also the average size of UK businesses taken over by foreigners is more than double the average size of foreign EU firms purchased by residents of the UK. There is no 'level playing field' where cross-border European Union mergers and acquisitions are concerned (Kay 1993). Specific barriers to takeover activity in Continental EU nations are as follows:

(a) Bank and family financing in conjunction with the absence of substantial equity markets in certain countries.

(b) The higher reserves conventionally held by companies in some EU states which result in their being better equipped to resist unwanted attempted take-overs. Belgian, French and German companies must, by law, create a reserve of at least ten per cent of their share capital. Italian companies have to retain a 20 per cent reserve; in Denmark the reserve has to be 25 per cent; and in Greece 33.3 per cent. Additionally the laws of many of these countries allow companies to create special (tax free) contingency reserves during highly profitable years (to cover possible environmental risks, currency exchange rate uncertainties, etc.) and then to write them back into their mainstream accounts in loss-making periods.

(c) The extensive use of bearer shares in many EU nations, which makes it difficult to identify shareholders willing to sell their equities.

(d) Availability of special voting rights to particular groups of shareholders. In Germany for instance, shares with high par values have more voting rights than shares with low par values. French law permits companies to grant more voting powers to long-standing shareholders than others. France, Germany, Belgium and the Netherlands permit companies to restrict the voting powers of any single shareholder to a low level (e.g. that no one person or institution may cast more than ten per cent of all votes, regardless of the magnitude of their actual shareholdings). This prevents individuals with large blocks of shares from transferring majority voting powers to takeover predators. Cross-shareholdings deals among friendly companies, with each partner holding large blocks of votes in the other, are common in Continental states.

(e) The compulsory industrial democracy arrangements that large companies in many Continental EU nations are obliged to implement. These can act as a barrier to mergers and acquisitions in that employee representatives on a Supervisory Board might argue against accepting a bid from another firm for fear of possible redundancies. Also the legal requirement that employee representatives be informed and consulted on takeover attempts (as matters affecting their fundamental interests) causes delays that take the heat out of attempted takeovers. Indeed, in Germany and the Netherlands employee representatives have the legal right to delay decisions on mergers and acquisitions for several weeks (longer in certain circumstances).

Note moreover that the concealment of the names and addresses of shareholders is lawful in Belgium, France, Spain, Italy, Germany and the Netherlands.

11. Control of M&As

Control over M&A activity occurs at the European level via the 1978 Third Directive on Company Law, which stipulates basic requirements for the protection of creditors and shareholders following a takeover, through the 1989 Merger Regulation which enables the European Commission to veto high-value cross-border EU mergers or acquisitions that would distort existing market structures or restrict freedom of choice for consumers, and the Merger Control Directive 1990 (Neven et al 1993).

The latter prohibits countries from taxing capital gains arising from mergers, acquisitions or capital transfers in EU member countries. This was considered necessary because the market values of the assets acquired through a company merger are typically well above their book value and, in principle, liable to capital gains tax, which would prevent many desirable cross-border mergers, management buy-outs or company rationalisations from taking place. Additionally there are two Draft Directives intended to harmonise national rules on takeovers and reduce barriers to cross-border takeovers, as follows:

(a) The Tenth Draft Directive on Cross-Border Mergers of PLCs 1985

This would restrict the defensive measures which the board of a target company may implement in order to fight off a bid (*see* **8**), strengthen shareholders' rights *vis-à-vis* the appointment and dismissal of directors, prevent the issue of equities with multiple voting powers and restrict the number of non-voting shares a company may possess. Also it would become difficult for a subsidiary to purchase shares in its parent (hence preventing these shares falling into a predator's hands); companies would also be prohibited from buying back more than 10% of their shares without shareholders' approval.

(b) The Thirteenth Draft Directive on Takeover and other General Bids

Under this proposal predators would have to bid for all remaining shares in target companies once a third of the voting shares in them have been purchased. The bid would have to be made at the highest price paid for shares previously acquired. National governments will be free to apply a lower threshold percentage if they so wish. Bids would have to be accepted not before four weeks and at most ten weeks from the publication date of the offer document, in order to allow shareholders to consider their position and to ensure that the target business's operations are not disrupted for too long a period. Advance notice of the bid would have to be given to the supervisory authority and the bid's details published in a mass circulation newpaper. The information provided would have to include details of how the predator intends raising the money needed to finance the acquisition, its intentions towards the target firm, and how the predator's level of indebtedness will be affected. Then, anyone owning more than 5% of the voting shares in the target will have to advise the supervisory authority of all dealings in them (to curb insider dealing), and shareholders must be kept fully informed of such transactions.

Further requirements of the Draft Directive are that all shareholders in target firms be treated equally, that predators publish informative offer documents, and that target companies be prohibited from issuing new shares and from completing 'exceptional transactions' during a bid (e.g. altering the basic structure of a firm's assets and liabilities or taking on major fresh commitments). Each EU country would have to establish an independent supervisory body to oversee contested takeovers.

12. The Merger Control Regulation 1989

This applies to cross-border M&As involving all of the following elements:

(a) An aggregate worldwide turnover in excess of five billion ECU. The turnover calculation has to include the sales of the entire group of companies to which the undertaking that is party to the merger belongs, unless just a subsidiary of another business is being acquired.

(b) EU-wide turnovers of at least 250 million ECU for at least two of the merging companies.

(c) Each of the companies concerned doing more than one-third of their EU business in different EU states.

The Regulation covers situations where *either*:

- two or more previously independent businesses merge to become one new independent undertaking, *or*
- an individual or firm controlling one business acquires direct or indirect control of another.

Hence joint ventures that perform on a permanent basis all the functions of a separate legal activity and all takeover bids fall within the second category. 'Control' means the exercise of decisive influence on an organisation via ownership, the right to use its assets, or the ability to exert a significant effect on shareholder voting. Thus effective control can involve a less than 50 per cent shareholding. The European Commission will adjudge each case on its merits in the latter situation.

The Commission is empowered to prohibit any merger that satisfies the previously mentioned criteria and which is considered anti-competitive or harmful to consumers, or may order its reversal if the merger has already been completed. Fines of up to ten per cent of annual turnover can be levied on firms that ignore the Commission's instructions. Sometimes mergers are allowed only on condition that the companies involved formally undertake to relinquish their interests in certain businesses, cancel exclusive distribution agreements, etc.

An intended merger falling within the scope of the Regulation must be notified to the European Commission within one week of the conclusion of the agreement and actions to implement the merger suspended for three weeks, during which period the Commission will decide whether to initiate an examination. If so the Commission has one further month in which to commence proceedings and then four months within which it must declare the proposed merger compatible with the requirements of the Single Market, or alternatively issue a prohibition order. The Commission is empowered to impose fines of up to ten per cent of annual turnover on companies that fail to give proper notice of intended mergers and/or which supply incorrect or misleading information.

Under the terms of the Regulation the Commission is obliged to take into account a number of factors when deciding whether a merger is likely to impede competition, notably:

- likely future developments in competition within the sector
- the consequences of a merger for competition
- the extent of non-EU international competition
- the merger's influence on barriers to entry to the industry.

The fact that a merger, of itself, will create or strengthen a dominant position is not sufficient to warrant its prohibition. These consequences must be pan-European in nature and not concern just one country. 'Dominance' has to be assessed in relation to the relevant product market (i.e. the market for products supplied by the merging companies that can reasonably be regarded as substitutable for each other – *see* 4) and the geographic area in which the merging firms' products are supplied. This area covers only those regions which have 'similar competitive conditions', thus excluding adjoining areas where these conditions might be different. Although the Regulation does not define what is actually meant by the term 'dominant position', the Commission suggests that a post-merger market share of more than 25 per cent could indicate that a merger might be incompatible with the public interest.

Joint ventures (JVs)

JVs are subject to the Merger Control Regulation because they might, of course, be used to camouflage what in reality are cartel situations. Accordingly, the EU Merger Regulation prohibits 'concentrative' JVs considered by the European Commission to constitute disguised company amalgamations. A concentrative venture is one which takes over a significant part of its parents' businesses and operates in the long term as a self-managing entity. Nevertheless, the Commission recognises the usefulness of joint ventures as a means for integrating the internal European market, particularly in relation to technology transfer, developing new products, strengthening the competitive position of smaller enterprises, and promoting innovation. Accordingly it is prepared to overlook many of the anti-competitive effects that joint ventures sometimes create. Action will be taken, however, if a JV raises entry barriers, leads to blatant market sharing and/or unduly intensifies market power.

Individual JVs can be exempted from EU competition law provided they satisfy two positive and two negative criteria. To qualify for exemption, a venture must:

(*i*) improve the production or distribution of goods or promote technical or economic progress, *and*
(*ii*) allow consumers a fair share of the resulting benefits.

These are generally known as the 'public policy' criteria. Examples of JV activities avoiding prohibition via the public policy argument include the following:

- General improvement of distribution channels.
- Facilitation of the sharing of technical knowledge.
- Increasing the productive capacity (and hence employment potential) of EU enterprises.
- Development or testing of experimental products at the fringes of new technology.
- Improvement of the ability of European industry to compete against non-EU countries, especially the US and Japan.
- Standardisation of products or processes which increases interchangeability and reduces production costs.

The negative criteria are that a JV must not:

(*i*) impose unreasonable restrictions on participants; *or*
(*ii*) contribute to the elimination of competition in relation to the product.

Partners in a joint venture normally agree not to compete with each other in relation to the development, production and sale of the product. Such agreements necessarily infringe Article 85 of the Rome Treaty even if they are not explicitly stated. A key factor here is whether the JV will have consequences for related ('spill-over') markets and, if so, whether their magnitudes will be 'appreciable'. To assess the latter the Commission will consider the sizes and existing market shares of JV members and the effects of the venture on distribution systems in relevant markets. More generally, the Commission has published a set of guidelines that it considers relevant to the decision of whether a joint venture contravenes EU competition law. These can be summarised as follows:

(a) Contractual restrictions on JV partners must be 'indispensable' to achieving the objectives of the project.

(b) Restrictive JVs are permissible if no individual partner has access to the technology, finance, know-how, sources of supply of input products or production facilities necessary for the project.

(c) JVs are most likely to infringe EU competition law when the parties are in direct competition with each other, including 'upstream' competition in research and technical development.

NATIONAL DIFFERENCES IN RULES ON COMPETITION

13. Differences in national legislation

EU competition law is binding on all member countries, although national governments are free to operate their own additional legislation. The essential features of EU countries' competition law are as follows:

Austria Any intended merger or acquisition likely to result in a dominant market position has to be pre-registered with the Vienna Appeal Court, which will sanction the deal only if it is in the interests of the consumer. Otherwise there is little anti-trust law other than that necessary to satisfy EU requirements.

Belgium This country relies almost exclusively on EU rules to control monopoly situations. Transfers of at least one third of the shares in large companies with capitals above a certain threshold must notify regional authorities prior to the deal. Straight takeover bids for firms must be notified to the Belgian Banking Commission, and disclosure rules apply.

Denmark The nation's Competition Act 1989 demands the complete transparency of cartel operations. Any agreement or tacit concerted practice likely to exert a dominant effect on the market must be notified to the country's Competition Council within 14 days of its conclusion. Failure to register can result in daily fines. No pre-merger or pre-acquisition public disclosures are required, and no prior public consents are necessary. However, M&As that lead to monopoly situations are subject to review by a judicial 'Competitive Board'.

Finland Finnish competition law now relies almost totally on EU legislation.

France Any 'concentration' of businesses that controls more than 25% of the sales, purchases or other transactions of a given market is prohibited. A concentration is defined as any situation in which a company or group can directly or indirectly exercise a decisive influence on another company. Laws on takeovers are stringent. Accepted bids must be registered with the state authorities and their details published in order to inform the creditors of the takeover target about the situation. These creditors may be entitled to take the amounts owing to them from the predator at the time of the transaction. Persons or groups of persons acquiring 5, 10, 20, 33, 50 and 66 per cent of a quoted company's share capital must disclose this to the French Stock Exchange Council within five days of the event. At the 20 per cent threshold the predator must publicly declare its intentions for the target company. When the 33 per cent limit is reached the buyer must offer to purchase the remaining 66 per cent of the firm's voting share capital.

It is illegal to use a company's assets as security against the repayment of debt incurred to finance an attempted acquisition. French companies may not purchase their own shares (with limited exceptions). Under French law, measures intended to exert a 'decisive influence' over other firms may be deemed to represent a *de facto* merger. Examples are interlocking directorships and (importantly) minority mutual shareholdings among groups of companies. Infringements of French merger law attract fines of up to five per cent of the guilty firm's domestic turnover over its last financial year.

Germany Cartels and monopolies are illegal unless they serve the public interest by rationalising and/or structurally reorganising important industries. Any merger resulting in a firm controlling 20% or more of a market, or having at least 10,000 employees or a turnover in excess of a certain prespecified limit, must be registered with the Federal Cartel Office in Berlin, which has four months to investigate and (if appropriate) prohibit the merger from going ahead. Any acquisition of more than 25 per cent of another firm's voting shares can be regarded as a 'merger'. Formal cross-company shareholding agreements involving less than 25 per cent of each participant's share capital might also be viewed as 'mergers' in certain circumstances. Any undertaking with more than one third of the relevant market is presumed to be a monopoly, and an 'uncompetitive situation' is assumed to exist if either (i) two or three firms in a market are responsible for more than 50 per cent of sales, or (ii) four or five businesses collectively hold at least a two-thirds share of the market.

Greece The country's 1977 Monopolies and Oligopolies Act prohibits dominant market positions, restrictive practices, unfair competition and 'abusive exploitation' of markets. Mergers or takeover bids require a two thirds majority vote of shareholders of the target company.

Ireland Ireland's Minister for Industry is empowered to break up a monopoly via its division into competing units and/or the sale of certain assets. Mergers and acquisitions are subject to the nation's Mergers, Takeovers and Monopolies Act 1978, and subsequent amendments. M&As exceeding certain threshold values and/or in specific industries must be notified in advance to the Ministry of Industry and Commerce and may not be concluded until the Ministry's permission has been obtained.

Italy Any merger resulting in a turnover that exceeds a certain threshold has to be pre-notified to the state authorities, which have one month to investigate and prohibit the merger if appropriate. Failure to notify a merger to the Italian authorities can result in a fine of up to one per cent of the firm's turnover for the previous year. Fines of between one and ten per cent of annual turnover may be imposed on companies that fail to comply with an order to cancel an intended merger. Mergers of listed companies are subject to a three-month moratorium to allow creditors of either business to object, and the merger cannot proceed unless creditors are given security against outstanding balances. Companies are not allowed to purchase their own shares but leverage buy-outs are possible.

Luxembourg There are no special regulations on mergers and acquisitions in this country.

Netherlands The Dutch Minister of Economic Affairs is able to intervene and prevent violations of fair competition although monopolies are not illegal in this nation. All exclusive distribution agreements have to be filed with and approved by the authorities.

Portugal Portugal has stringent anti-trust legislation. It is totally illegal to establish minimum prices, apply discriminatory prices or sales conditions for similar goods or services, or refuse to render services. Any agreement which restrains fair competition is unlawful and likely to attract heavy fines. Directors of merging companies are legally obliged to produce a merger proposal which outlines the aims and circumstances of the amalgamation and to deposit this with the Portuguese Commercial Register. Creditors have 30 days in which to object to the merger, which cannot proceed if a Court upholds creditors' objections.

Spain Any situation in which a company or group attains 25% or more of any given market or a certain prespecified turnover is exceeded is automatically investigated by the country's Anti-Trust Court. Directors of merging companies must draft and sign a merger proposal which is then placed before the share-holders of both businesses. Dissenting directors must indicate the grounds for their opposition. The local Mercantile Registry then appoints two independent experts to report on the proposal, the details of which must be published. Creditors to either company have one month in which to object to the planned merger.

Sweden Takeovers using funds from the target company are illegal. Sweden has an 'Anti-Trust Ombudsman' empowered to investigate M&A deals that might lead to a dominant market position.

United Kingdom British competition law relies heavily on EU legislation. There is a voluntary Code of Practice on takeovers and mergers; but little legislation other than the minimum required by European Union Directives. The UK Monopolies and Mergers Commission is empowered to investigate any merger resulting in a single supplier or group of suppliers controlling more than 25% of a market. All agreements between businesses to fix prices or regulate supplies must be registered with the UK's Office of Fair Trading, and are presumed void if the parties to them cannot prove they are in the public interest.

PUBLIC PROCUREMENT

14. Public purchasing

The public sector is an extremely important customer for many European companies: indeed it is estimated by the European Commission to account for as much as 15 per cent of aggregate EU gross domestic product. Completion of the Single Market has been accompanied by the opening up of public sector contracts to competitive bidding by an EU firm, regardless of its geographical location. It is intended that, within a few years, *all* public procurement will be subject to competitive tendering. Meanwhile, however, certain restrictions continue. At the time of writing, there are three types of tendering procedure (open, closed and negotiated) available for use by EU public bodies (i.e. 'associations governed by public law or bodies corresponding thereto formed by regional or local authorities'). 'Open' tendering means that *any* company may enter a bid. 'Restricted' tendering requires bidding companies to satisfy certain pre-qualifications set by the purchaser (e.g. providing evidence of their technical expertise and/or financial standing). 'Negotiated' procedures relate to direct discussions between the purchaser and chosen suppliers, without any competition. This may only occur (a) if no tenders have been received using the other procedures; or (b) in consequence of the highly technical nature of the goods (e.g. the need for compatibility with existing stocks); or (c) for reasons of extreme urgency. Purchasers can be forced to justify a decision to use negotiated procedures to the European Commission. Also they must specify in advance the criteria (price, quality, etc.) to be used in awarding contracts. Advance notice of all procurement plans exceeding appropriate thresholds must be advertised in the *Official Journal* of the EU, stating whether the call for tender is open or closed. Results of calls for tenders naming the successful bidders have to be declared in the *OJ*. Tenders submitted under the open procedure can be accepted for up to 52 days from the dispatch of details to the applicant firm. For restricted and negotiated procedures the deadline is 37 days from dispatch of details, or 40 days from the issue of a written invitation to bid.

Under the EU public procurement legislation, calls for tender *must* specify only EU rather than national technical standards. In the absence of a pan-European standard for a particular product the most general national or international standard should be used, provided this will not oblige purchasers to accept items that are incompatible with equipment already in use. Standards are irrelevant, of course, for situations where the product purchased is a completely novel invention.

Benefits deriving from the liberalisation of public procurement in EU countries include lower purchase prices, a wider choice of products for buyers, and the breaking up of local monopoly suppliers. Smaller firms can expand and obtain economies of scale in consequence of cross-border sales to foreign public purhasers. Critics of liberalisation allege that governments are prevented from supporting employment in depressed local regions (bearing in mind the fact that national governments lawfully give large amounts of direct financial assistance to economically underdeveloped areas). Local procurement can be more reliable, faster, and be accompanied by superior after-sales services.

15. Types of public sector contract

Four categories of contract are covered by the present scheme: supplies, works, services, and utilities. 'Supplies' contracts involve the provision of goods to central, regional and local governments and similar bodies such as police forces or local health authorities, provided the value of the contract exceeds 200,000 ECU for local government or 130,000 ECU for central government. 'Works' contracts are for building and civil engineering projects for central, regional and local government and similar bodies. Only contracts worth more than 5 million ECU are covered.

'Services' contracts are analogous to works contracts but relate to service providers. They are governed by the 1992 Services Directive, which allows greater freedom to use the negotiated procedures previously mentioned. The Directive covers services contracts exceeding 200,000 ECU. In 1993 a 'Utilities' Directive was introduced to bring the previously excluded water, energy, transport and telecommunications sectors within the public procurement rules, albeit with greater flexibility. These sectors are required either (a) to adhere to certain detailed rules governing their procurement policies and procedures and then attest that the rules have been implemented; or (b) to devise their own purchasing procedures and subsequently submit to periodic external audits designed to ensure that their purchasing methods are truly competitive. The thresholds for supplies and services contracts are 600,000 ECU for the telecommunications sector, 400,000 ECU for the other sectors. For works contracts a threshold of 500,000 ECU applies to all sectors.

INDUSTRIAL POLICY

16. Nature of industrial policy

Industrial policy is far more than government intervention in industry and/or the payment of subsidies to certain firms. Rather it concerns the entire macroeconomic and cultural environment surrounding business and trade in a particular country. It encompasses:

- deliberate stimulation of certain industrial sectors
- promotion of tripartite links between business, trade unions and government
- development of national infrastructures (training, transport and communications systems, etc.)
- grants for research and development
- attempts to create an 'enterprise culture' within an economy through

giving special tax allowances to small firms and/or by relaxing bureaucratic administrative controls
- government interest rate policy
- state provision of advice and information services
- competition law
- statutory controls over collective bargaining and other aspects of industrial relations.

National industrial policy determines the overall framework within which government decisions on economic development are taken (Geronski 1989). And the government grants and subsidies emerging from a country's industrial policy are a crucial factor in the investment and operational decisions of large numbers of firms.

State concerns with industrial policy normally focus on:

- maintaining employment (often via regional subsidies for economic development)
- encouraging research and technical development
- providing incentives for the creation of new businesses
- establishing technical standards for industries so that individual firms have substantial markets for their outputs
- facilitating improvements in social welfare
- forecasting trends in industrial structure (in order to help companies cope with structural economic change)
- identifying those industries with the greatest potential and those which need to be run down
- minimisation of excess industrial capacity at the national level.

Examples of specific governmental industrial policies intended to achieve these objectives include:

- subsidising technology transfer in key industry sectors
- helping firms export to high growth foreign markets
- providing technical assistance to companies (especially with research and development)
- assisting the settlement of labour/management disputes
- monitoring merger and acquisition activities, allowing some mergers while prohibiting others
- giving tax reliefs for the employment of additional workers
- promoting labour mobility via relocation grants and allowances.

17. Problems with industrial policy

Critics of national industrial policy allege that it:

- generates government bureaucracy and red tape
- wastes taxpayers' money on 'no-hope' projects
- stifles initiative and entrepreneurial activity
- impedes the necessary reallocation of resources away from inefficient industries towards profitable new ventures

- creates among firms a (debilitating) climate of dependency on state handouts, rather than stimulating genuine competitive advantage and awareness of customer needs
- causes countries to compete against each other in the provision of lucrative packages of state assistance intended to attract foreign investment
- requires civil servants without industrial experience to take critical decisions concerning the futures of major businesses
- encourages firms to develop lobbying skills and expertise in preparing grant applications, at the expense of getting on with the job
- can lead to the existence of large but unprofitable conglomerations capable of distorting competition and taking too high a market share.

Industrial policies invariably involve government intervention in industry and hence decisions by the state regarding which projects should be supported. This creates gainers and, of course, losers among competing industries and firms. The practice of 'picking winners' is extremely difficult, and politicians and civil servants have proven just as inept and unreliable when attempting this as any market system. It is easy for public servants (especially elected politicians) to confuse economic objectives with broader social aims, and government decisions on the allocation of state assistance are likely to be influenced by party political factors (such as the timing of elections).

Even if there is an incontrovertible case for public subsidy, determining the correct level of assistance for a specific project is extremely problematic. Note moreover that state-financed R&D and related activities could simply reduce privately funded research that would have occurred in any event, and that all government assistance has to be paid for via higher taxes, which themselves might depress the national economy.

18. EU industrial policy

EU industrial policy originated with the Treaty of Paris, which initiated a series of interventions in the coal and steel industries. The Treaty of Rome allowed for further measures for the support of industry, particularly via loans and grants from the European Investment Bank and the Regional Development Fund (*see* **23**). Most support was for R&D, training, and new investments designed to create jobs. Pressures for the further development of a coherent pan-European industrial policy intensified during the 1970s consequent to the rapid and severe declines of Europe's textiles, footwear, coal, steel and shipbuilding industries. There was an urgent need to encourage rationalisation, reorganisation and conversion to other lines of work within these sectors.

In 1983 the Council of Ministers adopted a 'Transnational Plan' designed to improve the competitiveness of European industry through:

- promoting new technologies and industrial innovation (defined as 'the introduction of new products, services, production methods, marketing and management techniques')
- preventing the duplication of effort

- encouraging co-operative arrangements and cross-border joint ventures
- increasing the flow of information to and between enterprises via the creation of (i) advanced information services and (ii) an efficient market in information.

The Single European Act shifted the emphasis of EC industrial policy towards the rapid removal of internal non-tariff barriers to trade, the improvement of communication infrastructures, harmonisation in the fields of new technologies, and the protection of intellectual property rights.

19. Small businesses

Small to medium sized enterprises (SMEs) dominate the majority of EU industries. Only in manufacturing is it the case that large firms (i.e. those which employ more than 500 workers) comprise more than half of one per cent of the sector. For analytical purposes the European Commission divides SMEs into three size categories: 'micro' (zero to nine employees); 'small' (10 to 99 employees); and 'medium' (100 to 499). The Commission's Directorate-General XXIII collects data on the activities of the EU's small to medium sized enterprises, summaries of which are published biennially.

According to the most recent of these surveys (CEC 1996), 91 per cent of the EU's 14 million SMEs are classed as micro and 8% as small. About 15% are manufacturing businesses – approximately the same percentage as for building and construction. Most others are service firms (primary industries are excluded from these statistics). Around 85% of manufacturing SMEs are micro businesses.

Overall, micro businesses account for nearly 30% of all EU jobs. Firms with between 10 and 499 workers provide about 40% of total employment; large businesses account for the remainder. The only European industries in which big firms are responsible for the majority of jobs are energy and water (75%), minerals and chemicals (55%), and transport and communications (51%). There are significant national differences in the pattern of employment. For example, large enterprises employ half of all workers in Germany, but only 10% in Spain. SMEs provide nearly 100% of jobs in the building and construction industry in Italy; 75% in the UK. In the Netherlands SMEs contribute 60% of jobs in the service sector, while for Spain the corresponding figure is 90%.

20. Aid for small businesses

In recognition of the crucial importance of SMEs for the economic development of the EU, the European Commission has for many years sought to support the small business sector and to encourage the creation of new small businesses. DG XXIII has established a special task force to co-ordinate assistance programmes, which have included, *inter alia*:

- Attempts to develop general economic environments conducive to the welfare of SMEs. Examples of specific measures intended to attain this objective include the provision by national governments of information and advice services, the identification of bureaucratic laws and regulations that impede SME activities, and financial assistance for the management training of owners and employees of small businesses.

- 'Compliance cost assessments', i.e. the critical examination of the likely effects of proposed new EU legislation on the small business sector.
- Helping SMEs find joint venture partners.
- Increasing the availability of research and development funds to small businesses.
- Subsidising the costs of engaging business consultants.
- Provision of venture capital, normally in association with private sector venture capital (VC) organisations. Venture capital is a minority shareholding in a young business taken by an outside body, e.g. a merchant bank. Usually the VC agreement provides for (i) the resale of the shares to the company at a (high) predetermined price, and (ii) some involvement of the VC provider in the management of the company.

In Britain, venture capital has long provided medium-term equity development finance for young high-risk businesses. France has an active venture capital industry, as (to lesser extents) do Germany and Spain. Other Continental countries, however, have negligible venture capital markets, presumably because on the Continent families, banks and industrial companies frequently invest long term in risky small businesses, but without attaching the strings that UK venture capital providers often impose on client companies. Nevertheless, the European Commission is actively promoting the extension of venture capital financing among EU firms, seeing venture capital as a potentially invaluable means for funding European research and technical development undertaken in small but rapidly expanding high-tech enterprises. A major problem is the shortage of venture capitalists with genuine experience and competence in transitional VC projects. Assessing the risks attached to a venture in a strange country is extremely difficult, and to date few VC providers have been willing to attempt the task.

Justifications for these (considerable) expenditures are the vulnerability of small firms to the greatly increased level of competition within national markets resulting from European economic integration, and the fact that tomorrow's successful big businesses will emerge from today's better small enterprises – which need to be nurtured and encouraged to grow (CEC 1990b).

REGIONAL AID

21. Legality of regional assistance

The legality of state aid to industry is governed by Article 92 of the Treaty of Rome, especially section 2 which prohibits state assistance that might distort or threaten to distort competition through favouring particular enterprises or the production of certain goods in situations *where inter-EU trade is affected*. However, section 3 of Article 92 lists various categories of state aid that are permissable, notably aid which:

- promotes the economic development of areas where living standards are low or where there is exceptionally high unemployment
- makes good *ad hoc* disruptions of a national or regional economy
- helps implement an investment project with pan-EU benefits
- facilitates economic activities which do not affect trading conditions to the detriment of the Single European Market.

Other classes of state aid may be declared lawful by qualified majority voting of the Council of Ministers on proposals from the European Commission. In practice, moreover, the Commission has always been prepared to ignore the anti-competitive effects of state subsidies which improve employment and living standards in poor areas, help restructure a declining industry, facilitate research and development, or develop new industries. Indeed, there are a number of positive reasons for the Commission actively to encourage governments to provide regional incentives, including the following:

(a) Expansion in the underdeveloped regions can relieve the over-crowding and congestion in the Union's core industrial areas.

(b) National grants and subsidies complement Union efforts under the Structural Funds initiative (*see* 23).

(c) New business start-ups in depressed regions create a commercial environment that encourages existing large companies to expand into these areas.

(d) Disparities in the economic performances of a country's regions might impede social cohesion in the entire European Union.

(e) Regional grants and subsidies from national governments may be used to supplement EU R&D grants for important research projects.

Hence, a wide range of national and Union level investment subsidies is available, including loans, direct grants, special tax reliefs and the provision of commercial and technical information. The Commission requires, however, that the assistance given be used to solve problems and not simply postpone inevitable business shutdowns, and that it be moderate and restricted to the level needed to achieve reasonable objectives. Also the government involved should have a long-term intention to phase out grants and subsidies progressively.

Article 93 of the Rome Treaty compels the Commission to monitor all forms of aid granted by member states, and to ban assistance that is not compatible with the Single Market or which is being misused. If a government wishes to implement fresh aid measures it must pre-notify the Commission, which examines the proposal and determines whether it is compatible with the Rome Treaty. Appeals against prohibitions are heard by the European Court of Justice. Notification is to the Commission's Directorate-General of Competition (DG IV), which has compiled and attempts to maintain a comprehensive list of all state aids available in EU member countries. Unfortunately, countries do not always report the full extent of the subsidies they are providing, and sometimes they conceal them within other statistical categories. Of particular concern has been the alleged use by some countries of 'research and development' grants for purposes which, in reality, are nothing more than general investment. State subsidy of unprofitable nationalised industries that compete with private companies in other EU countries is also a controversial matter, especially where the competition involves high unemployment industries.

22. Need for regional assistance

The Treaty of Rome requires the EU to promote the harmonious development of economic activity *throughout* its territory and to improve standards of living in regions in decline. Unfortunately, unequal distributions of economic activity occur in all EU countries, caused by the decline of traditional labour-intensive industries, plus the increasing use of mechanised methods in agriculture. The problem is severe: the difference in per capita income between the European Union's richest and poorest regions is now double the corresponding difference in income between the richest and poorest areas of the United States.

Regional disparities in living standards are socially divisive and impede the orderly development of national economies. Industrial infrastructures are weaker in underdeveloped regions, making the firms within them uncompetitive and extremely susceptible to the effects of downturns in national and international trade. It is hardly surprising, therefore, that about a quarter of all state assistance distributed within the EU Member States is for regional aid.

Typically, aid is channelled to two types of area:

1 'Traditional' underdeveloped regions that rely heavily on agriculture and where incomes have always been relatively low and unemployment levels high.
2 Formerly prosperous regions that are now in decline.

There are two approaches to the question of how this assistance should be allocated. The first relies on the theory that each region within a country possesses a particular set of resources (including human resources), industrial skills, and historical traditions which enable it to specialise in certain goods or services more efficiently than other regions. According to this argument, the government of the country should help regions develop these assets in order to establish healthy local economic infrastructures. The government should pick winners and selectively subsidise specific enterprises, projects or types of activity. The problem, of course, is that the predicted winners frequently lose, their failure arguably being encouraged by the featherbedding created by public support. Also, discretionary awards:

- require public servants to take important commercial decisions
- are administratively complex, expensive and troublesome both for the applicant firms and the grant-awarding authorities.

The alternative approach is for government to subsidise industrial development measures that benefit *all* firms and workers, regardless of lines of work. General tax allowances and employee training programmes are examples of this type of policy. Hence, some businesses will receive subsidies they do not need, while others might obtain them in forms that are not appropriate for their requirements (e.g. tax reliefs are useless for firms that earn negligible profits). Inefficient businesses might be subsidised, and the authorities cannot monitor the effectiveness of the grants awarded to particular companies. Advantages to automatic grants and subsidies include:

(a) Certainty, so that firms know in advance the value of the assistance they will receive for authorised projects, thus facilitating their financial planning.

(b) Transparency and equality of application. Civil servants and/or politicians do not have to decide which investments shall receive government funding.

(c) Administrative convenience. Governments simply determine eligibility criteria for the subsidy. They are not required to select specific enterprises for subsidy.

Types of assistance

Allowances are payable to firms for locating their premises in certain EU areas, for undertaking research and technical development, for creating new jobs and for other specially designated purposes. It is important to note how the completion of the Single Market means that *any* EU business is now eligible to receive national investment and other grants and subsidies on the same basis as local firms, regardless of the nationality of its majority owner – provided the latter is resident within the EU. Thus, for example, a British firm that establishes subsidiaries in (say) Germany and Portugal is entitled to receive exactly the same research and development (R&D), regional development and training grants as are available to local Portuguese or German owned enterprises. Grant availability and values differ among EU countries, and the regional aid packages offered in specific areas can be a key factor when choosing a location for a foreign EU subsidiary or branch.

All EU countries give capital grants for regional development. Interest rate subsidies are available in Belgium, Germany, Italy and Greece. Special tax concessions for firms locating in poorer regions apply in France, Greece, Italy and Luxembourg. Regional employment subsidies can be claimed by businesses in Germany, France, Italy and Portugal. Automatic (rather than discretionary) grants apply in Italy, Greece, Belgium, Portugal, the Netherlands and, for firms employing less than 25 workers, in the UK. Maximum values for regional incentive packages (capital grants plus interest rate subsidy) vary from 10% to 15% of total project value in five of the EU countries. In Germany the figure is 16% (higher in East Germany); 26% in the UK; about 40% in Spain, Greece and Ireland; and 50% in Portugal and Italy.

23. Regional aid at the EU level

EU funding for regional development comes predominantly from two sources: Structural Funds, and loans from the European Investment Bank for special projects.

Structural Funds

These comprise the European Regional Development Fund (ERDF), the European Social Fund (ESF) and the European Agricultural Guidance and Guarantee

Fund (EAGGF). The normal eligibility criteria for Structural Funds distribution are: (i) that national governments contribute to the project and (ii) that EU grants be additional to money which the national government would have donated to the project in normal circumstances. The European Commission has specified five priority objectives for the use of Structural Funds, as follows:

1. Economic development and structural adjustment of the poorest regions.
2. Improvement of regions seriously affected by industrial decline.
3. Combating long-term unemployment.
4. Facilitation of the occupational integration of young people.
5. Promotion of the development of agricultural areas.

In practice, Structural Funds may be applied in one of more of the following situations:

(a) Where regional per capita gross domestic product (GDP) is less than 75 per cent of the EU average. In the UK this covers all of Northern Ireland.

(b) Where the effects of industrial decline have been especially damaging.

(c) Where unemployment among workers who are over 25 years of age and have been unemployed for more than one year are abnormally high.

Additionally, regions suffering chronic unemployment among those aged 25 or under and depressed agricultural areas may receive Structural Funding. Since Structural Funds are used largely to finance public works (especially roads, ports, telecommunications and transport systems, and support services for small to medium sized enterprises), individual firms may only benefit through participating in an EU approved national aid programme, although direct EU assistance can be given if no state scheme currently exists for an accredited purpose. Applications may only be made by a national government or public authority.

The European Regional Development Fund

Prior to 1972, the (then) EEC left regional development to the discretion of national governments. However, the ever-increasing magnitudes of the gaps between prosperous and depressed EEC regions led to the determination of regional aid policies and, in 1975, to the establishment of the European Regional Development Fund (ERDF) through which assistance was to be channelled. Completion of the European Single Market in 1992 greatly facilitated the ease with which capital could cross national frontiers, hence exacerbating regional problems. Hence the amount of money allocated to the ERDF was doubled during 1992. Even so the Fund accounts for less than ten per cent of the total EU budget in most years. Grants from the ERDF are available for two types of project:

1 Industry and services investments, i.e. schemes intended to create new jobs or protect existing ones (modernisation of manufacturing plant for example).
2 Infrastructure investments designed to help the economic development of an entire region, e.g. road building or the improvement of telecommunications systems.

Loans from the European Investment Bank (EIB)

EIB loans are available for regional development projects, infrastructure invest-ment and environmental protection. A loan can cover up to half the investment costs of a project, including working capital requirements and expenditures incurred in the acquisition of patents, licences, know-how and other intellectual property. Most loans are for seven to 12 years, although loan periods of up to 20 years can be negotiated for infrastructure schemes and major energy sector investments.

Aid for rural areas

Special assistance for new investments in rural areas is available via the Euro-pean Agricultural Guidance and Guarantee Fund (EAGGF), which is concerned with improving agricultural productivity and increasing the incomes of resi-dents in agricultural regions. Funding occurs predominantly through national aid schemes, except (occasionally) for projects involving the processing and marketing of fishery and agricultural products. 'Processing' means all aspects of food preparation following production and includes activities related to the treatment and preservation of any food item. Aid can be obtained under a number of headings, as follows:

- Measures to facilitate the introduction of new technology to the fishery and aquaculture industries, e.g. through upgrading quality or hygiene systems or bettering the storage, handling and smoking of fisheries products.
- Investments that will improve the processing and marketing of farm crops, rationalise marketing channels, encourage the use of agricultural by-products and/or contribute to long-term structural development in rural regions.
- Projects for improving communications or irrigation or for protecting and conserving the environment (particularly *vis-à-vis* forests and wood-land) in agricultural areas.
- Investments intended to diversify rural economies towards tourism, craft and artisan industries and the manufacture and distribution of farm products.

The criteria applied to the selection of the projects that are to receive funding include (i) the extent to which projects are 'rural' in nature, (ii) their likely impact on local employment and (iii) how significantly they will help diversify the local economy and stimulate local incomes. Capital grants of up to 25 per cent of eligible investment expenditures are payable, provided the project is also funded in part by a national government.

Problems with EU regional development funding

Problems with the EU's regional development policies are as follows:

(a) Further enlargement of the Union is likely to bring in poorer countries that possess severe regional economic problems.

(b) Certain regions already receiving substantial assistance are continuing to decline.

(c) Still more European industries are liable to collapse in the not too distant future, creating yet more heavy unemployment in particular regions.

(d) National governments do not always use the money they receive from EU regional development funds for appropriate purposes. The poorest areas do not necessarily get the most money.

RESEARCH AND TECHNICAL DEVELOPMENT

24. Nature of research and development

Research and development (R&D) concerns the acquisition of new technical knowledge, particularly regarding new products, processes, materials and working methods. Activities might be initiated by a firm's marketing staff (having identified new consumer demands) or by production personnel as they seek new methods of manufacture. 'Pure' research is normally funded by the state or an entire industry. Its aims are exploratory and very general; immediately applicable results are not expected. Applied research, in contrast, investigates specific practical questions. Applied work is typically initiated and paid for by the individual company. The aim of applied research is quick improvement of a particular situation. 'Development' means the practical application of the results of research.

The need for R&D arises from the dynamic nature of contemporary business and the inescapable fact in many international commercial situations that materials and competitors' outputs are constantly improving, leading to a sharp reduction in the average life of the typical product. Extensive research and development spending implies the needs for large markets (in order to absorb the costs of heavy research expenditure). It also carries the danger of triggering 'research and development wars' as competitors respond to a firm's innovative behaviour in international markets. Key decisions concerning research and development include:

- the minimum returns that must result from R&D projects in a prespecified time period if the projects are not to be terminated
- whether R & D personnel are to be involved in the determination of the company's overall corporate strategy
- whether to undertake basic or applied research, or a mixture of the two (and if so then in what proportions).

Basic strategic options are as follows:

(a) Purchase patents and know-how from external sources.

(b) Seek to invent entirely new products in-house.

(c) Commission other organisations to invent new products.

(d) Improve existing products.

119

(e) Engage outside bodies to develop existing products.

Costs and benefits of R&D

Possible benefits arising from R&D include improvements in the technical aspects of existing products, introduction of new products, and lower costs of production. Whether the greatest benefits accrue to pure or applied research is a perplexing question. Applied developmental research seemingly offers more scope for the immediate application of fresh knowledge, and may itself provide the impetus for major theoretical breakthroughs. Yet truly original thinking – leading to the complete overthrow of an existing technology – might not be possible using a developmental approach. Unfortunately, the new theories that emerge from pure research may have value only to other theoreticians and be justified solely in academic terms. The sponsoring organisation may have contributed to the advancement of science, but have created no immediately tangible benefits (Cheng 1993).

Each day an R&D project continues it costs money. There is a danger that once a large amount of resources has been invested in a project that has so far been unproductive the firm will continue to fund the project in (possibly hopeless) attempts to recoup its initial investment. The situation is analogous to that of a gambler on a losing streak who gambles increasingly heavily on the assumption that his or her luck must eventually change. Hence, specific research and development timetables are essential. If targets are not met within a predetermined period or budget limitation then the project should be abandoned, unless there are outstandingly high probabilities of immediate success.

Research costs include salaries, equipment and facilities (laboratories for example) and the consequences of resources possibly being tied up for long periods with no financial return. Note moreover that labour turnover within a research department may be high. Scientists are frequently more interested in the subjects of their research than in building a career with a particular company, and thus might leave the firm when an interesting project has been completed. Retention of high calibre research staff may require the availability of a series of challenging new projects. Hence it might be better to arrange for projects to be completed sequentially rather than concurrently, thus employing fewer staff but accepting that overall research objectives may take longer to achieve.

Evaluation of R&D

Evaluation of R&D is perhaps best achieved through asking a series of questions, such as the following:

(a) Which of the firm's new products are the result of R&D activities?

(b) How does the firm's R&D effort compare with that of competitors?

(c) What would happen if all the organisation's R&D were to cease?

(d) What financial benefits (cost savings, increased sales, etc.) are directly attributable to R&D?

It is essential that the benefits of an R&D project be predicted at its inception, and budgetary constraints imposed in line with this prediction. Otherwise, one line of unproductive research might lead to other equally fruitless investigations which seek to correct deficiencies in the initial project. Nevertheless, the decision to terminate a project should not be taken lightly, and the long-term implications of the termination must be carefully evaluated. Will it result, for example, in the company losing market share? (This may actually be acceptable in comparison with enormous and escalating research expenditures.) Does termination mean that existing plant and processes are doomed to obsolescence? What are the implications for other research and investment projects?

25. EU support for research projects

The Treaty of Rome did not contain any meaningful statement concerning Community research policy, and it was not until 1974 that the Council of Ministers explicitly recognised the need to support R&D. Thereafter the European Commission became increasingly concerned about the extent and quality of European industrial R&D. For example, by the early 1980s over half the microprocessors and 80 per cent of microcomputers used in EC businesses were imported from non-EC sources, as were three quarters of all video recorders and similarly high proportions of many other categories of high technology consumer goods. It was obvious that the impaired international competitiveness of European firms in high-tech activities implied by inadequate R&D would impose many economic and social costs and inhibit business growth through the (then) European Community. The European Commission is extremely anxious to promote research and technical development within EU businesses. R&D policy aims to improve the competitiveness of European industry and to encourage firms to take full advantage of possibilities for continental-wide collaborative research activities (Peterson 1992; Sharp and Pravitt 1993). Support occurs via Framework Programmes.

The Framework Programmes

Every five years the Council of Ministers approves a fresh Framework Programme specifying the various scientific and technological fields in which EU funding is to be available. The following principles apply to the allocation of grants under the Framework Programmes:

(a) Application has to be made direct to the European Commission and not through intermediaries.

(b) Transnational collaboration of researching firms and/or educational institutions is obligatory.

(c) The bulk of the money is used to fund precompetitive R&D that lies between basic fundamental research and applied commercial development.

(d) Proposals are evaluated on a competitive basis in relation to how closely the work satisfies the guidelines and objectives specified by the relevant part of the Programme. This approach has been criticised in that it results in the rejection of some high quality proposals simply because they do not 'fit in' with the criteria laid out in the current Framework Programme.

Cross-border collaborative research

Firms benefit from cross-border collaborative research through (i) being able to market the results of their research efforts in more than one country, and (ii) the synergy and fresh ideas likely to emerge from the pooling of research activity. In the past, research and technical development has been undertaken mainly by large firms. Increasingly, however, small to medium sized enterprises participate collaboratively in R&D. Note moreover that although few small businesses conduct basic research, many SMEs are concerned with the *application* of new technologies. Robotics and advanced information technology are extensively available to small companies, enabling them to implement sophisticated manufacturing and management information and decision support systems, the latest just-in-time procurement and inventory procedures, and so on. Obtaining the best from these high technology systems might itself require the firm to undertake some sort of research.

Collaboration between smaller firms wishing to engage in R&D enables the sharing of research costs, personnel, and project failure risks. It helps concentrate resources into the most productive areas; facilitates the dissemination of information; enables firms to obtain know-how from research partners; enhances the career prospects and occupational mobility of research staff; and avoids the duplication of effort in small enterprises. Help with finding research partners is available via the EU's Business Co-operation Network (BC-Net) which acts as a clearing house for requests for co-operation from firms in EU states. The Network's database also includes names and addresses of management consultants and business advisers active in the European field. To use BC-Net the firm approaches an adviser who is a member of the system. (Many UK Chambers of Commerce and trade associations now undertake this function.) The adviser enters the nature of the co-operation sought plus the business's particulars on to a standard proforma 'company profile' which is then instantly and automatically compared with the existing stock of offers within the system. In the case of a positive outcome to the search, both the applicant company and the firms offering co-operation are informed immediately. Otherwise, all business advisers within the geographical area covered by the request are sent a 'flash profile' advising of the opportunity in case an adviser has a company on its books that may be interested in the application. Note that BC-Net extends beyond the frontiers of the European Union.

26. Nature of EU research funding

The European Commission draws an important distinction between pre-competitive, competitive and generic research. The former (which is sometimes referred to as 'pre-normative' research, although occasionally the term pre-normative is used to denote research 'further upstream', i.e. basic research affecting a wide range of subjects) concerns applied research beyond the fundamental level but which does not of itself generate immediately marketable processes or products. Rather, it influences industry standards and the strategic orientations of participating companies. Most grants for this type of research go to large organisations, even though in principle small businesses also qualify for support. Often, government establishments and/or industry or public research institutes belong to consortia specifically formed to complete pre-competitive investigations. 'Competitive' R&D, conversely, has precise operational objectives and typically involves technology-sharing agreements or co-operative research leading to licensing and cross-licensing in separate product markets. The third category, generic research, is for situations where the dividing line between pre-normative and competitive elements is indeterminate. Current EU policy is to fund mostly pre-competitive research. However, there is (usually) no objection to firms patenting the results of funded technical research, on the grounds that the profits generated will then be available to finance additional research in enterprises which have *proved* their innovatory ability.

Proposals need to demonstrate their ability (i) to improve the competitiveness of European industry and/or the quality of EU technical training, or (ii) to promote the harmonisation of EU technical standards, or (iii) to enhance social cohesion within the EU. Proposals must specify exactly how the results of the research are to be implemented. At least two partners from different EC countries must participate in a project, although this does not preclude collaboration between a large company in one nation and a small one in another. Many EU programmes are open to partners in specified non-EU European countries, although the Commission will not contribute directly to the research costs of non-EU organisations. Grants are allocated according to merit, not proportional to national or regional quotas.

Evaluation of proposals

The starting point for applications is normally a 'Call for Proposals' made under a particular programme and published in the *Official Journal of the European Communities*. Interested parties then have a standard three-month period in which to submit proposals. Selection is by a Commission-appointed advisory panel consisting of representatives from national EU governments, plus technical experts. Criteria applied will include project feasibility, scientific merit and possible commercial consequences. The calibre of the personnel who will undertake the research is obviously a critical factor. Research with outcomes likely to have industry-wide repercussions is generally preferred to research leading to long-term market advantage for specific organisations.

27. Management of EU-funded projects

Two types of funding are available: *contracted cost sharing* whereby the EU meets half of project costs, or *concertation funding* through which the EU pays all project co-ordination costs (meetings, travel expenses, etc.) but does *not* contribute to direct research expenditures. The consortium must appoint a project co-ordinator to oversee all aspects of the work. The grant is paid into the co-ordinator's account and the interpretation of the funding agreement and procedures for settling disputes are subject to the laws of the project co-ordinator's country. 'Contractors' to the project operate under the direction of the co-ordinator. They sign an agreement to complete certain specified tasks and, once this has been done, are free to exploit the outcomes to their assignments. Contractors hold all intellectual property rights to the results of the research but are expected to disseminate these (on payment of licence fees in appropriate circumstances) for use in other bona-fide research and technical development projects. 'Associate contractors' assist with various activities but do not sign the funding agreement and need to determine their rights to consequent intellectual property via separate deals with the main contractors. 'Sub-contractors' supply technical services in return for a fee, without any other rights or obligations.

Universities, other higher education establishments and non-commercial bodies not devoted entirely to research have a further funding option. The Commission accepts that such organisations are unlikely to possess costing systems which enable them to determine accurately the specific projects to which their research expenditures are attributable. Thus, it offers these institutions a special 'contract with reimbursement of additional costs' whereby the Commission pays 100 per cent of all the institution's marginal costs that arise from the research (e.g. the costs of extra staff hired specifically to work on the project or the costs of research materials). Thereafter the EU makes no other contribution, although a further sum equal to twenty per cent of the value of the additional costs incurred because of the project can be claimed by the institution as 'indirect costs' (overheads), thus adding substantially to its total grant income.

28. National grants for research and development

All EU governments provide tax rebates, cash grants and other incentives to firms that engage in R&D. And it is a fundamental tenet of the Single Market that all European Union businesses operating within a particular territory be eligible to apply for these subsidies on an equal basis regardless of the owner's nationalities. It is interesting to note moreover that a number of EU countries operate special schemes to help and encourage individual inventors to patent and exploit their work. In Denmark and Greece for example, government-funded bodies will provide advice and assistance to inventors wishing to promote and license their patents. The French and German governments tax earnings from potential inventions at a special low rate. In Ireland the national Patents Office will advise inventors on the best ways to patent and exploit their inventions. According to OECD figures, Germany is Europe's most research-oriented country, due perhaps to the size and strength of its buoyant manufacturing sector and high educational standards among employees. Aggregate R&D expenditure in Germany (more than two thirds of which is privately financed) is nearly three per cent of national income. The proportion of private R&D in the total has risen by a tenth since the 1970s. Basic research accounts for 20 per cent of Federal R&D spending. A fifth of all state R&D is concerned with defence. Portugal and Greece are Europe's least R&D-oriented countries, spending negligible amounts on technical research. Spain is another low research expenditure country. A major reason for the paucity of R&D in the latter three nations is probably their heavy dependence on inward foreign investment by multinational enterprises which undertake most of their research in other countries.

Progress test 6

1. How might unfettered business competition lead to inefficiency?

2. What are the objectives of EU competition policy?

3. How can an individual firm seek to enforce Articles 85 and 86 of the Treaty of Rome?

4. What is meant by the term 'relevant market' in the context of competition law?

5. Explain the role of the European Commission in enforcing EU competition policy.

6. What is a block exemption? Why were block exemptions considered necessary?

7. How can a company avoid being taken over by another business?

8. Why is it more difficult to acquire firms in some EU countries than in others?

9. What is the purpose of the Thirteenth Draft Directive on Takeover and other General Bids?

10. To which types of cross-border mergers and acquisitions does the 1989 Merger Control Regulation apply?

11. Explain the difference between a supplies contract and a works contract.

12. What is meant by the term 'industrial policy'? What are the purposes of industrial policy?

13. What is a micro enterprise?

14. List the major assistance programmes initiated by DG XXIII.

15. Certain forms of state assistance to industry are illegal under Article 92 of the Treaty of Rome. What are they?

16. Give four examples of how national governments subsidise businesses in economically underdeveloped regions?

17. What are the EU's Structural Funds?

18. List the main benefits that might accrue to firms that engage in research and technical development. How can Research and Development be evaluated?

19. How can small enterprises benefit from collaborative research and development?

20. Define 'pre-competitive research'.

7

THE LEGAL, POLITICAL AND CULTURAL ENVIRONMENTS OF EUROPEAN BUSINESS

THE LEGAL ENVIRONMENT OF EUROPEAN BUSINESS

1. Code law and common law

Businesses engaged in cross-border EU trade confront different laws and legal systems in the various countries in which they do business, and are subject also to supranational EU legislation. Fortunately, however, there are many similarities in the legal systems of several Continental countries, due in large part to the 1804 French Code Napoleon, which was subsequently imposed on Belgium, Italy, Luxembourg, the Netherlands, Spain, Greece, Portugal, and those regions of Germany (Westphalia, Baden and the Rhineland) occupied by France during the Napoleonic Wars. The fundamental difference in European legal systems lies between countries that have a written Code for determining legal matters and those (notably Britain and the Republic of Ireland) which rely on historical precedent, specific cases and *ad hoc* legislation to make and interpret law. Common law approaches apply throughout the English-speaking world, including most countries of the former British Empire (English common law being imposed on these countries by the British during the period of colonial rule). Countries with Code law systems have all their laws written down in Criminal, Civil and/or Commercial Codes which are used to determine all legal matters. Hence, 'the law' on a particular issue can be looked up in the appropriate Article of the relevant Code. Austria, (modern) Germany, Denmark, Finland, Greece and Sweden developed their own legal codes. Other EU nations (apart from the common law countries of Ireland and the UK) have legal systems based on the Code Napoleon.

Although they are quite different in principle, common law and Code law systems do have similarities in practice. A large part of the law of common law countries in fact derives from statutes and legally binding government regulations, while Code law systems rely heavily on judicial interpretations of the meanings of the words embodied in legislative Codes.

Note that the six original members of the EEC all had Code law systems, so it is hardly surprising that the Code law model dominates EU approaches to law making.

Domestic law and international law

The domestic law of every nation deals with aspects of international business. Foreigners – whether individuals or firms – are regarded as if they were citizens of the country in question and are treated and protected on the same terms as native inhabitants. 'International' law (or the 'law of nations' as it is sometimes called) applies to sovereign states (rather than individual citizens) and imposes rights and duties on nations in their dealings with each other. It derives from international conventions which establish rules agreed by contesting states; from international custom accepted as law within all nations; and from internationally recognised legal principles. Prior to the Treaty of Rome, businesses in signatory countries could not themselves resort to 'international law' in the event of a conflict of interests across national borders. Businesses were subject entirely to the national laws of the countries in which they operated, although some of these laws might themselves be based on international agreements. In other words, an international business embroiled in a legal dispute had to seek redress from the national Courts of the country in which the action was heard and could not obtain relief from any 'international legal system'.

The Treaty of Rome changed the situation by creating a new type of law that provided individual persons and businesses with the right to bring cases – on their own accounts – to a supranational legal body. Equally, individuals and businesses assumed obligations extending beyond those imposed by the national legal systems of the countries in which they functioned. Thus, for example, EU companies are subject to laws on competition established at the pan-European level, while employees can (and frequently do) appeal to the European Court of Justice (which can override the national courts of any EU member country) on equal opportunities matters.

EU law is supranational, uniform and autonomous. It transcends national law and if the ECJ (*see* 1:**9**) rules that domestic legislation is in breach of one of the foundation Treaties or an agreed Directive or Regulation then national law must be amended.

Legal personality of the European Union

On accession to the European Union (i.e. on signing the Rome, Euratom and ECSC Treaties – *see* 1:**1**), member states transferred some of their legislative, executive and judicial powers to permanent institutions outside their national jurisdictions. The following points relating to this transfer of powers should be noted:

(a) The transfer is definitive, i.e. it is not subject to challenge through the Courts by individual citizens of particular member states.

(b) Once the powers were transferred the transfer could not be renounced by a member country. The transfer was irreversible: the powers transferred could not thereafter be returned to national jurisdiction.

(c) There is no mechanism for the withdrawal of a member state from the Union.

(d) The Treaty of Rome has an indefinite duration.

(e) As legally constituted bodies, the institutions of the European Union may only exercise such powers as have been conferred on them by the Treaties signed by member states. These institutions (the European Commission for example) must act strictly within their authority and cannot assume additional powers or extend their activities to cover new areas.

Actions against member states

Articles 169–170 of the Rome Treaty create a mechanism for dealing with countries that (allegedly) fail to meet their obligations, as follows:

(a) If the European Commission believes that a member state has not fulfilled a Treaty obligation it informs the country concerned and invites comment. Then the Commission delivers a reasoned opinion on the matter. If the country does not comply with the opinion within a period specified by the Commission, the latter may put the issue before the European Court of Justice.

(b) A member state can itself bring a matter before the ECJ provided it first informs the European Commission.

EU institutions such as the European Commission may be put before the EJC by a member country if they infringe the Rome Treaty or fail to act to enforce its provisions. However the institution concerned must be given two months in which to define its position, legal action commencing after a further two months have elaped. Private individuals can bring actions against EU institutions for infringement or failure to act on the same terms as governments.

2. Similarities and differences in the national laws of EU countries

The following general principles of commercial law apply in all EU countries:

(a) Freedom of contract. In general, no permission from the state or from third parties is needed prior to a lawful contract being concluded. Parties to a contract may freely determine its contents and stipulate whatever terms and conditions they desire.

(b) Contracts do not require a special form of expression. In general they need not be in writing, although governments sometimes legislate to create specific exceptions to this rule.

(c) Contracts bind only the parties that entered the agreement (with the exception in some states of collective bargaining between trade unions and employers associations).

(d) Right to own, use and dispose of private property.

(e) Availability of limited liability for companies.

(f) Personal responsibility for actions. Anyone who inflicts damage on others must pay compensation for the losses incurred.

(g) Freedom to engage in business activities.

Thereafter however numerous differences in law, interpretation and legal methods apply to commercial litigation in each nation, and conflicts between the legal systems of specific countries frequently occur.

Important disparities among the business laws of various EU countries include:

(a) Laws concerning the circumstances in which an offer may be withdrawn without penalty vary in detail between nations. Normally the law of the country in which obligations arising from a contract were intended to be performed will apply to this matter, although many disputes arise over the question of where exactly the performance was supposed to take place.

(b) The types of contract that need to be in writing vary from state to state. For example, in Denmark, written contracts are required for most consumer credit transactions. Leases exceeding certain durations must be in writing in Germany, Greece, Ireland and Italy. In Portugal written contracts are necessary for matters relating to insurance and the transportation of goods.

(c) The amount of monetary compensation payable following a breach of contract in identical circumstances in various EU countries can differ considerably from state to state. This is because some national legal systems constrain damages strictly to actual losses incurred, while others allow generous compensation for expected future losses resulting from the breach of contract.

(d) Codes based on Napoleonic law (*see* **1**) require detailed formalities for the termination of a contract where one of the parties has defaulted on its terms. In other countries the aggrieved party may simply cancel the contract 'on the spot'.

(e) Some countries draw important distinctions between 'commercial' and 'non-commercial' contracts, with a lower burden of proof being necessary to establish the existence of the former, and disputes arising from commercial contracts being heard in special Commercial Courts. A higher standard of commercial responsibility may be expected of a trader, and penalties for breach of contract, fraud, etc., might be heavier than for ordinary members of the public. Conversely, proceedings in a Commercial Court are faster, cheaper and less formal than in the rest of the country's legal system, and the rules of evidence might be less severe.

(f) The intervals beyond which cases become 'statute barred' (so that no one can sue for compensation) differs among countries. In Britain, for example, the period for most classes of contract is six years; in France it can be up to 30 years, while in Germany it depends on whether both the parties to the contract are traders.

(g) Consideration does not *necessarily* have to be proven prior to suing for breach of contract in certain nations. Examples of 'consideration' are the price paid for goods, the wages of employees (as consideration for providing labour), the hire fee paid for a lease of equipment, etc. Under English law a contract *cannot exist* without consideration.

(h) National differences occur *vis-à-vis* the legality of exemption clauses and penalty clauses included in contracts.

(i) In certain countries it is necessary to 'protest' unpaid debts prior to suing for payment. This means getting a notary public (i.e. a local person legally qualified to attest and certify documents) to ask the customer for payment or for reasons for non-payment. The latter are put into a formal deed of protest which is then placed before a local court as evidence of refusal to pay.

3. Where cases are heard

Each party to a contract is likely to want any dispute arising from it to be settled in that party's own country according to that nation's laws. But this is obviously not possible when businesses from different countries are involved. Often, therefore, contracts include 'jurisdictional clauses' which specify that the law of a particular country will apply, as agreed by the parties to the contract. This ensures that both sides know for certain their legal rights and obligations. Often the law of England is specified even though neither party resides in the UK. The reason for this is that English law has dealt with questions of international trade for many centuries, is well-documented, and has ready-made answers for most questions arising from international transactions. This may of course lead to Courts outside the UK having to interpret English law. If a contract has no jurisdictional clause then the rules set out in the Brussels Convention will apply.

The Brussels Convention on the mutual recognition and enforcement of judgements 1968

Initially this Convention covered just the six original members of the EEC, but was updated and extended to include new entrants to the (then) EC in 1978, 1982 and 1992 and today covers 20 countries, including some non-EU states. It lays down a set of rules to determine the country in which a case involving parties from more than one signatory nation will be heard. The Convention also provides for the recognition of judgements and hence the ability to enforce them in all member states, although certain categories of legal action are excluded, namely:

- bankruptcy and company insolvency
- arbitration agreements
- matters relating to social security
- probate and matrimonial property
- customs duties and taxation.

The main principle of the Convention is that the defendant shall be sued in his or her 'country of domicile', which normally means the defendant's country of residence. In disputes involving contracts, however, the defendant *may* be sued in the country of the place of performance of the obligation arising from the contract. Hence the plaintiff might have a choice of nations in which to proceed, i.e. the country of the defendant's residence or the country of performance of the contract. In either situation it is invariably the case that a successful plaintiff will want to enforce the judgement in the defendant's country of residence.

4. International Conventions

A number of international agreements govern the legal frameworks to be applied to particular aspects of cross-border trade. Laws concerning the carriage of goods at sea follow the Hague-Visby Rules in the majority of the world's trading nations. And notwithstanding this fact, nearly all bills of lading (*see* Chapter 11) include clauses explicitly stating that at least some of the Hague-Visby rules will apply. The Hague Rules were drafted in 1921 and subsequently extended (to become the Hague-Visby Rules) via the 1968 Brussels Protocol. Hague-Visby rules formally determine the legal status of the bill of lading and specify upper limits and a formula for calculating the carrier's liability for damage to cargoes. Claims must be lodged within one year of delivery or the date a cargo was lost.

Air transport is covered by the Warsaw Convention 1929 (subsequently amended) which sets maximum limits on liability for negligence and regulates the legal relationships between air carriers and consignees. Conditions and performance of contracts for rail transport are governed by the 1985 Convention Relative aux Transports Internationaux Ferroviaries (COTIF). European road haulage is governed by the 1956 Convention de Marchandises par Route (CMR Convention) which lays down standard international contractual conditions for road transport, covering liability for loss or damage to goods and the maximum value for insurance claims against the haulier. Under the Convention the carrier is fully responsible for the acts and omissions of employees and agents, and specific documentations must be used. The Convention extends to contracts involving 'successive carriers', e.g. road, rail, sea and air.

Two international Conventions have sought to harmonise the legal rules concerning the international sale of goods. The Hague Convention of 1964 drafted Uniform Laws for (i) the sale of goods across national frontiers and (ii) the formation of contracts for international sales. These Uniform Laws were reconsidered, extended and developed by the United Nations Commission on International Trade Law (UNCITRAL), which organised a Vienna Convention to draft a commercial code for use in all international transactions. The resulting code included a clearly defined procedure for arbitration. UNCITRAL does not itself provide arbitration facilities; rather it lays down a model set of rules and procedures which other bodies can follow.

The intention of the Hague and Vienna Conventions was that agreed Uniform Laws be incorporated into the domestic law of all United Nations countries. This has indeed occurred in many states, including the USA, France, Italy, the Netherlands, and in Scandinavia. In countries that have not acceded to the Conventions (Britain for example) the Uniform Laws only apply if both parties agree to this happening.

Uniform Laws

UNCITRAL Uniform Laws are extremely valuable for dealing with national differences in the law of contract. The basic requirements for the existence of a contract are that there be an offer and an acceptance, intention to create legal relations, and consent to the terms of the agreement. Also the contract must be legal and technically capable of being completed and, in some countries (including the UK), there has to be consideration (*see* 2). National laws on these matters are similar in most respects, but with notable exceptions. Specific UNCITRAL rules on contract (which apply automatically in some states, elsewhere if the contracting parties agree that this shall happen) are as follows:

(a) Consideration is *not* necessary for the existence of a contract.

(b) An offer that is accepted is deemed to have been accepted at the moment of receipt and not the moment the offer was transmitted (as is the case under English law).

(c) An offer must be addressed to one or more particular people or organisations. Otherwise proposals not addressed to specific persons are not 'offers' but merely invitation to members of the public themselves to make offers to buy the goods. Examples of offers not addressed to specific persons include catalogues, circularised price lists, advertisements, etc. This does not contradict English law, but does reverse the rules on these matters of certain nations.

(d) If the party making an offer says it will remain open for a period, then it *cannot* be withdrawn during that period once the offer has been received by the other side.

THE POLITICAL ENVIRONMENT OF EUROPEAN BUSINESS

5. Nature of the political environment

The European political environment comprises all the policies, attitudes and decisions of politicians, civil servants and public officials who control political events and systems within nations plus the constraints imposed at the supranational level, notably by the EU, but also by such bodies as the World Trade Organisation, the International Monetary Fund and the United Nations. Political factors determine the overall legal environment in which business operates, particularly with respect to the law of contract and rules on advertising and consumer protection. Other areas in which political considerations play a crucial role are industrial policy (including national competition law and the extent of assistance given to small businesses), the relative importance of various pressure groups within a country, tax regimes and the nature of regulatory frameworks. Note how economic and political environments interrelate: political decisions affect the economy; while economic success or failure influence the electorate's choice of politicians.

6. National politics

National politics are concerned with (i) the direction and administration of states, (ii) government, and (iii) the control of aggregate social relationships. 'Government' involves making and implementing laws, representing the state, and routine public administration. A 'state' is an association of people formed for specific common purposes, with a clearly defined territory, a system of laws, and an organised government. It is important to realise that a 'state' is not necessarily the same as a 'nation', i.e. a group of people who feel they have certain things in common such as a common ancestry, history or traditions, language, culture or religion. A nation does not necessarily have an independent state in which to live.

7. European political co-operation (EPC)

Mechanisms for securing European political co-operation were established following the publication of the 1970 *Luxembourg Report* which recommended that the Foreign Ministers of member states should meet regularly in order to co-ordinate national foreign policies and take joint political action in appropriate circumstances. To date, joint position statements have been issued on terrorism, East/West relations, security policy and the non-proliferation of nuclear weapons. However, military and defence matters are normally excluded from EPC procedures, as such issues are dealt with through NATO and other more general international groupings. The development of a common EU defence policy was envisaged by the Treaty of European Union (Maastricht Treaty) ratified in 1993, although significant practical manifestations of this have yet to emerge.

Responsibility for the administration of EPC lies with the country currently holding the Presidency of the European Commission. Member countries contribute civil servants from their Foreign Ministries to an EU Political Committee that runs day-to-day EPC operations, which include the drafting of common position statements, the reception of political leaders from non-EU nations, and the organisation of fact finding missions.

Key issues in the area of European Political Co-operation that will have to be addressed in the future include:

- the role and authority of the European Parliament
- whether political 'opt-outs' (such as that of the United Kingdom in respect of the European Social Charter) are to be allowed indefinitely
- the extent to which the principle of subsidiarity will apply to non-industrial matters
- reform of EU institutions.

The Common Foreign and Security Policy (CFSP)

The Treaty of European Union (Maastricht Treaty) calls upon EU member states to define and implement a common foreign and security policy intended to:

- safeguard the common values, fundamental interests and independence of the Union
- strengthen the security of the Union and its Member States in all ways
- preserve peace and strengthen international security, in accordance with the principles of the United Nations Charter as well as the principles of the Helsinki Final Act and the objectives of the Paris Charter
- promote international co-operation

133

- develop and consolidate democracy and the rule of law, and respect for human rights and fundamental freedoms.

Further requirements of the Treaty in relation to political matters were:

- the establishment in due course of a common defence policy
- co-operation in relation to the administration of justice and home affairs (e.g. allowing the European Commission to decide whether third country nationals need visas to visit the EU
- intergovernmental rather than national determination of the following:

    combating drug trafficking and international fraud
    customs co-operation
    judicial co-operation on both civil and criminal matters
    police co-operation to prevent terrorism and to organise the EU-wide exchange of police formation.

Immigration and asylum policy concerning third country nationals is also determined inter-governmentally, including entry and residence conditions and rules on physical movement between EU states, family reunion and access to employment, and the issue of work permits.

THE CULTURAL ENVIRONMENT OF EUROPEAN BUSINESS

8. National culture

A national culture is the set of beliefs, perspectives, motivations, values and norms shared by the majority of the inhabitants of a particular country. It is reflected in the laws of the country and in its institutions and social standards, though note how laws and institutions may themselves help to form a national culture. Within a nation there might exist a number of subgroups, each with its own subculture. These subcultures can be very important in shaping a country's destiny, and may conflict violently with the national culture as a whole. Determinants of national culture include a variety of historical and environmentally determined factors, including religion, education system, national resources (which affect living standards and hence the nature of the experience of residing in a particular nation), and political and economic institutions. Note however that each of these variable is *itself* affected by national culture. For example, the forms and devices through which religion is practised in various countries are subject to cultural influence. Within Europe national cultures differ with respect to such variables as:

- family values
- attitudes towards authority
- the degree of formality of interpersonal relationships at work
- the role of women in society.

Cultural differences are especially important for European marketing because their existence might inhibit the development of a homogeneous market for certain types of good.

Nature of culture

Culture is easier to recognise than to define, involving as it does a complex set of interrelating beliefs and ways of living (Leeds *et al* 1994). A nation's culture represents a collective frame of reference through which a wide range of issues and problems are interpreted. It determines how symbols, sounds, pictures and behaviours are perceived by individuals, and affects socialisation, friendship patterns, social institutions, aesthetics and language (Usunier 1993). Culture has three primary characteristics: it is *shared* by a group; it is something that people *learn*; and it depends on *environmental* circumstances. A crucially important function of culture is that it helps the individual define *concepts*. A concept is a conscious linking together of images, object stimuli or events. Individuals receive huge numbers of messages, so the brain needs a system for classifying them into groups, which can then be dealt with efficiently. For instance, apples, oranges and bananas are all separate and unique items, but the brain will categorise them into a single concept of 'fruit'. Conceptualisation helps the individual to manage data, identify relations among events and objects, and to discover similarities and differences which enable the comparison of items of information. This is vitally important for the design of advertising images because culturally based conceptualisations can determine how a message is interpreted (as good or bad, conservative or risqué, etc.) and *how* the message recipient responds to its contents.

Convergence of cultures

A number of factors have encouraged the convergence of certain aspects of culture among West European nations, notably:

- improvements in transport and communications and a huge increase in the number of European who visit foreign countries
- globalisation of media, with similar television programmes, newspaper and magazine articles, etc., appearing in all EU nations
- similarities in the tastes and consumption patterns of young people
- the operations of MNCs across the European continent, supplying standardised products and frequently using undifferentiated marketing strategies
- a seemingly worldwide increase in consumers' willingness to accept fresh ideas and to try new products.

9. Importance of culture

Managers of European businesses need to know about cultural differences between various EU nations in order to be able to:

- communicate effectively with customers, suppliers, business associates and partners in other countries, and with foreign employees (Subhash and Tucker 1995)

- conduct negotiations and understand the nuances of the bargaining postures of the other parties to a negotiation
- predict trends in social behaviour likely to affect the firm's foreign operations
- understand ethical standards and concepts of social responsibility in various countries (Ferraro 1990)
- predict how cultural differences will affect consumer reactions to advertisements and other promotional forms.

Some of the more important cultural influences on business and society can be grouped under the following headings:

(a) *Business environments*

Relationships between trade union confederations and employers' associations. Role of government in business affairs. Employment conditions. Extent of employee participation in management decisions. How meetings are conducted. Degree of formality of personal relationships.

(b) *Marketing*

What people buy (local tastes, historical traditions, etc.). When people buy. Who does the purchasing, and the overall pattern of consumer buying behaviour. Which consumer needs are felt more intensely. Which family members take which purchasing decisions. Attitudes towards foreign-supplied products. How the female form may be used in advertising. The acceptability of nudity and / or what parts of the human body may be shown in advertisements. The extent of an advertisement's display of physical contact between people (of the same or of differing sexes). The degree of elegance, quality, urbanity, etc., expected of advertisements. The nature of the national media that carry advertisements, e.g. whether the country has a tabloid press, the editorial content of magazines, newpapers, and radio and television programmes, and the attitudes expressed by the media towards national issues (manifest in non-coverage of 'taboo' subjects, adoption of ideological 'lines', etc.).

(c) *Social attitudes*

Attitudes towards work and material possessions, entrepreneurship, politics, religion, the role of women in society, wealth accumulation, willingness to accept risk, morality, social class, respect for the law and social institutions, etc. A firm needs to become progressively more aware of foreign cultures as the nature and extent of its foreign operations alter. Exporters, for example, need only consider those cultural factors likely to affect the foreign marketing of their products. A company that engages in licensing or franchising will need to know something about the general business cultures of the nations in which licenses will be issued. Firms with foreign subsidiaries have to manage local labour and thus require a knowledge of local norms concerning employee relations, attitudes towards work, and so on.

Language and culture

Languages and culture are intimately intertwined, as language is the vehicle through which ideas and perceptions are expressed. Many aspects of a community's culture are reflected in the language it uses, and a detailed knowledge of that language provides illuminative insights into the relevant culture. Equally, ignorance of the nuances of a particular language creates boundless opportunities for the misinterpretation of messages. This creates many difficulties for translation between languages because the cultural concepts underlying particular words and phrases need to be matched as well as (or rather than) the words themselves. Examples of absurd (and commercially damaging) translations abound. For example, a translation into German of the slogan 'Come alive with Pepsi' turned out as 'Rise from the grave with Pepsi'. Schweppes tonic water became Schweppes bathroom water when translated into Italian. 'Chrysler for power' translated into 'Chrysler is an aphrodisiac' in Spanish.

Culture affects how people think, quite independently of what they do or the words they utter. Examples are whether people approach issues analytically rather than intuitively, and whether individuals inwardly feel they should be organised and methodical rather than 'taking life as it comes'. Attitudes towards space and time also differ between nations. Turning up late for an appointment is regarded as highly improper in some countries, as normal in others, or as acceptable only for top ranking people.

10. Stereotyping and self-referencing

A manager's awareness of national differences should not be clouded by stereotyping, i.e. the attribution to an individual by other people of a number of characteristics assumed typical of the group to which the person belongs. Self-stereotyping can also be important, and create problems. Thus for example managers from countries generally regarded as superefficient may regard *themselves* as superefficient, regardless of whether this is actually the case. Equally serious is the problem of cultural 'self-referencing', i.e. the (unconscious) presumption by an individual that the culture of his or her own country is the appropriate one against which other cultures should be assessed. Rather it is necessary to look at problems and issues from *foreign* as well as home country norms and perspectives and identify clearly the difference between the two. Local nationals should be consulted, as they will be sensitive to local cultural influences and will understand the 'inner logic' of the local way of life. *Ethnocentrism* can cost an international business a lot of money. Ethnocentrism is the tendency to regard one's own nation, group or culture as superior and to compare the standards of other nations, groups or cultures against this belief. It can lead to fundamental misunderstandings of foreign consumer attitudes and business practices, to inefficiency, and bad relations with host country governments. Ethnocentrism contrasts with polycentrism, which regards other nations, groups and cultures as different but of equal value, and with *geocentrism* that sees some but not all nations, groups and cultures as being of equal status. (The term geocentric is also used by some writers to describe the management approach adopted by companies which co-ordinate all their activities on the global scale, planning and resourcing without regard for national considerations.) A possible disadvantage with polycentrism is that it can cause a firm (inappropriately) to avoid transferring excellent home country practices intact to other nations. Also, delegation of duties to local subsidiaries may be excessive, leading to problems of control and co-ordination.

To overcome potential biases when evaluating foreign cultures, the following procedure might be adopted:

(a) Define the issue or problem to be studied in terms of the cultural norms, traits and perspectives of the home country.

(b) Repeat this exercise, without applying value judgements, using the cultural norms, traits and perspectives of residents of the foreign country.

(c) Compare the results of (a) and (b) and identify cultural differences that emerge from the analysis.

(d) Consider how these cultural differences might influence the interpretation of the original issue or problem.

(e) Redefine the issue or problem having removed cultural bias.

Culture and motivation

Many aspects of motivation have a cultural dimension. The factors that motivate people in one society might only have a limited effect in others, and it would be mistaken for managers to assume that personnel in foreign branches and subsidiaries can be motivated using the same approaches as in the head office country. What is clear, however, is that the same basic motivational process seems to apply to people in all West European nations, namely the existence of an unsatisfied need, followed by attempts to satisfy the need and (hopefully) eventual need gratification. Individuals pursue goals that they value, but the particular goals that they work towards may well be heavily influenced by national culture. In other words the specific 'needs' felt by individuals can have a cultural foundation. The problem is that in many countries there are numerous subcultures, each generating its own unique set of need perceptions. Hence the task of identifying the cultural factors underlying motivation in a particular country becomes extremely complex.

11. Norms and values

A major part of cultural analysis is the identification and characterisation of group norms within various societies. Group norms are shared perceptions of how things should be done or common attitudes, feelings or beliefs. As norms emerge, individuals begin behaving according to how they feel other group members expect them to behave. Entrants to an existing society will feel isolated and insecure and hence will actively seek out established norms that will act as a guide to how that person ought to behave. Norms, therefore, facilitate the integration of an individual into a social group, and thus will be eagerly accepted by new members.

Social values are moral principles or standards against which the desirability of certain modes of behaviour may be assessed. Values help determine what an individual considers important, personal priorities, and how he or she assesses other people's worth. Values change over time; some may disappear entirely as environmental circumstances alter. Also, values may vary across industries and from state to state. Nevertheless social values contribute greatly to 'national temperament', a concept easier to recognise than to define, encompassing as it does such matters as tolerance of opposing viewpoints, of emotion, self-discipline, degree of formality of relationships, etc. National values affect the acceptability of specific messages and symbols, and make important contributions to national culture. For example, 'masculine' values help determine the influence of advertisements that contain assertive messages, that emphasise toughness and vigour, and appeal to the competitive instinct. 'Individualistic' values within consumers imply a preference for pursuit of self-interest, self-control, etc. Other core values might relate to honesty, social responsibility, ambition and so on. The aim is to discover the existence of similar values within groups of consumers in different countries and hence present a common value-specific theme when promoting a product in disparate states.

12. Evaluating cultural differences

Managers of companies engaged in pan-European business need to assess the importance of the cultural factors likely to be encountered when doing business in various foreign markets. A thorough understanding of another country's culture can only be obtained by learning its language (and becoming aware of the significance of differences in regional dialects); knowing its history; mixing with host nationals socially as well as in working situations; and living in the country for several years. These are obviously impossible tasks for the great majority of managers of international businesses. But it is feasible to identify those cultural influences most likely to cause problems for the firm. One approach to this task is to take an overall view of the cultures of particular nations; another is to focus on just a handful of key variables. The problem with the former method is the enormous number of cultural influences that could be considered. In practice therefore it is more common to seek to identify a handful of key variables believed critically relevant to the firm's operations in each of the countries in which it does business and to examine their implications in great depth. The variables involved might relate to material culture (attitudes towards the possession of objects, accumulation of wealth, etc.), motivation to work, social institutions and social structure, and so on, according to the nature of the enterprise's work. Examples of the methods that might be adopted when applying this partial approach are:

- conducting research in order to describe a typical day in the life of a local consumer of a certain type of product
- an in-depth analysis of the employee relations system of a certain nation, with a view to exposing the underlying attitudes of workers towards employment and their employers
- studies of the factors that cause local customers to be attracted to a specific category of goods.

The difficulty with partial cultural assessment is that although it might identify critical variables relevant to an issue at a particular moment, these variables might change very quickly (see below). Culture, moreover, depends in large part on the *interrelations* between such variables as well as on the elements themselves. And it is easy to assume (wrongly) that a difference between nations is 'cultural', whereas in fact the difference relates to a mundane matter such as firm size, nature of the technology used in production, form of ownership of the enterprise, etc. Note also that in a number of nations there exist regional and social class distinctions within the country that outweigh the effects of dissimilarities between the culture of that particular nation and others. People undertaking the same occupation in disparate nations may share more in common with each other in terms of attitude, lifestyle, housing conditions and so than they share with fellow nationals. Indeed, some analysts have suggested that the influence of culture on customer preferences is overexaggerated. Theodore Levitt, for example, contended that provided a company supplies reliable high quality products at attractive prices then customers throughout the world will be happy to purchase them in a standardised form (Levitt 1983). He suggested moreover that to the extent that international firms do modify their outputs for local markets, this results more from managerial presumptions that differences in local preferences exist than from actual variations in national preferences! Culture represents just one of several environments within which a company operates. Political considerations and/or economic laws of supply and demand frequently outweigh cultural effects.

Predicting cultural change

National cultures change over time, possibly in consequence of the following forces:

- Immigration and emigration, especially if the people coming in have a different religion and lifestyle than members of the existing population.
- Rising (or in some cases falling) living standards.
- Improvements in education systems.
- Economic destabilisation (as occurred in East Europe in the early 1990s for example).
- The influx of new ideas from other countries.
- Increased opportunities for consumption (a wider range of products, shorter working hours, longer holidays, etc.).
- Improvements in state welfare provision: old age pensions, child support, national health services and so on.
- Introduction of new technologies which necessarily change working practices and relationships.

Examinations of trends in these and similar variables can help a firm predict cultural changes likely to affect its operations in a particular country.

13. National jurisdiction

A state has exclusive jurisdiction over its territory and its government is the only legal representative of the state in relation to other states. The government can enter into or abrogate any agreements with foreign states or with its own citizens. And it may use physical force to attain its ends.

Sovereignty

Much of the current debate on whether the supranational powers of the European Union should be extended relates to the question of sovereignty. The term 'national sovereignty' means the ultimate absolute power of the state to coerce and control its citizens. Two problems immediately arise:

(a) In the modern world few (if any) states can claim to be able to make genuinely independent decisions. Countries rely on each other for goods, markets, mutual economic assistance and defence. Capital is internationally mobile and no one nation can afford to lose foreign investment, whether physical or financial.

(b) It is unclear as to exactly *where* national sovereignty is to be found. Does it exist in the head of state, or in Parliament, the Prime Minister, collectively within the cabinet, or in 'the people' and/or various interest groups.

In practice, debates on national sovereignty tend to revolve around such matters as:

- who shall represent a particular state, a national government or a wider body (such as the European Union)
- whether the national parliament is solely entitled to levy taxes of whatever amount and whenever it wishes, and can spend tax revenues on its own volition
- whether decisions of the national parliament can be overruled
- whether parliament can legislate on any matter it chooses.

National interest

A government's concept of 'the national interest' will depend on the cultures, backgrounds, perceptions and learned experiences of the decision makers involved, and will change over time and according to circumstances. An interest considered vital today (and over which the state is not prepared to make any concessions) might be relegated to secondary status (for which compromises are possible) tomorrow. Each country has a potentially huge list of national interests, and cannot possibly realise all of them. Hence it is necessary to choose carefully which national interests actually to pursue.

Progress test 7

1. Explain the difference between Code Law and Common Law.

2. What is meant by the term 'international law'?

3. The Treaty of Rome created a mechanism for dealing with governments that fail to meet their obligations under the Treaty. What is the mechanism?

4. List six general principles of commercial law that apply in all EU countries.

5. What was the purpose of the Brussels Convention 1968?

6. Define the term 'national sovereignty'.

7. What are the objectives of the CFSP?

8. Define 'culture'.

9. What are the main determinants of national culture?

10. What factors have encouraged the convergence of certain aspects of the cultures of West European nations?

11. Why do managers of European businesses need to know about cultural differences among EU states?

12. Define 'ethnocentrism'.

8

HARMONISATION OF BUSINESS LAWS AND PRACTICES

1. Purposes of harmonisation

The standardisation of national legislation pertaining to business rules and practices in EU countries is (explicitly) required by the Treaty of Rome as a means for ensuring the free movement of goods, services and capital and that fair business competition occurs throughout the integrated European market. Company law in individual member nations has had to be changed to comply with EU directives, as have technical product standards, industrial health and safety requirements, the law on intellectual property, public procurement arrangements, laws on advertising, marketing and sales promotion, agency law, consumer protection regulations, the law on business competition, and rules concerning company mergers, acquisitions and financial control. A number of these matters are dealt with in the following sections; the remainder are covered in other chapters.

Benefits of harmonisation

Harmonisation of business laws and practices results in a common understanding of how businesses should behave, easier cross-border selling, standardised procedures, and the ability of staff trained in one country to transfer their skills and knowledge to other EU nations. Further benefits include:

- more intense competition among EU businesses, leading to lower prices and improved customer care
- greater potential for EU firms to obtain economies of scale
- lower costs in consequence of not having to apply different business methods in disparate countries.

COMPANY LAW HARMONISATION

2. EU Directives concerning companies

These emanate from Article 54 of the Treaty of Rome, which requires the removal of obstacles to the freedom of establishment of businesses throughout the European Union. Major legislation so far adopted is as follows:

(a) *The First Directive on Company Law 1968,* which imposes minimum requirements regarding company formation documents, company accounts, and winding-up procedures.

(b) *The Second Company Law Directive 1976* that sets down standards for the nominal and paid-up capitals of public companies. This also harmonised the ways in which EU countries distinguish between private and public companies.

(c) *The Directive on information concerning company acquisitions and disposals 1988,* which obliges owners of shares in companies listed on EU Stock Exchanges to disclose their shareholdings when they reach any of five thresholds: 10, 20, 33.3, 50 and 66.6 per cent.

(d) *The Twelfth Directive on Company Law 1989* that introduced the single member private limited company whereby it became possible to set up a company with just one shareholder.

Other significant legislation includes the Fourth and Seventh Directives (1978 and 1983 respectively) on company accounts (*see* **3**), the Third Company Law Directive on mergers 1978 intended to protect the interests of minority shareholders where the merging companies are in the same member state, and the Sixth 1982 Directive concerning shareholders' rights following the splitting up of public companies. The Eleventh Company Law Directive 1989 relates to the information that has to be disclosed when companies establish branches in other EU member states. Minimum qualifications for the auditors of company accounts were imposed by the Eighth Company Law Directive 1984. This created the occupation of Registered Auditor, i.e. someone able to 'furnish proof of the legal knowledge required' to undertake company audits, e.g. through having successfully completed a recognised course of study, normally of three years duration. However, a Registered Auditor does not automatically qualify for membership of a national accountancy body. A Registered Auditor must be independent and of good character, and is obliged to undertake company audits with professional integrity.

Types of company

All EU nations are required to recognise the distinction between private companies (set up primarily to restrict shareholders' liabilities for company debts) and public (joint stock) companies mainly established in order to raise capital by selling shares to the general public. Finland and Sweden did not distinguish between private and public forms of company prior to their entry to the EU in 1995. The domestic company law of these countries is being amended to bring it into line with EU standards. Private limited companies cannot invite the general public to subscribe to their shares or debentures. The overwhelming majority of limited companies are private. They exist primarily to avoid the owners being personally responsible for their companies' debts, so that the size of their share issues is not an important consideration.

In the UK many private companies have a nominal share capital of £100, of which only a small part is actually called up. In Germany it costs at least ten times this amount (depending on the currency exchange rate) to establish a private company (the German GmbH). The time taken to set up a private company also varies between countries: in Britain companies may be purchased 'off the shelf', whereas in some other nations (France for instance) registration takes several weeks.

3. The Fourth Company Law Directive 1978

This imposed standard formats for the layout and contents of company accounts. Profit and loss accounts and balance sheets may be presented either vertically or horizontally. The profit and loss account can show expenditures according to type of disbursement (wages, stationery, etc.), or by function (e.g. marketing, production, administration and so on). Companies must identify clearly the relationship between turnover and net profit. The Directive also requires that accounts be accompanied by a director's report intended to put the figures presented into a meaningful context. Under the Directive, accounts must give a true and fair view of a company's financial situation, and should be consistent and prudent. Small and medium sized companies are allowed to disclose less detailed information to the general public than large firms, although they must still provide the full data to their own shareholders. A 'small' company is defined as one that has fewer than 50 employees and turnover and/or asset values less than certain thresholds. 'Medium' sized companies are those with under 250 workers and less than specific balance sheet values and/or turnovers. A small firm need not disclose its profit and loss account; does not have to publish a director's report; and may disclose just the main headings of its balance sheet (excluding, for example, director's salaries). Medium-sized companies can begin their profit and loss account from a figure for gross profit without revealing turnover. Note however that the governments of individual countries are free to prohibit the restricted disclose concessions for SMEs if they do not believe this to be appropriate. The Directive requires each country to have a central registry at which all companies operating within its borders must deposit their published accounts and make them freely available for public inspection.

Benefits resulting from the Fourth Directive include a general increase in the amount of financial accounting information available on European companies and easier interpretation of the information presented. Problems with the implementation of the Directive are as follows:

(a) Some of the countries for which public disclosure requirements are highest are also the countries where the proportions of all companies having to make full disclosure are the least. This results from generous interpretations of what constitutes a small or medium sized enterprise that qualifies for restricted publication of accounts. Germany, Denmark and Ireland in particular have stringent company disclosure rules, yet allow large numbers of companies not to publish full accounts.

(b) The accessibility of published accounts differs among countries. Accounts are filed with the local Commercial Court in Belgium and France; with a National Registry in Denmark, Ireland and the UK; and with the local Trade Register in all other EU countries except for Greece, where accounts are not filed anywhere but instead have to be published in a government gazette and in at least two newspapers.

(c) Most nations do in fact make extensive use of exemptions permitted under the Directive whereby small companies need not publish their full accounts.

(d) Certain governments (notably in Spain and Italy) have been lax in enforcing the Directive and have not prosecuted companies failing to present their accounts in the approved manner.

In 1983 the Fourth Directive was complemented by the Seventh Company Law Directive (also known as the Consolidation Directive) concerning consolidated accounts for groups of companies. Under the Directive investors need to be able to examine consolidated accounts in order to see the financial position of a group as a whole, rather than just the accounts of the particular recipient of their investment (the principal shareholder of a group could be using one of its members to subsidise less successful subsidiaries). The Directive specifies how and in what circumstances group accounts should be prepared and published and requires that the accounts give a true and fair picture of the financial position of the group in its entirety, i.e. treating the various undertakings within it as if they were a single entity. Intra-group transactions must be eliminated from the consolidated accounts.

Directives Four and Seven were further extended by a 1990 Directive requiring any partnership wherein all partners have limited liability to prepare annual accounts in accordance with the requirements of the Fourth and Seventh Directives.

The Fifth Draft Directive on Company Law (latest version 1989)

This important proposal has many implications for employee representation on company boards. It is discussed at length in 10:**9**.

4. Insider dealing

The Directive on Insider Dealing 1989 compels EU countries to make insider dealing illegal and to co-operate by exchanging information in order to endorse the Directive. The Directive covers both 'primary' insiders, who acquire knowledge through their employment, and 'secondary' insiders, who knowingly receive insider information. 'Insider' information is defined as confidential information of a 'precise nature' that is not available to the general public and which, were it generally known, would cause the market prices of a company's shares to change significantly. The Directive specifically prohibits insiders from passing on insider information, improperly making use of inside information when buying or selling securities, or advising other people to buy or sell on the basis of insider information. This broad approach to the definition of 'insiders' encompasses consultants, analysts, lawyers, auditors and journalists; indeed anyone who – although not directly connected with a company – may have an informational advantage through their employment. Note how financial journalists and investment advisors spend much of their lives searching for 'inside' information.

Efficient pan-European capital markets are impossible without controlling insider dealing, which has constituted a major problem on the European stock exchanges. Neither the investing public nor capital-seeking firms can have full confidence in the system if insider dealing is known to occur. Yet the prevention of insider dealing is, in practice, extremely difficult. Incontrovertible proof that it has happened is almost impossible to obtain, financial policing is expensive and the practice itself is seen as 'victimless crime' by many people. In fact, the victim in the case of a price increase is the person who sold the stock to the insider not knowing that the price was almost certain to rise, while in the opposite case the victim is landed with stock the price of which is about to fall sharply.

Enforcement

Despite the availability of severe penalties for persons convicted of insider dealing, the fact is that very few cases involving alleged insider dealing ever come to trial, and in those that do the accused persons invariably declare themselves bankrupt and as such unable to compensate victims. Yet the administrative costs of prosecutions are enormous. Cases can last for months, and juries are often unable to understand the complexities of insider dealing legislation. Acquittals are common. The suspension of a company's quotation while allegations of insider dealing are investigated disrupts capital markets and punishes the ordinary shareholders, not the individuals responsible for the insider dealing.

Arguably, the prime reason for the lack of success in enforcing the Directive is the fact that in all EU countries insider dealing has been made a *criminal* rather than a civil offence. Hence a high burden of proof is placed on the prosecution, with the result that many cases are dismissed for lack of evidence.

5. Financial services

Residents of any EU country may purchase services from any EU provider regardless of where it is based. Firms and individuals can borrow money *anywhere* in the EU, while savers may deposit their funds in any EU-based bank or other financial institution. Residents of any member country may buy and sell shares in any European company no matter where it is situated. The effects of these measures include the availability of a wider range of financial products as providers vie for a competitive edge, greater use of open account transactions for intra-EU foreign trade, and the need for new tax inspection procedures to prevent tax evasion by individuals and companies that bank in several countries.

Problems with the new regime relate mainly to consumer protection and the practical difficulties of harmonising the (extensive) government regulations that control banks, insurance companies and other financial service institutions in various member countries. Accordingly the European Commission has laid down minimum standards for 'financial security' and for the management procedures to be adopted by financial service providers. Financial security relates to (i) basic rules for the protection of insurance policy holders, investors and other interested parties, and (ii) the extent of the information to be included in providers' publicity materials, prospectuses, brochures and so on. Supervision of institutions is to remain the responsibility of the government of the country where the provider is based, rather than where the services are offered. Further key EU Directives concerning financial services are as follows:

(a) All banks and building societies must maintain a prespecified minimum proportion of their assets in reserve.

(b) The insolvency law of an EU credit institution's *home country* shall apply if it is wound up.

(c) Directors of investment companies must be 'of sufficiently good repute and standing'.

(d) Prospectuses for share issues that meet the legal requirements of one member country shall be legally acceptable in others, subject to certain minimum conditions.

(e) The accounts of banks, credit institutions and insurance companies have to follow a standard format.

Additionally, the Commission has published recommendations regarding the nature of the contractual relation between credit card holders and card-issuing institutions. These recommendations concern the extent of a cardholder's liability for a lost or stolen card and the burden of proof in disputed transactions.

At present financial services providers must adhere to the national rules and regulations of the countries in which they do business, and these vary from state to state. Current negotiations focus on how best to develop a standardised pan-EU regulatory framework so that, having once obtained authorisation to operate within their home country, firms may then trade financial services throughout the Union without any further need to register with national authorities or to alter the services provided or working methods.

The future of European banking services

The nature of the provision of European banking is changing rapidly in a number of fundamental respects, notably through the application of information technology to the banking field. Other important trends include:

- increased use of the telephone to execute banking transactions
- more and more companies bypassing banks and raising funds directly from capital markets
- an extension of EU regulation of financial services
- more automated banking and fewer branch offices
- decreases in the volume of bank lending to small businesses (Economist Intelligence Unit 1994)

- customer demands for higher levels of quality in respect of financial services
- a proliferation of new products in the banking sphere
- much more banking disintermediation than in the past (disintermediation occurs when borrowers and lenders bypass banks and create credit between themselves)
- a reduction in the spread of interest rates between banks and other financial institutions.

TECHNICAL STANDARDS

6. Harmonisation of technical standards

Pan-European technical standards are established by two bodies: CEN (Comité Européen de Normalisation) and CENELEC (Comité Européen de Normalisation Electro-technique). CEN and CENELEC are based in Brussels and represent, in effect, federations of all the national standards-making institutions of the EU plus those of Norway, Iceland and Switzerland. Additionally there is the European Telecommunications Standards Institute (ETSI) established to harmonise national telecommunications standards through co-ordinating the activities of CEN and CENELEC in the telecommunications field. The aim of ETSI is to ensure compatibility between networks and terminals and hence to create an EU-wide market for telecommunications equipment. To underpin its commitment to harmonised telecommunications (and information technology) product standards, the Union now requires all member states to specify EU standards in calls for tender for public procurement contracts.

The need for common technical standards has long been a priority within the EU. Harmonised standards stimulate research and development in companies through ensuring that outcomes to research efforts which conform to EU technical standards are guaranteed a large pan-European market. Also, differing standards in various countries impede the free movement of goods and prevent European companies from obtaining the economies of scale in production available to United States businesses that manufacture for an enormous home market to technical specifications acceptable in all regions.

7. Standards-setting procedures

Officials of the European Commission (possibly acting on the advice of national governments or industry trade associations) decide which standards are to be processed via the CEN/CENELEC system. Then the various national standards authorities (DIN in Germany, AFNOR in France, the UK's British Standards Institute [BSI], etc.) discuss the matter and agree a joint position. Typically an existing national standard is used to begin a debate; otherwise an entirely new standard has to be drafted – either by a national standards body, by a small committee of representatives from several national standards bodies, or by an expert outside consultant. In the overwhelming majority of cases, however, an existing standard forms the initial basis for the fresh specification.

Thus, the national standards organisations with most pre-existing standards are necessarily the most influential when pan-European standards are being produced. Of all the EU countries, Germany's DIN system has the greatest number of standards on its files, and is the biggest producer of new standards (about 1400 per year, more than double the annual output of BSI). This means that large numbers of pan-European standards are being based on German DIN standards, which obviously benefits German firms that are already producing to these standards. New standards are adopted through weighted majority voting by the national standards-setting bodies. Eventually these new standards will replace all existing national specifications.

The problems involved

Critics of the harmonisation of technical standards sometimes allege that their existence stifles creativity and innovation in the development of new products, and that the creation of pan-European standards might serve merely to strengthen the positions of US, Japanese and other Pacific Rim suppliers, increasing their competitive strength and facilitating their assault on EU markets. The main practical problems experienced have related to the complexity of the issues involved and the resolution of competing interests among nations. To help overcome these difficulties the (then) EC introduced (i) the Information Directive of 1983 and (ii) the 'New Approach' to technical harmonisation and standards of 1985. Under the Information Directive, national standards-making bodies are legally obliged to advise other EU countries prior to their introducing fresh national standards. The standards bodies of other nations may then study the proposals, comment on them and make recommendations. Obviously, the standards authority of the initiating country has a large incentive to accept these recommendations, since their incorporation into the technical specifications of the resulting products will enhance their saleability in other markets. A major consequence of the Directive was to encourage still further the concentration of standards setting into the hands of just a few national bodies, notably the German DIN, France's AFNOR, and Britain's BSI. Increasingly, standards produced by these bodies act as pan-European standards.

The New Approach of the EU to technical standards is for the Commission to specify the overall level of safety and other 'essential requirements' that a product must satisfy and describe (a) how these requirements can be met and (b) the evidence ('Attestation') needed to prove that requirements have been satisfied for a particular item. Any product that complies is then legally entitled to be sold throughout the Union. However, the actual function of devising detailed standards is undertaken by national standards-making bodies. Until an EU standard exists for a product, national standards are deemed acceptable.

CE Marks

These are marks placed upon products to attest that they conform to all the requirements of relevant EU Directives and have been tested in accordance with those Directives. To qualify for a CE Mark an item must comply with the appropriate national or pan-European standard, and have its 'fitness for use' confirmed by an approved national certification body (BSI for instance). Note however that a CE Mark does not guarantee any particular level of quality. Certain products *must* carry a CE Mark before they can be sold. Examples of such products are toys, electrical, construction, telecommunications and medical equipment and personal protective clothing.

8. Packaging

Typically firms wish to use forms of packaging which minimise breakages and pilferage at the lowest cost, given the length of the distribution chain and the sorts of transportation needed. Other relevant considerations include the amount of intermediate handling the goods will receive, the value of the items, and the aesthetic appeal of the packaging. There is an EU Directive on packaging (see below), and the packaging selected might have to comply with additional national rules on the disposal or compulsory recycling of packaging materials. Germany for example has laws which require retailers, manufacturers and distributers to accept back all returned packaging, including crates, cardboard boxes, plastic containers and drums. Laws introduced in Germany in 1993 require all packaging used in that country (including consumer packaging) to be produced from environmentally friendly materials, and the minimum amounts of packaging have to be used. Manufacturers *and* retailers are obliged to take back transport packaging, which then has to be reused and not dumped. Industry (rather than local authorities) is required to collect and recycle 80 per cent of all packaging waste. Packaging that satisfies environmental standards is identified by a green dot.

The EU Packaging Directive 1994

The justification given for this Directive was that since various EU countries have disparate rules on packaging then nations with the highest standards on ecologically sound packaging and requirements for firms to dispose of packaging waste would, in the absence of pan-EU legislation, be at a cost disadvantage compared to companies in countries where packaging standards are lax. Aims of the Directive are:

- to reduce the overall impact of packaging waste on the environment
- to encourage waste recovery
- to minimise the amounts of waste packaging going to landfill (at present about 80 per cent of packaging ends up as landfill – this would have to be reduced by ten per cent)
- to reduce the total amount of packaging material used.

The Directive covers all primary, secondary and tertiary packaging except for road, rail, air or ship containers, and all packaging waste regardless of the materials used or whether it is released at industrial, commercial, shop, office or household level. By 30 June 2001, between 50 and 65 per cent by weight of all packaging waste must be recovered, and 20 to 45 per cent by weight of the totality of all packaging materials embodied within packaging waste must be recycled – with a minimum of 15 per cent for each packaging material. Further targets will be established in the year 2001. EU countries are required to establish recycling centres and, by 1998, devise identification marks to go on packaging. Users of packaging must be advised of where they can return packaging for recycling, etc. Packaging should be designed to be re-useable and, wherever possible, biodegradable or capable of composting. The volume and weight of packaging must be restricted to the 'minimum adequate amount needed to maintain safety and hygiene'. However, customer expectations regarding the appropriate amount of packaging for a product may also be taken into consideration. Thus if manufacturers can demonstrate that consumers will only purchase an item if it is covered by three or four layers of (objectively wasteful) packaging they may continue to overpackage.

Criticisms of the EU Directive

The arguments against the Directive are that it will increase business costs, impose unreasonable demands on manufacturers and retailers, and that the volume of waste materials sent for incineration will be so huge that waste disposal units will not be able to cope. Also attempts to reduce the amounts of packaging used could create health hazards (especially for foodstuffs) and dangers of accidents during transit.

Progress test 8

1. List the main benefits likely to result from the harmonisation of business laws and practices across the European Union.

2. What is the main requirement of the 1988 Directive on information concerning company acquisitions and disposals.

3. What is a registered auditor?

4. How did Finnish and Swedish company law differ from that of other EU countries at the time of their accession to the European Union in 1995?

5. Outline the problems that have been experienced with the implementation of the Fourth Company Law Directive 1978.

6. What is insider dealing?

7. Explain the roles of CEN and CENELEC.

8. Why is the European Commission anxious to harmonise technical standards across the EU?

9. What is a CE Mark?

10. Outline the major requirements of the EU Packaging Directive 1994.

9

EXTERNAL TRADE RELATIONS

EU CONTROL ARRANGEMENTS

The European Union is one of the largest and most prosperous trading blocs in the world, accounting for nearly a quarter of the world's imports and exports and, if intra-EU trade is counted, a third of total international trade.

1. The common external tariff

Since its inception in 1957 the EEC (and subsequently the EC and then the EU) has imposed a common external tariff on imports into the Community/Union, regardless of the country through which items enter the single market. However, once entry has occurred the goods face no further tariffs and minimal control over cross-border movement within the area. Uniform documentation and trading procedures apply to imports to all EU nations, and the goods then have equivalent status to items produced within the EU (Mayes 1993). The common customs tariff (CCT) was actually implemented in July 1968, based on the arithmetical average of the six nations which then made up the EEC. Nearly all EU customs duties are *ad valorem* (i.e. calculated as a percentage of the value of imports) rather than 'specific' (a lump sum applied to each unit imported). The CCT involves two types of tariff: autonomous and conventional. *Autonomous* duties are those which the EU determines unilaterally; *conventional* tariffs arise from international agreements negotiated via the WTO.

It is important to realise that the European Union has numerous trade agreements with other countries. Preferential rates of tariff apply to developing countries in Latin America, various African, Caribbean and Pacific (ACP) states, and to East European nations. The conditions of EU trade with non-member countries are regulated by Articles 110-116 of the Treaty of Rome, which oblige the EU, *inter-alia*, to:

- Contribute to the harmonious development of world trade, the lowering of customs barriers and the progressive removal of international trade restrictions.
- Adopt a common commercial policy based on uniform external tariffs, the adoption of common positions when negotiating international trade agreements, and common internal measures to protect against dumping by outside nations. EU member states must act as one in their dealings with the WTO (*see* 5), OECD, etc. Trade policy is not a matter for

individual member nations; it has to be determined collectively for the Union as a whole (Maresceau 1993).

2. Import controls

In general, quantitative restrictions on imports to the EU (quotas, import licence requirements, or other controls on the numbers or values of imported items) may only be imposed at the Union level. There is however a 1982 Regulation which permits national governments to apply selective quantitative restrictions against imports from particular third countries for the following purposes:

(a) *Surveillance*. The European Commission can authorise a member state to require that importers from non-EU countries likely to threaten or cause injury to EU producers of similar items must complete special import documentation before the goods are put into free circulation (CEC 1993).

(b) *Protection*. Quotas and other quantitative limits may be applied (subject to the European Commission's permission) if the volume of imports to the EU of a certain product might seriously harm EU producers.

Any protective measure used by the EU as a whole has to conform to the provisions of the GATT agreement, i.e. that controls are only permitted if imports are being 'dumped' (*see* 3) and/or they are likely to disrupt the importing nation's market for the product involved. Allowable restrictions in these situations include:

- Import quotas
- Anti-dumping duties intended to raise the price of the imported item to a reasonable level
- 'Counterveiling duties' imposed to offset the price effects of government grants and subsidiaries given to foreign producers
- Measures available under the EU's New Commercial Policy Instrument 1984 which enables the Union to retaliate against any non-member country engaging in illicit commercial practices. These measures include raising import duties, suspending existing concessions, and physically restricting imports.
- *Voluntary restraint agreements* (VRAs). Here foreign countries agree to restrict their exports to the EU to specified limits (exports of Japanese cars are an example). VRAs are not legally enforceable, although the European Commission may threaten further action if a VRA is infringed.

3. Dumping

Dumping is the practice of selling an item in an export market at a price less than its normal value, allowing for transport and other export costs (Matsumoto and Finlayson 1990). A 1988 EU Regulation defines 'normal' value as the usual price of a 'like product' in the exporter's home country. The dumping margin is taken as the difference between normal value and the price charged to the *first* purchaser in the European Union (rather than the end consumer). Under EU rules the price considered is that which the exporting firm charges to non-related local distributors, not the price paid by final consumers. A non-related local distributor is one that is not tied to the supplying firm via an agency agreement or exclusive dealership. If all distributors are in fact 'related' to the supplying foreign firm then the price charged to end consumers is used. Problems arise in assessing reasonable values for mark-ups attributable to transport, distribution and other costs involved in foreign selling, and from the common situation whereby firms supply a market with units of the same item produced by subsidiaries in *several* different countries, so that there is no single 'domestic' price for the purpose of comparison.

Firms engage in dumping to undercut foreign competitors and drive them out of business, to use existing spare capacity in order to develop foreign markets, and/or to shift end-of-range stock. Because dumping is universally regarded as an unfair business practice, governments are allowed to seek to prevent it (under Article 6 of the GATT agreement) wherever it occurs persistently and is clearly intended to damage local competition (although firms can dispose of [genuinely] surplus stock at very low prices on an *ad hoc* basis).

4. Customs classification

The Harmonised Description and Coding System (usually referred to as the HS system) is a universally accepted product classification scheme used for customs valuation and the compilation of import and export statistics. It has 21 sections according to type of industry plus a twenty-second section for special classifications. Each category is then broken down into sub-divisions, resulting in a ten-digit code for particular products. The HS system forms the basis for TARIC (Tariff Intégré Communitaire), which is the EU's integrated customs tariff that provides information on tariff levels for various items, preferential rates, quotas, etc., alongside relevant commodity codes. Hence importers can identify their customs duty obligations very quickly, and the necessary documentation can be processed more easily. It is obviously important that the customs authorities of each EU nation classify items under exactly the same tariff headings: otherwise different rates of duty would apply to identical products in various member states and hence might lead to exporters despatching goods to the country with the most favourable rate. Accordingly the European Commission prepared in 1992 a Customs Code harmonising the basis upon which imports are categorised and valued for customs purposes. Under the Code, imports are valued at their transaction value, i.e. the price actually paid or payable for the goods in the destination country, minus allowable costs for commissions and transport. If this cannot be established then the transaction value of identical goods exported to the EU at around the same time as the items in question will be used. Should no identical goods exist, the value of similar products will be looked at. If there are no similar items, national customs authorities will attempt an assessment of the total value of the inputs, labour, freight charges, etc., connected with the goods.

Rules of origin

Because the EU has preferential trade agreements with various groups of countries it is necessary to establish the origins of imported items in order to determine the correct level of tariff. Goods produced in a single nation are easily dealt with; products to which value is added in several different countries, however, can be extremely difficult to assess. EU rules for determining origin distinguish between 'preferential' and 'non-preferential' trade as follows:

(a) *Preferential trade.* This means transactions covered by bilateral or multilateral trade agreements. Lower tariffs apply to goods originating in particular nations (Simpson 1991). Special rules of origin are negotiated with each foreign country benefiting from the arrangement. These rules differ between countries and groups of countries according to the trade agreement involved.

(b) *Non-preferential trade,* trade with non-EU countries not subject to special agreements. Hence the origin of a product is taken as the nation in which the last 'substantial' stage of manufacture took place. More than ten per cent of the value added to a product needs to occur in a country in order to give the product the origin of that country.

Local content requirements

Items produced within the EU can be sold anywhere in the Union without payment of import duty. Non-EU companies are sometimes accused of establishing 'screwdriver' establishments intended merely to assemble imported components, and then passing off the resulting product as having been made in the EU. Accordingly the European Commission requires that certain minimum percentages of products be derived from local sources. The percentage varies from item to item. For example, radios and television sets must have at least 35 per cent of their value added in the EU; for motor cars the figure is 60 to 90 per cent, depending on the nationality of the assembling company. The problem lies in the measurement of local content. Should this occur through counting the number of imported elements (and if so at what level of detail), or by assessment of monetary values? In the latter case should cost value or market value apply? So contentious are these issues that the European Commission has set up a Committee of Origin to assess where the majority of value added took place in respect of disputed items.

THE EU AND THE WORLD TRADE ORGANISATION

5. The World Trade Organisation (WTO)

Prior to 1994 the World Trade Organisation was known as the General Agreement on Tariffs and Trade (GATT). It is a Geneva-based institution founded in 1947 to encourage multilateral (as opposed to bilateral) trade and to minimise tariff levels and non-tariff trade barriers. Its 116 members include all the industrialised nations, over 70 developing countries, and a number of East European states. To date there have been eight rounds of negotiation (the eighth being referred to as the 'Uruguay Round') resulting in 180 treaties. WTO rules now cover 90 per cent of world trade, and are based on the following principles:

(a) *Non-discrimination,* meaning that each member country must apply the same rates of tariff to imports from all member nations, although customs unions and free-trade areas are permitted and special arrangements apply to underdeveloped countries. This principle is sometimes referred to as the application of Most Favoured Nation treatment to all WTO members.

(b) *Resolution of disputes via consultation,* though note that the 'dumping' of exports at less than their cost of production may be counteracted by retaliatory measures targeted at the offending country.

(c) *Non-legality of quantitative restrictions on imports,* unless a country is economically underdeveloped, is experiencing severe balance of payments difficulties, or if an agricultural or fisheries product is involved.

Countries in dispute first try to settle their problems bilaterally. If this fails a working party is convened to investigate the matter and make a recommendation. Should the offending nation ignore the recommendation the aggrieved country is permitted to retaliate.

The Uruguay settlement

Conclusion of the Uruguay Round in December 1993 created the most significant trade agreement in GATT's history. Tariffs will fall by an average 40 per cent throughout the world by the year 2000. The USA and the EU each cut tariffs on the other's product by 50 per cent immediately, with more cuts to follow. GATT itself was restructured, renamed as the World Trade Organisation, and its powers extended. The deal included new measures relating to (i) the protection of intellectual property and the prohibition of trade in counterfeit goods, (ii) the reform of national agricultural subsidies, and (iii) trade in services. Matters relating to agricultural support were hotly disputed during negotiations. The EU's agricultural price support system (*see* Chapter 5) has led to enormous surpluses of EU-supplied food products. Hence the EU has not been prepared to make tariff concessions on agricultural items available either to crop-dependent under-developed countries or to the United States. Instead, non-EU agricultural produce must pay import duties to bring its selling prices up to internal EU levels. The US government (itself a major agricultural producer) objected strongly to this state of affairs as it wished its farmers to have free access to the (lucrative) European market. In reply, the EU argued that the USA itself pays high subsidies to its farmers, hence enabling them to export food at artificially low prices!

The eventual settlement of the agricultural issue required that agricultural subsidies be cut over a six-year period. Domestic farm support is being reduced by 20 per cent, export subsidies by 36 per cent (by value). Tariffs are to be the only permitted barrier to the import of agricultural goods. Restrictions are being placed on countries' abilities to dump subsidised food exports on the rest of the world. Adjustments on the European side are occurring under the EU's own plans for common agricultural policy reform.

In relation to intellectual property the Uruguay settlement provides for the following:

(a) Patent protection for 20 years regardless of where an item is invented or whether it is imported or locally produced.

(b) Limitations on the use of compulsory licensing (*see* 13:4) for patented products (licences are easily obtained in some underdeveloped countries).

(c) Copyright protection for at least 50 years from the creator's death. This is to include computer software and compiled databases.

(d) All countries will have to introduce laws to prevent the unauthorised disclosure of trade secrets.

(e) Provision of equal treatment for domestic and foreign intellectual property holders.

Benefits and problems of the WTO

Since 1947 GATT has reduced international tariff levels significantly across a wide range of products. It has encouraged 'good behaviour' in the conduct of international trade, and led to much useful dialogue and communication among nations. Fresh measures prejudicial to international trade (other than a number of hidden non-tariff barriers) have not been initiated since the first GATT negotiations. The European Union will benefit enormously from the 1993 agreement in a number of areas, including:

(a) The extension of WTO rules to cover trade in services (notably banking, insurance and telecommunications), which today accounts for 20 per cent of all international trade by value. Note how private sector services now contribute just under 50 per cent of the EU's aggregate GDP and employ 42 per cent of its workers. Industry, conversely, provides just a third of total GDP and 32 per cent of employment.

(b) The opening up of world markets (especially in North America and Australia) to European exports of agricultural products, natural resources, and textiles originating in Italy, Greece and Portugal.

(c) Significant international tariff reductions for chemicals, pharmaceuticals, scientific equipment and spirits – all of which the EU exports in large quantity

(d) The limits that will be placed on national governments' capacities to subsidise inefficient local industries.

Apart from the ongoing debate on the degree to which the principle of reciprocity should be applied (*see* 6), the main problems associated with the WTO are that:

- The wording of the original 1947 GATT agreement is vague and complicated, making it quite easy to circumvent commitments.
- The WTO cannot itself impose sanctions.
- Policing the use of hidden non-tariff barriers has proven difficult. As soon as one variety of hidden barrier is outlawed, another might be invented.

- An increasing number of governments outside the major trade blocs are currently advocating *bilateral* trade treaties as a means for counteracting the power of the regional trade groupings. To the extent that bilateral agreements are concluded they undermine the WTO's position and international influence.
- Underdeveloped countries have been just as unwilling to renounce excessively protectionist import controls as have economically advanced nations been reluctant to accept more imports from the Third World.
- Rule changes require a two thirds majority of members. The principle of one vote per country is applied regardless of the sizes of the nations involved.

Obligations under GATT

All EU nations are members of the WTO and as such must accept the Most Favoured Nation principle embodied in Article 1 of the GATT agreement, namely that:

'any advantage, favour, privilege or immunity granted by any member country to any product originating in or destined for any other member country shall be accorded immediately and unconditionally to the like product originating in or destined for all other member countries'.

In other words, member nations must offer equivalent treatment to *all* third countries without discrimination (provided the latter are members of the WTO). Exemptions to the Most Favoured Nation principle are available, however, and the EU does have preferential trade agreements with certain groups of countries, as outlined in **1**.

6. The Generalised System of Preferences (GSP)

GATT's operations were severely criticised by many underdeveloped countries, particularly in relation to the application of the principle of reciprocity, i.e. that underdeveloped as well as economically advanced nations were required to reduce tariffs, even though this worsened the balance of payments positions and foreign exchange shortages of poorer states. Such concerns led to the formation in 1964 of the United Nations Conference on Trade and Development (UNCTAD), as a permanent body attached to the UN. Its successes to date have included international action to create a fund to help stabilise the prices of exports of primary commodities from developing nations, and (importantly) the implementation in 1971 of the Generalised System of Preferences (GSP) whereby the export of most categories of manufactured industrial product from underdeveloped to developed countries receive duty-free treatment. Under the GSP, tariff preferences are:

- non-discriminatory, i.e. they apply without distinction to *all* countries defined as 'developing' by UNCTAD
- autonomous, in that they are not the result of negotiation with particular beneficiary nations

- non-reciprocal, so that developing countries do not have to make equivalent reductions in customs duties
- generalised, i.e. they are granted by all industrially advanced GATT members, not just the EU and USA.

Accordingly the EU grants tariff preferences to a large number of underdeveloped countries. However, ceilings on manufactured imports entering the EU under GSP may be imposed and, once these have been exceeded, the common commercial tariff applies.

RELATIONS WITH NORTH AMERICA

7. Trade with NAFTA

The North American Free Trade Agreement (NAFTA) came into being in 1994 with a view to eliminating all tariffs and trade obstacles between member countries by the year 2009. Internal tariffs on a large number of product categories were removed immediately. A free trade agreement between the USA and Canada was signed in 1989. Its extension to Mexico presents Canada (a small population economy that is nevertheless resource rich and highly industrialised) and the US with a large consumer goods market, while the US is a major importer of Mexican manufactures and oil. NAFTA has a population of 363 million, making it one of the most important economic trading areas in the world, clearly able to compete effectively against the European Union. Government procurement markets in each member country are being opened up to suppliers from other NAFTA nations, subject to minimum values for the contracts involved. Residents of any NAFTA country may freely invest in any NAFTA nation. The agreement sets out specific requirements regarding the protection of intellectual property within each member state. Further measures include:

- Simplification and harmonisation of product standards across the region
- Easy border crossings for business personnel
- Application of stringent local content rules to prevent non-NAFTA firms assembling goods in Mexico and hence avoiding US and Canadian tariffs and quotas. Third-country products imported into one country cannot be re-exported to other members as if they were domestically produced goods, *unless* certain minimum percentages of their manufacturing costs have been incurred in the importing nation. For Canada and the US the figure is 50 per cent; for Mexico the local content requirement can be as high as 80 per cent. Each country continues to operate its own system of tariffs against non-NAFTA states.

The formation of NAFTA should generate fresh business opportunities for European exporters as national markets expand (especially Mexico, which is developing extremely rapidly) and create a stable environment for foreign investors. As NAFTA is a free trade area rather than a common market, NAFTA countries maintain their own independent relations with the outside world; the

EU has no formal trade treaty with NAFTA as a corporate body – trade agreements continue to operate with each of the three member states. The USA is, of course, the dominant NAFTA nation. Indeed the US is the world's biggest international trader, and the extent of its foreign trade is increasing. Overall the pattern of America's trade has shifted away from Europe and towards the Pacific Rim, notably Japan, Taiwan and South Korea. Nevertheless, the European Union remains a critically important trading partner, taking about 20 per cent of US exports and furnishing nearly the same percentage of its imports. Overall, relations between the USA and the EU have been satisfactory, although the completion of the Single European Market has given rise to a number of complaints by various US interest groups (Featherstone and Ginsberg 1993). Specific allegations are as follows:

(a) The Common Agricultural Policy is unfairly discriminatory.

(b) EU local content rules are too severe (*see* 4).

(c) Because movies and television programmes are a major US export, European Commission encouragement to national governments to induce TV companies to source programmes locally wherever practicable represents a direct threat to the US economy.

(d) Pan-European technical standards (*see* Chapter 8) are being established without regard to existing standards on the other side of the Atlantic. There is no provision for US participation in the work of CEN and CENELEC, despite the fact that the American National Standards Institute has been prepared to consider representations from European standards-setting bodies. The US authorities fear that new European standards will be devised as much with the intention of keeping US goods out of the Single Market as with quality and/or health and safety considerations.

(e) The common external tariff has led to an outflow of capital from the US and into the European Union. US direct foreign investment in the EU twelve doubled during the 1980s, suggesting a strong desire by American firms to establish a firm base in the Single Market. Arguably this led to job losses within the United States.

TRADE WITH ACP AND MEDITERRANEAN STATES

8. The Lomé Convention

The European Union extends many preferences to a large number of the world's poorest countries via the Lomé Convention, which itself emerged from the special trading arrangements that were negotiated (through the Yaoundé Convention of 1963) between the founder members of the EEC and their former colonial territories. Extension of the Yaoundé Convention was necessitated by the United Kingdom's accession to the EEC in 1973. Accordingly the first Lomé Convention (named after the capital of Togo) was signed in 1975 and incorporated an extra 20 underdeveloped African, Caribbean and Pacific (ACP) states. The Convention is updated every few years and currently covers around 70 ACP countries plus the EU fifteen. Collectively the Lomé countries have trade agreements with Mediterranean and Latin American states, effectively taking in half the countries of the world. All the signatories to the Convention itself are eligible for EU technical and financial help plus tariff-free and quota-free access to EU countries, without reciprocity, except for a handful of agricultural products.

9. Trade with the Mediterranean countries

The EU has bilateral trade agreements with Algeria, Cyprus, Egypt, Malta, Morocco, Tunisia and Turkey; and further east with Israel, Jordan, Lebanon and Syria. These treaties differ significantly one from another, ranging from co-operation agreements or Association Agreements (*see* Chapter 3), through to full free trade agreements. All the Treaties provide for tariff-free access to the EU for industrial products, subject to ceilings on the annual levels of imports of certain types of item. Note however that many of the previously mentioned countries are major industrial suppliers.

10. Foreign aid

The EU operates four major foreign aid programmes, covering the following regions:

The ACP nations

Asian and Latin American (ALA) countries

Eastern Europe

The non-EU Mediterranean states of Morocco, Algeria, Tunisia, Jordan, Syria, Lebanon, Israel and Egypt.

Additionally there are separate programmes for humanitarian and for food aid. Typically between 50 and 65 per cent of all EU aid goes to non-Lomé countries. Assistance to Lomé nations is channelled through the European Development Fund (EDF) established by the Treaty of Rome and financed via direct contributions from member states.

Trade versus aid

The issue of whether the EU should give substantial amounts of foreign aid has been hotly disputed ever since the EDF commenced operations (Grilli 1993). Advocates of aid argue that it directs resources to the areas where it is most needed; that it is distributed immediately; can be used to target specific projects; and is justified on purely humanitarian criteria. Arguments against the distribution of aid are that:

- It might have little impact on long-term economic development.
- Donors (including the EU) are liable to cut aid budgets without notice when their domestic economic circumstances become unfavourable.
- Recipients come to rely on external handouts rather than tackling fundamental economic problems head on.
- Aid could be misdirected towards inefficient uses.

- Widespread bribery and corruption might accompany the aid distribution process.

Hence the stimulation of commercial trade is arguably more beneficial to poorer countries. Trade should increase output and employment, improve export earnings and develop new markets for underdeveloped countries' products. On the other hand, additional trade could worsen a nation's balance of payments situation and/or lead to bad working conditions (long hours, low wages, etc.) for employees in Third World countries. There is no *guarantee* that extra trade will improve living standards.

Progress test 9

1. How was the EEC's common customs tariff initially computed?

2. Explain the difference between autonomous duties and conventional duties.

3. List the obligations stated in Articles 110-116 of the Treaty of Rome.

4. What is the purpose of import 'surveillance'?

5. List the measures available under the New Commercial Policy Instrument 1994.

6. Define 'dumping'. Why do firms engage in dumping?

7. What is the HS system and what is its purpose? How does TARIC relate to the HS system?

8. Outline the main contents of the EU's 1992 Customs Code.

9. State the EU's rules on the definition of the country of origin of imported goods.

10. What is the WTO and what is its role?

11. How does the Generalised System of Preferences operate?

12. Examine the implications for EU exporters of the signing of the North American Free Trade Agreement.

13. What is the Lomé Convention?

14. List the advantages and disadvantages of (i) increased EU trade with ACP countries, and (ii) increased levels of foreign aid given by the EU to ACP countries.

10

BUSINESS ORGANISATION IN WESTERN EUROPE

FORMS OF BUSINESS ORGANISATION

Similar forms of business organisation are found in all EU nations except for Finland and Sweden, which (currently) do not distinguish between private and public limited companies (*see* **2** and **3**). The latter countries will, of course, be changing their domestic company law to bring it into line with EU Company Law Directives (*see* Chapter 8) in due course. Each nation has its own peculiar types of business, but the general legal structures of firms are essentially the same throughout the EU. The European Commission has sought to harmonise national rules on partnership, company formation, disclosure and audit requirements, dissolution, mergers, etc., in order to facilitate EU-wide freedom of establishment for businesses and the creation of a 'level playing field' where these matters are concerned. However, a number of significant differences continue to exist, including:

(a) Businesses in several EU countries must, by law, join a local Chamber of Commerce. This provides the Chambers of Commerce of such nations with large subscription incomes which can be used to provide support services (training, information gathering, help with finding agents, etc.) to member firms.

(b) Branches of foreign companies are viewed as distinct legal entities in some (but not all) EU states. Co-operatives are also regarded as a separate form of business (with limited liability) under the laws of several nations.

(c) In some EU countries (notably Italy) the shares of certain companies are not divided into units of equal par value. Rather, each investor receives a 'quota' which reflects his or her financial contribution. Hence quotas may vary in value, although for all practical purposes they can be regarded as exactly the same as shares.

(d) The majority of EU nations require all businesses to register their details with a state Commercial Register. Information from these Registers (which can be used for mailshots or for collecting data on potential competitors) is normally available to the general public.

1. Sole traders and partnerships

The most basic form of business ownership is the single-person firm without limited liability. This is referred to as a *sole tradership*. Proprietors of sole trader-ships run them personally and are responsible for all the debts of their busi-nesses. If the enterprise fails the owner's personal possessions are sold off to raise the money needed to settle outstanding balances. Profits accrue entirely to the proprietor. In about half of all EU countries sole traders have a distinct legal status in that disputes over contracts between traders and ordinary members of the public or between pairs of traders might be heard by a special Commercial Tribunal, and specific rights and duties attach to 'commercial' as opposed to non-commercial contracts.

Larger businesses are possible through *partnerships* of two or more individu-als. Each partner usually contributes capital, and will often have skills and talents not possessed by other partners. All partners are jointly liable for the debts of the business. It is common therefore for a written agreement to be drafted regulating the partnership's activities. This agreement should define authority and responsibility structures within the business; what and how much work each partner should do; how profits will be distributed, etc. The entire partnership is bound by contracts entered into by any partner, unless the contract is beyond the commercial scope of the business or is clearly for that partner's personal benefit. Partnerships are not limited-liability organisations and have no existence separate from their members. Thus, a contract with a partnership is a contract with all its members, who are equally liable for discharging the contract. An important implication of joint personal liability for debts is that if some partners are insolvent when a debt is recovered from the partners, the remaining solvency partners are responsible (to the extent of their personal estates) for all the outstanding amount. This obligation is referred to as the 'joint and several' liability of partners.

Limited partnerships

These are a special form of partnership whereby the liability for the business's debts of one or all of the partners is restricted to the value of the individual's financial investment in the firm. Limited partnerships are permitted in all EU states. Certain nations provide for a special kind of partnership in which some or all of the partners are themselves limited companies. These firms have a unique legal status with particular rights and obligations specified by national legislation. In Germany it is possible to form a 'civil law partnership' which is a joint venture arrangement by which members agree to pool expertise for a specific business purpose. France and Luxembourg have a similar arrangement for non-commercial partnerships used to hold property, conduct research, etc. Luxembourg's law also provides for the *Association Momentanee*, a joint venture arrangement formed for a particular task without having a trade under a specific name. Participants have unlimited liability for the business's debts.

In Britain a member of a partnership can be a 'sleeping partner' who contrib-utes capital but leaves the running of the business to other partners. A sleeping partner can obtain protection against liability for the debts of the business by registering the firm as a limited partnership with the UK Registrar of Companies. In this case the sleeping partner is legally prohibited from taking part in the management of the business, and he or she cannot write cheques or enter contracts on behalf of the firm. France has a similar legal form, the 'silent partnership' which has a senior partner without limited liability plus sleeping partners whose liability is limited but whose identities are not made known to the public. If sleeping partners' names are disclosed the individuals concerned lose their limited liability.

Spain has the EU's most complex laws on the formation of joint ventures (elsewhere joint ventures are regarded as partnerships among firms – assuming of course that a separate company has not been created to undertake the venture's operations). In Spain, joint ventures (JVs) can be developed as associations of enterprises or as a 'contract of joint accounts'. The former may be established with or without an independent legal identity. JVs with independent legal identity are separate businesses created by at least three members, which can be companies or individual persons. No participant can hold more than a one-third share in the business. Unlike other Spanish companies, joint venture companies constituted in this way pay negligible company formation tax. JVs without independent legal identity exist to promote the common interests of the participants in some way. They do not pay any tax in their own right. Rather, profits are shared by the members of the arrangement who then include these profits in their own tax returns (even if the profits are temporarily retained within the joint venture itself). Such a venture requires prior approval from the Ministry of Commerce and must be evidenced by a written agreement specifying each participant's financial contribution and profit share. There are three varieties of this organisational form:

1 *Agrupaciones de empresas,* which are loose collaboration agreements between enterprises to further a common interest.
2 *Uniones temporales de empresas,* which are agreements to undertake specific *ad hoc* projects.
3 *Cesiones de unidades de obras,* which are subcontracting arrangements.

Contracts of joint accounts comprise businesses conducted by one party (the promoter) on behalf of several other parties. Profits are distributed to the members according to a predetermined formula. The arrangement is useful for Spanish businesses which undertake collective assignments for a number of foreign firms (establishing joint warehousing or distribution facilities, for instance).

Joint ventures without legal identity are common in Spain because the resulting organisation can trade without a common name, can be set up by word of mouth and, most important, enjoy substantial tax advantages.

2. Private limited companies

Owners (shareholders) of a limited liability company are responsible for its debts only to the extent of their shareholding. A limited liability company has its own legal personality. It can enter contracts in its own name, and can sue as an entity quite separate from its owners.

Private limited companies cannot invite the general public to subscribe to their shares. The overwhelming majority of European limited companies are private.

They exist primarily to avoid the owners being personally responsible for their companies' debts, so that the size of their share issues is not an important consideration. All EU countries now permit the existence of single member private companies, following the introduction in 1992 of the EU Twelfth Directive on Company Law which demanded this facility. Prior to 1992 single-person companies were only available in a few EU countries; notably France and Portugal, where they enjoy a separate legal status.

Important differences in national laws concerning private limited companies apply to the following:

(a) *Length and complexity of the process of company incorporation.* Companies are formed (incorporated) by completing a series of documents and depositing them with a country's national company registration authorities. The major documents involved are:

(*i*) the company's Articles of Association which specify the rules and conditions governing internal relations between directors and members of the company, e.g. shareholders' voting rights, share transfer regulations, election of directors, etc.

(*ii*) the Memorandum of Association that states the objects (contractual powers) of the business plus details of its share capital.

In Britain the process of incorporation is straightforward. Indeed there exist businesses which specialise in company formation and which advertise 'off-the-peg' companies in the financial press. These 'company registration agents' spend all their time documenting and registering companies, which they then sell for as little as £150 for a private company or £1250 for a public company. In France, conversely, it is almost impossible to buy private companies 'off-the-shelf' because of the many notices and announcements that have to be declared and the long delays they necessitate. Registration procedures can be costly and tedious in a number of other EU countries.

(b) *Share call-up requirements.* The 'nominal' (or 'authorised') capital of a company is the maximum amount its articles of association specify that it can raise through selling shares. This may differ from 'issued' (or 'allotted') capital, which is the proportion of nominal capital actually sold. Payment for shares is 'called up' from shareholders in instalments. 'Paid up' capital is that part of issued capital that has been called and for which payment has actually been received. Shareholders who fail to respond to calls are liable to forfeit their shares. Shares in private companies have to be fully paid up on incorporation in about half of all EU countries. In Italy, Ireland and the UK conversely there are no significant call-up requirements. Danish company law requires that shares in private companies be paid up within one year of incorporation. Elsewhere, share capital has to be partly paid up (e.g. 25 per cent in the Netherlands, 50 per cent in Portugal).

(c) *Voting rights of shareholders.* The commonest type of share in Western Europe is the 'ordinary' share. Ordinary shareholders carry the risk of the business and receive dividends only if profits are made. And if the company collapses they are repaid their investment only after all the firm's other debts and obligations have been settled. In most EU countries the rule of one vote per share applies. Non-voting ordinary shares may be issued in Denmark and the UK; multiple vote shares are permitted in Ireland and Denmark. Restrictions on the maximum voting rights of individual shareholders are imposed in Belgium, the Netherlands and Portugal.

(d) *Restrictions on share transfer.* In most countries there are no restrictions on a shareholder's ability to sell or otherwise transfer his or her shares in a private company. Shares in a Belgian private company cannot be transferred without the consent of at least half the company's shareholders representing a minimum of 75 per cent of share capital. In France and Luxembourg share transfers need the permission of existing shareholders accounting for at least 75 per cent of the company's share capital.

3. Public limited companies (joint stock companies)

Public limited companies may raise capital from the general public. They are not obliged to do so but in practice the majority of public companies do in fact invite the public to subscribe. Major differences in national laws relating to public companies apply to the following matters:

(a) *Minimum capital requirements.* The Second EU Directive on Company Law 1977 requires that all EU public companies have a nominal share capital of at least 25,000 ECU, although this is the *minimum* figure and national governments are free to impose whatever higher amount they so wish. The purpose of imposing minimum capital requirements is to give creditors of a public company a degree of protection by ensuring that the company has at least some assets to disperse to shareholders if the company fails. These minimum values vary from state to state. In most EU countries, 25 per cent of the minimum capital requirement must be paid in at the time a public company is formed (in Italy and Portugal the figure is 30 per cent). Elsewhere the entire amount of the specific minimum value has to be paid on incorporation.

(b) *Periods of appointment of company directors.* A few EU countries impose no statutory restrictions on this matter. The majority insist that directors be re-elected every six years (five years in Austria and Germany, three years in Italy).

(c) *Specification of persons who may not become directors.* Apart from Luxembourg and Portugal, all EU nations prohibit certain classes of people from serving on the boards of PLCs. Bankrupts are the commonest category of excluded person. Other proscriptions include:

- members of national Parliaments (France and Greece)
- civil servants (Spain, France, Greece and Belgium)
- non-shareholders (France)
- bank managers (Denmark)
- persons who have served prison sentences (Belgium)
- persons certified as insane (UK and Italy)
- certified alcoholics or drug abusers (Italy).

(d) *Minimum number of directors.* This varies between one and three according to the country involved.

(e) *Minimum number of shareholders.* This varies between two and seven.

(f) *Penalties on directors who mismanage a PLC.* All EU countries permit shareholders and/or creditors to sue directors of public companies for damages caused by the latter's misconduct. In Britain and the Netherlands a company, acting as an independent 'legal person', can itself sue members of its own board of directors. Dutch directors have unlimited personal liability for company insolvencies caused by their own negligence. Acts committed by Dutch directors intended to damage their companies are criminal offences for which the individuals responsible can be heavily fined or imprisoned. Contracts entered into by Italian directors and which are *ultra-vires* to a company's objects (*see* 2) are still binding if the other party acted in good faith.

(g) *Share call-up requirements.* The commonest rule is that 25 per cent of each of a PLC's shares must be paid up. Shares in France and Portuguese public companies must be fully paid up within five years of their issue. Spain and Italy require at least 30 per cent of each share to be paid up on incorporation.

(h) *Shareholders' voting rights.* As is the case with private companies (*see* 2), some countries strictly apply the rule of one vote per share, others permit the issue of multiple vote and/or non-voting shares.

(i) *Employee representation on company boards.* This is considered in 7 below.

4. Statutory reserves

The majority of EU countries legally require companies incorporated within their borders to create and hold substantial cash reserves. Arguably, the 'retention culture' this encourages in companies domiciled in these nations leads to cash-rich businesses better able to take over other companies in other EU states (and themselves to avoid being taken over via the use of their extensive reserves). Also, it has been alleged, accumulated profit retention creates sounder financial bases for companies in these countries, enabling them to survive recessions more readily than companies elsewhere. Businesses with extensive reserves are able to adopt long-term perspectives, to develop long-term plans and to invest for the future. The general problem of 'short termism' is discussed in Chapter 11.

Companies in Austria, Belgium, France, Germany and Luxembourg must place five per cent of their annual profits into reserves until their reserves equal ten per cent of the value of paid-up share capital. In Denmark, ten per cent of profits has to be paid into reserves each year until the reserve equals ten per cent of share capital; thereafter five per cent of annual profits must be transferred until the reserve reaches 25 per cent of share capital. Greek companies are required to put five per cent of each year's profits into reserves until the latter equals one third of share capital. The same applies in Italy except that the threshold figure is 20 per cent. Compulsory transfers to reserves of five per cent of each year's profits apply in Spain and Sweden, again until 20 per cent of the value of share capital has been accumulated. Finland does not require its companies to hold minimum levels of reserves, but does offer generous tax allowances to any company that elects to do so. Up to 30 per cent of annual profits can be transferred to reserves without tax liability, although the ways in which such reserves can be used are constrained (to the purchase of fixed assets, for instance).

5. Supervision, audit and disclosure requirements

Supervisory (as opposed to executive) boards (*see* **6**) are compulsory for certain classes of company in Austria, Denmark, Germany and the Netherlands, and are a legal option in Portugal and France. The advantages, disadvantages and implications of supervisory boards are discussed in **6** to **9**.

Audit requirements

At the time of writing *all* UK, Danish, Irish, Finnish and Swedish companies are legally compelled to have their accounts audited by an independent qualified accountant. This is not the case in other EU nations however, and audit requirements and practices vary considerably from state to state. Belgian, Greek and Dutch companies with more than 50 employees and/or with turnovers or asset values exceeding certain thresholds have to be audited, as must all Luxembourgian public companies and private companies with less than 25 shareholders. In France and Germany, audits are compulsory for all public companies and for private companies above a certain size (measured by asset value, turnover and number of employees). Italian companies with more than a prespecified share capital are subject to audit, as are firms in receipt of state assistance. Spain has minimal audit requirements: only large businesses with turnovers and asset values above certain levels need to have their accounts externally audited.

Disclosure

In the majority of EU countries, companies' annual accounts must be deposited with a government body and then made available for public inspection. The government body concerned might be a Registrar's Office (as happens in Denmark, Germany, Spain and the UK), a local Commercial Court (France), or the National Bank (Belgium). Dutch companies have to file their accounts with a Chamber of Commerce, where they are open to public view. Exceptions to this general rule are as follows:

(a) In Portugal, only companies with 50 or more workers and/or certain turnover and asset values are required to publish their annual accounts (in the Official Gazette of the Commercial Registry).

(b) Only those Italian companies that are listed on the country's Stock Exchange are obliged to publish their accounts; otherwise disclosure requirements are minimal.

(c) Greek public (but not private) companies have to file their accounts with the Ministry of Commerce and publish them in the government *Gazette* and prescribed daily newspapers.

BOARDS OF DIRECTORS

6. Two-tier boards

In Austria, Germany, Denmark and the Netherlands there exist legal requirements compelling large companies to have two-tier boards of directors. The
lower tier is an *executive board*, comprising managerial employees of the firm
responsible for the day-to-day operational management. Above this is a *supervisory board*, which takes strategic decisions in relation to the overall direction of
the enterprise. By law, employee representatives must sit on the supervisory
boards of companies in these countries. The functions of supervisory boards
include:

- the appointment and dismissal of executive managers and the determination of their remunerations
- deciding the overall direction of the enterprise (its products, markets,
  major new investments, etc.)
- matters concerning mergers and takeovers and how the company is to be
  financed.

Two-tier boards were first used in Germany in the 1860s, when the German
banks began making large financial investments in industry and demanded
representation at board-room level in order to protect their interests. Today all
German (and Austrian) public and private companies with more than 500
workers must have a supervisory board. In Denmark supervisory boards are
compulsory for all companies (public and private) with at least 50 employees
and a certain minimum share capital. For the Netherlands the rule is that
companies employing 100 or more workers and with asset values above a
specific minimum level must have a supervisory board. Portuguese and French
public companies may opt to have a supervisory board, although an alternative
may be selected. Once a Portuguese PLC forms a supervisory board it is bound
thereafter by special laws on how the business of the supervisory board is to be
conducted. A similar situation applies in France, where a public company may
be managed by either:

(*i*) a board of between three and 12 directors (*conseil de administration*) all
members of which must be shareholders in the business and who serve for
(renewable) six-year terms; or
(*ii*) a two-tier system comprising a supervisory board (*counseil de surveillance*)
and, below that, an executive board of two to seven managers.

The advantages claimed for the practice of having a separate supervisory board
are that:

- General policy-making is undertaken objectively and independently
  without interference from executives with vested interests in outcomes.
- Interpersonal rivalries among lower level managers can be ignored.
- Employee interests may be considered in the absence of line managers
  who control workers.

- Tough decisions that adversely affect senior line managers can be taken more easily.

Problems with supervisory boards are that:

- The people who determine basic strategy might be remote from the day-to-day realities of executive management.
- Decision-making is slowed down by the need to go through two separate boards on certain issues.
- Confusions could arise between executive and supervisory boards, with the decisions of each not being properly understood by the other.

7. Employee representation on company boards

This is required by law in six EU countries. In France, voluntary arrangements are possible which, once implemented, then have a legal status and cannot be revoked. National systems operate as follows:

(a) *Denmark.* Between two and half the number of shareholder's representatives must serve on the boards of all firms with more than 35 employees. Worker directors serve four-year terms and are directly elected by the workforce.

(b) *France.* Any size of business may choose to have employee representatives on its board of directors. Four workers have to be elected (five in a quoted public company) by the workforce, or alternatively one third of the total size of the board. The individuals appointed serve six-year terms. Although the system is initiated voluntarily, it thereafter has the force of law.

(c) *Germany and Austria.* There is compulsory employee representation on the supervisory boards of public companies and any other form of business employing in excess of 500 people. Worker directors have to make up between one third and one half of the board depending on the size of the firm. In the latter situation the casting vote lies with the chair of the board. There are no statutory limitations on periods of office.

(d) *Luxembourg.* One third of the main board of any company employing more than 1000 workers must consist of employee representatives directly elected by the workforce for three-year terms.

(e) *Netherlands.* Boards of public companies with more than 100 workers and assets exceeding a certain value need to contain at least one person nominated by the firm's works council (*see* **10**) but who is not an employee of the enterprise (a trade union officer for example). Works councils are legally entitled to object to any appointment to a Supervisory Board.

(f) *Finland.* Firms employing more than 150 people are required to have worker directors, their number depending on the size of the company's workforce.

(g) *Sweden.* Companies with more than 25 workers must have at least two directors appointed by trade unions active within the company.

Advantages and problems of having worker directors

The essential argument for having worker directors is that since many employees devote much of their working lives to a particular firm, they are entitled, through elected representatives, to some say in how the firm is run. Against this is the fact that firms are owned by entrepreneurs and / or shareholders who put their personal capital at risk. Owners of firms may resent the imposition of worker directors who, in part, will control the owners' assets without having been elected by the owners themselves. Specific problems facing worker directors could include the following:

(a) Reluctance of other board members to disclose confidential information to employee representatives, in case it is passed on to union negotiators. But if worker directors agree not to reveal sensitive data, they face criticism from union colleagues who expect them to divulge information gained in board meetings. To whom does the worker owe loyalty, management or the union?

(b) Hostility and social ostracism from other board members, who might conduct secret board meetings to decide key issues without the presence of worker directors.

(c) The fact that special privileges afforded to worker directors – higher status, preferential treatment, expenses, time off for board meetings, perhaps even higher wages – might cause them to lose contact with the workers who elected them. Hence they might become integrated into the management system, adopt management perspectives and become reluctant to challenge management decisions. Effectively the worker director's role disintegrates to being nothing more than explaining, justifying and / or apologising for management's actions.

(d) Although a company's board of directors is nominally the most powerful body in the enterprise, real power might in fact lie elsewhere.

(e) To the extent that a worker director can influence the board's decisions, he or she will be presenting arguments as an individual and not as an employee representative as happens with collective bargaining: there is no question of negotiation occurring during board meetings.

(f) Worker directors may be patronised but effectively ignored.

(g) Company boards take *strategic* decisions the outcomes of which might not be visible for several years, so the employees the worker director represents may not see any tangible short-term benefits to electing worker directors.

(h) Boards of directors have to deal with a wide variety of issues, not just employee relations. Board members other than worker directors will have been selected for their knowledge of and ability to contribute to these wider discussions. Worker directors who have no experience of practical management but who wish nevertheless to express opinions on all matters could impede effective decision-making.

(i) Worker directors may not be able to relate their immediate workplace concerns with the need to adopt an overall perspective on the enterprise. Can worker directors realistically be expected to think strategically?

Perhaps the most immediately useful functions of a worker director are to voice criticism of management's stated intentions and to articulate the workplace point of view. Management is confronted with new and different interpretations of issues. Also, the presence on the board of employee representatives underlines senior management's commitment to employee welfare, and a climate of mutual confidence and co-operation between management and labour may emerge.

Specific implications of having worker directors on supervisory boards are as follows:

(a) The knowledge and experience of employee representatives can be directly applied to *strategic* decisions without employee representatives having to argue with line managers.

(b) Matters concerning human relations are automatically elevated to the highest level of decision-making within the organisation. Note that since the supervisory board appoints and dismisses senior managers then the latter will be highly sensitive to worker directors' views, and to human relations issues generally.

(c) Arguably, the presence of employee representatives on a supervisory board facilitates the financial stability of the company, because worker directors' concerns for employees' continuity of employment invariably cause them to argue in favour of profit retention and the accumulation of reserves to guard against temporary economic downturns. Also, employee representatives will oppose any merger or takeover that could result in redundancies.

8. The proposed European Company Statute

In 1970 the European Commission first recommended the creation of a special form of European Company to be known as a *Societas Europeas* or SE. Progress towards implementing the proposal has been slow, however, partly because of its insistence that SEs have compulsory employee participation in management decisions: a demand vigorously opposed by business interests and successive governments in the UK. Under the proposal three options are to be available for securing employee participation in management decisions, as follows:

- between one third and one half of its supervisory or administrative board must consist of employee representatives; *or*
- a separate works council could be established, meeting at least once every three months; *or*
- the SE may adopt the employee representation model of the country in which it registers, provided this model offers *at least* comparable participation rights to worker representatives as those embodied in the SE proposal.

Regardless of the precise form of participation, employee representatives would have to be informed of any proposal with 'significant implications' for workers, and to be consulted about any planned takeover or disposal of part of the business valued at more than 5 per cent of the SE's share capital (this percentage may be increased to up to 25 per cent in certain circumstances). Consultation would also be necessary prior to the conclusion of major loan agreements or supply contracts.

Precise details concerning the formation and operation of SEs have yet to be agreed, although the following general features of the European Company have been determined:

(a) An SE will be governed not by the laws of any one members country but by a set of fresh rules and procedures applicable throughout the EU.

(b) Such companies will be able to offset profits and losses between activities in various member countries, hence avoiding complications arising from double taxation.

(c) A European Company that holds more than half the shares of a subsidiary will be entitled to set all the latter's losses against its own profits.

(d) If an SE has branches in several EU nations then profits earned by a branch in one country will automatically be offset against losses incurred by branches in other EU states.

(e) An SE's profits will only be taxed in the country in which its head office is domiciled.

(f) SEs will register their existence with the European Court in Luxembourg, but will then be subject to the insolvency and other business laws of their countries of residence. An SE will require a minimum share capital of at least 100,000 ECU.

9. The Fifth Draft Directive on Company Law

The initial 1972 version of this proposal stipulated that all European Community based companies with more than 1000 workers would have had to set up a two-tier board of directors with compulsory employee representation on the supervisory board, or worker participation in management through a separate works council with representation on the board, or an equivalent body established by collective agreement (provided the body affords at least the same rights as alternative devices). However, the Draft was amended in 1983 to offer companies the option of a single board with a majority of non-executive directors (empowered to appoint and dismiss executive directors) instead of having a two-tier board. Between one third and one half of a single or supervisory board would consist of employee representatives.

Benefits possibly resulting from this arrangement are discussed in 7. A number of objections have been raised against the proposal (particularly within the UK), including the following:

(a) Agendas of board meetings could become dominated by personnel management and industrial relations issues, at the expense of considering strategic and operational matters.

(b) Businesses affected by the Directive would need to train employee representatives in the principles of management, company structure, finance, market environments, etc., in order to enable them to understand board-room discussions.

(c) Companies operating in several EU countries would experience severe practical problems resulting from their boards having to include employee representatives from several countries, speaking different languages (thus requiring the presence of interpreters at board meetings), from widely disparate trade union backgrounds, and with contrasting cultural perspectives.

(d) Conflicts might be created between agreements reached by worker and other directors at the board level, and settlements concluded via plant-level collective bargaining in divisions and subsidiaries of the firm.

WORKS COUNCILS

10. Works councils in EU countries

Works councils (referred to as works committees in some countries) are an important feature of the continental European business scene, though not in the United Kingdom. They are compulsory for certain sizes of firm (normally defined in terms of a minimum number of employees) in Austria, Belgium, Denmark, France, Germany, Greece, Luxembourg, the Netherlands, Portugal and Spain. In Sweden, firms are legally obliged to inform employees of important plans and discuss these with trade unions (although management retains the ultimate right to take all decisions). At present works councils are not a legal requirement in the UK, Italy or the Irish Republic, but the latter two of these countries are actively considering how they can be introduced on a compulsory basis. In countries where they are required, councils are normally legally obliged to *discuss* particular (specified) matters, and entitled to *take decisions* (effectively giving employee representatives a right of veto) on others.

The range of issues involved differs substantially from country to country. Decision-making powers vary from internal works rules (e.g. the operation of grievance procedures) to recruitment methods and whether the firm is to take on part-time or temporary workers. In Germany and the Netherlands, employee representatives on works councils have the legal right to delay certain important management decisions (on company mergers for instance). Examples of issues that are subject to decision-making by works councils are as follows:

- criteria for hiring temporary staff and for selecting workers for redundancy (Belgium)
- profit-sharing arrangements (France)
- changes in working hours, training agreements, recruitment and disciplinary procedures (Germany)

- operation of job evaluation schemes, appraisal and grievance procedures, working hours (the Netherlands).

Matters subject to discussion by works councils in various EU countries include:

- financial plans and company structures
- acquisitions, physical investments and divestments
- working practices and the introduction of new technology
- proposed incentive schemes and wage payment systems
- company sales, profits and prices
- personnel policies (including recruitment methods)
- health and safety at work.

In Belgium, members of the works council are (legally) bound by confidentiality, and can be prohibited from disclosing sensitive information to other employees. Employers can apply to the Belgian Ministry of Labour to withhold certain information from the works council, although in practice this is extremely rare. German and Portuguese works council members are also statutorily bound by rules on confidentiality. For detailed information on the rights and duties of works councils in various EU nations see *Human Resources Management*, published in this series.

11. Advantages of works councils

Benefits claimed for the practice of having works council in firms include the following:

(a) The existence of a works council compels management to seek consensus with employee representatives on many important issues, hence avoiding conflicts and disruptive industrial action.

(b) Employees assume *obligations* for the operation of the business as well as rights to consultation. Works councils come to execute certain management functions (allocation of overtime, decisions on working methods, determination of promotion criteria, etc.) that otherwise would have to be undertaken by alternative (and perhaps more costly) management committees. Also, discussions between management and labour encourage the latter to propose new ideas, offer alternative solutions to problems and generally adopt constructive and useful perspectives.

(c) Change can be introduced more easily, since a works council provides a useful forum for explaining the needs for and implications of new methods.

(d) Management benefits as it is quickly made aware of any problems relating to intended developments that are likely to provoke hostile opposition from the workforce and hence can alter its plans in order to remove or minimise employee resistance.

Although it is known that employee apathy frequently results in works councils not operating within many companies in countries where employee representation is legally required, the *existence* of legislative procedures itself can create an environment in which managers are extremely sensitive to the need to consult with and win over the workforce, leading perhaps to greatly improved management/labour relations.

12. Criticisms of the works council system

Opponents of works councils argue as follows:

(a) Wages and conditions of employment in firms with active and influential works councils tend to be higher than elsewhere, possibly causing companies operating works councils to lose competitive advantage.

(b) The administrative costs of running a works council (executive time, rooms, secretarial support, etc.) can be substantial.

(c) Employees may adopt short-term perspectives, and might oppose decisions that would benefit the company in the long run but do not offer many rewards to employees in the immediate future. Innovation and enterprise may be discouraged.

(d) Decision-taking can be slow, and many employee representatives will not have the technical knowledge upon which they can base decisions.

(e) Efficiency improvements that involve shedding labour might be impeded.

(f) Councils can easily degenerate into vehicles for plant-level collective bargaining, undermining normal management/union negotiating machinery.

13. The Works Council Directive 1994

In 1991 the European Commission issued a Draft Directive that would require EU-wide companies with more than 1000 European employees and at least two establishments in EU states to establish cross-border group or company-wide works councils. Management would be legally obliged to inform and consult these councils on matters relating to job reductions, the introduction of new technology, and changes in working practices. The proposal was vetoed by the British government, but the (then) other eleven EU countries decided to go ahead with the Directive under the procedures established by the Maastricht Protocol (*see* 1:4) agreed in December 1991. Accordingly the UK exercised its opt-out so that when the Directive was finally adopted in 1994 it did not apply within the UK. Note however that British transnational companies employing substantial numbers of workers in subsidiaries in any two of the other 14 EU states (plus Iceland and Norway for this particular piece of legislation) are bound by the Directive in respect of their operations in these states (EIRR 1994).

Under the Directive a cross-frontier group or company-wide works council must have up to 30 members and the right to at least one meeting with management each year. A second meeting can be called in exceptional circumstances. A group or company is not compelled to form such a works council if its employees do not want one, but if the workers express a wish to have a cross-border works council and management fails to respond to a written request for a council to be implemented then legal processes can be invoked to force management to comply with the demand.

The Directive applies to:

(i) *EU scale undertakings*, i.e. those with at least 1000 employees within the EU and at least 150 employees in at least two member states; *and*

(ii) *EU scale groups of companies*, i.e. groups controlled by a single parent and with at least 1000 employees within the EU and possessing at least two undertakings in separate EU states each with at least 150 employees.

The nature, composition and *modus operandi* of a European works council must be set out in a written agreement between management and a 'special negotiating body' (SNB) elected by employee representatives and containing at least one worker representative from each EU state (except Britain) in which the company operates. Negotiations must begin within six months following a request from the SNB, and the council must be established within the next three years. The process of forming a works council is activated when the central management receives a written request from at least 100 employees or their representatives in at least two EU states (or Norway and/or Iceland).

The written agreement itself needs to cover the scope and powers of the council, number of members and their durations of office, election procedures, consultation mechanisms, and the resources and assistance to be given to the council by central management (such assistance is required by law to be of 'appropriate' dimensions). Council members are entitled to paid time off work to attend meetings. Consultations must be 'timely', and conducted on the basis of a report prepared by the central management. However, confidential information that if disclosed would 'substantially damage' the business may be withheld from the council. Whether a specific item of information might cause substantial damage is open to legal challenge. All council members are obliged not to disclose confidential information to third parties. The council is entitled to have professional help of its own choosing, paid for by the management. Even if a workforce decides not to have a works council, its representatives must still be informed of any management proposal likely to have serious consequences for employees in more than one EU state (excluding the UK); notably in relation to mergers, relocations, planned redundancies and intended closures of establishments, organisation changes, and/or the introduction of substantially new technologies or working methods.

BRANCHES, SUBSIDIARIES AND EEIGs

The difference between a branch and a subsidiary is that whereas a branch is regarded in law as a direct extension of the parent firm into a foreign country (so that the parent is legally responsible for all the branch's debts and activities), a subsidiary is a separate business from the parent company. A subsidiary is responsible for its own debts and (unlike a branch) is subject to exactly the same taxes, auditing, registration and accounting regulations as any other local business. A branch and its parent are regarded as parts of the same legal entity, so that the profits/losses of the branch are held to be the profits/losses of the parent (and shown as such in the latter's accounts). A branch does not require its own capital or directors with statutory responsibility for its affairs. Rather, the parent organisation is legally liable for all aspects of the branch's activities. Subsidiaries, on the other hand, are separate legally constituted entities, operating and taxed as if they were any other form of domestic business. Normally, subsidiaries are constituted as private limited companies; raise capital alongside local firms; and maintain their own accounts independent of the parent enterprise.

14. Branches

Typically foreign branches are concerned with the transport and storage of goods, marketing, the provision of after-sales service; and liaison with local banks, advertising agencies, suppliers and distributors, and so on. Local assembly and/or manufacture is normally undertaken by other means. Branches may or may not be required to declare their existences with governmental or local authority business registration offices, but will always be subject to the laws and regulations (including laws on contract and employment) of the host country. The advantages to having a branch (as opposed to a subsidiary) in another EU country include the following:

(a) Branches are easy to set up and dismantle. Registration procedures are usually straightforward, comprising the deposit of a simple form plus translated documents attesting the whereabouts and solvency of the parent firm. No special authorisation to set up a branch in another EU country is necessary; only compliance with local laws concerning the registration of branches of domestic businesses. The normal procedure is for the parent firm to (i) complete a form declaring the branch's existence and detailing its activities, and (ii) deposit with the local tax authorities its translated Articles and Memorandum of Association and/or other statutory documents of the parent company (or comparable details if the parent is some other type of business). In some countries the branch must specify the name and address of at least one person responsible for liaising with the local tax authorities and upon whom legal notices may be served.

(b) Branch accounts do not have to independently audited.

(c) Because a branch is regarded in law as part and parcel of the same firm, cash transfers between branches and their parents can usually be treated as internal company transactions, so that no withholding taxes are involved. (Withholding tax is the percentage of dividends, interest payments, etc., deducted at source as tax by the host nation's fiscal authorities.) Also assets can be transferred from the parent company to the branch without incurring tax liability (i.e. there is no change in the ownership of the assets, as occurs when assets are transferred to a legally autonomous subsidiary). Services also can be 'sold' by head office to the branch.

(d) The contracts of employment of the staff working in a branch can be with the parent organisation. Hence, staff may be paid direct from a head office in another country, possibly creating significant tax advantages.

(e) Losses incurred by a branch can be offset against the parent company's domestic tax (in contrast to losses incurred by subsidiaries, which are treated as losses made by independent firms).

National differences in branch regulation

Tax and management rules for branches can vary enormously from state to state. In Belgium, for example, foreign branches must declare the name and address of a local representative (who need not be a Belgian national) explicitly authorised to enter contracts on the parent's behalf. Failure to register a branch properly in Belgium results in it not being able to initiate legal proceedings (against debtors for instance) within that country. Unusually for European countries, Belgian branches of foreign firms are regarded as separate entities for tax purposes. Income earned by a Belgian branch is calculated and taxed as if it were income accruing to an autonomous subsidiary. A similar situation applies in the Republic of Ireland.

Danish law only recognises branches of foreign limited companies which are officially recognised in their home countries and which possess substantial share capitals. Branches have to register with the Danish Registrar of Companies, and the parent must (i) pledge that its branch will be subject to Danish law in all matters, and (ii) formally authorise named branch managers to enter contracts on its behalf. Copies of the parent's annual accounts have to be deposited with the Danish Registrar of Companies within one month of their publication. In France, a special withholding tax is levied on branch profits, all of which are assumed to be remitted to head office.

Germany recognises two types of branch: dependent and independent. The latter must register as a separate business with the German Trade Registry, and is legally responsible for its own debts. Owners of dependent branches, conversely, assume full liability for all branch activities. Branches pay a special flat rate of tax which differs from the variable tax rates applicable to German companies.

Greece has a regulation whereby branches of foreign companies are only allowed if the parent's share capital corresponds to the minimum requirements applicable to Greek companies. In Spain, the branch of a foreign company can opt either to be taxed as if it were a Spanish business, or may remit its profits to head office and pay a special withholding tax as an advance against Spanish corporation tax, the balance to be paid at the end of the tax year. Austria, Finland and Sweden tax foreign branches in exactly the same way as local firms.

15. Subsidiaries

Potential benefits resulting from the establishment of a subsidiary rather than a branch include:

- Limited liability (thought note how a company can set up a subsidiary limited company in its own country, which then establishes in a foreign nation a branch that, by nature of its ownership, possesses *de facto* limited liability)
- The ability to apply for government regional development assistance and R&D grants on the same terms as any other local business

- A local identity
- The capacity to raise capital in the subsidiary's own name and (importantly) to sell shares to outsiders
- Not having to disclose the annual accounts of the parent organisation
- The ability to undertake internal company reorganisations without having to report this to the foreign authorities
- Possibilities for repatriating profits via a variety of arrangements: dividends, interest payments, royalties, share issues etc., in order to optimise the parent's overall tax position. Note how a subsidiary company may itself be part of a local group of companies that offsets profits and losses.
- The ability to sell off the shares in the subsidiary as soon as it has no further value to the parent company.

A common reason for preferring an independently constituted subsidiary to a branch is that disadvantageous tax situations can arise for branches in certain EU nations where local tax authorities are empowered to tax branch offices on profits deemed to accrue to the parent firm's worldwide operations in consequence of the branch's activities in the country concerned.

Subsidiaries versus branches

In most EU countries branches are required to disclose the accounts of their parent organisation so as to enable the local tax authorities to ascertain how much of the parent's income has been generated by the branch. Exact disclosure requirements are governed by the 1989 Eleventh EU Directive on Company Law, which relieved branches of companies registered in other EU countries from the need to prepare detailed separate accounts, but required them to divulge substantial information concerning the parent company. Further problems with operating a foreign branch are:

(a) Since branches have no share capital they could be more difficult to sell off once they cease to be useful to their parent organisations.

(b) It could be more difficult to optimise the parent's overall tax position when trading through a branch. A subsidiary can repatriate its profits via a variety of arrangements, dividends, interest payments, royalties, share issues, and so on. Also a subsidiary can itself belong to a local group of companies that offset profits and losses.

(c) Changes in organisational relationships between a branch and its parent might have to be reported to the foreign tax authorities.

The critical factor determining whether it is better to own a foreign subsidiary rather than a branch is how quickly the business is expected to move into profit. Normally initial set-up costs, unfamiliarity with local markets and commercial practices, lack of contacts with local business services, etc., result in losses being incurred for the first couple of years of operation. Often it is preferable to run a branch rather than a subsidiary during loss-making periods, essentially because the parent organisation can immediately deduct a branch's losses from its own profits where a separately constituted subsidiary would need to set this year's loss against profits earned in future years. In many EU countries there are no withholding taxes on remittances from branches to their parent companies, whereas (under the 1990 EU Directive on this matter – see below) a five per cent withholding tax will usually be deducted from dividend payments made by a subsidiary. It is not unusual for parent organisations to establish foreign branches in the first place, but then convert these into locally incorporated subsidiary companies as soon as they cease making losses.

Note how branches might themselves be limited liability companies, freshly incorporated or purchased from existing shareholders in the relevant nation. In most (but not all) European countries a business's status as a 'branch' of a parent organisation depends entirely on the fact that the branch has been declared as such to the national business registration authorities, rather than the precise legal structure the operation adopts (company, sole trader, partnership, etc.).

The EU Directive on the Taxation of Subsidiaries 1990

Withholding taxes (*see* above) vary significantly among EU countries, hence greatly influencing the decision whether to establish a subsidiary or a branch in a particular nation. This problem was addressed by the 1990 EU Directive on the Taxation of Subsidiaries in Member States, which eliminated all withholding taxes on remittances from foreign EU subsidiaries. Under the Directive:

- Dividends are taxed at normal rates in the country in which they arise but are then tax free as far as head office (defined as a company with at least a 25 per cent shareholding in the subsidiary) is concerned (although the tax authorities of the head office country have discretion to increase head office's taxable profits by up to five per cent of the value of dividends received); *or*
- Head office pays full domestic corporation tax on dividends received and claims back from the local domestic tax authorities any amount already paid to the tax authorities of the state in which the subsidiary is situated.

Financing subsidiaries

A foreign subsidiary can be financed through borrowings from local banks, issue of shares to the parent, or loans from the parent. Local borrowing is appropriate if the host country has low interest rates. Equity financing creates a share capital which may then be sold to third parties. Frequently, however, loans from the parent company are the best means for financing a subsidiary, because interest payments on loans are regarded in all EU countries as a tax-deductible business expense. The loan can be made in any one of a variety of national currencies, and the scheduling of interest repayments can be varied. The rate of interest charged on the loan by the parent can be as high or as low (including a zero rate of interest) as the parent determines. Also there is none of the administrative work that otherwise would be attached to registering a share issue; no payment of stamp duties, etc.

In order to prevent companies from using unreasonably high interest repayments as a tax-free means for repatriating the subsidiary's earnings back to the parent, certain EU nations (notably France, Luxembourg, Finland and the Netherlands) impose limits on the extents to which loans to a subsidiary may exceed the value of the latter's share capital. Beyond these limits, all interest repayments are taxed as if they were dividends.

16. European Economic Interest Groups (EEIGs)

In 1985 the European Commission introduced a Regulation establishing a procedure whereby combinations of European businesses (companies, partnerships, sole traders, etc.) which extend over at least two EU countries may form legal structures in order to pool common research and development of marketing activities or to manage particular projects. However the EEIG must not seek to make profits 'in its own right'. An EEIG has a separate legal identity, but individual members have unlimited liability for the debts of the entire group. EEIGs need not have any capital and are not required to file annual reports or accounts. The member businesses of an EEIG must themselves decide how the group is to be financed and its revenues distributed. If there is no explicit agreement on this point it is assumed that all participants will contribute equal shares and receive equal revenues. The contract which establishes an EEIG must specify its name (which has to include the words 'European Economic Interest Group' or their initials), address, the objects for which the grouping is formed, details of participants, and the duration of the contract (unless this is indefinite). The contract is then registered in the country in which the EEIG has its head office. A Group can be wound up by a unanimous decision of its members, or will automatically end on expiry of a stated contract period or when the purpose for which the group was set up has been accomplished.

Advantages and problems of EEIGs

The EEIG was made available as a distinct form of European business organisation so as to provide EU firms with a convenient device for undertaking cross-border joint ventures and thus for obtaining the economies of scale available from combining the operations of several enterprises. Benefits accruing to EEIGs include the retention of independent status by each member organisation; the provision of a vehicle through which small firms may collectively bid for large contracts; the pooling of risks; and the ability of a small business to enter new lines of work and unfamiliar territory. Problems with EEIGs are that they are not permitted to employ more than 500 persons, and no single participant is allowed a majority of votes in its management. Hence the EEIG is not a suitable device for implementing cross-border take-overs. Further difficulties with EEIGs (some of which explain why the EEIG has not in fact become a popular means for conducting pan-European business) include the absence of limited liability, their inabilities to seek profit openly and/or to raise equity capital from the general public, and that they offer no significant tax advantages compared to other forms of enterprise.

SPECIAL FORMS OF EUROPEAN BUSINESS

17. National differences in business regulation

Despite the European Commission's numerous attempts at harmonising national laws on business structure there remain many significant differences in the forms of business operating in EU states. Britain for example has 'companies limited by guarantee', i.e. limited companies without share capital where the members guarantee that if the company ceases to trade then each guarantor will make a small contribution (usually £10) towards settlement of the company's debts. Such companies are widely used for educational and other non-profit-making organisations which, nevertheless, required limited liability.

Several EU countries recognise the *co-operative enterprise* as a distinct legal form, with limited liability. Co-operatives are businesses that follow the principle of one vote per member, regardless of the extent of a member's shareholdings in the firm. In Britain a co-operative can acquire limited liability either by registering as a limited company under the Companies Act 1985 and by incorporating co-operative principles into its memorandum and articles of association, or by registering under the Industrial and Provident Societies Acts (IPSA), which defined specific requirements for the administration of co-operatives registered in this way.

German law recognises the status of a trader or merchant (*kaufman*) and some parts of the country's Commercial Code apply only to these individuals. The implication of being a *kaufman* is that (i) a higher level of business awareness is assumed, and (ii) a lower degree of proof is needed to establish the existence of a commercial contract. In the Netherlands there is legal provision for 'professional partnerships' wherein each partner is only liable for an equal share of the firm's debts. If a partner cannot contribute his or her full share to total liabilities then the creditors cannot claim the shortfall from other partners. In Austria there is a special type of partnership, *Kommanditgesellschaft* (KG), that involves companies. This is known as GmbH & Co KG.

Danish company law recognises Associations (*Foreninger*), Foundations (*Fonde*), and Public Corporations (*Offentlige Foretagender*) that trade as distinct forms of business, usually with limited liability. (The same is true for the Netherlands.) Luxembourg permits a special arrangement whereby a holding company is exempt from business taxes on dividends, interest or royalties received from foreign subsidiaries, and there is no withholding tax on dividends paid by the parent organisation to foreign shareholders. The holding company itself might only be a very small firm. A peculiarity of Greek company law is its special provision for 'dispersed' public companies as ongoing legal entities. A dispersed public company is one that has been dissolved but not liquidated and its assets transferred to other public companies. Shareholders are given newly issued shares to evidence their continuing ownership of these assets.

Progress test 10

1. What is a limited partnership?

2. Explain the difference between a private limited company and a public limited company.

3. Give four examples of national differences in laws concerning private limited companies.

4. What is the basic requirement of the Second EU Directive on Company Law 1977?

5. In most EU states, certain classes of people are prohibited from serving on the boards of PLCs. What are these classes of people?

6. What are the implications of the 'retention culture' evident within many continental European companies?

7. What is a Supervisory Board and what are its functions?

8. List the advantages to having employee representatives on company boards.

9. Outline the major provisions of the proposed European Company Statute.

10. What is a works council? What are the main criticisms of the works council system?

11. Explain the difference between a branch and a subsidiary.

12. What are the EU rules concerning withholding taxes on profits earned by subsidiaries?

11

FINANCIAL ASPECTS OF EUROPEAN BUSINESS

CORPORATE FINANCE

1. The financing of European companies

A fundamental difference applies to the approaches to company financing adopted in the UK as opposed to continental EU countries. In Britain (and the USA) companies are regarded as commodities to be traded in exactly the same way as any other marketable item, leading – advocates of the Anglo-American system allege – to optimum efficiency as the forces of supply and demand direct scarce resources towards the most efficient businesses. The shares of many continental European companies, conversely, are held by family and institutional investors, hence making it difficult to acquire companies on the open market. Representatives of banks frequently occupy seats on company boards and help control businesses. There is much debenture and loan financing in continental countries, and many medium/large sized enterprises are family owned. In Italy, for example, there are barely 200 Stock Exchange listed firms, with only two of these having more than half their share capitals in the hands of the general public. (Fiat, Benetton and Olivetti are well known examples of Italian family-owned firms.) Cross-shareholdings between families are common and, of course, this helps to make it difficult for outsiders to acquire Italian companies. In both Spain and France, around 50 per cent of the top 200 companies are family-owned. Nearly half of France's top 200 companies exhibit large (often controlling) family shareholdings.

According to data collected by the European Union's DG II and published in the biennial *Panorama of EU industries*, nearly a quarter of a typical French public company's capital resources during the early 1990s consisted of medium and long term borrowing, compared to just eight per cent in the UK. For Germany the figure was about 18 per cent; in Spain 15 per cent. Italian companies on average had only ten per cent of their capital in the form of medium/long term debt, but compensated for this by drawing 55 per cent of their capital from short-term borrowings. To the extent that continental companies are financed by share issues, these typically involve private placings with large investors, especially banks. Germany is a leading example of how the continental system operates. German companies themselves own about half the country's equity, with banks also holding large blocks of company shares. Banks, moreover, frequently act as proxies for the votes of smaller shareholders. The Supervisory Boards of most German companies include a bank representative. At the same time leading industrialists sit on the boards of all the main German banks hence creating effective two-way communications between the manufacturing and financial sectors.

2. The problem of short-termism

It is sometimes argued that the fact that most continental European companies are difficult to acquire on the open market enables them to adopt long-term perspectives, to plough back profits and to expand and diversify without having to worry about hostile takeover attempts by other firms. Conversely, the ease with which outsiders can acquire significant shareholdings in UK companies results in the latter being obliged to incorporate plans for avoiding being taken over into their overall corporate strategies: causing them perhaps to pay too much to shareholders in the form of dividends; to distort their market share prices; or to assume obligations intended to make them unattractive to predators (selling-off valuable assets for example) when they should instead be concentrating on developing the firm. This 'short termism', as it is known, is also blamed for the continuation of old production methods and the failure to exploit new technologies, since to the extent that managements seek quick financial returns they will be unwilling to invest long term in advanced manufacturing techniques.

Examples of measures that might lead to short-run increases in profit at the expense of long-run growth include:

- Not advertising at all for several months (possibly longer). This saves substantial amounts of money, boosting short-term profits at little cost because sales will continue at previous levels for some time in consequence of consumer loyalty to a brand and the firm's pre-existing reputation. Eventually, however, sales will decline as competitors attack the market and as the brand in question loses public exposure. The cost of subsequently recapturing marketing share could be enormous.
- Cancelling or running down research and development projects.
- Not maintaining buildings, plant and equipment.

3. Disadvantages of the continental approach

A number of problems are created by the continental (especially the German) company financing system. In particular, an 'uneven playing field' *vis-à-vis* merger and takeover activity in different EU nations has emerged. British firms sometimes find that the need to concentrate on short-term issues causes them to lack cash and immediately realisable assets, placing them at a disadvantage compared to continental rivals that possess extensive reserves accumulated over many years. Also the corporate cultures of many European countries are not attuned to the cut and thrust of hostile acquisitions, and shareholders often have to be cajoled and seduced into parting with their shares. Interest rates differ among countries, so that funds for financing acquisitions can be borrowed less expensively in some countries than elsewhere. Moreover, profit retention by firms that do not have to worry about the adverse effects of internal financing on dividends (and hence the market price of the company's shares) have resulted in a large number of cash-rich predator companies in certain nations.

There is an acute shortage of high quality companies for sale in some countries, consequent to the high proportion of continental firms owned by private families and/or that have large blocks of their shares in the hands of large banks and other institutional investors. And even when companies do become available for purchase, the absence of an active share market means there is no market mechanism for valuing them objectively. Share prices represent an acid test of how the astute and commercially knowledgable outside investor sees the worth of a company and its future prospects. Note how the low numbers of companies listed on continental Stock Exchanges has meant there has been little to encourage the development of the company research and information-gathering facilities that exist in Britain, Ireland and certain non-EU nations (especially the USA).

4. The future of continental European equity financing

A number of historical factors account for the differences in company financing arrangements that have arisen between the UK and continental Western Europe during the post-Second World War years. In the past there have been relatively few private pension schemes (which are big investors in equities) in certain European nations; while the non-availability of extensive share trading systems encouraged insurance companies to invest in regional savings banks or government bonds rather than in shares. (German insurance companies, for example, only hold about five per cent of their funds in the form of equities.) There are however a number of reasons for believing that continental attitudes towards equity issue and share trading might change. Long-term economic growth could lead to demands for finance so extensive that they outstrip the capacities of banks, families and institutional investors to satisfy them. And the growing economic power and increasing importance in the global financing systems of France and (particularly) Germany are naturally causing them to become leading financial centres in their own right. This should create an environment generally conducive to the development of financial services industries in these countries and, concomitantly, to more extensive international as well as domestic share trading.

Political stability and steady economic growth during the last 40 years means that Europeans born in the richer EU countries in the next century will inherit wealth, much of which will be invested. Rising levels of affluence have resulted in many continental Europeans having high disposable incomes, some of which is now being invested in shares. For instance, the number of German shareholders increased by 50 per cent between 1987 and 1994 (albeit starting from a low base). Also, younger Europeans are perhaps less risk adverse than the older generation and hence more willing to purchase equities. An important factor here is the implementation of various EU Directives compelling companies to disclose far more information about themselves than previously was the case, so that potential buyers of shares in continental businesses now have hard facts upon which to base their decisions. Share financing, moreover, is particularly suitable for West Europe's emerging high technology industry sectors, which require risk capital that (risk averse) banks are not willing to supply.

EUROPEAN STOCK EXCHANGES

5. European equity markets

Continental European share markets are 'thin': Stock Exchanges have low capitalisations compared with the UK; share trading is irregular and share price movements infrequent. The total value of shares quoted on the London Stock Exchange (i.e. its aggregate 'market capitalisation') is more than double that of the German, Italian and French Stock Exchanges combined. Nevertheless, every European Union country has a Stock Exchange, and their market capitalisations are continuously increasing. Moreover, all EU Exchanges other than the one in Denmark have a well-developed *unlisted securities market* [USM] whereby companies that do not qualify for a full quotation on the nation's main Stock Exchange (e.g. because the firm is too small or has existed for too short a period of time) may raise equity capital and have their shares traded and share prices regularly published in an orderly and regulated way. The reason for Denmark's slow progress towards establishing a substantial USM is that the Copenhagen Exchange only started to develop in the late 1980s (prior to 1986 there was very little competition among Danish share dealers) so that many Danish companies chose to obtain listings on the Luxembourg or London Stock Exchanges rather than at home. Many exchanges also provide a further market for recognised but minimally supervised share transactions. These are sometimes called 'Third Markets' or 'Over-the-Counter' markets, depending on the rules and circumstances of the Exchange of the country concerned.

Major differences between European Stock Exchanges occur in relation to the following:

(a) The bases upon which national share price indexes are constructed vary from state to state, making it difficult to compare average equity performances in different countries in meaningful ways. Most Exchanges have an all-share General Return Index which includes capital gains as well as dividends, and a 'spot' index which excludes the latter. Thereafter however a plethora of share indices exist, varying in relation to the number of securities included (e.g. the top 25, 50 or 100 shares) and the criteria used for their selection. The latter might be company size, value of shares, or how actively the shares are traded.

(b) The types of shares transacted: voting, non-voting or multiple vote securities (the latter two categories are not allowed in some countries); preference or ordinary; bearer or non-bearer. Ordinary shares are shares that have no special rights or privileges in relation to dividends or the division of assets on dissolution of a company. Ordinary shares with votes are called B shares; those without,

A shares. Preference shares are non-voting shares which (i) carry a fixed rate of dividend payable from a company's profits before ordinary shareholders receive any dividend and (ii) take precedence over ordinary shareholders for the repayment of capital when the company is wound up. Bearer shares belong to and may be traded by the person who possesses them at any given moment. Registered (non-bearer) shares, conversely, can only be sold by the person listed as their owner in the company's register of shareholders.

(c) Involvement of pension funds and/or insurance companies in the market. The extents to which these organisations may lawfully invest in shares are restricted in some countries.

(d) Whether open share trading may occur outside a nation's authorised Stock Exchanges. Third and/or over-the-counter markets operate in many countries, and the stringency of the rules that control them varies substantially between national Exchanges. The laws of France, Belgium, Spain and Italy insist that all open share trading (i.e. excluding private one-to-one share transfer deals) be undertaken via Stock Exchange controlled and supervised markets; Britain, Germany and the Netherlands have no such restrictions.

(e) Commission rates taken by share dealers. These vary from 0.25 per cent to two per cent according to transaction size and country.

6. Pan-European share trading

Formation of a fully integrated pan-European equities market would create many benefits for European companies and investors, and progress towards the establishment of an all-European Stock Exchange is actively encouraged by the European Commission. Specific potential advantages include:

- facilitation of an efficient and competitive Single Market in financial services
- open access to all EU Exchanges for finance-seeking companies and private and institutional investors
- the development of mechanisms for transmitting investor information instantly between national Exchanges
- construction of comparable share price indexes in different states
- encouragement of wider share ownership and equity financing by European firms
- increased availability of company finance
- downwards pressure on share dealers' commissions and share flotation expenses in consequence of an intensification of (pan-European) competition.

Unfortunately, however, all attempts at integrating European Exchanges have so far failed. Indeed it is arguable that integrative measures are not even necessary because a *de facto* pan-European share market already exists, based on London and supported by SEAQ (the London Exchange's computerised trading system). Deals are concluded by telephone rather than screen-to-screen and, critically, the market is not regulated. The anxiety sometimes expressed within

191

European Exchanges is that formalisation of pan-European share trading arrangements is almost certain to lead to EU-level regulation and the imposition of bureaucratic inhibitory rules.

Many difficulties arise in relation to the choice of information technology to be used in an integrated pan-European system. All EU Stock Exchanges are now computerised, but use different hardware and software. SEAQ International is firmly embedded in the UK system, yet has a number of incompatibilities with France's Eurolist and Germany's Ibis. Changing the system in some Exchanges will be expensive and it is unclear who should bear the cost. Another major problem is the continuing need to issue written share certificates following every share transfer. It has been agreed in principle that this should cease (i.e. that evidence of share ownership be 'dematerialised' and that some sort of transactions receipt be used as proof of title).

7. EU Directives concerning Stock Exchanges

Quoted (Listed) companies are those which are recognised by the relevant national Stock Exchange and whose shares are traded on the main market of the Exchange. The market prices of these shares are published on (at least) a daily basis. European Stock Exchanges are subject to three EU Directives on procedures for share listing:

1 The Admissions Directives of 1979, which lays down minimum conditions for the admission of securities to Stock Exchanges in EU countries.

2 The 1980 Directive on Listing Particulars that sets out the information to be published by a company when obtaining a listing. This was subsequently amended by the 1987 Directive on the Mutual Recognition of Listing Particulars in order to ensure that a company listed on the Exchanges of one member state could easily obtain a quotation on others.

3 The Disclosure of Information Directive 1982 which specifies the information to be regularly published by listed companies.

Additionally the 1989 Directive on Prospectuses specifies the minimum information to be provided in prospectuses that invite the purchase of transferable shares in unlisted companies. Under the Directive, a prospectus approved for this purpose in one member state is automatically acceptable in others. Further EU legislation to control USMs and Third Markets is planned. The case for strict regulation of off-market trading concerns the need for investor protection and the desirability of 'share price transparency', i.e. that share prices reflect true market forces and not be manipulated behind the scenes by off-market operators. The trend in national legislation on this matter is towards greater regulation, with securities firms in an increasing number of European countries being required to report on a daily basis all share transactions completed outside official Stock Exchanges.

The Directive on Collective Investment Schemes 1985 sets out certain requirements for the establishment and administration of unit trusts and the information that must be provided to unit holders. A trust that complies with the

Directive may market itself in any EU state, subject to local financial services advertising regulations. The Directive also guarantees free cross-border trade in unit trusts.

A problem for the European Commission when drafting proposed legislation on share issue and transfer is that different types of Stock Exchange regulatory body operate in various EU countries. In Germany the national banking authorities have ultimate control over securities markets; in Spain and the Netherlands there is direct government supervision; the UK relies entirely on voluntary regulation via internal Stock Exchange Codes of Practice; while Ireland and France have a mixture of legislative and voluntary controls. Critics of the self-regulatory approach allege that the financial rewards for ignoring voluntary guidelines are so great that abuse is inevitable. Equally, however, policing statutory controls is extremely difficult and, some argue, they stifle enterprise and initiative. And it is virtually impossible to draft laws that are precise enough to cover every conceivable eventuality.

FINANCE OF CROSS-BORDER TRADE

8. Management of foreign exchange risk

A business which invoices its foreign customers in terms of local foreign currency, or which accumulates foreign currencies for some other reason, runs the risk that the exchange rates of these foreign currencies will depreciate in value relative to the firm's home country currency between the moments that contracts are signed and when the money is actually received. Hence less domestic currency is obtained for a given amount of foreign currency after the exchange rate has moved in the home country's favour. To avoid this risk the exporter can sell to its bank, in advance, the foreign currency that its customers have been invoiced to pay. The bank will quote a fixed forward exchange rate for these transactions, which will apply to the conversions regardless of the actual spot exchange in force one month or three months (say) from today.

The bank will demand a reward for its services and therefore will quote an exchange rate for forward currency transactions which differs from the current spot exchange rate by an amount sufficient to cover the bank's exposure to risk and make a profit. This obviously represents a (significant) cost to the exporter.

An exporting firm that invoices in local currency and which expects the spot exchange rate to move in its favour (so that it stands to raise more domestic currency when it eventually comes to convert than if it converted today) may decide not to bother with forward cover. Another possibility available to exporters scheduled to receive foreign currency payments over a long period is to enter into an *option contract* with its bank whereby the exporter is given the right to sell to the bank foreign currency up to an agreed limit at a predetermined rate at any time within the next twelve months. If the spot exchange rate moves in one direction the exporter will exercise the option; if it moves in the other the option will not be taken up, forfeiting thereby the fee paid to the bank to purchase the option.

Further devices for avoiding foreign exchange risk include the following:

(a) *Swap arrangements* whereby two or more firms in different countries agree to lend their surplus cash to each other on a reciprocal basis. Suppose for example that a French company needs German Deutschemarks to pay for imports from Germany. It might have an arrangement with a German business whereby the latter lends (at low interest) to the French firm the Deutschemarks necessary to settle the import transaction. When the German company imports from France and requires Francs it borrows these from the French firm. The two loans will then be balanced-off against each other at a predetermined currency rate of exchange. This can be cheaper than using the forward exchange market and (importantly) may be used to circumvent national exchange control regulations.

(b) Inclusion of *renegotiation clauses* in all sales contracts to enable an exporter automatically to change the contract price in the event of significant exchange rate fluctuations.

(c) Accumulation of (interest earning) foreign currency balances in various countries, to be exchanged for other currencies at appropriate moments or used to purchase local products for subsequent exporting to other markets. Note how this imposes additional costs and inconvenience on the exporting company relative to locally based rivals.

9. Settlement of international transactions

Payment by cheque or credit transfer is known as *open account* settlement. Exporting businesses that are not prepared to accept the risks of customer default attached to open account trading may be able to use bills of exchange or letters of credit (see below) to finance international transactions. Alternatively, the exporter can use the services of an export *credit factoring* company which will purchase, at a discount, invoices issued to foreign customers as the goods are supplied. This is discussed in **15** below.

Bills of exchange

A bill of exchange is a written instruction sent by an employer to an importer ordering the importer to pay to the exporter, or anyone specified by the exporter, a certain sum of money either on receipt of the bill, or at a specified date in the future (e.g. in three months' time). A bill that requires payment immediately or within three days of acceptance is called a sight bill or draft; one that is to be settled in the future is referred to as a term, usance or tenor bill. The seller is the 'drawer' of the bill, the buyer the 'drawee', the seller's bank is known as the 'remitting' bank and the importer's bank the 'collecting' bank.

10. Uses for bills of exchange

Bills of exchange can be used for acceptance credit transactions, for documentary collections, or for forfaiting (*see* **11**). Acceptance credit transactions occur when the exporter sends a bill of exchange to a foreign importer, who 'accepts' it (by signing the bill) and returns it to the exporter. Once accepted the bill becomes a *negotiable instrument*, i.e. it can be sold to another party. Hence one possible way of dealing with an accepted bill is for the exporting firm to sell it to its own bank at a discount. The bank then collects the money when the bill matures. Thus the bank assumes the risk of non-payment. A documentary collection involves the exporter handing over a bill of exchange to its own bank, together with various documents (e.g. the insurance certificate, invoice, transit documents) required by the customer prior to taking delivery. The exporter's bank now sends the bill to the customer for acceptance. If the bill is a sight bill, the customer accepts it and returns it to the exporter's bank, which now becomes responsible for collecting the money. All the documents which provide title to the goods are handled by the exporter's bank, which will only release them to the customer at the time of payment.

It is of course open for the exporting firm to keep the bill until it falls due for payment and itself collect the money, or borrow the money from its bank using the accepted bill as security. In the latter case the bank might want a guarantee that the bill will definitely be settled, e.g. by requiring the importer's bank to promise to honour the bill if the importer defaults. The term *avalised bill of exchange* is applied to a bill that carries such an undertaking. If the bill is not avalised and the buyer defaults then the bank will still expect the exporting company to repay the loan. This is known as 'with recourse financing', i.e. the bank can demand compensation from the exporter if the customer defaults.

In the event of a customer defaulting on a bill of exchange the first step towards recovery through local courts is to have the bill protested. This means getting a notary public (i.e. a local person legally qualified to attest and certify documents) to ask the customer for payment or reasons for non-payment. The latter are put into a formal deed of protest which is then placed before a local court as evidence of dishonour.

11. Forfaiting

A company engaged on a long-term and expensive project with a large customer can have the latter accept a bundle of bills of exchange, each maturing on a different date. The first bill could be payable after six months, the second after 18 months, the third after three years, etc., up to the last bill maturing on completion of the project. These accepted bills may now be discounted *en bloc* with the company's own bankers.

The advantages of forfaiting are that it is financing without recourse (although the exporter's bank may insist that the bills of exchange be avalised) and that since bills of exchange are sold to the bank at today's known rate of discount the exporter pays what is in effect a fixed rate of interest on the money raised. The amount available to the exporter is known with certainty and there is no risk of currency exchange rate depreciation, so that forward planning is facilitated.

Problems with forfaiting include the loss of revenue resulting from discounting the bills, bankers' administrative fees, and the need to persuade customers to accept bills of exchange issued for work that will not be completed or goods that will not be supplied until a long time in the future.

12. Letters of credit

Foreign importers who are little known in the exporter's country will experience difficulty in ordering goods because suppliers (and their bankers) will fear non-payment of accounts. Thus, importers commonly arrange for established banks (preferably in the exporter's country) to guarantee final payment. Banks which agree to do this will issue to foreign importers *letters of credit* in which they formally assume responsibility for settling importers' debts, subject to the conditions laid down in the letters of credit. These conditions normally relate to the receipt by the importer's bank of a number of properly completed documents (including documents of title) relating to the transaction, notably the transport document (bill of lading, air waybill or whatever), the invoice, insurance certificate and (where appropriate) dangerous goods notices, packing lists, pre-inspection certificates, bank indemnities, and so on. A bill of exchange might also be included in the bundle. A 'confirmed' letter of credit is one the settlement of which has been guaranteed by a bank in the exporter's own country. The exporter is paid by its local confirming bank, which then collects the money from the foreign bank issuing the credit. The confirming bank has no claim on the exporter if the credit is not honoured. Currently, nearly all letters of credit are irrevocable, meaning that they cannot be arbitrarily cancelled by the customer.

13. Settlement by letter of credit

The first step in letter of credit settlement is for the foreign customer to approach its bank (called the 'issuing' or 'opening' bank) and ask it to open a letter of credit in the exporter's favour. The letter of credit will specify when payment is to be made (e.g. on presentation of documents or at a later date) and which documents must be submitted prior to the paying bank releasing the money. On issuing the letter of credit the bank assumes liability for the debt. Then the exporter or its bank (known as the 'advising' bank) is informed that the credit has been opened and of the exact conditions to be met prior to releasing the money. The goods are now sent off and the documents forwarded to the bank that is to pay the money. A bill of exchange may or may not be included in the documents depending on the precise terms of the credit. On receipt of the documents the paying bank checks them and, if they are in order, releases payment. Alternatively, if payment is to be through a bill of exchange, the bank accepts and returns this on behalf of the customer. In the latter case it is the bank and not the customer that honours the bill of exchange when it matures.

CREDIT MANAGEMENT

To compete successfully in the European Single Market firms must be prepared to quote local currency prices, accept foreign currency cheques as payment, and offer whatever credit is customary in the country concerned. Why otherwise should customers bother buying from a foreign supplier rather than from nearby businesses? These realities have led to a significant rise in the magnitude of outstanding cross-border debt. Economic recession, moreover, has caused significant expansions in the numbers of bankruptcies in all EU states. Accordingly, supplying firms need either (i) to remove (at a cost) the risks of customer default through factoring or invoice discounting (*see* **15**) or by purchasing insurance against non-payment, or (ii) to develop expertise in the techniques of cross-border debt collecting.

14. The 1994 EU Recommendation on Credit Periods for Commercial Transactions

Average credit periods lengthened sharply in several EU member states during the early 1990s. In 1994, for example, over a quarter of all EU enterprises had to wait more than three months for payment; eight per cent waited for more than 120 days. The average contractual credit period was 66 days. In Italy it was 90 days, France 70 days, Belgium 57 days and Germany 43 days. Late payments (i.e. those received after the contracted credit period) were creating major problems for small businesses. Payments were late by an average 23 days in the UK (double the EU average of 13 days), and by 20 days in France and Italy (Justica 1994). It seemed moreover that over a third of all late payments were intentional (43 per cent for cross-border transactions). In response to this situation the European Commission put forward in 1994 a Recommendation on Credit Periods for Commercial Transaction, with a view to turning the Recommendation into a Draft Directive in 1997 if late payment periods did not reduce. The Recommendation advises national governments to:

- create legal frameworks that will allow victims of late payment easily to enforce contracted credit periods. This could be achieved via low-cost procedures for reaching out-of-court settlements and by simplifying litigation processes.
- ensure that public sector purchasers do not insist on excessively long credit periods, and never longer than 60 days
- establish the legal right to interest on delayed payments
- remove any tax benefits that might accrue to delaying the settlement of bills
- generate information on the problem and how it can be solved
- encourage firms to improve their training of staff dealing with payments.

The Draft Directive on Cross-Border Credit Transfers 1994

Europeans expect to pay for goods supplied from other EU countries using their own currency and on the same terms and conditions (including credit arrangements) as are available from local firms. They are not generally interested in bills of exchange, letters of credit, or any other paraphernalia concerned with non-EU international trade. Currently about eighty-five per cent of cross-border EU transactions are settled by cheque, and the figure is increasing. Cross-border money transfers have therefore become a major issue for many European firms. The purpose of this Draft Directive is to help small businesses combat difficulties experienced when making cross-border payments. These problems include delays, high fees, double charging, and difficulties arising from unsuccessful bank transfers. If implemented the Draft Directive will require the following:

(a) Banks will have to complete cross-border payments within the time scale agreed with the customer. In the absence of a specific agreement, the bank of the party originating the transaction (i.e. the 'originating bank') must complete the transfer within five working days. The bank of the beneficiary then has to ensure that the latter receives the money within one further working day.

(b) If the transfer is not effected within the contracted period (or five working days if no formal agreement exists), the originator's bank will be required to pay interest to the client making the transfer (unless the latter was responsible for the delay). Similarly the beneficiary's bank will be liable for interest if any delay exceeds the agreed time scale (or one working day *in absentia*).

(c) Double charging will be prohibited. This arises when both the originator's bank and the beneficiary bank deduct charges from the transfer despite instructions from the originator's bank that all charges have already been levied. Any amount overcharged will have to be reimbursed. The beneficiary's bank will be able to impose an administrative charge, but this must not exceed the amount applicable to a comparable domestic transfer.

(d) Banks will be required to provide precise written information in advance to their customers on (i) how long it will take to transfer the money to the beneficiary's bank, (ii) the charges payable, and (iii) procedures for obtaining redress if things go wrong. Charges must be clearly itemised in the customer's bank statement. If the originator authorises the deduction of a charge from the amount transferred, the beneficiary must be informed of this by his or her own bank. These provisions are known as the 'transparency' aspect of the Draft Directive.

(e) Clients must be reimbursed for unsuccessful transfers. The onus will be on the bank to inform its client that money has not been transferred.

15. Factoring and invoice discounting

Factoring involves the outright sale (at a discount) of debts owed to the company to an outside body in exchange for cash. The factor takes over the administration of the client company's invoices, collects the money and (importantly) assumes the risk of customer default. How much is paid for the invoices is subject to negotiation but will depend ultimately on the magnitudes of debt involved, the degree of risk, and the extent of the paperwork needed to collect payment. The cost of the factor's services typically breaks down into four components:

(a) A service charge of perhaps one or two per cent of the value of sales to cover the cost of administering invoices.

(b) A financing charge (equivalent to loan interest) on the money turned over to the company by the factor. This will normally be three to five per cent above bank base rate and is payable on the period between the company's receipt of cash from the factor and the dates when creditors settle their bills.

(c) A premium of about one per cent to cover the cost of bad debts.

(d) Extra charges for legal fees incurred by the factor while collecting money owed against invoices.

Advantages to factoring include the following:

(a) Regular cash flows are assured. Hence the company can settle its own bills promptly (possibly obtaining cash discounts from suppliers) and hence will acquire a high credit rating (Hawkins 1993).

(b) Other lines of credit are left open.

(c) Low administrative costs for managing the firm's sales ledger, and no debt collecting.

(d) The method is simple and convenient.

(e) Gearing (i.e. the ratio of a firm's indebtedness to the value of its assets) is not affected.

(f) Factors are expert in debt-collecting techniques and may be able to persuade recalcitrant debtors to settle their outstanding balances more convincingly than could the company's own accounts staff.

(g) Many factors offer ancillary services to their clients, e.g. information on customers' credit status; industry norms for prices and terms and conditions of sale; news about which regions and/or industries are experiencing recession (evidenced by exceptionally late payments by firms in these industries/regions), and so on.

With invoice discounting, the company receives a cash payment (effectively a loan) from the invoice discounter against the value of the invoices issued to customers, but retains responsibility for debt collection and for an agreed proportion of bad debts.

Factoring and invoice discounting can avoid disruptions in cash flow caused by customers delaying payment for their credit purchases. They are sources of finance in the sense that cash is rapidly injected into the business following the sale of goods, thus enabling the firm to avoid having to wait for payment or borrow from other sources.

Problems with factoring and invoice discounting

Factoring and invoice discounting, while convenient, can be expensive compared to the interest payable on loans. Also, the client company is usually expected to sign a twelve-month agreement with the factor or discounter so that it becomes locked into using factoring/discounting services.

A problem with factoring is the client company's loss of contact with its customers where debt settlement is concerned. Either the factor will collect debts under its own name – which might irritate the client's customers – or under the client's own letterhead. In the latter case, however, it will still purchase long-outstanding debts vigorously – in the client's name – regardless of possible damaging effects on customer relations.

Factors and invoice discounters are not usually interested in contracts with very small businesses. While it is possible to arrange factoring/discounting for smaller firms, the fees charged will be high relative to the turnovers of such enterprises.

16. Payments insurance

In all EU countries insurance against foreign customers not paying their bills may be obtained from private insurers and/or from government-backed schemes. Cover may be comprehensive or specific. Comprehensive policies offer guarantees against all short-term credit for projects involving major capital goods. Comprehensive cover applies to transactions involving up to six months' credit and will indemnify losses incurred through insolvency of or failure to pay by the foreign customer, the latter's refusal to accept goods already despatched and extra handling or transport charges owing to the necessary diversion of a consignment from its planned route, if these cannot be recovered from the buyer. Export credit insurers will not offer full indemnity to exporting firms, which must normally bear 10 to 15 per cent of the loss. Full indemnity might encourage firms to exercise insufficient care in choosing potential customers.

Throughout the world, national governments subsidise the cost of export credit insurance offered by the state-backed insurer in order to give their domestic firms a competitive edge in international markets. To prevent this, 22 of the world's leading industrialised nations concluded in 1978 a Consensus Arrangement aimed at limiting state subsidy of export insurance. Minimum interest rates and maximum repayment periods were specified in order to avoid 'interest rate wars' between countries as national governments increasingly contributed to firms' export insurance costs. There is moreover an EU Draft Directive that seeks to harmonise European practices on these matters, as outlined below.

The Draft Directive on the harmonisation of export credit in Europe 1994

All EU governments offer state-backed credit insurance facilities to exporting firms. This encourages exports and can give companies cost advantages over foreign rivals when bidding for contracts. Critics of the practice allege that:

- Competition among firms in various EU countries is distorted because different governments provide different levels of subsidy.

- The costs to national governments are enormous. In the three years 1991-93 the (then) EU twelve spent seven billion ECU on underwriting export credit insurance.
- Countries outside the EU are impelled to retaliate by offering even larger insurance subsidies to their own exporters.

If implemented the Draft Directive will establish common principles for guarantees and the fixing of premiums in relation to state-supported medium to long-term credit insurance, and will require transparency of cover policies (i.e. clear statements of how premiums are calculated and the precise cover involved) in order to identify differences in the premiums charged for the same policies in various nations. The Draft Directive sets guidelines for the types of risk that should and should not be covered in insurance contracts, the percentages of losses to be covered, and other rules. It specifies premium levels for various categories of risk, and the criteria to be used to determine the extent of the cover that is to be made available for exports to particular countries. Key aims of the proposal are that:

- Premium levels should reflect the degrees of risk attached to transactions and, in the long-term, should cover the costs arising from claims.
- Exporters and export credit granting agencies should be encouraged to make responsible judgements when deciding to insure particular transactions. Hence a proportion of the loss must be left with the exporter.
- Premiums and cover details should be progressively aligned among EU member nations, although the latter will still be able to vary policies and charges as market circumstances alter.

17. Cross-border debt collecting

Debt collecting in foreign countries is troublesome, time-consuming and expensive. Foreign lawyers may have to be engaged; procedures are lengthy and outcomes uncertain. Correspondence and/or telephone calls need to be made in foreign languages; customers cannot conveniently be visited in order to discuss their debts; and there are major differences in the legal measures that can be taken against customers who persistently refuse to pay. Enforcement of Court orders is straightforward in some countries, complex and tedious in others. The laws of most EU countries provide for the following remedies (or their local equivalents):

(a) Attachment of earnings orders whereby the debtor's employer must pay the debtor's wages directly to the judgement creditor.

(b) Garnishee orders under which a third party owing money to the debtor has to remit it to the creditor.

(c) Warrants of execution that direct the Court bailiff to seize and liquidate the debtor's assets.

(d) Writs of equitable execution, to confiscate the debtor's income from rent and/or the sale of land.

(e) Orders to prevent debtors selling their assets until their debts have been settled.

(f) Bankruptcy of the debtor.

TAX AND VAT

18. Taxation

Progress towards the harmonisation of the tax regimes of EU countries has been slow, essentially because tax changes are a crucial weapon for managing an economy and governments are (to say the least) loathe to surrender national sovereignty in this respect (Jeffcote 1993). Each EU country has the right to tax its citizens and businesses as it wishes (subject to a handful of EU Directives relating to cross-border transactions) and, at the time of writing, there are no plans to establish a harmonised Union-wide business tax system with standardised rates, allowances, and so on. Important disparities in national tax systems exist in relation to levels of corporation and personal income tax, periodicity of tax payments, rates and treatment of withholding tax on dividends, the taxation of mergers, and whether the tax authorities levy tax on the source of a transaction or on the recipient of the revenue arising from the deal. Companies in some countries pay tax on the basis of the figures contained in their annual accounts; in others according to published changes in the net worth of the business as shown in its balance sheet; or according to special rules imposed by national tax authorities (quite independent of internal or published accounts).

Numerous problems emerge from this situation. The pattern of competition is distorted across the entire EU, especially in areas where substantial government grants for regional development and / or research and technical development can be obtained. Pan-European mergers and acquisitions may be impeded; there is less incentive for businesses to operate in certain EU nations. A company that operates throughout Europe will find that the enormous ranges of tax reliefs, tax payment arrangements, bi-lateral double taxation deals between various pairs of EU countries, etc., lead to substantial disparities in post-tax rates of profitability in different states, with the choice of location of a company's head office drastically affecting its net tax position. Hence it is possible for EU nations to compete against each other through offering higher and higher tax concessions intended to attract foreign investment.

In 1991–92 the European Commission convened a committee of experts under the chairmanship of Onno Ruding (a former Dutch finance minister) to examine the sources and consequences of distortions in the internal EU market likely to arise from differences in taxation among EU states. This committee concluded that it would not be possible to harmonise direct taxes across the EU until a common currency and full economic and political union had taken place. In the meantime, the committee recommended the establishment of a minimum rate for corporation tax across the EU (to prevent tax competition among EU nations); total transparency of corporate tax incentives; a general tightening and extension of the scope of existing Company Law Directives; and immediate harmonisation of double-taxation agreements (Ruding 1992).

Political arguments prevented the adoption of the Ruding proposals, although the European Commission has promised to put forward several of the major recommendations as Draft Directives over the next few years.

19. Value added tax

Value added tax (VAT) is a tax levied at each stage in the production and distribution process. A business charges VAT to its customers but may reclaim the VAT it pays when purchasing its own supplies, i.e. it pays tax only on 'value added' to inputs. At present, cross-border sales are free of domestic VAT, but are subject to import tax (now known as *acquisition tax*) levied at the domestic rate of VAT applicable in the importing EU country. This tax is levied on the CIF value (*see* 15:**17**) of the imported goods. However, firms selling across national EU borders must (1) quote the customer's VAT number on each invoice, (2) prepare a quarterly return stating the total sales to each VAT registered customer, and (3) be able to provide a full description of the goods. If foreign customers are not registered for VAT in their own countries they must be charged the domestic rate applicable within the exporter's country and the fact that this has been done reported to the exporting country's VAT authorities.

For mail order distance selling the exporter must charge the exporting country's rate of VAT to any non-VAT registered foreign EU customer *until* the exporting firm's annual sales in each country exceed certain threshold levels, at which point the firm must register with their VAT authorities and thereafter charge local VAT and hand this over to the VAT authorities in each country in which the threshold is exceeded. Unfortunately, threshold values vary from country-to-country. There are no customs duties on goods moving between EU member states, although excise duties are payable on certain items (alcohol, for instance).

ACCOUNTING SYSTEMS

20. Financial accounting systems

Major differences in national accounting laws, standards and conventions apply, *inter alia*, to the following matters:

(a) Methods for taking profit on long-term contracts, e.g. as a single lump on completion of the project or through spreading the revenues over several periods. German companies, for example, must record the profits resulting from long-term investments only in the single accounting period in which the profits are realised, leading to peaks and troughs in observed profitability (although the profits may, of course, be smoothed out for tax purposes).

(b) Valuation of intellectual property and whether it can be depreciated.

(c) The formulae applied to the depreciation of fixed assets (plus the writing-down allowances permitted by national tax authorities and the range of assets that may be depreciated). Note that in the Netherlands, fixed assets are always valued at their replacement cost rather than at historical cost as is the general continental practice.

(d) Treatment of monies paid-in to company pension funds. In the majority of EU nations, companies do not have to disclose their expected future obligations *vis-à-vis* meeting retired employees' company pensions. Yet this is a formal requirement in Denmark, Ireland, Finland and Sweden.

(e) Valuation of inventories and work-in-progress. The basis upon which inventories are valued has to be disclosed in accounts prepared in Germany, the UK, Norway and the Netherlands, but not in Luxembourg or Finland. In Germany, inventories may be valued using a wide variety of methods other than the conventional 'lower of cost or market value' (which is legally necessary in several EU nations).

(f) Whether and/or in what circumstances companies are permitted to revalue their assets and, if so, whether the revaluations attract tax penalties.

(g) Extent of 'creative accounting'. The book values of profits in UK firms are frequently reported as being higher than in the accounts of comparable continental businesses. Wider shareholding and equity financing in the UK means that companies must appear to be profitable in order to defend their share price and attract new investment. Bank and family financing of companies (common in other EU countries) removes this need. Creative accounting is virtually unknown in the Netherlands, where accountants have traditionally adopted a strict 'economic' approach to the valuation of assets. It is difficult also in France and Germany, where accounting is effectively a branch of the law and where there exist detailed legal prescriptions over how accounts have to be presented (Alexander 1993).

Role of auditors

Auditors in the UK and Ireland must certify that a company's accounts are 'true and fair'; whereas auditors in France, Germany and Italy have to declare that the accounts are legal. The stringency of audits varies from state to state, and there is much discussion within accounting circles as to whether the EU should legislate to make auditing requirements more or less rigorous. To date there has been little EU-level legislation in this area other than the Eighth Company Law Directive 1984 concerning the level of ability of persons responsible for auditing company accounts. Under the Directive, auditors must:

- have a basic education of university entrance level, have completed a minimum of three years' practical training and passed a university level examination, or – for people whose basic education has not reached university entrance level – have 15 years' relevant experience or have combined seven years experience with a course of practical training and (in all cases) passed the same university level examination

- be independent and persons of good repute
- complete audits with 'professional care'.

An auditor who qualifies in one EU country may become a member of the relevant professional body for auditors in another without having to requalify. If there are significant differences in the nature and extent of the training needed to become an auditor in each of the two nations then the person may be required to take a test or undergo a period of supervised practice not exceeding three years.

The European Commission has proposed the abolition of the requirement that exists in some EU countries for the accounts of all small companies to be audited. Arguments in favour of abolition are that compulsory audits impose an unjustified expense on small firms (which by law have to pay high fees for work that normally has no practical consequence), and that some of the most spectacular business swindles in history have been perpetuated by firms whose accounts have been declared 'true and fair' by independent auditors. Counter-arguments are that statutory audits (i) discourage casual lawbreaking by small companies and (ii) provide at least some information to those who need to trade with them.

Need for harmonisation of accounting standards

Harmonisation of accounting standards and practices across all EU member countries is desirable because the adoption of comparable standards, method-ologies and financial reporting procedures in EU states should greatly facilitate the consolidation of the Single Market: investors and others will be able to compare like with like when analysing companies in various EU nations; newly established firms should be able (through examining competitors' accounts) to identify the most profitable fields of operations; and national governments will be able to adopt common positions on the taxation of companies (Gammie 1992). Crucial disparities in national accounting practices have arisen in consequence of historical differences between, on the one hand, countries in which the principle of financial accounting was to satisfy the requirements of government tax authorities, and on the other, nations with developed equity capital markets where meaningful published accounts were necessary in order to provide information to shareholders. Accounting regulation in nations where tax con-siderations predominated became highly legalistic, and even today follow gov-ernment rules rather than standards established by professional accounting bodies. This makes the accountant's job more straightforward, but the depth of the financial information generated has not been as extensive in these countries as in other states. An important consequence of the distinction between the two approaches is that whereas accounts prepared for tax purposes tend to under-state a company's performance in order to save tax, the reverse is true where the intention is to raise capital from external sources. Another influence on the extent of detail contained within company accounts has been the role of local banks in supplying business finance, since the extensive use of bank financing reduces the impetus for firms to produce sophisticated accounts for examination by equity investors.

The European Commission is anxious to harmonise accounting standards. It has set up an Accounting Advisory Forum, to which all EU national accountancy bodies, standards setters and representatives of main users of accounting information belong (Hegarty 1993; Van Hulle 1993). National EU accounting bodies have themselves formed the International Accounting Standards Committee (IASC), which is devising common standards to recommend to the European Commission. Convergence of accounting practices within the EU is also encouraged by the fact that qualified European accountants may practise in other EU member states (subject to their passing a test on local commercial law and taxation) and cross-border mobility is encouraged by the improved comparability of accounting practices in EU member states. There are, however, arguments against the compulsory harmonisation of standards at the pan-European level, as follows:

(a) Legislation is not necessary, because firms which refuse to provide full information about themselves will not be able to attract investors or obtain credit so that laws compelling disclosure are not required.

(b) The need to publish detailed accounts may discourage firms from taking risks and spending large amounts on research and technical development (for fear of adverse shareholder reaction).

(c) Disclosures by small businesses could make them vulnerable to attack from larger rivals, e.g. through divulging a small firm's heavy dependence on certain sources of income or by revealing a perilous cash flow situation. Knowledge of the latter might impel a large competitor to initiate a price war intended to knock the small firm out of business. Also a small company forced to disclose that it is highly profitable could become the target of unwelcome attempted takeovers.

(d) Irrespective of legal rules on disclosure, companies can still manipulate their accounts to appear more favourable than is actually the case.

Future of European financial accountancy

The market demand for qualified accountants in European Union countries has been stimulated by various EU Company Law Directives which have prescribed standard formats for balance sheets and other published accounts, for the valuation of assets and for the structure of consolidated accounts issued by groups of companies based in EU territory. The Fourth Directive (*see* 8:**3**) is especially important in requiring that company accounts be 'true and fair', although it fails to provide detailed rules or guidance on what this actually means in practice.

According to the European Commission, the overwhelming majority of the EU's accountants reside and practice in the United Kingdom, which has nearly four times the number of qualified accountants as Italy, the next most 'accountant-intensive' nation in Europe. Italy itself has three times more accountants than France, and eight times more than Germany (although the latter has in addition about 40,000 'Steuerberater' who, although they must pass an elementary examination in book-keeping, are not accountants in the normal meaning of the term). The UK has more than 50,000 accountants who practice as auditors (out of over 100,000 qualified to do so). This is a huge number compared to other EU states. For example, the French national auditing body has less than 10,000 members; in Germany the figure is below 5,000 while in Greece it is barely 100 (CEC 1994). The number of accountants and auditors in continental EU nations will increase dramatically if EU national governments move quickly to harmonise their domestic company tax rules and information requirements. Convergence of national accounting practices on tax-related issues would then follow. Another stimulant would be a move towards continental EU businesses raising equity capital, thus necessitating the provision of financial data to potential investors.

Progress test 11

1. A fundamental difference applies to the financing of companies on the European continent compared to companies in the UK. What is this difference?

2. What is meant by the expression 'short-termism'?

3. List the main disadvantages of the continental European approach to company financing.

4. What is an unlisted securities market?

5. Explain the difference between bearer shares and registered shares.

6. What are the potential benefits of an integrated pan-European equities market?

7. Explain the major EU requirements for the listing of company shares on European Stock Exchanges.

8. What is a bill of exchange?

9. How can letters of credit be used to facilitate the settlement of import transactions?

10. Define 'forfaiting'.

11. Why has the European Commission recommended legislation on credit periods for commercial transactions?

12. What is the purpose of the 1994 Draft Directive on Cross-Border Credit Transfers?

13. Explain the difference between factoring and invoice discounting.

14. List the criticisms of state support for export payments insurance.

15. Debt collecting in foreign countries is troublesome and expensive. Why is this the case?

16. State the recommendations of the Ruding Committee on the harmonisation of EU business taxes.

17. Outline the rules concerning the payment of VAT on cross-border mail order sales.

18. Give six examples of important national differences in accounting laws and standards.

19. What are the EU rules on the qualifications of auditors?

20. What is the Accounting Advisory Forum and what is its role?

12

METHODS OF CONDUCTING CROSS-BORDER OPERATIONS

European Union based firms can do business in other EU nations via exporting, licensing and franchising, joint ventures, contract manufacture, or direct foreign investment.

1. Exporting

Exporting means the sale abroad of an item produced, stored or processed in the supplying firm's home country. Some firms regard exporting as little more than a convenient way of increasing total sales; others see it as a crucial element of overall corporate strategy. *Passive exporting* occurs when a firm receives orders from abroad without having canvassed them. *Active exporting*, conversely, results from a strategic decision to establish proper systems for organising the export function and for procuring foreign sales. Exporting may be direct or indirect. With direct exporting the exporter assumes full responsibility for the transfer of goods to foreign customers, for customs clearance, local advertising and final sale of the goods. Indirect exporting uses intermediaries.

Advantages of exporting are that it is cheap, convenient to administer, and carries no risk of failure of direct foreign investments. The revenues from foreign sales accrue entirely to the exporting company (rather than it having to repatriate profits from foreign agents, distributors, retail outlets, etc.). Direct exporting provides total control over the selling process; avoids the need to share know-how with foreign partners; and cuts out expensive intermediaries. Exporting can be highly profitable, although the development of an export facility can place a severe strain on the business's resources. Other reasons for *not* actively exporting include language problems, the higher degree of risk typically involved in selling abroad rather than in the home country, and the difficulty of forecasting sales in foreign countries rather than in the firm's home nation. Sales forecasting can be far more difficult for foreign countries than in the firm's home base. Changes in the political, legal, social and economic superstructures of other nations are hard to predict, as are the behaviours of actual and potential competing companies. Also there are the costs and inconveniences of finding foreign agents and distributors and of investigating the market characteristics and trading rules of various foreign countries, plus the cost of financing long periods between obtaining export orders, delivering the goods to distant destinations and getting paid. The firm has to find the resources necessary to have its managers visit foreign markets regularly, monitor and control agents and distributors, meet important customers, attend foreign exhibitions, etc. Note moreover that the money needed to sell abroad might be more profitably employed in building up the home market, and that foreign sales may encourage a company to delay introducing new products and / or to ignore the threat of domestic competition.

Firms committed to exporting must be prepared to adapt their products to meet foreign requirements and to research the needs and characteristics of foreign customers.

2. Licensing

Licensing is appropriate where the firm has legal control over its intellectual property (via registered patents and / or trademarks), where transport costs or the cost of establishing local manufacturing facilities would be prohibitive, or where rapid installation of a manufacturing capability in a particular market is necessary in order to beat the competition. Other circumstances in which licensing is likely to succeed are where:

- Images of locally produced items will improve sales
- The licensee will have to purchase input components or materials from the licensor
- The licensor is already exporting directly to more markets than it can conveniently handle
- It is not technically feasible to establish a permanent presence in a particular country
- The foreign market is small and does not justify the expense attached to alternative forms of market entry
- The licensor is a small company with limited resources
- There are possibilities for 'technology feedback' from the licensee
- The technology transferred under licence is 'perishable' so that the licensor has considerable bargaining power through its ability to supply new technology in the future
- Licensing can be a means for testing and developing a product in a foreign market, perhaps with a view to subsequent direct foreign investment
- Auxiliary processes rather than a core technology can be licensed.

Licences can take many forms, ranging from a permit to exploit an existing patent, to extensive and complicated arrangements on industrial co-operation. There are a number of types of licensing agreement. With an *assignment*, for instance, a firm hands over all its intellectual property rights in relation to a particular patent, trademark, design or whatever, to a licensee. The latter may then use these rights as it wishes. If the firm issues a *sole* licence, however, it retains rights but agrees not to extend licences to anyone other than a single licensee during the period of the agreement. *Exclusive* licences require licensors not to use their patents, trademarks, etc., for their own businesses while licensing contracts are in force, leaving these rights entirely to licensees for prespecified periods. *Know-how licensing* means the licensing of confidential but non-patented technical knowledge. The advantages of licensing are that:

- No capital investment is necessary.
- Licensees avoid research and development costs, while acquiring experience of manufacturing the item.
- The licensor has complete legal control over its intellectual property.
- A manufacturing capability can be quickly established in an unfamiliar market.
- Licensees carry some of the risk of failure.
- The nucleus of the parent organisation can remain small, have low overheads, yet control extensive operations.

Disadvantages to licensing are:

- Profits are sacrificed through allowing other firms to make the parent company's goods.
- The risk of a licensee company setting up in competition once it has learned all the licensor's production methods and trade secrets and the licence period has expired.
- Possible ambiguities and interpretation difficulties in relation to minimum and/or maximum output levels, territory covered, basis of royalty payments (including the frequency of payment and the currency to be used) and the circumstances under which the agreement may be terminated.
- Deciding how to control the licensee in relation to quality standards, declaration of production levels, and methods of marketing the product.
- Problems arising if the licensee turns out to be less competent than first expected.
- Possible failure of the licensee to exploit fully the local market.
- Acquisition by the licensee of the licensor's technical knowledge.
- The need for complex contractual arrangements in certain circumstances.
- The numerous opportunities that arise for disagreements and misunderstandings.

The Technology Transfer Regulation 1996

Licence agreements typically violate Article 85 of the Treaty of Rome as they invariably forbid the licensee from selling the licensed product outside a designated territory, restrict the licensee's production or involvement with competing items, or limit the range of customers to whom the product may be sold. However, a block exemption has applied to most patent and know-how licensing agreements, as outlined in 6:6. In 1994 the Commission proposed replacing the block exemption with a new Technology Transfer Regulation, introduced in 1996. Under the Regulation an exclusive licence is not legal without individual exemption unless the licensee has a market share of less than 40 per cent or the market is not *oligopolistic*. An oligopolistic market is defined as one in which *either*:

- the parties to the agreement plus another company enjoy a 50 per cent or more market share, *or*
- the parties to the agreement plus five or less companies collectively hold a two thirds market share, provided the licensee's share exceeds ten per cent.

The Commission justifies its emphasis on high and low market share on the grounds that businesses with little market power should be able to enter into more restrictive licensing agreements. Also the Regulation distinguishes between 'necessary' and 'unnecessary' patents. A necessary patent is one which is fundamental to the achievement of the objects of the licensed technology; an unnecessary patent cannot be used to restrict a licensee's behaviour, even if the licensee only has a small market share.

Under the Regulation the licensee can be contractually prevented from:

- placing the licensed product on the market in territories licensed to other EU licensees in response to unsolicited orders for a period of up to five years; *and/or*
- actively soliciting sales of the licensed product from other licensees' territories for up to ten years.

The Regulation explicitly prohibits a number of types of clause which, if included in a license agreement, will render it void and expose the parties to the risks of large fines and/or actions for civil damages. The following are banned:

(a) Restrictions on the quantity of goods which one party may produce.

(b) Requirements for the licensee to assign to the licensor any technical improvements discovered by the licensee.

(c) Price restrictions.

(d) Restrictions on the specific customers that may be served within the licensee's territory.

(e) Non-competition restrictions following expiry of the agreement.

(f) Restrictions on parallel imports (i.e. the licensee buying the item cheap in one market and reselling it in others).

An 'opposition procedure' applies to the Regulation, i.e. companies with licences not containing any of the above types of clause can simply notify the Commission and if no objections are received within four months the agreement is automatically allowed to proceed.

Licence contracts

These need to specify royalty and other fee payments, criteria for and the timing of remittances, the geographical area to be covered, permissible selling prices, and provisions for terminating the contract. Procedures concerning quality control should be detailed, plus the licensee's ability to become involved with competing products and the remedies available if the licensee fails to meet its obligations. Sometimes the experience acquired by the licensee in operating the licence leads to further technical development and inventions, so it is essential to determine at the outset the ownership of any fresh patents that emerge. Other key elements that need to be included in the licence contract are:

- the licensee's capacity to sub-contract
- minimum production levels
- extent of the support services to be given by the licensor
- permissible selling prices
- termination and renewal arrangements
- confidentiality requirements
- procedures for settling disputes and which country's laws shall apply to the agreement.

3. Franchising

The EU block exemption on franchising (*see* 6:6) defines franchising as 'a package of industrial or intellectual property rights relating to trade marks, trade names, shop signs, utility models, designs, copyrights, know-how or patents, to be exploited for the resale of goods or the provision of services to end users.' In other words, franchising is a form of licensing whereby the franchisee adopts the parent company's entire business format: its name, trade marks, business methods, layout of premises, etc. The franchisor provides (in return for a royalty and lump sum fee) a variety of supplementary management services: training, technical advice, stock control systems, perhaps even financial loans. Hence it retains complete control over how the product is marketed, but the franchisee carries the risks of failure and the franchisor's capital commitment is typically low. Accordingly, international franchising allows companies to expand rapidly from a limited capital base. It combines the technical experience of the franchisor with the intimate local knowledge of the franchisee. Franchisees are self-employed, not employees of the parent company, and rarely possess rights against a parent organisation in the event of either the entire system or just an individual outlet collapsing (Abel 1991; Welsh 1992). The European Commission has always sought to encourage franchising on the grounds that it improves the provision of goods and services within the EU, and facilitates new business startups thus increasing inter-brand competition (Singleton 1995). Hence the Commission has been extremely lenient when applying EU competition law to franchising agreements, and many more restrictive provisions are allowed under the franchising block exemption than under the corresponding block exemptions for exclusive distribution and purchasing (*see* 6:6). This has meant that it can be advantageous to distribute goods via franchise arrangements than by other means, so that firms have been tempted to pass-off what are in reality restrictive distribution contracts as 'franchise' deals. To qualify for the franchise block exemption the contract involved must include obligations concerning the application of a uniform presentation of premises, a common name or shop sign, the transfer of know-how and long-term provision of assistance by the franchisor to the franchisee. Otherwise it is treated as a normal distribution agreement. Franchise arrangements between companies producing similar competing goods are not allowed under the block exemption.

Normally, franchisees must follow standardised business techniques, layouts of premises, and are subject to some control by the franchisor. Franchisees are sheltered under a protective umbrella of specialist skills, resources and experiences already possessed by the parent organisation. They obtain a well known name and set of activities with a proven reputation. Franchisees are required to protect the franchisor's good name through maintenance of minimum quality standards, adoption of a uniform appearance, adherence to standard opening hours, and so on. If the franchisor is a manufacturer, the franchisee is usually required to purchase supplies (for example, meat for hamburgers, spare parts, ingredients for alcoholic or soft drinks) from the franchisor at prices predetermined by the parent firm (which buys raw materials in bulk at big discounts).

Franchising began when inventors of new machines, processes or business methods were forced by lack of finance or inadequate knowledge of the business world into allowing other parties the right to manufacture or otherwise adopt new inventions in exchange for a licence fee. Initially, therefore, business expertise was provided by franchisees. As the system developed, however, franchisors assumed responsibilities for business organisation, trade marks, advertising and sales promotion. Today, franchisors impose levies on franchisees to cover national advertising and servicing costs. The cost of local advertising is borne by franchisees. Successful franchising requires that the product or service involved has a distinct and unique image which is conceptually dissimilar to competing lines. Also, demand for the franchised product should be genuinely international, and expected to continue in the long term. Franchising is not suitable for fashion products with short lives. Business methods associated with the product, its presentation, ingredients, style and design, must be capable of standardisation.

As franchising represents a restraint on free competition it violates EU competition law. (Note how franchisees are often tied to taking supplies from the parent organisation.) There is however a block exemption on franchise agreements, as outlined in 6:**6**.

Types of franchise agreement

There are three basic forms of franchise agreement: unit, area development, and master (Mendelsohn 1993). A *unit agreement* covers the rights and obligations of a single franchised outlet, specifying the territory allocated, protection of intellectual property, duration of the contract, nature and extent of the services to be provided by the franchisor, etc. An *area development agreement* is appropriate for situations where a franchisee wishes to operate many outlets in the same area. In effect the franchisor hands over an entire territory for development by another party under licence. Hence this type of contract needs to contain details of:

- the legal protection afforded to the franchisee *vis-à-vis* his or her exclusive right to develop the region
- how and by when the franchisee will establish multiple outlets
- the development programme
- procedures for selecting and approving locations
- responsibilities for training and supervising staff in the various outlets
- who shall decide the number and distribution of outlets within the region

- whether the developer can sell his or her rights to a third party.

With a *master franchise agreement* the franchisor contracts to a sub-franchisor the right to create and subsequently dispose of individual franchised outlets for the main franchisor's product.

Withholding taxes

The arrangements concerning withholding taxes on transfers between a parent company and its subsidiaries discussed in 10:15 do *not* apply to payments from franchisees to franchisors, as in law the two parties are separate and independent businesses. Hence the tax position of a franchisor with franchisees in several countries can become extremely complicated. A major problem is that franchise fees are treated differently in disparate countries. In some nations they are regarded as royalties; elsewhere as straightforward profits, or as management fees or service income. The intellectual property transferred through a franchise contract is viewed as a capital asset in certain states; as a source of revenue in others. (This is important because money paid for capital assets can normally be offset against tax.) It could be tax efficient for a franchisor to set up a local subsidiary company to operate franchised outlets in particular countries (the Netherlands for instance).

Advantages and disadvantages of franchising

Advantages to franchisors include the following:

(a) As franchisees are self-employed (rather than employees of the parent firm) they will be highly motivated to succeed in their own business. There are no strikes, go-slows, work-to-rules, or other industrial problems.

(b) While franchisors retain control of distribution systems, new and unfamiliar market segments can be entered using the skills, experiences and local background knowledge of neighbourhood-based franchisees.

(c) Since large distribution networks are tied to supplies from single companies, there exist opportunities for bulk buying of raw materials at big discounts.

(d) As a franchise operation grows, trade marks, brand names and product styles become more widely dispersed and familiar to the public. The franchisor's name becomes internationally recognised.

(e) The nucleus of the franchisor's organisation remains small, and overheads are low. Large profits can result from a limited capital base, yet risks are shared with franchisees. Moreover, routine administrative problems are dealt with by outlets, not central office.

Similar benefits accrue to franchisees. A franchise can be purchased (often with a loan arranged by the franchisor) for less than usually has to be paid for an existing business. Outlets receive advice on book-keeping, tax liability, training of staff, stock control, layout of premises and related matters.

Advertising is dealt with by franchisors, leaving outlets free to concentrate on day-to-day operations. Technical advice and training will also be available.

Another advantage is the product and marketing research activities undertaken by franchisors that small firms individually could not afford. Also, the competition faced by an outlet within a specific locality is restricted by the fact that franchisors will not permit more than one of their franchisees to operate there.

Drawbacks relate to the fact that franchisees' working methods are controlled. Product specification, quality, layout of premises and so on are predetermined. Little discretion is allowed. Royalty payments could be high, making unprofitable an otherwise successful business. Unjustifiably high raw material prices might be charged by franchisors, and interruptions in supplies (indeed, inadequate backup services generally) can ruin an individual outlet. Unlike ordinary businesses, franchised outlets cannot be sold without the franchisor's permission. Also:

- The brand image of the franchised product may deteriorate for reasons beyond the franchisee's control, including policy mistakes made by the parent organisation.
- Since royalties are invariably expressed as fixed percentages of turnovers, hard-working and successful franchisees will have to pay ever increasing sums to their franchisors, thus discouraging the more able. Yet, franchisees who fail lose everything.
- Franchise contracts cover relatively short periods, normally five years. A successful franchisee who has increased the profitability of an outlet will find that it reverts to the franchisor following expiry of the franchise contract. The franchisor will then demand higher royalties in line with the increased value of the outlet. During the contract period, however, the franchisee is tied to a particular product, unable to modify the good or introduce alternatives.

Franchisors too face disadvantages. They control only the overall format of outlets, not day-to-day operations. Badly managed outlets offering poor quality and inadequate presentation of the product can ruin a carefully nurtured public image. Sometimes, franchisors insist on inspecting franchisees' premises, but this can arouse resentment and cause disagreements over how that outlet should be run. Franchisees are not employees, they cannot be dismissed, and termination of a contract might be difficult. Typically, franchisees regard themselves as owners of their outlets (which they are not) and begrudge interference from the parent firm. A common problem is that franchisees can learn a business from top to bottom while under contract, and then set up competing outlets (perhaps under disguised ownership) nearby the moment their contract expires. Franchisors must rely on outlets to declare honestly their monthly receipts (for the purpose of computing royalty payments), to promote their product vigorously, and to employ suitable staff.

Obviously, aggregate returns to a franchisor are less than would be available were all outlets directly owned and controlled since then all revenues would accrue to the franchisor, not just percentage royalties. On the other hand, franchisors avoid start-up and developmental costs, and they share the risk of failure. Relatively little administrative work is necessary, and fewer staff are needed within the parent firm.

4. Joint ventures

Joint ventures (JVs) are collaborative arrangements between unrelated parties which exchange or combine various resources while remaining separate and independent legal entities. There are two types of JV: equity and contractual. The former involves each partner taking an equity stake in the venture (e.g. through setting up a joint subsidiary with its own share capital); the latter rely on contractual agreements between the partners. Joint ventures are an example of the wider concept of the 'strategic alliance', which embraces knowledge-sharing arrangements, mutual licensing, measures to control and utilise excess capacity, etc. (Lorange and Roos 1992). Usually JVs are formed to undertake a specific project that has to be completed within a set period. JVs are a flexible form of business arrangement; can be quickly entered into and shut down; enable the sharing of costs; yet are frequently just as effective a means for entering markets as more direct forms of foreign investment. Often they are used to establish bridgeheads in a foreign market prior to more substantial operations within the market by individual participants. Advantages to joint ventures include:

(a) Firms can expand into several foreign markets simultaneously for low capital cost.

(b) Costs of administration are shared between the partners.

(c) Participants can avoid the needs to purchase local premises and hire new employees.

(d) Risks of failure are shared.

(e) JVs are less costly than acquisitions.

(f) Returns are higher than with licensing/franchising.

(g) Firms can gain instant access to local expertise and to partners' distribution systems.

Problems with JVs include possible disagreements over organisation and control, methods of operation, and the long-term goals of the venture. Other disputes might arise concerning pricing policy, the confidentiality of information exchanged between members, and about how underperformance by any one of the participants is to be dealt with (e.g. whether equal compensation shall be payable to each of the parties if the project is abandoned). Further potential difficulties are listed below.

(a) Partners may become locked into long-term investments from which it is difficult to withdraw.

(b) Arguments may arise concerning which partner is responsible for budget overspends and how these should be financed.

(c) Co-ordination may be difficult.

(d) Profits have to be shared with partners.

(e) There might be differences in management culture among participating firms.

(f) Completion of a JV project might overburden a company's staff.

(g) Intellectual property may have to be shared.

(h) It might be difficult to integrate a JV into a firm's overall corporate strategy.

(i) Partners are not free to act independently.

(j) The corporate objectives of partners may conflict.

(k) The prices at which goods are passed between partners might be subject to dispute.

(l) The importance of the venture to each partner might change over time.

Selection of JV partners

Local partners in a foreign country should have proven knowledge, expertise and experience of local business conditions and practices. A prospective partner should be able to conduct or commission local market research and possess extensive contacts with local banks, businesses and providers of specialist services. Obviously the partner needs to have resources (staff, technical facilities, management systems, etc.) sufficient to undertake the collaboration (Harvey and Lusch 1995). Further selection criteria are (i) the firm's track record, how long it has existed and its general business reputation; and (ii) how readily the quality of the potential partner's work can be appraised. Ideally, participants should be able to pool complementary skills. For example, one partner might supply the technological know-how, another raise the necessary finance, while the third provides local marketing expertise and facilities. Crucial to the selection process is the exercise of 'due diligence' in relation to an intended collaborator. This means verifying the other business's value and activities and will normally involve an assessment of its creditworthiness (probably undertaken by an international credit reference agency), inspection of its accounts, and the evaluation of its technical and managerial competence.

Joint venture contracts

These need to specify the venture's legal form and capital structure, details of who is to manage the project, financial contributions and the division of profits and losses, the confidentiality of information provided by each partner and the ownership of resulting intellectual property. Further matters that need to be determined include:

- geographical coverage of the venture's activities
- procedures for resolving disagreements
- partners' abilities to transfer their shares in the venture to third parties
- how an unsuccessful JV will be wound up
- methods for establishing transfer prices
- the proportion of profits to be ploughed back into the JV
- responsibilities for training employees involved in the venture

- how policies are to be determined, and which partner is to take which decisions
- division of tasks and responsibilities, including duties relating to quality management, liaison with other firms, information gathering and analysis, and the administration of the venture's employees
- reporting procedures and control systems.

European Commission attitudes towards joint ventures

The Commission recognises the importance of joint ventures as a means for technology transfer and small business development. Accordingly it operates an information service (BC-NET) for small and medium sized businesses seeking joint venture partners. At the same time, the Commission is aware that JVs can be used to circumvent EU laws on monopoly and restrictive practices. Hence, concentrative JVs are illegal under the 1989 Merger Regulation (*see* 6:**12**), although a block exemption applies to normal JV activities.

5. Contract manufacture

This involves the firm placing orders with local foreign businesses for the production of goods which it then sells locally or exports. Local manufacture can be dovetailed to the needs of local distribution arrangements and numerous cost savings may be obtained. A 'home-grown' image is attached to the goods, and delivery and customer service mechanisms should improve. Further advantages to contract manufacture include:

- easy withdrawal from markets that do not live up to expectations
- not having to invest large sums of money in capital equipment
- the potential to undertake large-scale operations from a small capital base
- avoidance of involvement in industrial relations with foreign manufacturing workforces
- existing production facilities are not overloaded.

Problems with contract manufacture include the difficulties of monitoring and maintaining quality levels, of protecting any intellectual property embodied within the manufacturing item, and preventing the other firm from setting up in competition (perhaps covertly) once it has acquired expertise in making the product. Note moreover that the company to which the contract is awarded may require substantial technical back-up, possibly extending to the training of its employees.

6. Direct foreign investment (DFI)

Residents of any EU country may set up businesses in other EU nations on the same terms as citizens of the latter states. As West European integration progresses, moreover, a significant increase in the number of European enterprises wishing to establish permanent presences in other EU states is almost certain to occur. Several advantages accrue to having a fixed presence in a foreign EU market: the firm trades as a local business; can obtain local investment grants and subsidies; has immediate control over local market research, advertising, the granting of credit, etc. and (importantly) creates a local image for its operations. Foreign establishments are especially useful if local assembly or part-manufacture of a product is required, or if local agents/distributors are unreliable or difficult to find. A local subsidiary can recruit local staff who are experts in the nuances of the local market, fluent in the language of the host country, and who possess wide-ranging contacts with local businesses and institutions. Staff are, nevertheless, entirely subject to the direction of the parent organisation, and no conflicts of interest are involved. Competitors' activities can be closely observed, and there should be better co-ordination of marketing, distribution, after-sales service and so on. Communication difficulties with *ad hoc* representatives, lack of commitment on the part of commission agents, and costly margins taken by independent distributors are further possible reasons for wanting to set up a branch or subsidiary business with its own facilities.

Other possible motives for direct investment in foreign EU countries include:

- undercapacity at home
- lower operating costs available in certain countries
- high transport costs associated with exporting
- local foreign competitors perhaps reacting more vigorously against the actions of foreign rivals than against domestic businesses
- customer perceptions that the parent is fully committed to a permanent presence in the country concerned
- especially favourable economic conditions in particular countries: buoyant markets, rising consumer incomes, easy access to finance, low interest rates, etc.
- wanting to spread the risk of downturns in particular markets.

Total ownership of a foreign subsidiary means there is no scope for arguments with partner firms; there is complete and immediate control over operations; and subsidiary operations can be fitted into the parent company's overall corporate strategies. The close link between local production and local marketing might enable more rapid product modification in response to changing local demand.

An obvious problem with DFI is, of course, the substantial capital investment it requires. This cannot be sacrificed easily, whereas cancellation of (say) a contract manufacture agreement is (subject to the details of the contract) a cheap and straightforward matter. Apart from the local availability of manufacturing resources (labour, materials, etc.) the decision whether to invest in foreign manufacturing capacity will normally depend on such factors as the extent of government investment grants and subsidies, and wage and other costs.

New versus existing businesses

An investment can involve setting up an entirely fresh operation from scratch, or the purchase of an existing business. The advantages of buying a local firm outright include the avoidance of start-up delays and expenses, and the immediate possession of a functioning administrative system with staff, distribution arrangements, etc. This presupposes of course that a suitable local business can be found and that its price is reasonable.

On the other hand the acquired business has to be integrated into the parent firm's organisation and management systems; old and technologically out-of-date equipment may be acquired; and implementing change in the purchased firm's operating methods might prove difficult. Also the purchasing business acquires (under a number of EU Directives) all the existing firm's obligations to its customers, creditors and of course employees. The financial costs of rationalising the workforce of a purchased company can be extremely high in certain European states.

Progress test 12

1. What are the advantages of exporting?

2. Explain the difference between a sole licence and an exclusive licence.

3. List the main contents of the Technology Transfer Regulation 1996.

4. What are the advantages of franchising from the viewpoint of the franchisor?

5. What is an area development agreement?

6. Explain the difference between an equity joint venture and a contractual joint venture.

7. What criteria should be applied to the selection of joint venture partners?

8. What are the disadvantages of contract manufacture?

9. Give six possible motives for direct foreign investment in EU nations.

10. What are the benefits to purchasing an existing foreign business outright as opposed to setting up an entirely new operation?

13

INTELLECTUAL PROPERTY

1. Nature of intellectual property

The term 'intellectual property' is used to describe rights over patents on: inventions; trade marks; industrial designs and models; works of literature, art or music; films, sound recordings or broadcasts; computer software, and any other copyright material. The 'rights' embodied in intellectual property normally involve the exclusive possession of the benefits arising from the property and the ability to take legal action against any person or organisation attempting to appropriate those benefits.

Intellectual property and EU competition law

Protection of intellectual property is obviously important for firms concerned with research and development (R&D) and new product innovation. Firms need to be able to recoup their investments in research and technical development and/or to protect the goodwill they have accumulated over time through the use of brand names or other trade marks. Clearly, however, the exercise of rights over intellectual property might interfere with the free movement of goods and could distort the pattern of competition within the EU. In particular, the granting of exclusive licences by a patent holder to other firms enabling them to exploit the former's invention necessarily causes the licensor to contravene Article 85 of the Treaty of Rome, and might create a 'dominant position' under Article 86 (*see* 6:**2**). Nevertheless, the European Commission recognises the need for a strong European patent protection system (in order to encourage research and innovation), despite its monopolistic implications. Patenting makes it possible for firms to announce their inventions earlier than otherwise would be feasible (hence giving fresh ideas to other would-be inventors), and ensures that the money invested in developing an invention is not wasted. Accordingly the Commission has adopted a liberal view on the application of competition law to intellectual property matters, with the important exception that it will not allow owners of intellectual property to use their rights to prevent the sale of goods in particular countries. Cases concerning intellectual property brought before the European Court since 1970 have led to the application of the doctrine of 'exhaustion of rights' throughout the European Union. This means that a patent holder (or owner of other intellectual property) cannot use patent rights to prevent the item on which he or she holds the patent from being marketed in specific EU nations. The item must be available everywhere, or not at all. The exhaustion of rights principle applies to all EU patents, no matter where they are registered.

Harmonisation of intellectual property law

Article 222 of the Treaty of Rome states that the Treaty shall 'in no way prejudice the rules of member states governing the system of property ownership', hence effectively guaranteeing national sovereignty where intellectual property matters are concerned. There is however a general consensus among EU governments that harmonisation of intellectual property law is necessary in order to facilitate the free movement of goods, persons and capital within the Union and to prevent the fragmentation of the European market. Accordingly a number of important EU Directives have been adopted in the intellectual property field, as outlined in the following sections.

COPYRIGHT

2. Copyright

Copyright protection does *not* extend to ideas or themes, however original they might be. Only words, drawings, photographs, musical or dramatic works, sound recordings, films or television or radio broadcasts may be protected. Thus it is necessary to convert ideas into material form before copyright can be claimed, and it is the material form (e.g. drawings or words written on paper) that enjoys protection – not the ideas from which they emanated. If an idea is copied in a different material form, this is not a violation of copyright. Hence a second party may independently produce a very similar piece of work based on an idea generated by the first party and put into words, drawings, etc., by the first party; yet there is no infringement of the latter's rights provided the words, drawings, etc., used are not actually copied. The only remedy that might be possible in this situation is to bring an action under national consumer protection law to prevent the 'passing off' of a piece of work in such a way as deliberately to mislead potential buyers into believing the similar work is in fact the original. To prove 'passing off' it is necessary to demonstrate (i) the probability of confusion in the minds of buyers, and (ii) actual damage to the complainant's business or trade.

No formalities are required to establish the existence of copyright, which arises the moment the work is drawn, composed or written. The work does not have to be printed or published, it can be typed or handwritten. To enjoy protection the work has to be original and/or involve some skill and/or labour or composition. Copyright itself has two aspects: personal rights conferred on the creator of a literary or artistic work; and 'neighbouring' rights which protect those who contribute to activities giving rise to copyright materials. The distinction is extremely important in some EU countries. Until 1 January 1994 the standard copyright period was 50 years from the death of the creator in all Community countries except Spain (where it was 60 years) and Germany (70 years). The period has now been harmonised at 70 years for written work; 50 years for performances and broadcasts.

Although the details of national copyright law vary from country to country, *all* EU member states belong to both the Berne Convention and Universal

Copyright Convention (UCC) and adhere to the principles required by these Conventions, which give protection to literary and artistic works in most countries of the world. The Berne Convention was originally agreed in 1886 and today has around 95 members, including all major industrial states. It extends copyright protection to all member countries without the need for any formality, provided that the author is a citizen of a member country or that the work is first published in a member state. The UCC began in 1955 and has around 90 member nations. Under the Convention the government of each member state is obliged to offer exactly the same copyright protection to foreign works originating to a member country as it provides to its own citizens, provided the work predominantly displays the UCC copyright symbol © plus the name of the copyright holder and date of publication.

In recognition of the increasing importance of copyright to the business community the European Commission produced in the 1980s a number of proposals designed to bring copyright law into the modern high-tech age and to establish minimum legal standards. Specific suggestions were for a Directive(s) covering:

- a licensing scheme for users of commercial audio tape duplicating equipment
- standard rules whereby the producers of films, videos and sound recordings can authorise their reproduction, plus similar rights for performing artists.

Another major concern was the absence of Union-level law on the protection of computer software. This was dealt with via a 1991 Directive as outlined in the following section.

3. The Directive on the protection of computer software 1991

Developments in information technology during the 1970s and 80s created copyright problems that did not conveniently fit into existing national rules on intellectual property. Governments responded to this challenge by making available widely disparate devices for software protection, including orthodox national copyright law (i.e. treating a computer program as if it were a piece of literary writing); national patent law (i.e. regarding a program as an 'invention'); laws on trade secrets and know-how, etc. An effective system for protecting computer software was obviously necessary, both for enabling Europe's computer industry to compete effectively with US and Japanese rivals and for helping to minimise the costs of software piracy among the general public (estimated to reduce the software industry's revenues by ten per cent annually). Unfortunately, a number of special problems arise when attempting to define the scope and nature of copyright on computer software. In particular, the fundamentals of computer programming are so well known that it is arguable that particular configurations of steps (which anyone might be able to write given sufficient effort) should not be regarded as novel innovations. Most software is not technically an 'invention' as such, and hence copyright law might not be appropriate for computer software because, unlike literary writing, software programs are addressed to machines rather than to people so that software construction is not really 'writing'. Note moreover that minor changes in a program can radically alter its composition, yet still duplicate its essential outputs.

The eventual decision was to regard computer programs as essentially literary creations, meaning that any program produced within an EU nation now qualifies for 70 years' protection following the writer's death, and that through the Berne Convention and the UCC (*see* above) the copyright automatically extends to all industrially developed non-EU countries. Under the 1991 Directive, all EU member states must grant copyright protection to writers of computer programs, regardless of a program's contents, quality, or aesthetic considerations. A computer program is defined as a sequence of instructions designed to be used directly or indirectly in a computer system in order to obtain a certain result. Updates and derivative programs are regarded as integral parts of the original program. Decompiling is authorised only in the case of interfaces and when it is necessary for the 'interoperability of programs created independently'. Protection applies to programs that are fixed in form and original (i.e. the result of the writer's own intellectual effort). Interfaces and access protocols are covered (sometimes these constitute a quarter of the work involved in devising a program) although interfaces based on ideas and general principles are not protected. The requirement for fixity in form means that copyright does not arise from a program's temporary existence in the memory of a computer; the program must be permanently recorded. Programs are legally protected from the time they are written; there is no requirement that they be registered.

A problem with the 1991 Directive is that *reverse engineering* is not prohibited. This means translating a program from machine code to source code in order to discover the rules and procedures used in the program's construction. Permission from the copyright owner to perform reverse engineering is not necessary, even though it reveals the fundamental structure of a program. However, any fresh program resulting from reverse engineering will constitute a breach of copyright unless the end product is recognisably different from the one analysed. Another difficulty is that minor modifications to programs can be technically illegal (e.g. altering a software supplier's program to work with a laser printer rather than with a dot matrix).

At the time of writing the European Commission is developing measures intended to extend copyright protection to the producers of computer databases, proposing that electronic database producers be protected against unfair copying for ten years from the date of registering a database with a central authority. Also the 'mode of compilation' of a database will be protectable.

PATENT RIGHTS

4. Patents

A patent is an official document granted to the inventor of an entirely new product or manufacturing process allowing the inventor a monopoly over the production, use or sale of the invention for a certain period from the date the patent application was filed. To obtain a patent the inventor must supply full details of the invention to a national patent office, which has to be satisfied that the invention contains original features. Patent holders may legally prevent other people from copying or using their inventions, may licence the patent, sell or exchange it for money or goods. The temporary monopoly is given in recognition of the inventor having disclosed the invention which, at the end of the patent protection period, enters the public domain (i.e. it can be copied by anyone). It is the responsibility of patent holders to enforce their rights, not the national patent office that grants patents.

Increasing competition, more R&D within European companies, free cross-border capital mobility across national EU frontiers, the free labour mobility of research workers, widespread introductions of new technologies to European firms, and a greater willingness to finance risky projects made possible by easier access to Europe's financial capital markets have led to a sharp increase in the number of EU patent applications. Patents can be registered separately in individual EU nations, or throughout Europe via a single application under the 1977 European Patent Convention. The latter covers 17 West European countries including all EU states plus Switzerland, Monaco and Liechtenstein. To use this system the inventor must apply (through his or her national patent office) to the EU Patent Office in Munich specifying which EU countries the patent is to cover. The inventor then receives a bundle of national patents relating to those countries. Renewals of the patents can be undertaken through the inventor's national patent office. Application can be in any one of three languages: English, German or French. On being granted, the patent is translated into the other two languages plus the languages of any other EU countries to which the patent is to apply. Opposition to the patent must be filed within nine months of when it was granted. Patent protection lasts for 20 years from the date of filing the application.

As the inventor receives a bundle of national patents rather than a single document, subsequent litigation must be carried out separately in each country. However the EU member nations have agreed a further Patent Convention under which EU-wide patents will eventually be granted. These will be subject to the rules of the Convention rather than national laws on patenting. Disputes will be resolved through special Patent Courts established in each state, the judgements of which will be binding throughout the Union. Advantages to the proposed EU patent include convenience, lower overall registration costs, the need to pay only one set of renewal fees, and the fact that actions to prevent infringement of a patent will have effect throughout the entire European Union (Maronick 1988).

The problems that patent licensing creates in respect of EU competition law were mentioned in section 1. Similar considerations apply to *know-how* licensing. Know-how is confidential non-patented technical knowledge, and it can be licensed. Arguably, know-how (and patent) licensing is a barrier to free competition and could be used to sustain a monopoly. Equally, however, licensing is a major vehicle for the fast and efficient transfer of new technologies across national frontiers, and needs to be available to enable firms to protect the rights of those who research, initiate and develop new methods. Accordingly, two important block exemptions (*see* 6:6) from EU competition law apply to intellectual property, as follows:

1 The 1984 Regulation on Patent Licensing Agreements, which allows patent holders to grant territorially exclusive licences to other firms for periods of five years beginning from the date a new product is introduced to the EU. Limited exclusivity is permitted thereafter, provided the customer can easily obtain the item from other sources. Also, exclusive licences outside the scope of the block exemption can be notified to the European Commission through a special procedure and, if they are not opposed within six months, are automatically exempted.

2 The 1988 Regulation on Know-How Licensing Agreements. This allows the insertion of territorial restrictions in know-how licensing agreements so as to prevent licensees from exploiting the licensor's know-how in territories not covered by the contract.

Compulsory licensing

Patents registered in various countries need to be 'worked' – i.e. the patented product must actually be produced and / or sold – periodically. Patents that are not exploited for a certain period (this varies according to the law of the country concerned – two years is typical) may be subject to 'compulsory licensing', i.e. another firm can apply to a court for permission to utilise the patent under licence from the inventor. The court can compel the latter to issue a licence on terms that the court considers reasonable.

5. Utility models

A utility model is an invention that is not sufficiently original to qualify for a full patent but which, nevertheless, can be legally protected in all EU countries except the UK, Sweden and Luxembourg. Other terms used to describe utility models in some of the nations where they are permitted include 'short-term patent', 'petty patent', and 'utility certificate'. Unfortunately, EU countries have widely disparate laws concerning utility models, so in 1995 the European Commission published a proposal for the harmonisation of national legislation in the field. The proposal defines a utility model as a *registered* right conferring exclusive protection on an invention that must 'possess novelty' and involve an 'inventive step', although the latter need not be as substantial as for the grant of a proper patent. An important feature of utility model protection is that it is granted without a prior search to establish originality. Hence registration is faster and cheaper than for a patent, albeit with a lower degree of protection. Thus, utility model registration can be used as a temporary measure to protect intellectual property prior to obtaining a full patent. The latter process can take up to three years in some nations, whereas only six months on average is required for a utility model. Also a firm can test market its invention to see whether it has sufficient commercial appeal to justify the cost of total patent protection.

The proposal itself calls for the establishment of utility model registration facilities in all EU nations, and for a multi-country registration scheme similar to that available via the European Patent System (*see* **4**). It also suggests the following harmonisations of national rules on utility model registration and protection:

(a) No prior search should be required to establish originality, only a *prima facie* investigation. However, applicants should be able to commission an optional search if they so wish in order to reinforce their legal positions.

(b) The novelty of an application should be established by reference to the international (rather than national) 'state of the art' in the relevant field. A successful challenge to the novelty of an application by a third party should not take effect until 12 months after the date of the decision in favour of the third party.

(c) Registered rights over utility models should be transferrable without restriction.

(d) The maximum protection period should be ten years, reached through periodic renewals of one to three years.

(e) In the event of a dispute over originality, a national court should initiate a search and adjudicate the issue.

(f) The same exclusions that apply to conventional patent protection should also apply to utility models, e.g. discoveries and mathematical models, aesthetic creations, and certain production processes.

6. Designs

Governments grant designers the equivalent of patent rights over designs in order to encourage the introduction of novel designs for products and to stimulate industrial research and technical development. A 'design' is a pattern or shape, configuration or ornamentation applied to an article by an industrial process. It involves the appearance of a product resulting from the features of the lines, contours and colours applied to its make-up. For a design to be protectable the shape, configuration or ornamentation must not be dictated solely by the function which the article has to perform. Design is a crucial competitive weapon in industries such as machinery, electronics, domestic appliances and clothing.

The 1994 Draft Directive on Designs

This is intended to harmonise EU law on design protection and to create a system for pan-EU registration of design specifications. As is currently the case with the European Patent Convention (*see* **4**), existing national design law will remain in existence and operate in parallel with the new procedures, and it will still be possible to register a design in just one or a few EU countries. Under the Draft Directive, protection would last for five years in the first instance, renewable up to a maximum of 25 years. However, if the design is incorporated into a 'complex product' then third parties will be able to use the design after three years following the product being put on the market, subject to certain conditions. Protection will only be available for new designs of individual character. If the technical functions of a product are such that the producer cannot exercise discretion in relation to the product's appearance then the design may not be protected. Designs will not need to be registered in order to enjoy protection, but if they are not the protection period will only last for three years.

TRADE MARKS

7. Trade marks and branding

A trade mark can be any word, symbol or collection of words and/or symbols used to identify goods and to distinguish them from the outputs of other businesses. In some countries the first user of a trade mark becomes its lawful owner. Elsewhere, formal registration with state authorities is required. Another important difference is between countries which require owners of registered trade marks to use them during specific time intervals (usually three to five years) or accept that other firms may appropriate them after the specified interval has elapsed. The process of registering trade marks can be quite expensive. Legal actions to protect trade marks are also very costly. Note how in some countries it may be necessary to register a brand name at frequent intervals, with any brand name not registered in the correct manner becoming available to any other business.

Trade marks may be registered separately in every country where protection is required (except for Belgium, Luxembourg and the Netherlands, which have a common registration procedure giving protection throughout the Benelux union). Alternatively, pan-EU protection can be acquired via the EU Trade Mark Regulation agreed in 1993 and currently being implemented. This does not interfere with national trade marks already registered in each EU country, but instead creates a procedure that enables nationals of EU (and certain other) states to obtain from a central EU Trade Mark Office (EUTMO) an EU Trade Mark that is valid and enjoys identical legal protection in all EU countries. An EUTM can be obtained as an alternative to a national trade mark. For existing trade marks, the equivalent national trade mark will be suspended once an EUTM is registered, although national trade mark registration systems will continue to co-exist alongside the EUTM scheme, which is voluntary.

Applications for EU Trade Marks can be made through national patent offices or direct to the EUTMO in Alicante. Registration will be refused if the trade mark is not sufficiently distinct (in order to differentiate it clearly from competing trade marks) or if the name is likely to mislead the public or is otherwise contrary to EU public policy. Obviously the name must not already be in use within an EU state. It is up to aggrieved parties to petition the EUTMO for prohibition on the use of their trade marks by other firms. Appeals against the decision of the EUTMO are to be heard first by a Board of Appeal and then by the European Court of Justice. Civil actions for damages resulting from an infringement of a registered EUTM are heard in the national courts of the country in which the violation allegedly occurred.

Owners of registered EUTMs enjoy all the legal rights available to the owner of intellectual property in any EU country. These rights may be transferred, offered as security against bank loans, or licensed (for use in the entire European Union or just certain parts of it) to other businesses. An EUTM will have a life of ten years from the date of registration, and is renewable. Registration empowers an EUTM holder to prevent any other person or organisation from using the same trade mark for similar goods or services or from imitating the trade mark, e.g. by changing a few letters in the name while retaining its essential character so as to 'pass off' products. Other firms are not permitted to exploit the commercial value of the trade mark, e.g. by mentioning it in the promotional literature of other businesses. EUTMs cease to have effect if they are not used for five years, of if the acts or omissions of the EUTM's owner allow it to become a generic product title. It is up to a third party to make a formal application to the EUTMO to have a EUTM revoked.

The EUTM Regulation was preceded (and made possible) by a 1988 Directive on the harmonisation of trade mark legislation, which obliged countries to harmonise national rules *vis-à-vis* the rights conferred on registration of a trade mark and the tests applied when deciding whether a trade mark can be registered.

National versus EUTMO registration

There will of course be cases where firms will have to continue registering national rather than EU trade marks, e.g. if two businesses in different parts of the EU are independently using the same trade mark. Also national registration can be cheaper than using the EUTM scheme, especially if the firm operates predominantly within just one or two EU countries.

Brands

A brand identity may emerge from words, symbols, or a combination of the two. It follows that there is no essential difference between a trade mark and a brand. Hence the laws that apply to trade marks are equally applicable to brands. The importance of this fact has increased enormously following the completion of the Single Market and the consequent rise of the pan-European brand. In countries where trade mark protection is only available through formal registration the possibility of 'brand piracy' arises, i.e. the practice of people other than the original brand name user registering the brand name of a company just about to enter a country in which formal registration is necessary, and then 'selling' the brand name back to the company concerned.

Failure to take legal action to protect a brand name can result in it falling into the public domain as a generic product title. Examples of brands that have suffered this fate include kerosene, celluloid, thermos, aspirin and linoleum. All these began as brands, but may now be used by any manufacturer. This problem is especially severe when there is no generic term that adequately describes a broad type of product, resulting in the name of a well-known brand being commonly used as a proxy for the entire product category.

INTERNATIONAL PROTECTION

8. International organisations concerned with intellectual property

A number of international agreements have been concluded in order to facilitate the protection of intellectual property abroad. The longest established is the International Convention for the Protection of Industrial Property, originally signed in Paris in 1883 and repeatedly revised since then. This Convention has over 100 signatories and covers patents, models, trade marks and industrial designs. According to the rules of the Convention, an inventor who obtains a patent in one member country must then apply for protection under the national patent laws of other member countries, pay additional fees, and run the risk that these further applications may be refused. However, the applications take priority in these other countries over subsequent competing applications, provided they are filed within one year (six months for trade marks) from the date of the application in the inventor's home country. The owner's rights over the intellectual property are automatically maintained during this period. Signatory nations are obliged to extend to inventors from foreign member countries all the rights, protections, privileges and remedies as are available to home country nationals. No compulsory licence (*see* 4) may be granted within three years from the grant of a patent, even though the patent has not been worked.

The Madrid Agreement 1982 established the World Intellectual Property Organisation (WIPO) with headquarters in Geneva and through which trade mark holders in participating states can obtain protection in about 30 countries. On receipt of an application for registration, the WIPO circulates the trade mark to all signatory nations, where it is processed according to local intellectual property law. When the exercise has been completed the applicant receives a bundle of national trade mark registrations, at much lower cost than if a series of separate applications had been registered. A Protocol to the Agreement was signed in 1988, representing in effect a completely new Treaty with less stringent membership conditions than the earlier Agreement. This was necessary because the national intellectual property laws and practices of certain states (including some EU countries) were incompatible with the provisions of the original Agreement, even though these nations wanted to participate in the system. Under the Protocol, intergovernmental organisations can become members of the WIPO, despite particular states belonging to these intergovernmental organisations not themselves having signed the Madrid Agreement. The EU intends joining the WIPO as an intergovernmental organisation. Thus, any holder of an EUTM will be eligible to apply for WIPO protection in non-EU countries even if the holder's home state is, for technical reasons, not a signatory to the Madrid Agreement.

9. Piracy and counterfeiting

In the context of intellectual property law, piracy means the unauthorised reproduction of copyright works for commercial purposes. Examples are the illicit copying of books, video recordings, films and compact discs. Counterfeiting on the other hand, results from the unauthorised copying of products, packages, labels or trade marks, and is a major problem for certain industries, notably cosmetics, wrist watches, pharmaceuticals, chemicals, fashion clothing, books and computer software which are particularly susceptible to copying. Low-quality copies of a company's product devalue the company's image (product guarantees on counterfeits are obviously worthless) and deprive it of income, although some counterfeit goods are of very high quality. Indeed, counterfeit goods can find their way into official distribution systems and hence into reputable retail outlets where they sell alongside the original version. Tracking down counterfeits, compiling dossiers, gathering evidence, bringing court actions and enforcing judgements is costly and inconvenient. Hence companies sometimes do deals with counterfeiting firms, awarding them bona fide contracts to manufacture their products on condition that counterfeiting activities immediately cease.

An EU Regulation of 1986 enables governments to prevent the importation and free circulation of counterfeit goods – defined as those bearing other firm's valid trade marks without authorisation. Also the settlement of the Uruguay Round of the GATT negotiations changed GATT rules to enable patent and trade mark holders to have counterfeit goods confiscated and sold off. Measures to develop faster, simpler and more effective procedures for customs seizure of goods that violate other parties' intellectual property rights are currently being implemented (Maskers 1993).

Progress test 13

1. What is intellectual property?

2. Why is the European Commission attempting to harmonise intellectual property law?

3. What is meant by the term 'passing off'?

4. List the main provisions of the EU Directive on the protection of computer software.

5. What is 'reverse engineering' and why is it a problem for the computer software industry?

6. How does the European Patent Convention operate?

7. What is meant by the 'compulsory licensing' of patents?

8. In what circumstances may a design be legally protected?

9. What is the significance of the EU Trade Mark Regulation 1993?

10. Explain the term 'brand piracy'.

11. Outline the main rules of the International Convention for the Protection of Intellectual Property.

12. What was the purpose of the Madrid Agreement 1982?

14

MARKETING IN EUROPE

FUNDAMENTALS

Enlargement of the European Union has created the second largest trading area (after NAFTA) in the developed world, generating numerous opportunities and threats for the individual firm. To succeed in pan-European marketing a company's management requires genuinely international perspectives, an awareness of market conditions in all EU states and, above all, the capacity to accommodate change.

1. Nature of European marketing

The UK Chartered Institute of Marketing defines marketing as 'the management process responsible for identifying, anticipating and satisfying customers' requirements profitably'. Cross-border European marketing differs from domestic marketing in that it requires multilingual communications, the consideration of numerous cultural factors, the possession by marketing managers of a wide range of marketing skills, and possibly the need to modify products and promotional methods to suit local conditions in other countries. Information on foreign markets will often be in foreign languages; may be hard to obtain; and is frequently difficult to interpret. Further problems that arise in the course of cross-border European marketing are:

(a) Trends in foreign market environments may be difficult to observe.

(b) Distribution channels could involve large numbers of intermediaries.

(c) Diverse national laws on advertising, consumer protection, sales promotions, direct marketing, etc., need to be taken into consideration.

(d) Pricing decisions have to take account of currency exchange rate fluctuations.

(e) Competitors' behaviour may be difficult to monitor.

(f) Special packaging and labelling is usually required.

2. The marketing concept and the European marketing mix

The *marketing concept* is the idea that a firm should seek to evaluate market opportunities before production, assess potential demand for the good, determine the product characteristics desired by consumers, predict the prices consumers are willing to pay, and then supply goods corresponding to the needs and wants of target markets. Adherence to the marketing concept means the firm conceives and develops products that satisfy consumer wants. For international marketing this means the integration of the international side of the company's business with all aspects of its operations, and the willingness to create new products and adapt existing products to satisfy the needs of *world* markets. Products may have to be adapted to suit the tastes, needs and economic and other characteristics of consumers in specific regions, rather than it being assumed that an item which sells well in one country will be equally successful elsewhere.

The marketing mix

Marketing is a collection of activities that includes selling, advertising, public relations, sales promotions, research, new product development, package design, merchandising, the provision of after-sales service, and exporting. The term *marketing mix* describes the combination of marketing elements used in a given situation. Appropriate mixtures vary depending on the firm and industry. Major elements of the marketing mix can be listed under four headings:

(a) *Promotion* – including advertising, merchandising, public relations, and the utilisation of salespeople.

(b) *Product* – design and quality of output, assessment of consumer needs, choice of which products to offer for sale, and after-sales service.

(c) *Price* – choice of pricing strategy and prediction of competitors' responses.

(d) *Place* – selection of distribution channels and transport arrangements.

A firm's marketing mix will normally (but not necessarily – *see* **3**) have to be adapted for international (as opposed to purely domestic) marketing in consequence of the many national differences that exist in relation to stages of economic development (manifest in income levels and lifestyles), social systems, technological environments, legal frameworks, competitive situation, business practices and cultural perspectives. Promotion policy, for example, has to consider disparate laws and regulations on advertising and sales promotions, while pricing policies need to take into account wide variations in credit and delivery terms practiced in various states.

Approaches to international marketing

Differentiated international marketing strategies involve the modification of products and promotional messages to take account of cultural, linguistic, legal and other national characteristics. An *undifferentiated* marketing strategy, conversely, means the application of an identical marketing mix in all countries, and is normally cheaper to implement than the differentiated approach. Here the firm offers exactly the same product using identical promotional images and methods in a wide range of markets. Differences in market segments are ignored. Products are designed and advertised in order to appeal to the widest possible range of consumers. *Concentrated* marketing involves focusing all the firm's attention on a handful of markets and applying a different marketing mix to each market. The markets involved could be particular countries, or types of customer with common characteristics but resident in several different countries.

The following sections outline the main considerations to be taken into account when determining price, product and promotion policies for European markets. Place policies are discussed in Chapter 15.

3. Product policy

The fundamental decision to be taken here is whether to supply to foreign markets the firm's existing product, or modify the product to suit the needs of each foreign country. Product modification is appropriate where there exist:

- significant differences in local consumer taste
- intense competition in foreign markets (creating the need to differentiate a firm's output from that of foreign rivals)
- special local requirements in relation to package size, technical standards, consumer protection laws and customer care facilities
- differences in local climate, living conditions, literacy (buyers in poor countries might need low quality products), and in the uses to which the product might be put in various markets (Whitelock 1987).

The aim of product modification is to increase pan-European sales of the firm's core products through (i) the satisfaction of different customer needs in various regions, (ii) retention of existing customers by keeping the product up-to-date, and (iii) matching the product attributes offered by competing firms. Complementary products might be introduced to stimulate sales of existing lines, e.g. by improving the usefulness of currently produced items (gardening tools or DIY power accessories for example). The need for extensive product modification is a common impetus for firms to establish local manufacturing or assembly facilities in foreign countries, as it could well be cheaper to set up a new establishment to produce what is essentially a new product near to end consumers rather than make major changes to existing production lines and procedures at home.

The case for standardisation

A number of problems apply to product modification, notably that:

- Extra promotional costs have to be incurred.
- There is duplication of effort within the business.
- The company may possess insufficient experience and technical know-how of different products and how to market them.
- Technical research and development efforts might become fragmented as increasing amounts of resources are devoted to issues pertaining to the special requirements of particular national markets.

Supplying a single unmodified product can provide several advantages:

economies of scale in production, concentration of technical research into a limited area, standardisation of marketing and distribution methods, fewer staff training requirements, and so on. It leads to reduced stockholding costs (because demand in any market can be met from a single inventory of the same item), facilitates the development of technical expertise in a narrow area, and allows the interchangeability of spare parts and input components between supply points in various locations. Accordingly, firms sometimes attempt to create universal products (hopefully) suitable for all markets in all regions. This might be suitable where:

- The essential need that the product aims to satisfy is basically the same in all national and market segments.
- After-sales service is easily standardised.
- There exists a large market across several countries and cultural differences do not necessitate adaption.

BRANDING

4. Branding for European markets

A product is anything a business has to sell, whether this be a physical good or a service. 'New' products could be completely fresh innovations, or modifications of existing products, or copies of other firms' products. *Branding* a product means giving it a trade name and/or logo and then seeking via advertising and other sales promotion to associate certain attractive characteristics with the branded item. Customers then *recognise* the product and, having once been satisfied by it, need not subsequently re-evaluate its worth. Thus, little fresh information about the product has to be provided to the customer after it has been branded. Note that failure to brand a product convincingly can result in the waste of much of the firm's advertising, since advertisements will promote the *generic* product category (including competitors' versions) to which the item belongs rather than the output of the firm in question (Littler and Schlieper 1995).

Brand images encapsulate whole collections of product attributes and special features. Consumers come to know what the brand represents and may thus satisfy their requirements without careful thought or research. Also they can avoid repurchasing unsatisfactory branded items. If the firm sells several products in the same foreign country it must choose whether to allocate separate brand names to individual products or establish a generic 'family' brand covering all versions of its output. The latter approach can be highly cost-effective, especially if the various products are closely related through associated usage (toiletries for example) or a common channel of distribution, a common customer group or similarity of prices. This is because the entire product range may then be advertised under a single brand name, thus cutting the cost of advertising individual brands separately. Moreover, additions to product lines are introduced easily and inexpensively since no extra advertising or promotions need be incurred. The new product is simply incorporated into existing advertising literature – the firm does not have to establish a completely new individual brand image. Separate brands are essential, nevertheless, if the firm wishes to appeal to different market segments (e.g. in consequence of cultural differences) or where products are markedly dissimilar.

Choice of brand name

Brand names used in foreign markets need to be internationally acceptable, distinct and easily recognisable, culture free, legally available and not subject to local restrictions. A brand name is far more than a device to identify the supplier of a product; it is an advertisement in its own right and a means for arousing in consumers a set of emotions and mental images conducive to selling the item. Short, simple, easily read and easy-to-pronounce brand names are usually best for foreign markets. Such names can be used in several countries simultaneously, for family branding (*see* above), and may be supported within advertisements by a wide variety of pictorial illustrations.

5. Brand positioning

Market positioning involves finding out how customers think about the firm's products in relation to competing products, with a view either to modifying the product (plus associated advertising and other publicity) to make it fit in with these perceptions, or to changing the product's position in consumers' minds. Positions depend on the nature of the product, competing products and on how consumers see themselves (the lifestyles to which they aspire, role models, etc.). The essential issue is whether to attempt to position a brand similarly in all the nations in which the firm wishes to sell its outputs or to attempt different positions for the item in each country (Johansson and Thorelli 1985). A number of factors should influence the decision whether to opt for a single or different position in various countries:

(a) The degree of direct and immediate subsitutability between the advertised output and locally supplied brands (if this is high the appropriate position for the product should be self-evident).

(b) The scope of the product's appeal: whether it sells to a broad cross-section of consumers (in relation to their ages, sex, income level, lifestyle, etc.) or only within small market niches.

(c) The extent to which a product's selling points are perceived similarly in different nations.

(d) Whether the item fulfils the same consumer needs in each market.

(e) Whether the brand name and/or product features need to be altered for different markets.

Positioning a brand in the same location in all foreign markets has a number of practical advantages:

(a) The firm can concentrate all its creative efforts on a handful of variables equally relevant to all markets.

(b) Standardisation of advertising is facilitated, leading to many cost savings.

(c) A similar price can be charged in each market, so that common price lists, catalogues and other price-sensitive promotional materials can be printed.

(d) Similar demographic and lifestyle variables will be researched in each country. Hence, the firm only needs to monitor a few key statistics in the nations in which the product is sold.

Sound reasons for seeking different brand positions in various countries include:

- The existence of numerous possibilities for national stereotyping (e.g. precision and reliability in Germany, flair and elegance in France, style in Italy and so on). Stereotyping enables the advertiser instantly (and cheaply) to associate desirable national images with certain brands. Consumers' perceptions of a brand may be significantly influenced by the image of the country with which it is associated.
- The availability of extensive creative possibilities when drafting advertisements with nationalistic themes (windmills in The Netherlands, *haute couture* in France, pasta in Italy, etc.).
- Local customers' possible perceptions that locally produced goods are superior in quality (Belgian, French and German consumers are known to exhibit this characteristic for certain products).

6. Valuation of brands

Brand names are valuable assets in their own right. They can be sold, mortgaged, assigned to others or licensed in return for a royalty or lump-sum payment. Increasingly, firms prefer to acquire local firms that already possess strong brand images in foreign countries rather than incur the expense of introducing and developing their own brands in unfamiliar markets. Also, brand values often appear as intangible assets in company balance sheets, and the amounts stated have significant implications for the borrowing powers of the firm. Ultimately, the only way to value a brand is to sell it to the highest bidder on the open market. Unfortunately, there is typically no genuine competitive market when a brand comes up for sale: bilateral haggling between the brand owner and a single possible buyer normally applies. The vendor will probably begin the negotiation from a brand valuation based on the worth of the brand when used in the vendor's own business, which will depend on factors such as:

- the amount that has been spent on introducing and developing the brand (market research and advertising costs, agency fees, sales promotions expenses, etc.)
- the competitive situation and the risk of new brands entering the market
- whether the brand is a market leader or a market follower
- the number of countries in which the brand can be used without significant adaptation
- trends in consumer fashion likely to affect brand performance
- an estimate of the difference between the retail price made possible by

selling the firm's output under the existing brand name and the price for which it would have to be sold if unbranded

- the long-term stability of demand (and hence of output and the use of productive capacity) created by consumer loyalty towards the brand
- relations between the brand image and the firm's overall corporate image.

A firm considering purchasing an existing brand, conversely, will be concerned with:

- fluctuations in annual sales and the expected life of the company owning the brand
- the brand's ability to stand alone and create profits without having to rely on the sale of other goods, brands or services
- the brand's market position
- consumer brand awareness and brand loyalty, independent of the company owning the brand
- the magnitude of the flow of income expected to be generated by the brand in comparison with the return to be had from investing in some other form of asset.

PRICING

7. Pricing considerations

The price a firm may charge for its output depends on many factors, including:

- consumers' perceptions of the attributes and quality of the product
- total demand for the good (which depends on consumer income, the size of the market and seasonal and demographic factors)
- the degree of competition in the market
- price elasticity of demand for the product (i.e. the extent to which a price change leads to an alteration in sales)
- competitors' likely reactions to a price cut
- consumers' knowledge of the availability of substitute products
- the product's brand image and the degree of consumer loyalty
- costs of production and distribution.

Special problems apply to international (as opposed to purely domestic) pricing, particularly in relation to lack of information, uncertain consumer responses, foreign exchange rate influences, and the difficulty of estimating all the extra costs (including overheads) associated with foreign sales. These extra costs might include translating and interpreting fees, export packaging and documentation costs, insurance payments, clearing agents' fees, pre-shipment inspection and wharfage costs, and many other items. Credit periods are very long in some countries. Government price controls apply in certain states.

8. Pricing strategies

A number of pricing strategies are available, as follows:

(a) *Penetration pricing*, whereby a low price is combined with aggressive advertising aimed at capturing a large percentage of the market. The firm hopes that unit production costs will fall as output is expanded. The strategy will fail, however, if competitors simultaneously reduce their prices. This is a long-term strategy intended to build market share. It is expensive and normally involves substantial expenditures on promoting the product. Pricing at low levels in certain foreign markets might also be necessary in consequence of lower levels of consumers, intense local competition from rival companies, or weak demand for the product.

(b) *Skimming*, which is a high-price policy suitable for top quality versions of established products. The firm must convince high-income consumers that the expensive model offers distinct improvement over the standard version. This policy requires the existence in the local market of significant numbers of high-income consumers prepared to pay top prices. Products should be designed to appeal to affluent consumers, offering extra features, greater comfort, versatility or ease of operation. The firm trades off a low market share against a high margin. A foreign image can help a product sustain a premium price, provided the image involves special qualities or features not available in home-supplied competing goods.

(c) *Cost-plus pricing* whereby the supplying firm predetermines the length of a production run, adds up all its anticipated costs – fixed and variable – and divides estimated total cost by planned output. Some percentage mark-up is then added to get a unit price. Cost-plus pricing is problematic for firms producing several different products. Allocations of overheads to the various items will be arbitrary, to some extent, so that individual products may be over- or under-priced. Also not all of a production run will necessarily be sold. Some units may have to be put into stock or scrapped, hence altering the unit production costs of the remaining items. And how should an international firm serving many foreign markets relate its overheads to particular markets? For example, what proportion of senior management time should be assumed to be taken up by the firm's foreign operations? Should the business seek to cover *all* its costs including the firm's overheads ('full-cost' pricing) or merely the *variable* costs of foreign sales, regarding the latter as a bonus that contributes to total revenue but need not absorb overhead expenditures.

(d) *Product life-cycle pricing*. Here the price is varied according to the product's stage in its life cycle. Initially, a high price may be set to cover development and advertising costs. The price might then be systematically lowered to broaden the product's appeal.

RESEARCHING WEST EUROPEAN MARKETS

9. Nature of marketing research

Discovery of foreign marketing opportunities requires the assembly of information about the following:

- The size of overseas market segments, their buoyancy and prospects for expansion.
- Demographic structures of prospective markets in terms of age, sex composition, family structures, geographical spread of the population, etc.
- Market stability, local rates of inflation and economic growth.
- Whether local cultural norms and values might affect consumer perceptions of the firm's product, and if so the implications of this.
- Foreign tastes, lifestyles and spending patterns.
- Average local incomes and the distribution of wealth; living standards, housing, education and so on.
- Number of competitors, their strengths and weaknesses and modes of response to other firms' activities.
- Competitors' prices, product quality, credit terms, delivery periods, after-sales service, etc.
- How easily the firm monitors competitors' behaviour (price changes, product modifications, etc.).
- How frequently competitors change their prices (this is a crude indicator of the stability of the local market and whether local firms do actually compete).
- The selling points that competitors stress in their local advertising, and why these characteristics are emphasised.
- Local technical product standards and labelling requirements.
- Local preferences regarding package size, colouring and design, weights and volumes, shapes and ease of package disposal, etc.
- Local taxation; investment grants for establishing subsidiaries and/or owned distribution outlets.
- Nature of local distribution channels.
- Availability of commercial services (advertising agencies, debt collectors, warehousing facilities and so on).
- Frequency and whereabouts of local trade fairs and exhibitions.

Businesses can commission international marketing research from large agencies in their home countries (these agencies having international connections), or from local research firms based in foreign markets. Research companies apply the full range of MR techniques to their international work, including:

- Consumer sampling through questionnaires and interviews (undertaken by local employees of the research company)
- Market surveys

- Test marketing
- Canvassing competent local business people about a product's likely appeal
- Interpreting foreign statistical classifications, assessing data reliability, etc.)
- Conducting local telephone surveys
- Estimating the market shares of local competitors
- Obtaining details of the ownership and control of competing firms
- Assessing growth prospects in the local economy
- Establishing *why* competitors choose to distribute their products through certain channels
- Measuring local consumers' reactions to the firm's brand name and images
- Providing sales estimates for each of several possible selling prices
- Determining the costs and benefits of various distribution options
- Assessing the cost effectiveness of local advertising media
- Investigating various promotional possibilities
- Consulting local retail audits (i.e. continuously monitoring a panel of selected local retail outlets to check the level and periodicity of sales of the client firm's product).

Need for marketing research

Marketing research is necessary to decide which foreign markets the firm should enter and to determine the characteristics of the consumers they contain. It helps the firm formulate appropriate international marketing strategies, identify openings, and match the company's capabilities with opportunities to sell abroad. On completion of a marketing research exercise the company should be better able to select the best distribution channels, charge the right prices, use the most cost-effective advertising media, and know whether it should customise or standardise its products and campaigns.

10. Information for marketing research

Facilities for researching European markets are better and more extensive than ever before and the costs of undertaking significant market research have fallen substantially in recent years. The latter is due mainly to the increasing numbers of information providers – including national statistical services – that now make their outputs available via computerised on-line systems and/or CD-ROM. All European nations have government statistical offices that collect data, conduct surveys and publish the results. Normally, a national statistical office will respond to written requests for information provided its acquisition is straightforward and does not require special research, although the correspondence will probably need to be conducted in the language of the country concerned. However most of the publications of national statistical offices provide English sub-headings for important tables and graphs.

Eurostat (the EU's statistical service) provides a number of statistical databases of interest to business researchers, notably CRONOS and REGIO. The former carries a wide range of statistics concerning the economic, industrial, financial and social situations of various EU member states. An important sub-section of this database is EUROSTATUS, which has macroeconomic data on all sectors of the economies of EU members for (at least) the last 15 years. REGIO is a demographic database; its contents include details of population characteristics, workforce and unemployment data, industry breakdowns, and the entire national accounts of each EU country. Eurostat also produces COMEXT, a databank of statistics on intra-EU and external trade. Other important Eurostat publications are its quarterly bulletin, *European Economy*, which outlines key economic trends in member states, and the *Panorama of EU Industries*, that covers 15 product groups and includes brief pan-EU industry surveys.

Further sources of information for in-house research include:

- statistics gathered by international organisations, notably the OECD, United Nations, European Commission and the International Monetary Fund
- trade and technical magazines
- directories and data books issued by private publishing companies (Euromonitor's *International Marketing Data and Statistics*, for example)
- databases held by database hosts such as DIALOG or FT PROFILE
- chambers of commerce and trade associations.

The European market research industry

Market research companies are available to conduct investigations in all West European countries. Estimates published by the European Commission indicate that the European Union has around 2000 significant market research (MR) organisations, including five of the world's ten largest research firms. Collectively, the Union's MR industry accounts for about 40 per cent of all market research undertaken in the world. Europe's ten biggest MR firms take half the industry's total revenue. Otherwise however, Europe's market research industry is fragmented and contains an extremely large number of one or two person firms (CEC 1996).

SEGMENTING EUROPEAN MARKETS

The European Union contains so many consumers that it is necessary for the firm to attempt to discover the *types* of person most likely to purchase its products. Then, either a standardised promotional campaign can be devised to communicate a common message to the same group in various countries, or a customised approach may be adopted with separate tailor-made advertisements for each group in each European state.

11. Market segmentation

This is the process of dividing the total market into sub-units and then modifying the product and/or the way it is packaged, advertised or otherwise promoted in order to satisfy the particular customer requirements of each market segment. Traditionally, markets have been segmented with respect to geographical location, socio-economic structure, age, sex, ethnic origin, religion, etc. Increasingly, however, attention is paid to the behavioural aspects of target segments, especially the relationship between spending patterns and the life styles (actual or desired) of various consumer groupings.

The objective of market segmentation is to identify specific consumer groups (e.g. high-income middle-aged women with no children living at home, who work in offices, have received a certain level of education and who cook using electricity), within which potential customers are as homogenous as possible, and then devise products and campaigns suitable for those markets. Accurate segmentation enables the firm to pinpoint and tailor its marketing activities to satisfy consumer needs (Day *et al.* 1988).

Data on consumers' ages, sex, income levels, occupations, educational backgrounds, marital status and social class can be extremely useful in identifying the whereabouts of potential markets. Each time a fresh variable is added to the analysis the narrower the target market becomes. This results in a more precise specification of the customer type being sought.

12. Demographic segmentation

Variables used to segment markets demographically include the sex, age, income, household size, occupation, physical whereabouts, social status, etc. of prospective customers. A number of EU countries follow the UK in having their national statistical authorities divide people into six categories: A, B, C1, C2, D and E. Grades A and B contain the upper middle class, professional and managerial people and others on high incomes; categories B and C1 are the middle and lower middle classes, including clerical and administrative workers on above-average incomes; C2 is the skilled working class earning average incomes; D comprises unskilled manual workers with below-average income levels; class E contains the elderly, the unemployed and other poor people. In the Netherlands, however, the statistical authorities divide the Dutch population into categories for Professional and Higher Managerial, Intermediate Managerial, Clerical and Skilled Manual, and Pensioners and the Unskilled. The German authorities segment Germans in terms of monthly household income. France combines 'senior management' with the self-employed, and has further classes for professional, white collar and blue collar employees. Greece divides its population according to residence in urban, semi-urban or rural areas. Further definitional and measurement discrepancies apply in many other demographic fields.

13. Psychographic segmentation

Consumers possessing identical demographic characteristics might nevertheless have quite different attitudes, perspectives and purchasing behaviour. For example, two households may be located in the same area and have equal incomes, yet exhibit enormous differences in their consumption patterns according to their lifestyles, attitudes and aspirations. Hence the incorporation into the analysis of a psychographic dimension to reflect consumer lifestyles, personality type, interests, leisure activities, perspectives and opinions may be needed in order to reduce the extent of the markets under review. The term 'psychographics' refers to the systematic study of consumer lifestyles, attitudes, interests, opinions and prejudices as they affect purchasing behaviour. Psychographics seeks to sketch profiles of particular consumer groups and hence identify demands for certain products from key variables that characterise consumer types. For instance, an outdoor type who enjoys sport, fast cars, action-packed television pro-grammes, etc. may be attracted by products with rugged images that correspond to these conceptions. This kind of analysis distinguishes between consumers in terms of their activities, interests and opinions; particularly *vis-à-vis* their use of leisure, mental priorities, stances on ethical and social issues, and attitudes towards themselves and the environments in which they exist (Baalbaki and Malhotra 1993).

Problems with psychographic market segmentation

Psychographic analysis rests on the assumption that consumers have *consistent* values, beliefs and attitudes that are not subject to sudden and unpredictable change. Yet this is not always true. Note moreover that the psychosocial cate-gorisations used in psychographics are highly subjective and open to numerous interpretations. What *exactly* is meant by terms such as 'sophisticated', 'reflect-ive', 'persuadable', 'refined', etc.? Implementation of campaigns resulting from segmentation exercises requires the existence of highly specialised advertising media (specialist magazines, cable TV programmes catering for special interests, etc.) capable of carrying specially devised messages to narrowly defined target groups. Critics of psychographic analysis might allege that the outputs from psychographic analyses offer little that is of *practical* value to advertising firms, and that relating psychographic concepts directly to consumer behaviour is extremely problematic.

14. The European consumer

The European Union is home to very many cultural, societal, socio-economic and other groupings, and European consumer behaviour is extremely diverse. Not surprisingly, therefore, several attempts at analysing EU cultural and atti-tudinal differences have been made in order to define the precise whereabouts of various target consumer categories.

European lifestyles

'Lifestyle' emerges from a large number of interacting variables: income, up-bringing, experiences, relationships with others, cultural influences, etc. It in-volves a pattern of living habits, methods for communicating with the outside world, leisure pursuits, types of entertainment purchased, and so on. Often, people buy goods they feel they ought to purchase in order to pursue a particular lifestyle, rather than products they objectively need! 'Vicarious participation' in a certain desired way of life (e.g. healthy, sophisticated, outdoor, 'man-about-town', etc.) is sometimes possible via consuming goods mentally associated with the lifestyle to which the individual aspires. Hence the firm needs to identify the lifestyle characteristics (real or imagined) of consumers likely to buy its goods so that it can focus its promotional and general marketing efforts in the most cost effective ways.

European lifestyles have been analysed and classified for a number of years (Burt 1989). The aim of these studies is to identify in consumers certain common characteristics, such as:

- whether their outlooks are 'conservative and traditional' or whether they are 'innovative and adventurous'
- attitudes toward home, family, security and the propriety of the status quo
- whether they are motivated by materialistic or non-materialistic drives
- the extent to which their main concern is merely to exist and survive rather than engage in luxury and/or conspicuous consumption
- the degree of logic and rationality they apply to purchasing decisions
- whether they are 'inner directed' (i.e. concerned with personal growth, individual freedom and human relations) or 'outer directed' materialists who gain greater satisfaction from physical consumption of goods.

Sub-categories may be discerned for each of these dimensions (e.g. ambitious achievers; the near-destitute struggling poor; the materialistic young, etc.) within various EU countries. With European consumers neatly categorised in these ways it may be feasible to launch a variety of pan-European products, each slightly modified to appeal to specific types of consumer. A crucial distinction emerging from these studies is between Europe's haves and have-nots. Among the haves there appear to be three groups: idealists involved in the higher realms of human affairs (art, music, ecology and so on); materialists with high profile spending habits; and a comfortably off suburban middle class exhibiting 'traditional' attitudes and consumer behaviour. It has been suggested that the first of these groups comprises around ten per cent of the populations of most EU nations; the second group about 15 per cent; and the third between 25 and 50 per cent.

European have-nots, it seems, divide into two categories: those who (while poor) have skills, jobs (albeit with occasional bouts of unemployment) and some prospects; and a disaffected underclass without cultural or economic roots, and which is prone to long-term unemployment. The latter section of the population normally resides in inner cities in northern Europe (particularly in Britain) and also rural areas in Europe's south. Better-off have-nots usually account for 20 to 25 per cent of the population of EU nations; the underclass (found predominantly in southern Europe, the Irish Republic and the UK) could constitute 20 to 30 per cent of the population of certain EU nations (around ten per cent in continental north European states).

EUROPEAN MARKETING COMMUNICATIONS

15. Advertising

The EU's definition of advertising is 'the making of a representation in any form in connection with a trade, business, craft or profession in order to promote the supply of goods or services, including immovable property, rights and obligations' (EU Directive on Misleading Advertising 1984). Objectives of advertising include:

- creation of consumer awareness of products, special offers and available discounts
- projection of favourable corporate loyalty
- establishment of brand loyalty
- development of feelings of need for specific goods
- encouragement of retailers to stock certain products
- reinforcement of brand images at or near points of sale.

Formulation of an advertising strategy requires the clear identification of target consumers and a definition of the product attributes they desire.

Advertising agencies

Agencies plan campaigns, design advertisements, create slogans, produce artwork and television commercials, and place advertisements in suitable media. They charge commissions to the media with which advertisements are placed and thus can offer their services to client companies at very low cost, though agency work related to ancillary activities such as market research, direct mail or public relations must be paid for at negotiated rates. Advertisers do not have to use agencies, and are free to contact media directly themselves. However, agencies possess wide-ranging experience of media administration, and often they can secure bulk discounts on advertising space. Advertising which attracts agency commissions (such as that which appears in the press, on television and on posters) is referred to as 'above the line' advertising, as opposed to (non-commission bearing) 'below the line' techniques of public relations, sales promotions (*see* 26) and so on.

Domestic versus foreign advertising agencies

Using a large agency based in the supplying firm's own country offers 'one stop shopping' to the client business. This type of agency will already possess extensive stocks of research data on international markets, on foreign consumer tastes and buying habits, and on the sort of messages that are likely to succeed in various countries. And there is easy liaison with agency staff. On the other hand, a domestic agency does not *necessarily* have better contacts with and information about local media than smaller foreign agencies within the countries concerned. Reasons for selecting a local foreign agency might include:

- its ability to give the exporting firm a local image
- potential for close and effective liaison with local distribution agents and/or other representatives
- possibly a higher level of effort and commitment on the part of local agencies, which need to offer a better service in order to compete with larger and better-known multinational rivals
- flair and creativity that is sometimes absent in big international agencies.

16. Advertising in the European Union

According to Eurostat (*see* 14:**10**) about 1.2 per cent of total EU GDP is spent on advertising. In terms of total (rather than per capita) spending, Germany is Europe's biggest advertising nation followed by France, the UK and Spain. If advertising is measured as a percentage of GDP, however, Spain is West Europe's most advertising-oriented country, followed by Denmark and Britain. It is least important, using the latter criteria, in Belgium and Italy, with Portugal and Greece also scoring low. EU advertising is controlled by domestic laws, national voluntary restrictions imposed by self-regulatory organisations (advertisers' associations or advertising stand-ards authorities for example) and, increasingly, by EU Directives. National laws and regulations differ with respect to the categories of product that may be advertised, the contents of advertisements (e.g. whether comparative advertising is permitted, restrictions on actors portraying members of the medical profession, the use of children as models, etc.), and the creative approaches that may be employed (for example, it is illegal in many countries to instil fear in consumers' minds in order to advertise products). The media permitted to carry advertisements and the amounts of advertising allowed on each also varies from state to state, and certain governments require a predetermined proportion of commercials to be locally produced (as in Luxembourg for instance).

Cultural differences

National advertising media (newspapers, TV, magazines, etc.) are influenced by national culture in terms of the spoken and written language used (differences between hi-brow and low-brow newspapers are critically impor-tant in some EU states); whether a country has a tabloid press; and the editorial contents of magazines, newspapers and radio and television pro-grammes. Attitudes expressed by the media towards national issues (manifest in non-coverage of 'taboo' subjects, adoption of ideological 'lines', etc.) are also subject to cultural influences. Culture affects the makeup of society (kinship patterns, social stratification, etc.), consumer behaviour, who makes purchasing decisions within families, and how national markets divide into sub-units. It influences such matters as how local consumers perceive the value for money of competing brands; how the female form may be used in advertisements; and the degrees of elegance, quality, urbanity, humour or factual contents expected in advertisements. Significant differences in national advertising style already exist. British advertising, for example, uses humour extensively, whereas German advertisements tend to stick to the facts. French and Italian advertising contains much sexual innuendo in comparison with advertising in other EU states.

17. Standardisation versus customisation of advertising campaigns

The key issue in cross-border European advertising is whether the firm should standardise its advertising messages or adapt them to meet the requirements of particular foreign markets (Anholt 1993; Agrawal 1995). Some advertising messages are applicable to several countries, others are relevant to only one. Much depends on the degree of homogeneity of target consumers in various countries, their lifestyles, interests, incomes and tastes. The advantages of uniformity are that it:

- requires less marketing research in individual countries
- is relatively cheap and convenient to administer
- demands less creative time to devise advertisements; a single message is constructed and used in all markets.

Customisation, conversely, might be necessary in consequence of;

- cultural differences between countries and/or market segments
- translation difficulties between different languages
- differences in the educational backgrounds of target groups in various countries
- non-availability of certain media (specialist magazines, for instance) in some regions
- differences in national attitudes towards advertising.

To the extent that alterations are needed they may take one or more of the following forms:

(a) Different media. For instance, listeners to commercial radio in different countries might typically belong to different socio-economic groups.

(b) Changes in symbols, e.g. using a male rather than a female model as the dominant figure in an advertisement. This might be necessary if males are the primary purchasers of the product in one market and females in another.

(c) Changes in advertisement headlines and body copy.

(d) Changes in the fundamental selling proposition. For instance, presenting a bicycle as a leisure item in one market, a fashion accessory in another, and as a commuting vehicle elsewhere.

The extent to which the same messages can successfully be applied transnationally depends on whether in various countries the product:

- is used in the *same way*
- satisfies the *same consumer needs*
- appeals to the *same consumer type*

- can be sold at *similar prices*
- is purchased in response to the *same consumer motives* (convenience, status, impulse buying, etc.)
- evokes mental images that can be manipulated using *pictures rather than words*
- can be advertised in the *same media*
- is *perceived* by consumers in a similar manner (e.g. technically complex electrical equipment may be seen as performing exactly the same function regardless of the customer's location) and is *evaluated using similar criteria*
- has just one or two universally intelligible *selling points*
- cannot by *law* be promoted in certain ways
- is purchased by consumers with *similar income levels*
- is typically bought by the *same family members* (wives, husbands, parents, etc.)
- is demanded in the *same package sizes and quantities*
- is purchased with the *same frequency* (weekly, monthly, irregularly)
- appeals to the *same cultural traditions*.

18. Misleading Advertising Directive 1984

This seeks to protect businesses and the general public against the effects of misleading advertising. The latter is defined as advertising that deceives or is likely to deceive the people it reaches and which, by virtue of its deceptive nature, could affect consumer behaviour or cause damage to a competing firm. Under the Directive the burden of proof lies with the advertiser and not with the consumer. National courts are empowered to halt the publication of misleading advertising.

The purpose of the Directive was to provide procedures for the overall *control* of misleading advertising – not to specify detailed rules. Hence, the Directive requires that each EU member state has a supervisory body capable of regulating misleading advertising, and sets out a general framework for the determination of what is not allowed, notably misleading information concerning either:

- a product (its characteristics, price, capabilities, fitness for purpose, where it was made, etc.); *or*
- the advertiser, e.g. the size of the firm, the advertiser's qualifications or true identity.

The national supervisory bodies demanded by the Directive may be self-regulatory (e.g. the UK Advertising Standards Authority) but, if this is the case, it must be backed up by government organisations with legal powers. In Britain the Office of Fair Trading fulfils this role.

Nature of deceptive advertising

Definition of misleading advertising as 'advertising that deceives' begs the question of what precisely is meant by 'deception'. The Directive defines advertising as follows:

Advertising means the making of a representation in any form in connection with a trade, business, craft or profession in order to promote the supply of goods or services, including immovable property, rights and obligations.

The term 'making a representation' in the above does not necessarily mean that the representation has to be literally true, although the representation presented should obviously create a fair impression. It took ten years to agree the final wording of the Misleading Advertising Directive, and much controversy preceded the eventual draft. The European Commission contributed to the debate via a memorandum setting out the Commission's opinions regarding the circumstances in which the public might be misled. Although the details of the memorandum were not incorporated into the 1984 Directive, it is instructive to note the Commission's comments as a means for determining what 'misleading' advertising actually involves.

According to the Commission, misleading advertising occurs when claims are made that are false, partially true and partially false, contain insufficient information, or which:

- create a false impression
- cannot be substantiated
- make offers that are unlikely to be fulfilled.

Further reasonable implications to be drawn from the Misleading Advertising Directive are that:

- Advertisements should not be allowed if they *intend* to mislead consumers, even if an actual deception cannot be proven to have occurred.
- Failure to disclose relevant facts is tantamount to deception.
- Statements can be misleading even if the separate phrases they contain are not untrue when taken individually.

Descriptions may be misleading in relationship to weights, sizes, quantities, place of origin, method of manufacture, contents, fitness for purpose, conformity to standards, identity or competence of the supplier. Pictures are covered by the legislation as well as words, e.g. a photograph of a country different to that of the country of origin of the item. Goods may be described through a label, a statement on a package, statements in documents (guarantees, for example) relating to the goods, or through signs on, above, alongside or near the goods.

Sellers can avoid liability if they prove that a false description was given due to a genuine mistake, or by accident, provided all reasonable precautions against mistakes and accidents had been taken.

19. The Cross-Frontier Broadcasting Directive 1989

Effective from 1992, this Directive guarantees freedom of transmission in broadcasting across national frontiers and lays down minimum rules on advertising. Responsibility for the control of advertising lies with the authorities of the country in which an advertisement originated. The Directive (a) set limits on the airtime devoted to commercials (no more that 15 per cent of total daily transmissions, with a maximum of 18 per cent during peak hours), (b) banned the TV advertising of tobacco and prescription pharmaceuticals, and (c) introduced guidelines for TV alcohol advertising, for advertising to children and the sponsorship of television programmes. In particular it bans the use in advertisements of pornography and gratuitous violence that could adversely affect young viewers.

The Directive recommends that broadcasters in each EU state attempt to use a majority of EU-produced TV programmes, excluding news and sports bulletins. Specific provisions are as follows:

(a) Advertisements aimed at children must follow the recommendations of a code of practice on this matter published by the International Chamber of Commerce.

(b) Alcohol advertisements may not target young people (or even show them drinking alcohol); link alcohol to driving, physical performance, social or sexual success; encourage heavy drinking or the consumption of drinks with an especially high alcohol content; or claim that alcohol is therapeutic or able to solve personal problems.

(c) Sponsors of televisions programmes must be clearly identified, may not influence editorial content and not recommend the purchase of specific items. Suppliers of tobacco or pharmaceutical products may not sponsor programmes.

(d) Tobacco cannot be advertised on television indirectly, e.g. through showing brand images, symbols or other identifying features of tobacco products.

The essential problem with the Directive is that whereas it attempts to maintain the cultural identity of European broadcast media (which implies restricting the frequency of commercial breaks), it is also necessary to recognise that advertising revenues are the life blood of the radio and television industries, and that limits on advertising necessarily reduce the extent and variety of available channels and programmes. Also, the lengths and makeups of programmes might be manipulated in order to circumvent whatever specific restrictions are imposed.

Satellite broadcasts

The European Commission cannot, of course, control satellite broadcasts emanating from beyond its frontiers. Accordingly, the European Commission has issued a set of guidelines to which advertisements should adhere. These guidelines request that advertisements do not:

- portray behaviour that is prejudicial to health and safety
- offend prevailing standards of decency and good taste
- engender fear in those watching the broadcast
- contain material encouraging racial or sexual discrimination
- offend religious or political beliefs.

Note the contradiction between the first of these recommendations and tobacco and alcohol advertising.

20. Commission proposals on comparative advertising

For some years the European Commission has been attempting to introduce a Directive on comparative advertising, which is illegal in some EU states, subject to stringent conditions in others, but free of all restrictions elsewhere. Comparative advertising was defined in the original 1991 Draft Directive as any which 'explicitly or by implication identifies a competitor or goods or services of the same kind offered by a competitor'. The intention is to harmonise EU member countries' currently diverse laws and regulations on comparative claims, and allow advertisers to make direct comparisons between competing firms and products – provided the comparisons are fair and verifiable. The proposals apply to advertisements, messages printed on packages, and all other kinds of promotional material.

The problems involved

Some EU member nations (Italy and Greece, for example) have already incorporated the provisions of the Proposals into their domestic advertising law. Other countries, however, are resolutely opposed to the intended measure, on the following grounds:

(a) The objective superiority of one brand over another is rarely demonstrable.

(b) Consumers do not normally possess the technical knowledge or information necessary to validate comparisons. An 'advertising war' based on comparative claims and counter-claims could erupt, leaving consumers hopelessly confused.

(c) Comparative advertising can be used to promote unfair competition in that one or more large and powerful companies can launch a campaign criticising a smaller business's branded output, without the small firm having the resources necessary to respond to the challenge. This could drive smaller enterprises into liquidation, leaving big firms free to exploit customers.

(d) Allegations made by advertisers against competing products are likely to be vexatious and intended to mislead.

The main argument in favour of comparative advertising is that it increases the amount of information available to customers. Advocates of comparative advertising allege, moreover, that:

- The ability to advertise comparatively is essential to ensure 'freedom of commercial speech'.
- Consumers can easily spot false comparisons.
- In practice, misleading comparative claims are unlikely because they bring into disrepute the credibility of the firms making them.
- It *stimulates* rather than inhibits competition, because the targets of criticism will be impelled to improve the quality of their products and levels of customer service.

In 1995 a new clause was added to the Draft Directive stipulating that in order to be lawful comparative advertising must not mislead; not cause confusion between the advertiser and a competitor or between the former's name, trade marks, goods or services and those of a competitor; and not discredit, denigrate or bring contempt on a competitor. Comparisons must *objectively* compare the 'material, relevant, verifiable and fairly chosen features of competing goods and services'. Under the Draft Directive, each member state must institute a means for obtaining legal redress against unfair comparative advertising. Courts must be able to order the cessation of misleading campaigns.

21. Public relations (PR)

The UK Institute of Public Relations defines PR as 'the deliberate, planned and sustained effort to establish and maintain mutual understanding between an organisation and its public'. A PR consultant will help the client firm (i) determine the various 'publics' it needs to influence, (ii) define the messages to which these publics will most favourably respond, and (iii) decide how best to reach target groups. This may involve research into how the firm and its operations and products are perceived by outsiders, and into the media seen most often by the company's leading publics (e.g. which newspapers are read by the people it most needs to influence).

Public relations consultancies operate in all EU states and the majority of large European companies include public relations as a key element of their corporate strategies. Europe's PR industry is more than double the size of that of Japan but is still only a quarter the size of that of the United States, so there is obviously scope for expansion. Europe's public relations industry is highly fragmented. There are many single-person firms, and it is common for employees of larger PR organisations to quit and take clients with them. Entry to the PR industry is relatively easy as there are no industry standards, little restrictive legislation on PR activities, and no obligation for PR practitioners to belong to national professional bodies. The industry's key resource is people: minimal capital investment in premises or equipment is necessary. PR activity is expanding in all EU countries. Major factors contributing to the increased demand for PR services include the following:

(a) Escalating costs of European above-the-line advertising media.

(b) The development of equity markets and wider share ownership in several European countries, leading to increased demand for PR assistance with investor relations.

(c) PR's ability to target precise groups of people whose attitudes are crucial for the well-being of the firm.

(d) Large-scale privatisation programmes in many countries (which boost the demand for investor, employee and consumer PR services). Mergers and acquisitions among EU companies also give rise to the need for PR activity.

DIRECT MARKETING

22. Nature of direct marketing

Direct marketing covers direct mail, telephone selling, catalogues and 'off-the-page' selling via cut-outs in newspaper and magazine advertisements, and is increasingly important as a selling medium through the European Union. Indeed, the European Commission estimates that direct marketing today accounts for about a quarter of all commercial communication expenditure occurring within member states. Note however that a small number of product sectors dominate the industry's turnover, notably insurance and financial services, consumer durables, foodstuffs, credit cards and business-to-business promotions.

Direct marketing is an increasingly important marketing tool. A major reason for this, of course, is the growing number of independent households in many countries resulting from falling birth rates, higher divorce rates and increased longevity, and hence fresh possibilities for the identification of distinct market segments among various types of family group (Baines 1995). Profiles of particular customers can be built up using information from the firm's accounting and sales files in conjunction with data about their neighbourhoods, businesses (where appropriate) or socio-demographic characteristics; consumers' names and addresses may be easily assembled for repeated direct marketing use and perhaps sold to other parties. Specific reasons for the expansion of the European direct marketing industry include:

- The increasing availability of good quality lists of prospective customers
- New developments in information technology (especially database technology and desk top publishing) which enable smaller companies to produce high-quality direct marketing materials in-house. Also, advances in mailing technology have greatly reduced the costs of distributing direct-mail literature.
- The rapid escalation of the costs of conventional advertising in many EU states
- The availability of interactive television facilities whereby consumers may order goods through a teletext system.

23. Direct mail

The volume of addressed direct mail is greatest in Germany (where nearly four billion items are mailed in the west of the country each year) followed by France (three billion), the United Kingdom (2.5 billion), Belgium and the Netherlands (approaching one billion each). Note the importance of direct mail in the latter two countries relative to the sizes of their populations. In terms of direct mail expenditures however the UK is on the same level as (western) Germany, reflecting the high costs of direct mail activity in Britain. Direct mail spending per head of population is greatest (by far) in Denmark, followed by the UK, (west) Germany and Spain (Baines 1995; Royal Mail International 1993). Differences in the media available to carry advertisements in various countries help explain divergences in direct mail expenditures.

Direct mail has many advantages as a medium for reaching EU businesses and end consumers. It is flexible, selective and potentially highly cost-effective. Messages can be addressed exclusively to a target market, advertising budgets may be concentrated on the most promising market segments, and it will be some time before competitors realise that the firm has launched a campaign. Also the size, content, timing and geographical coverage of mailshots can be varied at will: the firm can spend as much or as little as necessary to achieve its objectives. There are no media space or airtime restrictions and no copy or insertion deadlines to be met. All aspects of the direct-mail process are subject to the firm's immediate control, and it can experiment by varying the approach used in different countries. Further advantages are that:

- Personalised messages may be transmitted.
- Customers can be quickly advised about special discounts, credit offers, sales promotions, etc.
- A variety of informative and persuasive items can be included in the envelope.
- A number of response mechanisms are available, including international freephone telephone numbers.

List broking

Lists of names and addresses of potential customers can be rented from commercial list broking firms, which now operate in all EU states. List broking is expanding particularly rapidly in France, the Netherlands and Italy. Europe's worst countries for list availability are Spain, Portugal and Greece. In Belgium, the majority of purchasable lists are for individual named consumers rather than for named firms. The Belgian Post Office keeps lists of households that wish to receive information on various product categories. Accordingly, the Belgian Post Office can deliver publicity materials to its list of all people in Belgium with a certain interest, without the items having to be individually addressed. In Sweden and Finland the user of a list must state its source on promotional literature sent to addresses. List brokers take their profits by charging commissions to list owners (the standard international rate is 20 per cent), so that they can offer their services to clients either free of charge or at low cost (depending on the amount of work involved).

Mailing preference schemes ('Robinson lists') whereby individuals may register with a national list of people not wishing to receive direct mail literature operate in Belgium, France, the UK, Germany and the Netherlands. An EU-wide mailing preference scheme is currently being devised by the managements of the Robinson lists of these five countries.

The Draft Directive on Distance Selling 1992

This is intended to apply to contracts entered into without simultaneous physical contact between buyer and seller; to the supply of unsolicited goods (referred to as 'inertia selling'); to direct mail and catalogue selling; and to telephone, fax, electronic mail and television sales.

If adopted the Directive will cover all goods and services, with the following exceptions:

- goods or services intended for current consumption (foodstuffs or beverages for instance)
- services that require a reservation (e.g. theatre bookings or reservations for railway seats or hotel rooms)
- made-to-measure products
- automated vending machines and automated self-service outlets.

The Draft Directive also extends to credit and transactions where a credit card number is given to the supplier, but not the card itself, and where the validity of the transaction is disputed. Under the Draft Directive customers will be entitled to a seven-day cooling-off period (during which a contract may be cancelled without penalty) and any contract entered into will have to be performed within 30 days of the date of the agreement. Customers must be given clear information about the identity of the supplier, the full price, transport charges, and payment and delivery arrangements. Any agreement by the customer to waive the rights confered by the proposed Directive will not be legally valid.

24. The Directive on Data Protection 1996

By the year 1990, five out of the twelve EU countries had yet to implement significant data protection legislation (which is stringent in northern Europe; virtually non-existent in the south) while the remaining seven had legislated in different ways. The data protection laws of France, the UK and the Netherlands require that the holding of personal data be registered with a central authority. Elsewhere however, registration is not required (in recognition of the impossibility of policing registration in the modern business world, where virtually every firm has at least one microcomputer that holds personal information). Data collection methods must be 'lawful' in the Netherlands; while under British legislation they must be 'fair' as well as lawful; and in France 'not intended to deceive'. The period for which personal data may be stored is severely restricted in Denmark and Germany, but not at all in the UK or France. In Denmark, list brokers cannot lawfully pass a consumer's name and address to third parties without the consumer's express permission. The merging of lists from different sources is illegal. Most commercially available Danish lists are for business-to-business marketing, although even here company lists cannot be merged. Under German law, non-personalised direct mail literature may not be delivered to any household which displays a sign stating that the household does not wish to receive it. A consequence of Germany's strict approach to data protection is that many direct marketing agencies, list brokers, etc., serving the German market operate from Austria, where legislation is less severe (although even here it is illegal to cross-reference names and addresses with the known special interests of the individuals who appear on mailing lists). Finland has stringent laws on data protection which, *inter-alia*, limit the compilation of lifestyle databases to just one piece of information additional to the name, address and telephone number, profession, age and sex of the data subject. Unaddressed mail may not be delivered to any household that displays a sign indicating its unwillingness to receive unsolicited promotional literature. In Sweden, most direct mail is unaddressed, consequent to the restrictive data protection laws of this country. Greece, Spain, Portugal and Italy, conversely, have minimal data protection legislation.

The European Commission issued in 1990 a Draft Directive intended to harmonise national data protection legislation and 'ensure the free and un-fettered flow of data within the EU'. Under the proposals (which were agreed by the Council of Ministers in 1995), data subjects (consumers) will have to give their express permission to the use by firms of data about them. The onus will be on businesses to seek the consent of data subjects and to provide them with full details of all intended disclosures. Paper records as well as computerised records will be subject to control (at present paper records are exempt from the Data Protection Acts of several EU nations) and, impor-tantly, the profiling of consumers (i.e. deliberately collecting information on several dimensions of the lifestyles and activities of target groups) will be severely restricted (illegal in certain circumstances). The transfer of data to countries outside the EU that do not have equally stringent data protection laws will be forbidden, and blanket swapping between organisations will not be allowed. Even if a data subject gives permission for his or her details to be used, that person will have to be notified the first time the data is passed on to a third party.

Member states will have three years to implement the Directive (which at the time of writing has yet to be published in the *Official Journal*). Special provisions apply to the processing of 'sensitive' personal data, defined to include personal details that reveal racial or ethnic origin, political opinions, religious beliefs, trade union membership or matters relating to a person's health. Such data cannot be processed without the data subject's consent.

25. Telemarketing

This can be used both for consumer and business-to-business campaigns throughout the EU. The telephone can also be employed to undertake fast low-cost market research. Telemarketing covers cold calling by salespeople, market surveys conducted by telephone, calls designed to compile databases of possible sales prospects and follow-ups to customer requests for further infor-mation resulting from print and broadcast advertisements. Currently, the ma-jority of cross-border telemarketing campaigns focus on business-to-business contacts, essentially because of the combined telephone/fax/telex/database facilities that an increasing number of companies possess and, in consequence, the greater reliability of business-to-business communications. The European Commission estimates that at least 1000 telemarketing bureaux now operate in EU countries, and that telemarketing is the fastest growing sector of the direct marketing field. According to the Commission, the EU telemarketing industry has a turnover in excess of 3.5 billion ECU, This figure represents about 0.1 per cent of EU GDP and around six per cent of the sum spent on traditional advertising media (CEC 1996).

France has the European Union's most developed telemarketing industry, with a turnover exceeding 1200 million ECU each year. The Netherlands comes next, followed by Germany (though note that much German telemarketing is done via Austria in order to circumvent German legal restrictions on the activity). Telemarketing is least used in Portugal, Greece and Ireland. Cross-frontier telemarketing normally requires the use of a commercial telemarketing agency. Language skills are required, plus considerable skills and experience in identifying decision makers in target firms. Note how telemarketing agencies can be engaged to receive the incoming calls resulting from an EU-wide freefone number maildrop campaign. Switchboard operators taking such calls have to be competent to respond in any of the EU languages and then pass the call to someone sufficiently *au fait* with the caller's language to be able to follow up the enquiry. The major telemarketing agencies now have transnational arrangements enabling the local country processing of incoming calls.

SALES PROMOTIONS

26. Nature of sales promotions

Sales promotions can be a highly effective tool for marketing goods in EU countries. They can be used for much diverse purposes penetrating new markets, shifting slow-moving stock, encouraging consumer loyalty, stimulating impulse purchases, increasing the frequency of repeat buying, smoothing out seasonal demand, and generally drawing attention to the firm and its products. A wide range of promotional devices is available, including free samples and free draws, competitions, money-off coupons, and premium offers (e.g. send in a certain number of packet tops plus a small amount of money and receive the offered item at a very low price).

Directorate-General III of the European Commission periodically conducts surveys of the European sales promotions industry (the results of which are published in the biennial *Panorama of EU Industries*) that indicate very rapid growth in the sector. An average real growth rate of five per cent per annum was recorded for the (then) EU twelve during the early 1990s, with the Commission forecasting that the growth rate would more than double that of conventional advertising until the end of the decade. Factors contributing to the expansion of the sales promotions industry, according to DG III, are as follows:

- Possibilities for using sales promotions as a viable alternative to (more expensive) conventional advertising.
- The increasing employment of sales promotions as a key element of integrated pan-European promotional campaigns.
- Competitive pressures which cause companies to prefer marketing methods with directly measurable returns to those which (like media advertising) possess less quantifiable outcomes.
- Greater competition among European retailers.

- Higher levels of brand awareness among EU consumers, leading to the need for manufacturers to defend brand shares.
- Concentration of the European retailing industry into larger units, each capable of demanding improved service from supplying firms.
- Proliferation of brands (including own-label brands of the big retail firms) leading to intense competition for shelf space and the best shelf positions.
- Relaxation of the laws on sales promotions in a number of European countries (but see below).
- Developments in retail technology (electronic funds transfer at point of sale, in-store scanning, etc.) that enable the effects of particular promotions to be easily monitored.

27. Legal problems

Different laws apply to sales promotions in different EU countries. Hence it is not possible to employ the same promotional devices in all EU states. For example, a money-off voucher is legal in Spain but not in Germany; a 'lower price for the next purchase' offer is legal in Belgium, illegal in Denmark and could be illegal in Italy; cross-product offers (buy one item and get a big price reduction on something else) are illegal in Luxembourg; and free draws are illegal in the Netherlands. Coupons and door-to-door free samples cannot be used as easily in France as in most other EU states, while in Germany and certain other countries free gifts and premiums are forbidden if they constitute a genuine incentive to buy. Formal prohibitions on certain forms of sales promotion apply in Denmark, Belgium, France, Germany, Luxembourg and the Netherlands. In Italy the state authorities hold a number of reserve powers in relation to sales promotions, e.g. that promotions be licensed, that certain products may not be used as premiums (typically foodstuffs and non-prescription pharmaceuticals) and that the value of premium offers be restricted – normally to a maximum of eight per cent of the price of the principal item.

The case for control

The case for legislative control over sales promotions is based on the proposition that they interfere with natural market forces and impede fair competition. Free gifts in particular are said to be unfair because their distribution can be interpreted as a form of 'dumping', undertaken merely to force rival companies into liquidation. Arguably, large firms that possess the resources necessary to plan and implement extensive sales promotions campaigns enjoy an inequitable advantage over smaller rivals. Competition between large and small businesses should be based (so the argument goes) solely on the quality and value for money of the principal product. Also there are dangers of 'sales promotions wars' erupting as firms vie in order to provide bigger and better premium offers, leading to the collapse of some businesses that otherwise would have continued trading. Further criticisms of sales promotions are as follows:

(a) A promotion will *itself* have to be advertised, adding to the cost ultimately borne by the consumer. Sales promotions are expensive and must be paid for eventually through higher prices.

(b) The true value of the promoted item is concealed, since consumers are improperly influenced (arguably misled) by the special offer (free gift, money-off voucher, entry to a competition or whatever) accompanying the sale.

(c) Consumers cannot meaningfully compare the prices of similar competing goods because of the distortions and distractions that sales promotions introduce.

(d) Promotions encourage consumers to make unwise purchasing decisions, since they stimulate impulse buying while deterring the critical and objective evaluation of the real worth of an offered good. The normal processes whereby consumers rationally relate quality to price are deliberately disrupted.

Sweepstakes and lotteries

These are promotions involving prizes that are distributed by chance. A 'lottery' is any game or contest based on chance and which does not require the exercise of skill or discretion. A 'sweepstake' is a lottery in which the stakes of the participants constitute the prize. Both forms of promotion have been singled out for particular censure in that they are said, first, to encourage gambling, secondly to inculcate undesirable moral values in consumers' minds, and thirdly to deliberately mislead the public (on the grounds that entry can never in fact be 'free'; the stake is necessarily embodied in the higher price paid for the promoted item).

The counter-argument is, of course, that in a free society consumers should be at liberty to decide for themselves whether or not to purchase products accompanied by sweepstakes, lotteries, competitions or whatever types of promotion suppliers choose to present. Increases in sales consequent to vigorous sales promotions can lead to unit cost *reductions* rather than price increases; and the intelligent use of promotions by small businesses can enable them to compete effectively against larger firms. There is no evidence that any form of sales promotion actually harms consumers. On the contrary, they frequently benefit consumers by widening customer choice and cutting household costs.

CONSUMER PROTECTION

28. The consumer movement

European (and other) businesses have been criticised for incorporating 'built-in obsolescence' into their goods, for publishing misleading advertisements, failing to test goods adequately, not marking safety instructions properly and not recalling defective products. Consumerists demand four basic rights: information, choice, safety and redress. Lack of competition, they argue, denies consumers the ability to choose between products, while advertisements that focus on images at the expense of information foster ignorance (including ignorance of the potentially harmful effects of using certain products) among consumers. Hence, they suggest, laws are needed to guarantee basic consumer rights.

Opponents of consumerism allege that it encourages groundless petty complaints, creates unfounded fears about product safety, and that consumerist interference with commercial decisions causes inefficiency and increased production costs. If customers do not want the goods on offer – albeit with built-in obsolescence and extensive advertising – they will not be bought! Market forces, they assert, will ensure that customer requirements are met.

Benefits of consumerism

Consumerists have been able to draw public attention to the needs for quality, safety and reliability in products; so much so that many firms today consciously anticipate the reactions of consumer groups when drafting marketing plans. Indeed, in a sense the consumerist movement provides businesses with free market research – informing firms of customers' desires for better labelling, more effective after-sales service, reusable containers and so on. Consumerist activities, moreover, have induced several major industries to devise codes of practice covering such matters as product safety, quality control, avoidance of environmental pollution, and the establishment of independent procedures to investigate complaints.

29. EU consumer protection policies

Formal consumer protection policies were not formulated at the EU level until the 1985 Single European Act, although the preamble to the Treaty of Rome stated that the main objective of the Treaty was 'the constant improvement of the living and working conditions of the people'. (A preamble is an introductory statement attached to a statute, Treaty, etc., setting out its purpose.) Accordingly, the first EEC consumer protection measures were proposed in 1961, though no tangible results emerged until the mid-1970s, notably via the 1975 Paris Summit of EEC heads of government, which introduced a 'Social Dimension' to Community affairs resulting, *inter-alia*, in the establishment of a Consumers' Consultative Committee, an Environmental and Consumer Protection Service (later to become DG XI) and a programme of activities intended to protect consumer interests and provide consumers with legal means for obtaining redress. The absence of specific provision for consumer protection in the Treaty of Rome was based on the proposition that free competition would inevitably benefit the consumer.

Article 100(A)3 of the Single European Act committed the EU to consumer protection via its promise that 'the Commission in its proposals concerning health, safety, environmental protection and consumer protection will take as a base a high level of protection'. A number of initiatives accompanied and followed the SEA, notably the 1985 Directive on Liability for Defective Products (*see* 30), the establishment of the Consumer Consultative Council, the Distance and Doorstep Selling Directives (*see* 31), and attempts to harmonise product safety legislation on a sector by sector basis.

Current EU priorities in the consumer protection field (as stated by the European Commission) are as follows:

(a) Improved access to legal redress for consumers.

(b) Inclusion of representatives of consumer groups in EU committees that influence the formation of common policies.

(c) Explicit consideration of consumer issues when EU legislation is being drafted.

(d) Increased support for the development of consumer organisations.

(e) Formulation of a strategy for improving the amount of information given by producers to consumers.

(f) Laws to require that guarantees are honoured in EU consumers' countries of residence, regardless of where the product was bought.

(g) Provision of education on consumer matters to young people.

Consumer health and safety

The European Court of Justice determined in the *Cassis de Dijon* case of 1979 that every product legally manufactured and sold in one EU country should in principle be admitted to all other EU states. Hence national product standards should not be used to obstruct the import of goods; each member state must recognise the adequacy of the technical standards of other members. To prevent EU states from unfairly imposing technical requirements so as to discriminate against EU imports, it has been necessary since 1984 for every proposal for a new national product standard to be vetted by the product standard authorities of other EU countries, which can object to the proposal and cause its suspension if it is not strictly necessary in order to protect public health or consumers's interests. Harmonisation of EU technical standards is discussed in Chapter 8.

30. Product Liability Directive 1985

Prior to the implementation of this important Directive different EU countries adopted different approaches to the question of who was liable for damages caused by defective products. Some countries insisted that the producer is liable no matter what the circumstances. Others made suppliers liable if the injured party can *prove* negligence on the supplier's part. The Directive obliged countries to abandon the need for plaintiffs to prove the supplier's negligence when pursuing defective product claims. However, the Directive allowed nations an optional 'development risks' defence, so that the Directive does not go so far as to render suppliers absolutely responsible for defects in their products. Britain is one of the countries that has applied this caveat. Thus, in Britain a supplier is generally liable, but not if he or she can demonstrate that the 'state of scientific and technical knowledge' at the time the product went into circulation was *not* such that a supplier could be reasonably expected to have known about the defect the product contains.

The Directive had a number of significant consequences for European businesses (especially small firms) as follows:

(a) All businesses became liable to be sued by victims, with no upper limits on compensation.

(b) Insurance costs for cover against such liability can be substantial.

(c) Manufacturers have become increasingly reluctant to purchase goods from small businesses which cannot guarantee provision of full product liability insurance cover, because manufacturers are now liable to consumers for the inputs and raw materials they use and thus need to be sure they can pass back financial responsibility for defective inputs to initial suppliers.

(d) As purchasers of inputs from other firms, small businesses must ensure that their own suppliers have adequate product liability insurance, so that they do not end up being made financially responsible for defects in another firm's products.

Under the Directive, a 'producer' is not only the manufacturer of a finished article, or its raw materials (or the extractor of raw materials), or the manufacturer of component parts, but may also include any firm or person who imports, processes, distributes or otherwise supplies (e.g. by hiring or lending) the product.

Defences

Confronted with a claim, a firm may assert that:

- It did not supply the good.
- Someone else produced it and is therefore liable; although if the firm cannot pass back liability, either because it is in fact the producer or the actual producer has disappeared or is insolvent, then it is fully responsible for the damage caused (unless the firm is a 'retailer', see below).
- The goods are not defective.
- The state of technical knowledge at the moment of supply could not reasonably lead the firm to suspect the goods were defective.
- Defects arose not within the firm's product but through the way someone else made up or designed the final product into which they were incorporated.

Note, however, that liability cannot be avoided through exclusion clauses in sale agreements or through notices posted around the point of sale denying responsibility. Moreover, the firm must show that it was 'duly diligent' and took all reasonable steps in trying to avoid committing an offence.

It is illegal not only to supply unsafe goods, but also to:

- possess them (e.g. by holding them in stock)
- provide inadequate instructions for their use thereby causing accidents
- fail to provide proper warnings of dangerous aspects of the goods
- fail to apply all reasonable measures (having regard to cost and the likelihood of improvement) for improving the safety of goods.

Retailers have a special protection. They are not liable for the defective goods they sell provided:

(a) they did not know the goods were unsafe

(b) that such ignorance was reasonable in the particular circumstances.

It is interesting to note that tobacco is excluded from the Directive. Cigarettes therefore are not a 'defective product' despite the deaths and suffering they cause.

31. Miscellaneous consumer protection legislation

Notable EU interventions in the field of consumer protection include the following:

(a) *The Directive on Food Labelling 1979.* This is updated every few years and aims to facilitate the free movement of foodstuffs throughout the EU by ensuring that consumers are properly informed about the contents of foodstuffs. Labelling must be clear, legible, indelible, not obscured by misleading pictures or slogans, and in the consumer's local language. Under the Directive a food label *must* include lists of ingredients, use by dates for perishables, and the full postal address of an *EU-based* manufacturer, packer or seller. It must *not* claim that the item has properties it does not in fact possess, or that a foodstuff can prevent, treat or cure a human disease, or has special characteristics which all products of that general class also possess. The Directive applies to the catering trade as well as sale to end consumers. If a foodstuff is not prepackaged then the relevant information must be contained on trade documents.

(b) *The Doorstep Selling Directive 1985.* The major provision of this Directive is a seven-day 'cooling off period' during which buyers may cancel without penalty contracts entered into at their homes or places of work (apart from doorstep sales involving very low value items).

(c) *The Consumer Credit Directive 1987,* which specifies a common method for calculating the annual percentage rate of interest for consumer credit which must be quoted on all promotional and display materials used to advertise credit facilities.

(d) *The Dangerous Imitations Directive 1987.* This harmonised national laws concerning the imitation of food products where the imitation might result in injury.

(e) *The Price Indication Directive 1988,* which required that the selling prices of goods be openly displayed to consumers. Displayed prices must include extras such as installation or service charges, VAT, and should not refer to top end of the range models to create the impression that lower-price models have similar attributes. A price indication is misleading if:

- the actual price is higher than that shown
- the low price indicated depends on facts or circumstances not revealed to the customer
- additional charges are not disclosed
- the supplier makes out that the price will shortly be increased when this is not the case (e.g. the statement 'buy now to beat next month's price rise' when no such price increase is scheduled to occur).

Misleading price indications are unlawful in advertisements, catalogues, circulars and price lists as well as at the point of sale.

(f) *The Toy Safety Directive 1988.* The purpose of this Directive was to harmonise toy safety standards across the EU and ensure that only safe toys are supplied within member countries. Toys must conform to relevant CEN and CENELEC standards and bear a CE Mark (*see* 8:**6**) confirming compliance. The name and address of the manufacturer or importer must be clearly displayed.

(g) *The Package Travel Directive 1990.* This covers package holidays and package tours (i.e. those lasting more than 24 hours and including overnight accommodation). Promotional materials describing the tour must be accurate and not intended to mislead. The full price must be quoted and details of passport and visa requirements provided well before the start of the journey. If the tour organiser cancels the holiday the consumer is entitled to reimbursement or a replacement holiday.

(h) *The General Product Safety Directive 1992.* Effective from 1994 this Directive imposes a general obligation on producers, importers and distributors to supply safe consumer products. Manufacturers must provide full details of any risks associated with the use of their products.

(i) *The Unfair Contract Terms Directive 1993.* This is intended to protect the interests of consumers who contract to buy goods or services on supplier's written 'standard terms' by preventing suppliers from enforcing terms which put consumers at a significant disadvantage. Certain terms are automatically presumed unfair, notably any which:

- allow the supplier unilaterally to vary the terms of the contract
- give the supplier the right to increase the price, except when a specific price indexation clause has been inserted in the contract
- enable the supplier to cancel the contract on shorter notice than that required of the customer
- provide for renewal of an existing contract without the consumer being informed of the situation and having a reasonable time to decide not to renew.

The terms of a contract must be written in plain and clearly understandable language and, where there is any doubt about the meaning of words used, the interpretation most favourable to the consumer must be applied.

Additionally, important Directives relating to the safety of particular groups of products have been implemented, notably:

- household products containing radioactive substances
- electrical equipment using low voltages
- household gas appliances
- household chemicals
- cosmetics.

Progress test 14

1. Define marketing.

2. Why is pan-European marketing more difficult than purely domestic marketing?

3. What is the marketing concept?

4. List six advantages of modifying products to satisfy the needs of particular foreign markets.

5. How can the monetary value of a brand be determined?

6. List the major pricing strategies available to an international business.

7. Why do firms engaged in cross-border European business need to undertake marketing research?

8. List six examples of important sources of information on West European markets.

9. Explain the concept of market segmentation. What are the purposes of market segmentation?

10. What are the main problems associated with psychographic market segmentation?

11. State the European Commission's definition of advertising.

12. List the advantages of using a large multinational advertising agency for pan-European campaigns.

13. In what circumstances is it appropriate to standardise cross-border European advertising campaigns?

14. Define the term 'public relations'.

15. List the factors that have contributed to the rapid growth in direct marketing that has occurred in recent years.

16. How do list brokers make their profits?

17. Why does the Draft Directive on Data Protection represent a threat to the European direct marketing industry?

18. Why is it difficult to include sales promotions in pan-European marketing campaigns?

19. Why did the Treaty of Rome not contain any explicit statements concerning consumer protection?

20. What are the European Commission's current priorities in the consumer protection field?

21. Outline the major provisions of the EU Product Liability Directive 1985.

15

EUROPEAN DISTRIBUTION

AGENCIES AND DISTRIBUTION

1. Agents and distributors

Agents differ from distributors in that whereas the latter actually *purchase* a supplying firm's products (assuming thereby full responsibility for their condition, sale, and any bad debts), agents simply put their clients in touch with third parties but then 'drop out' of resulting contracts – so that the agreements are between the agent's client and third parties, without the agent being further involved. An agent will (for a commission) find foreign customers for a company's products, but if the goods are defective, damaged or delivered late it is the client and not the agent who is responsible. In practice, however, the distinction between an agency and a distribution agreement can become blurred, especially if the agent takes physical control over the goods. Distributors typically demand exclusivity. Note how exclusivity clauses in a distribution agreement can create legal difficulties, because exclusive trading arrangements are not generally permitted under the competition laws of most industrialised nations.

Rules on agency

Certain rules apply to agents in all countries:

(a) The agent cannot act for a third party as well as the client without disclosing the fact to everyone concerned.

(b) Agents are obliged to maintain strict confidentiality regarding their clients' affairs, and to transmit to them all relevant information.

(c) If an agent does not pass on money deposited with the agent but owing to a third party, the client is still liable for the third party debt.

(d) The client is liable for damages to third parties for wrongs committed by an agent 'in the course of his or her authority'.

(e) Clients are obliged to indemnify their agents for expenses incurred while reasonably exercising their duties.

Use of agents

Agents operate on a commission basis and may either be *brokers*, who simply bring together buyers and sellers without ever taking physical possession of the goods; or *factors* who do possess the goods until customers are found and who sometimes sell under their own names at prices they think best (Christou 1990). A *del credere* agent is one who, in return for a higher commission, indemnifies the supplying firm against customers' bad debts.

2. Choice of agent

Agents need to be fully familiar with local business conditions and practices, and capable of conducting local market research. Other criteria to be adopted when choosing an agent should include the following:

- Whether the agent has contacts with local businesses capable of supplying specialist services to the exporting company (repair and after-sales service for example).
- How easily the agent can be contacted.
- Whether the agent will represent a competing firm and, if so, the incentives that are needed to encourage the agent to promote the exporter's products enthusiastically.
- How much information and feedback on matters such as consumer responses to the product, the quality of local delivery arrangements, whether local translations of operating instructions are satisfactory, etc., the agent can provide.
- How easily the calibre of the agent's work can be evaluated.
- The agent's track record, how long the firm has existed and its general business reputation.
- How extensively the agent covers the market; how many branch offices it has and their location and whether the agent can genuinely cover an entire country.
- Whether the agent possesses sufficient resources for the task: staff, showrooms, technical competence, storage facilities, etc.
- The ease with which the firm can control and motivate the agent. Normally the agent will be asked to prepare quarterly sales forecasts and to explain significant deviations of actual sales from these predictions. The agent should keep a record of enquiries received, calls made, customer complaints, etc. and submit details on a monthly basis.
- Whether the agent requires a large amount of technical training about the product and sales training for promoting it effectively.

3. Support of agents

Supplying companies can support and motivate their agents through the provision of technical advice and training; regular meetings in the principal's country paid for by the supplying firm; regular circulation of information about the supplying firm's current activities, changes in personnel, new product developments, marketing plans, etc.; and significant local advertising and brand awareness development by the supplying company. Other devices for supporting agents include:

- incentive schemes such as competitions with cash prizes, free holidays, etc., for agents with the highest sales
- setting up regional offices to coordinate communications with the firm's agents or distributors in a particular area
- the principal's involvement in local exhibitions and trade fairs in conjunction with the local agent
- field visits to the agent.

4. Agency contracts

Agency agreements should be in writing and detail the parties to the agreement, duration (including the length of any probationary period), products and territory involved, confidentiality requirements, arbitration provisions and which country's law shall apply to the contract. Other matters that need to be specified are:

- termination arrangements
- the agent's discretion to offer special terms to customers
- the principal's right to inspect client's accounts
- requirements to disclose all relevant facts
- responsibility for credit checks on potential customers and for collecting debts
- commission rates
- extent of the agent's authority.

The agent's commission details must be tightly specified in relation to when exactly commission is payable (on receipt of an order, on delivery of the goods, or on payment of the resulting invoice); whether commission is still payable if an order is eventually cancelled; and whether the principal will pay commission on orders received from the agent's territory that did not pass directly through the agent but which might be indirectly attributable to the agent's work (repeat orders, for example).

5. The Commercial Agents Directive 1986

Agency law in the European Union has been harmonised via the Commercial Agents Directive 1986, under which any individual or company acting as an agent (excluding bankruptcy receivers and insolvency practitioners; partners, employees or officers of firms; or commodity dealers) has the right to receive the following on termination of an agency agreement:

(a) Full payment for any transaction predominantly attributable to the agent's work during the period of the agency, even if the transaction is concluded after the agency has been terminated.

(b) A lump sum not exceeding the agent's average commission for one year. To complete this average the agent's earnings over the last five years are considered (or less if the agency has not been in force for five years). The lump sum could be payable if the agency has ended because of the death of the agent.

(c) Damages for losses (e.g. loss of goodwill) in appropriate circumstances (Whittaker and Roney 1993).

The above represents the minimum level of compensation payable; national governments may impose further requirements if they so wish. Thus, for example, French agents are legally entitled to one month's notice for each year of service up to a maximum of three months and up to two years' past average commission is payable. In Germany, principals must give agents one to six months' notice, depending on the duration of the agreement. Dutch agents are entitled to four months' notice plus one extra month if the agreement has lasted for three years; two extra months if the agreement has lasted for six years, and may obtain payment for contributions to the principal's goodwill up to the value of one year's commission.

6. Distributors

Since distributors actually purchase the supplier's goods they assume full responsibility for selling the item and for all credit risks. An important potential advantage is that a local image for the product might be projected. Also the distributor has to pay for storing the goods. Note how the contract between supplier and distributor can specify precise selling prices and marketing procedures that the distributor is obliged to follow.

Distribution contracts need to cover most of the items mentioned in **4**, with additional clauses on discounts allowable, which party is to be responsible for defective items, selling prices (where appropriate), arrangements for after-sales service, and (importantly) exclusivity details. Even if no exclusivity arrangement is specified a distributor will almost certainly insist on receiving more favourable terms than other purchasers, possibly causing legal problems.

Most exclusive distribution agreements within the European Union are exempt from EU competition law via a block exemption. See 6:6 for a discussion of this matter.

7. Distribution options

A distribution channel is a route from the producer of a good to the final consumer. Functions of a distribution channel include the physical movement of goods, storage of goods awaiting transit and/or sale, transfer of title to goods, and their presentation to final purchasers. There are four main categories of distribution system:

(a) *Direct to consumers*, e.g. mail order or if the supplier owns and controls its own outlets. No intermediaries are involved, so prices can be lower and the firm can ensure that its goods are properly presented to local consumers. The method is commonest among companies (i) with very large volumes of international business (and thus able to justify establishing a separate sales organisation), (ii) with technically complicated products, and (iii) where customers are geographically concentrated and place high value orders.

(b) *Producer to retailer.* Here the retailer bears the cost of storing goods awaiting sale. The supplier must employ salespeople to canvass retail outlets and to merchandise the product. Retailers sell the goods, possibly offer credit, provide product information to customers, and ensure that goods are available in small quantities throughout the year. Franchising (*see* **12:3**) is a special case of this method.

(c) *Producer to intermediary.* The advantages of selling to an intermediary (an export merchant (*see* **9**) for example) include (i) less administration (there is no need for a salesforce, no warehousing costs, fewer deliveries, and negligible invoicing and debt collecting) and (ii) the transfer of the risk of product failure from the supplier to the intermediary. However, final prices will be higher and intermediaries typically handle competing lines.

(d) *Through agents (see* **1**).

Pan-European distribution differs from its domestic counterpart in the following respects:

(a) The range of available options is more varied. A firm can establish its own distribution system (purchasing or setting up from scratch its own distribution subsidiaries in various countries) or may opt to use locally controlled channels. In the former case a further decision has to be taken regarding whether to manage distribution subsidiaries through expatriate or locally recruited staff. Standardisation of the methods and procedures used by a company for international distribution is extremely difficult because of the big differences that exist in national distribution systems. Hence the firm's task is to identify and utilise that combination of directly owned foreign sales subsidiaries, wholesalers, import agents and other intermediaries, and retailers necessary to ensure that its products are available to customers where and when they are needed and at a reasonable price.

(b) Distribution channels are usually longer than for domestic business.

(c) Delays and hold-ups at various points in international distribution systems are common.

(d) Wholesaling and retailing systems differ from country to country.

Factors influencing national distribution systems include:

- Consumer demand patterns. Shoppers in some countries insist on buying their goods in small quantities from nearby stores which they visit frequently, elsewhere people prefer to shop in large retail outlets on (say) a weekly or fortnightly basis.
- Wage levels paid to retail workers.
- Competition rules within the country (which might discourage the development of large retail chains).
- Entrepreneurial attitudes within the nation. Establishing and running a small shop is more popular in some countries than in others.
- Local laws restricting the size and nature of retail outlets.
- Popularity of mail order buying.

8. Choice of system

In selecting a distribution system the producer should consider the following characteristics in respect of each alternative:

(a) Cost of the channel. This is affected by the need to give discounts, salespeoples' salaries and travelling expenses, costs of credit given, inventory holding costs of unsold output, and administrative costs (invoicing, debt collection, bad debts, etc.).

(b) Extent of the control that can be exercised over the channel.

(c) Whether the channel improves or worsens the image of the goods (e.g. high-quality expensive output would not be congruent in a low-price cash and carry discount store).

(d) Geographical coverage of the channel.

(e) Reliability of distributors in relation to:

- product presentation and the provision of information to customers
- ensuring continuity of supply
- adequacy of customer care and after-sales service.

(f) Consequences for the duration of the total order cycle, i.e. the period likely to elapse between the customer placing an order and the actual delivery of the goods.

(g) Probabilities of the non-availability of the product in certain markets through using certain channels and the impact on long run sales that occasional stockouts will exert.

USE OF INTERMEDIARIES

9. Types of intermediary

Firms that sell directly to foreign EU customers assume full responsibility for their transportation, local advertising and final sale of the goods. This might be achieved via the establishment of a branch office or subsidiary in the country concerned. The alternative is to use export intermediaries when selling to foreign EU markets. Export merchants, for example, reside in the exporter's country, acting as principals in export transactions (that is, buying and selling on their own accounts). They are wholesalers who operate in foreign markets through their own salespeople, stockists and, perhaps, retail outlets. Exporters are relieved of administrative problems, documentation, shipping, internal transport and so on, and do not carry the risks of market failure. However, they lose control over presentation of their products, and foreign sales may fall because of poor foreign retailing.

Confirming houses exist to represent foreign buyers who are not sufficiently well known for home firms to supply them on credit terms. The confirming house assumes the risk of customer default. In return it charges the buyer a commission.

10. Piggybacking

Smaller firms engaged in cross-border European trade sometimes 'piggyback' on larger companies which already operate in certain foreign markets and are willing to act on behalf of other businesses that wish to export to those markets. This enables larger companies to use fully their sales representatives, premises, office equipment, etc., in the countries concerned. The carrier will purchase the goods outright or act as a commission agent and may or may not sell the rider's product under the carrier's own brand name, depending on the form of the agreement. Sometimes the carriers will insist that the rider's products be similar to its own in view of the need to deal with technical queries and after-sales service 'in the field'. The rider obtains access to all the carrier's facilities and resources, and can conveniently sell its product without having to establish its own distribution systems. Carriers also benefit. They are able to sell items that fill gaps in their own product lines, without having to manufacture additional products. Economies of scale in bulk distribution become available, and the carrier's overall business image may improve. Problems with piggyback arrangements are the possible lack of commitment by the carrier to the rider's products; possible failure of the rider to supply the carrier on a continuous basis; and the fact that the rider becomes locked into the carrier's selling methods and territorial coverage.

Another means whereby a smaller business can distribute its products easily in foreign markets is to enter into 'sister company' agreements with foreign firms. A sister company is a business in another country offering similar products and which is of a similar size and nature to the one looking for a partner. Such firms act as a foreign agent, advise on local market conditions, translate documents, etc. Usually the sister company is engaged in complementary rather than directly competitive lines of work.

11. Advantages and disadvantages of using intermediaries

The advantages to an international business of handling its own distribution rather than engaging intermediaries include total control over the entire distribution process, the development of management skills in the international distribution field, the absence of commissions and discounts payable to outsiders, and possibilities for economies of scale and economies of scope in the distribution process. (Economies of scope are unit cost reductions resulting from a business undertaking a wide range of activities and thus being able to provide common services useful for each activity.) The staff involved will (or should) be committed to the well-being of the company, and there is continuity of the personnel involved in distribution matters. Staff are completely familiar with the firm's products and how they need to be presented, and have detailed knowledge of all the company's operations. They are fully accountable for their actions and their careers within the organisation depend substantially on the success of their work.

Advantages to using intermediaries, conversely, are as follows:

(a) The firm does not require an extensive foreign sales organisation.

(b) Intermediaries should be more objective in their assessments of the prospects for sales of the product in a particular region.

(c) The company does not need to train and develop in-house staff in specialist distribution functions.

(d) Savings on overheads should be available.

(e) Intermediaries have extensive contacts with experts in their field, and ought to possess up-to-the-minute knowledge of foreign market situations.

(f) Many (though not all) intermediaries take full possession of the goods and assume all the risks of foreign non-payment.

(g) Intermediaries have wide-ranging experience of the distribution problems of firms and industries other than their immediate clients and this experience should enable them to identify appropriate solutions and appreciate all the options available and difficulties involved.

Note moreover that a number of the benefits of using in-house staff to handle distribution assume that the people involved are competent and highly motivated. This is not always the case: staff might be apathetic and/or incapable of undertaking complicated duties. They might lack the specialist expertise and independent perspectives of high-calibre intermediaries.

Considerations that an international business should take into account when deciding whether to handle its own distribution rather than engage intermediaries include the following:

(a) Volume of sales. If sales within a particular market are modest it is rarely worthwhile handling the distribution of the goods internally within the firm.

(b) Nature of the product. High-tech items that require complex after-sales service are likely to be distributed direct by the producing company.

(c) Availability of good calibre distribution outlets in the local area.

(d) The ease with which feedback on how well the firm's products are selling in the local market can be obtained from local distributors.

(e) Whether the scale of sales can be increased substantially via intermediaries in the country concerned.

Selection of intermediaries

Major criteria to be examined when selecting an intermediary include the candidate's geographical coverage, product and market expertise, required margins, size of salesforce, credit rating, track record, corporate image, customer care facilities and ability to promote the supplier's products in an effective way.

TRANSPORT

Goods can be freely transported within the EU by road, rail, ferry or other shipping services, parcel post or air. Firms may organise some or all of the transportation of consignments to foreign EU customers, or may opt to use a freight forwarder who will manage all aspects of transportation from the collection of goods from the suppliers premises up to their final delivery abroad.

12. Freight forwarders

These are businesses which specialise in the international movement of goods and which advise clients on packaging and labelling, warehousing, and which modes of transport are most suitable for carrying a client firm's output taking account of its size, weight, characteristics and the urgency of the delivery. *Groupage* is the process whereby a forwarder collects at one of its depots numerous small shipments bound for the same destination and consolidates them into a single large consignment. Substantial discounts are available for the bulk transportation of consolidation consignments, part of which the forwarder will pass back to small business clients in the form of lower freight prices. Moreover, a forwarder can often avoid the losses resulting from lorries and containers having to return from particular destinations empty, since forwarders continuously liaise with each other and swap counter-directional loads. The problem with groupage is that a specific consignment may be stored at the forwarder's collection depot for several days awaiting a consolidation into which it conveniently fits.

Speed is essential for certain consignments, especially where customers operate just-in-time production systems or where the benefits of faster delivery greatly outweigh the additional cost. *Integrated carriers* are a type of forwarding firm offering immediate door-to-door collection and delivery services but without any need for groupage. They use scheduled services which run regardless of loading, so that goods are guaranteed to be delivered within a specific time.

13. Airfreight

Airfreight journey times are very short, although services are subject to weather delays, labour disputes at airports, and diversions are sometimes necessary. Air transport is not suitable for heavy, non-perishable consignments, although modern aircraft are increasingly capable of carrying heavy loads. Advantages to air transport include:

- Less stockholding and speedier settlement of invoices in consequence of faster delivery of goods.
- Avoidance of certain intermediate warehousing costs as consignments can move straight from the airport to customers' premises (the cost of warehousing can be as much as one third of the value of stored items).
- Its usefulness from the viewpoint of customers operating just-in-time production systems, because it becomes possible to satisfy small and frequent orders immediately.

- Convenience and ease of administration. Space can be booked direct with an airline or through a cargo agent. Either will help consignors to arrange shipments and documentation, and will organise goods collection services if required.

The basic document used in air transport is the 'air waybill', which is nothing more than a consignment note – it is not a document of title. Airfreight prices are fixed internationally via the International Air Transport Association (IATA), although competition does occur through a variety of special discounts offered to customers. Also IATA rates do not apply to consignments large enough to justify chartering an entire aircraft, charges for which depend on the urgency of the trip and the time of year the aircraft is needed. Note however that the charterer has to pay for the entire round trip if the chartered plane returns empty.

14. Seafreight

Seafreight is cheap compared to most other options, but slow, and transhipment (i.e. having to unload and reload consignments between different modes of transport) may be necessary. It is flexible in the sense that there is usually a choice of ships going to the required destination, although it is necessary to book space well in advance of the shipment and substantial documentation is needed. There are 'liner services' that set sail and arrive according to a strict timetable and which charge uniform freight rates regardless of the particular shipping company concerned; and 'tramp' ships that leave port only when they have a full cargo and which are liable to call at intermediate ports *en route* to load and unload *ad hoc* cargoes. Hence there is no firm commitment that a tramp service will arrive at a particular end destination within a prespecified period. Freight charges for tramp ships vary between vessels. Two main documents are connected with sea transport:

1. The *standard shipping note* (SSN), which is a form used to advise the shipping company about what is to happen to the goods on arrival at the foreign port, e.g. who will collect them, who is to pay unloading charges, whether the consignment is to be placed in a warehouse within the docks, etc. The document also acts as a formal request to the destination port authorities to receive and handle the shipment.
2. The bill of lading, which is the shipping company's receipt for the goods specifying whether they were loaded in a satisfactory or damaged condition. A 'clean' bill of lading refers to goods received on board in apparently good condition and with no shortages. Otherwise the bill is 'dirty' and will detail the shortfalls or damage to goods observed. A 'short form' bill of lading is one that does not show the shipping company's terms and conditions on the back. In the absence of any other evidence, the holder of a bill of lading is entitled to collect the consignment from the docks on its arrival, i.e. the bill is a *de facto* document of title. Without a bill of lading the customer can only obtain possession of the goods by giving the shipping company a bank letter of indemnity which protects the shipping company against subsequent claims. The bill of lading is the contract between the exporter and the shipping company and is a highly

legalistic document. For small loads and/or short journeys, however, the shipping company might issue a 'data freight receipt' (sometimes called a sea waybill) rather than a bill of lading *per se*. DFRs act merely as receipts for goods and as evidence of contracts of carriage. They do not relate to the ownership of goods.

A contract under which an *entire ship* is hired to a user is called a Charter Party (CP). There are two forms: non-demise CPs whereby the shipowner provides the vessel and crew, and demise CPs which furnish the vessel only. A 'voyage CP' is for a specific journey(s); a 'time CP' contracts the ship for a stated period.

15. Rail transport

This is suitable for bulky consignments sent over long distances. The cost-effectiveness of the method increases the longer the journey, especially in Continental Europe where there are many high-speed services. A problem with rail transport is the need for transhipment, although this can sometimes be avoided for consignments large enough to use 'swap body' containers, i.e. self-contained trailers on their own wheels that can be exchanged between vehicle cabs, as opposed to 'flat' trailers on to which containers have to be loaded. The entire swap body can be uncoupled from a cab, rolled on to a train for long-haul rail transport, and rolled off and attached to another cab at the final destination. Empty containers are re-routed by national railway companies via an internationally agreed system. The document under which goods are transported by rail is the International Consignment Note which lays down internationally agreed standard conditions of carriage.

The Channel Tunnel

Continuity of rail transport between Britain and Continental Europe has existed since the completion of the Channel Tunnel. Half the Tunnel's rail capacity is leased to the British and French Railways. The owner (Euro Tunnel Ltd) uses the remainder for its own shuttle services, which run between the Tunnel's two portals (at Folkestone in England and at Coquelles to the west of Calais in France). Track gauge is the same as the European main railway lines so that services can operate from all principal UK industrial centres to Continental rail destinations. Note, however, that although the French TGV (*très grand vitesse*) runs right up to the French terminal at Coquelles it does not thereafter run on to London or other UK destinations. Goods are shifted either on container freight trains travelling from the UK to various Continental destinations, or in lorries carried on special shuttles between Folkestone and Coquelles that operate around the clock and for which no prior booking is required.

A hub and spoke system operates for the transportation of consignments sent via container freight trains through the Channel Tunnel. Timetabled 'through trains' run between main distribution centres, normally on a daily basis, but at least three times per week. Although the need for customs clearance has been abolished for intra-community trade, some simple documentation is still required, especially for goods originating outside the EU. The processing of these documents is undertaken inland at the departure terminal. At each distribution centre (hub), wagons from through trains (and other trains made up on an *ad-hoc* basis) are transferred to other engines in order to make up complete wagon sets for transportation through a system 'spoke' to a particular distribution centre. If there are sufficient volumes of freight bound for certain destinations, 'full block' trains are made up and run direct to those destinations without entering the hub and spoke system.

Advantages and problems of the Channel Tunnel railfreight system

The Channel Tunnel has created a common railfreight distribution system with standardised procedures for shifting goods throughout the European Union with the exception of Ireland. Most EU destinations can be reached within 72 hours, with little need for intermediate goods handling. Services are fast, convenient, reliable and unaffected by high seas, fog and other climatic conditions. It is important to note however that rail transport is more economical the longer the distance involved. Thus, for journeys shorter than 250–300 miles, road / ferry freight services will probably continue to be substantially cheaper than rail. This is particularly true where door-to-door delivery is required. Also certain regions of Europe are not easily accessed via the Tunnel hub and spoke system and, in consequence, railfreight charges are not competitive in comparison with alternative modes of transport to such areas, which include most of the Netherlands and north west Germany (served as they are by the highly efficient sea port at Rotterdam), Normandy, Brittany and other regions accessible from the ferry Ro-Ro services of the English south coast.

16. Road transport

Road transport offers door-to-door collection and delivery of goods. There is no need for transhipment and minimal intermediate goods handling, thus reducing handling costs and pilferage losses. Lorries can go to remote rural areas, and may be re-routed at will as circumstances alter. The contract of carriage between an exporter and the road haulier is evidenced by a CMR note (*Convention de Marchandises par Route*), which acts as a receipt for the goods but does not provide evidence of ownership of the consignment. Under the CMR convention there are standard international contractual conditions for road transport, covering liability for loss or damage to goods and the maximum value of insurance claims against the haulier. Problems with road transport are its slowness over long distances; its vulnerability to bad weather; limited load sizes; and the fact that lorries often have to return empty.

Road and ferry

Road transport is often used in conjunction with Roll-on Roll-off (Ro-Ro) ferries which carry complete vehicles or the trailers of articulated lorries. Goods handling is reduced to the absolute minimum (no lifting gear is required, and marshalling is easy), so that ferries can turn around extremely quickly. Ro-Ro facilities exist along the entire European coastline.

Choice of transport method

Speed, cost and reliability are the main factors that have to be balanced when selecting a particular mode of transport for international consignments. Accordingly the supplier needs to consider:

- how quickly the goods are required by final consumers
- the weights, sizes and handling characteristics of transported items
- the value of consignments (which affects insurance costs and the likelihood of pilfering)
- the consequences for customers of late delivery (the impact on just-in-time production systems for example)
- costs of intermediate goods handling and storage, packaging, spoilage of perishable items, documentation, and the income foregone through having working capital tied up as goods in transit during long journeys.

17. Delivery terms

Today the norm is for companies to quote *delivered duty paid* (DDP) prices for cross-border European sales. This means the supplying firm delivers to the customers' premises and assumes all the risks and expenses associated with the journey. Standard definitions of what precisely is meant by DDP and other common export delivery terms have been drafted by the International Chamber of Commerce. These INCOTERMS, as they are known, can be incorporated into contracts of sale, price quotation, letters of credit, etc., and specify precisely the duties and obligations of buyer and seller and, in particular, the exact moment at which ownership of (and hence responsibility for) goods passes from one party to the other. Hence legal arguments about who is responsible for what, when and where, may be avoided as all these matters have already been defined in the INCOTERM that the contracting parties agree to apply. INCOTERMS are widely quoted and have a legal status in some countries. The commonest INCOTERMS are as follows:

(a) *Ex Works (EXW)* which requires the customer to collect the goods from the exporter's premises.

(b) *Free on Board (FOB)*, where the buyer takes delivery when the goods are loaded on to a ship in the exporter's country.

(c) *Cost, Insurance and Freight (CIF)*, whereby the exporter pays all transport and insurance costs to a named foreign destination.

(d) *Delivered Duty Paid (DDP)*, where the exporter assumes all costs and risks involved in delivering the goods to the customer's premises. Increasingly, this is the standard requirement for export sales.

Variations on the above include Free on Rail (FOR); Free on Truck (FOT); and Cost and Freight (C&F) which parallels CIF except that the buyer rather than the exporter is responsible for insurance. Additionally there are special INCOTERMS to cover multimodal transport. For example, Free Carrier (FRC) is the same as FOB but for any form of carrier. Ownership of the goods passes from supplier to purchaser when the consignment is handed to the carrier at a specified place. Likewise, 'Carriage and Insurance Paid to' (CIP) matches CIF but for any means of transport. The INCOTERM Delivered at Frontier (DAF) means the customer takes responsibility for the goods the moment they pass through a named national frontier.

18. The contract of sale

This needs to specify the currency to be used to settle the transaction; which country's law is to apply to the contract; and for sales involving letters of credit, the names and addresses of the buyer's and seller's banks handling the transaction, and who is to be responsible for bank charges. It should also incorporate details of the price of the goods, parties to the sale, delivery terms (CIF, FOB, etc.), the latest despatch date, the mode of transport to be used and the method of payment.

In certain (somewhat complicated) circumstances it is possible to incorporate a clause (sometimes called a *Romalpa* clause after the court case that established the precedent in these respects) in a contract of sale whereby goods supplied to the customer remain the property of the supplying firm until they are paid for. Thus, should the customer sell the goods to a third party before reneging on the debt the supplier can approach the third party and reclaim the items, which in law still belong to the supplier.

19. Warehousing

Companies can warehouse goods in their own premises or in (frequently subsidised) warehouses owned by airports and by docks and harbour authorities. Freight forwarders and large road hauliers also provide warehousing facilities. Factors influencing the decision where to warehouse goods include the whereabouts of concentrations of customers, likelihoods of breakage and pilferage, depot rental or acquisition costs, and the ease of transportation both to the warehouse itself and from the warehouse to major outlets, taking into consideration local road and rail links, traffic congestion, etc. A firm that warehouses its goods in multiple locations can get its products to customers very quickly, but only at higher administrative and storage costs. Also average overall inventory holding will be higher than if a single warehouse was used for a particular region.

Goods imported from outside the European Union (and which therefore are subject to the common external tariff) may be temporarily stored in *bonded warehouses* without paying import duty. While in a bonded warehouse goods may be blended, repackaged or otherwise modified. Duty is payable only as goods are released, and not at all if they are re-exported. National customs authorities exert tight control over bonded warehouses. Use of bonded warehouses is especially valuable where the imported goods are subject to a quota restriction, since the exporter can be sure that consignments will not be refused entry to the country on arrival if a quota threshold happens to have been exceeded. The items can be stored duty free until the next quota period.

A *freeport* fulfils the same function, but comprises a designated wider area at a seaport where goods can be stored and manipulated free of duty. Inland *freezones* are equivalent to freeports but usually located near airports. Freeports and freezones are to be found throughout the European Union.

EU TRANSPORT POLICY

20. The common transport policy

Although the Treaty of Rome required the establishment of a common transport policy to apply throughout the (then) EEC, progress towards achieving this objective has been slow. The main achievements to date have perhaps been the abolition of (i) restrictions on cabotage (i.e. the right of non-resident hauliers to collect and deliver goods within another member state) and (ii) the need for special documentation when sending consignments to other EU countries; goods may move freely throughout the Union without undergoing any customs control. Non-resident passenger carriers and freight hauliers can operate in any member state on the same conditions as domestic operators, while rules on the qualifications needed to run a road haulage business, recording equipment (tachographs for instance), handling of dangerous loads, etc., have been harmonised. Tourist coach cabotage has been allowed since 1996. The question of extending cabotage rights to scheduled bus services is currently under review.

Since 1993 the fleets of any EU member country have been free to provide shipping services between member states. Civil air transport is subject to three EU Regulations introduced in 1993, as follows:

1. *The Licensing Regulation* which established uniform criteria for the issue of licences to air transport operators throughout the EU. Carriers satisfying these criteria are entitled to a licence from the civil aviation authorities of any member state.
2. *The Market Access Regulation*. This requires that any licensed carrier be permitted to fly on all international routes within the EU, with the total abolition of restrictions on air cabotage by April 1997. Capacity constraints on individual carriers were abolished.
3. *The Fares and Rates Regulation* that introduced free pricing for cargo rates and for scheduled and non-scheduled air fares.

Problems experienced by the European Commission when attempting to achieve a common transport policy are as follows:

(a) Transport networks continue to be developed to satisfy national rather than pan-European interests.

(b) The railway systems of most EU countries receive government subsidy. Differences in the levels of national subsidy granted distort competition in the transport sector through distorting freight charges.

Progress test 15

1. Explain the difference between an agent and a distributor.

2. List the main contents of the EU Commercial Agents Directive 1986.

3. What is a distribution channel?

4. Explain the role of the export merchant.

5. What is a 'sister company'?

6. List the disadvantages of using export intermediaries.

7. What is a freight forwarder?

8. In what circumstances is rail transport suitable for the cross-border movement of goods?

9. Explain the operation of the Channel Tunnel hub and spoke system.

10. What factors should a firm take into consideration when selecting a means of transport for its products?

11. Explain the difference between FOB and CIF prices.

12. What is the purpose of INCOTERMS?

13. List the main points that need to be covered in a contract of sale.

14. Explain the function of a bonded warehouse.

15. What have been the main achievements to date of the EU's common transport policy?

16

EUROPEAN HUMAN RESOURCES MANAGEMENT

ELEMENTS OF HUMAN RESOURCES MANAGEMENT

1. Nature of human resources management

Human resources management (HRM) concerns the human side of the management of enterprises and employees' relations with their firms. Its purpose is to
ensure that the employees of a company, i.e. its human resources, are used in
such a way that the employer obtains the greatest possible benefit from their
abilities and the employees obtain both material and psychological rewards
from their work. A key element of HRM is, of course, *personnel management*
which is that part of human resources management concerned with staffing the
enterprise, determining and satisfying the needs of people at work, and the
practical rules and procedures that govern relationships between employees
and the organisation. In particular it involves (according to the UK Institute of
Personnel Development's published definition of the subject) the development
and application of policies governing:

- Human resources planning, recruitment, selection, placement and
  termination
- Education and training; career development
- Terms of employment, methods and standards of remuneration
- Formal and informal communication and consultation both through the
  representatives of employers and employees and at all levels through the
  enterprise
- Negotiation and application of agreements on wages and working conditions; procedures for the avoidance and settlement of disputes.

However, whereas personnel management is practical, utilitarian and instru-
mental, and mostly concerned with administration and the *implementation* of
policies, human resources management has *strategic* dimensions and involves
the total deployment of human resources within the firm. Thus, for example
HRM will consider such matters as:

- The aggregate size of the organisation's labour force in the context of an
  overall corporate plan (how many divisions and subsidiaries the company is to have, design of the organisation, etc.)

- How much to spend on training the workforce, given strategic decisions on target quality levels, product prices, volume of production, and so on, in order to ensure that the organisation has the competencies necessary to survive and prosper
- The desirability of establishing relations with trade unions from the viewpoint of the effective management control of the entire organisation
- The wider implications for employees of the management of change (not just the consequences of alterations in working practices).

The strategic approach to HRM involves the integration of personnel and other HRM considerations into the firm's overall corporate planning and strategy formulation procedures. It is proactive, seeking constantly to discover new ways of utilising the labour force in a more productive manner thus giving the business a competitive edge. Practical manifestations of the adoption of a strategic approach to HRM might include:

- Incorporation of a brief summary of the firm's basic HRM policy into its mission statement
- Explicit consideration of the consequences for employees of each of the firm's strategies and major new projects
- Implementation of programmes for changing organisational cultures
- Designing organisation structures to suit the needs of employees rather than conditioning the latter to fit in with the existing form of organisation.

Formulation of a human resources strategy implies recognition of the crucial importance of the HR function and the need therefore to have HR specialists in the senior management team, e.g. as members of the firm's main and/or subsidiary boards of directors.

2. National differences in HRM practices

A wide range of factors determine national HRM practices: social and economic circumstances, national culture, labour market characteristics, laws and customs, nature of the workforce (skills, attitudes, educational backgrounds, etc.), sizes and structures of business enterprises, identities of the main stakeholders in firms, levels of prosperity, role of the state in social affairs, and so on. Important national differences arise in relation to:

- The extent of employee participation in management decision making
- Legal regulation of employee relations (especially the roles of trade unions and collective bargaining)
- The importance of market forces in fixing wages and conditions of service
- Attitudes towards individualism and collectivism
- Backgrounds of persons engaged in the HRM function. In some countries (Germany for example) HRM professionals tend to have legal qualifications; elsewhere HRM is seen as a matter of financial efficiency, or in terms of sociology and human relations, or in certain nations as an occupation suitable for the 'gifted amateur'

- Whether HRM is regarded as a specialist or a general line management function.

Workers doing comparable jobs in different countries vary with respect to their motivation (e.g. whether there exists a 'work ethic' in a particular nation), commitment to employing organisations, wage levels, technical skills and educational backgrounds. Other determinants of national differences include the extent of unemployment (which often affects workers' attitudes towards their firms), age and sex distribution of the population, and expectations regarding working hours, holidays, etc. Managerial attitudes and behaviour also vary between nations. Differences in managers from disparate countries might relate to preferred management style (authoritarian approaches are more common in certain countries), values, personal objectives, approaches to problem-solving, salary expectations, use of management models and 'scientific' techniques, willingness to delegate, and attitudes towards risk. Planning and strategy formulation are more widespread in some countries than in others. Attitudes towards punctuality and the need to complete work on schedule can also differ among nations.

WORKING INTERNATIONALLY

3. Euro-executives

These are multi-lingual managers who feel at home in any European country, are familiar with EU business laws and practices, and regularly move between companies and countries. Qualities of Euro-executives include:

- Cultural adaptability, i.e. the ability to blend quickly into the local culture of any EU member nation
- Wide-ranging experience of European business management resulting from several changes of jobs and location
- Possession of generalist rather than function-specific management competencies
- Ability to communicate effectively and to exercise interpersonal management skills
- Knowledge of individual EU markets
- Selling and negotiating skills, and the ability to conduct hostile negotiations in more than one language
- Familiarity with EU product standards
- Knowledge of the documentation and procedures attached to cross-border EU marketing, including those needed for transport and distribution across the Union
- Willingness and ability to cope with rapid technical, organisational and environmental change
- Capacity to get on with fellow workers of different nationalities and to contribute to multinational project teams
- Acceptance of a lifestyle involving much foreign travel, frequent relocation and disruptions to normal family routines.

Problems attached to the employment and use of Euro-executives are as follows:

(a) Their high salaries (resulting from their short supply) which create large differentials between Euro-executives and other managers. Euro-executives are hired in consequence of their superior competencies and will demand remuneration packages comparable to those available in other countries. Additionally, they could demand compensation for the high cost of accommodation in prosperous areas (London for instance), for the cost of sending children to private schools that cater for a particular nationality, and for the loss of a spouse's earnings.

(b) Fitting them into conventional line and staff organisation systems, which might stifle their initiative and creativity.

(c) A high probability of their being headhunted by other firms.

(d) Their lack of intimate knowledge of their employing companies and associated products or of the local economy and local business cultures. Euro-executives might not stay in a country long enough to develop networks of contacts with local business people, banks, ancillary services, etc.

(e) Possible conflicts arising from different approaches to business adopted by Euro-executives compared to locally-recruited managers.

Euro-executives, moreover, could experience significant domestic problems that might reduce their usefulness to employing firms (Weiss and Grippo 1992), for example:

- Reluctance to accept a fresh assignment in another EU country because the manager's children have only just settled into a local school
- Opposition to an intended move from the manager's spouse, who may regard it as interference with his or her own career
- Traumas and tribulations attached to regularly moving house and resettling in other cultures
- Practical problems connected with finding suitable housing, arranging for pension transfers, tax arrangements, etc. (Brewster 1991).

4. Management of expatriate staff

An important consequence of the completion of the European Single Market is the ability of an EU business to set up subsidiaries and operate in any EU state, leading to an increase in the number of expatriate European employees working abroad for long periods. Use of home country staff for foreign assignments ensures that senior management has full knowledge of the capabilities, experience, attitudes and perspectives of those in charge of foreign operations; that managers are fully conversant with company policies and procedures; and that communications will be fast and efficient (Boyacigiller 1991). The local subsidiary will be run precisely as headquarters wishes, and since the expatriates themselves will depend on the parent organisation for future career advancement they can be relied upon to further the parent company's interests. Expatriates might have greater product knowledge and managerial expertise than local nationals.

Disadvantages to using expatriates include:

- Their lack of familiarity with the local language, culture and business practices
- The period needed for them to settle in to a new environment (up to a year in some cases) during which a manager's productivity will be lower than he or she achieved at home
- Dangers that individual biases and prejudices towards certain racial or other ethnic groups might emerge during a foreign posting, even though such negative attitudes were not apparent during the manager's home country service
- The possibility that expatriates might impose an inappropriate management style on host country employees, rather than adapting to the local environment
- The blocking of promotion opportunities for locally recruited staff, the most able of whom may well leave the firm.

Settling-in

Settling-in difficulties might result from the expatriate's family not adjusting to local conditions, children not making progress at school, or a spouse not finding local employment (Boyacigiller 1991). Experience suggests that female spouses frequently experience greater difficulty in adjusting to a foreign environment than their male partners, essentially because expatriate communities tend to be male dominated (the husbands' jobs representing the reason for the existence of the expatriate community) and since female spouses lack the continuity and stabilising influence provided by a job (Black and Gregersen 1991). The female may have given up work in order to accompany her spouse to the foreign country, and has to cope with new experiences in all aspects of life: accommodation, friendships, house care arrangements, etc. A spouse will probably find it easier to settle in to a foreign country that already has a large expatriate community from the spouse's home country. This community can help, support and share its experience with the individual in question; creates immediate opportunities for social intercourse; and will generally insulate the spouse from the shock of having to cope with a new environment.

Expatriate training programmes

These normally include the provision of information on the host country, housing, educational and medical facilities, living conditions, social norms, etc.; language training; and job-specific matters relating to local business laws and regulations, the tasks to be undertaken, performance targets, methods for communicating with head office, and so on. The programme might include visits to the country, briefings by other employees recently returned from abroad, and the supply of information to family members who will accompany the person to the new location (Carusgil *et al* 1992). While abroad, the expatriate might be kept in touch with head office affairs via the appointment of a mentor (typically a senior head office manager) who periodically meets with the expatriate to discuss the latter's progress and what is likely to happen to the expatriate on his or her return. Further training might be needed to prepare the person and his or her family for repatriation (Moynihan 1993).

Expatriate remuneration

Salary levels need to be of a level sufficient to attract, retain and motivate expatriate staff of a suitable calibre. This could involve paying expatriates salaries that are considerably higher than those of locally recruited managers, causing much resentment among the lower paid staff. Supplements to base salary are common, and could take the form of expenses payments (for cars, drivers, hire of domestic servants, etc.), special cost of living allowances to compensate for higher taxes, housing costs and so on encountered abroad. Alternatively a straight percentage premium on basic salary might be payable during the foreign posting. An important issue is the currency in which the expatriate is remunerated, since changes in currency exchange rates will affect the conversion value of local currency savings. Sometimes the expatriate is paid partly in local currency and partly in the currency of the host nation.

Repatriation

It is crucially important to plan the orderly re-absorption of a former expatriate into the head office organisation system following his or her return from abroad. Problems frequently experienced by returning expatriates include reductions in their real standards of living (loss of paid accommodation, termination of financial assistance with school fees, etc.), boredom (a headquarters job may be less varied and carry less responsibility), and 'reverse culture shock' as the individual adjusts to changes in the home country environment. The returning expatriate has to cope with head office organisational changes that will have occurred during his or her absence, possible communication difficulties with head office colleagues, new technical developments and alterations in head office management methods.

Selection of staff for foreign postings

Managers may be attracted to a foreign posting through prospects for a higher salary, long-term promotion (though often these are not actually realised), broader responsibilities and the acquisition of experience not available in the home country. Such aspirations could cloud an individual's judgement vis-a-vis the problems that expatriate assignments are likely to involve, and obscure the fact that expatriate work can be extremely demanding. The ideal expatriate is perhaps one who, in addition to being adaptable, is good at foreign languages, self-reliant and independent, emotionally stable and in excellent physical health, is sensitive to foreign culture, technically competent and genuinely enjoys working abroad. He or she needs to possess a working knowledge of business methods, cultures, organisation and policies in various countries and of best practice in foreign firms, and be able quickly and easily to transfer his or her knowledge and skills between firms and operational cultures. The person

289

should be a good communicator, capable of exercising interpersonal management skills in multicultural situations; willing and able to cope with rapid technical, organisational and environmental change; and capable of working with fellow managers of different nationalities and of contributing to multinational project teams.

Few managers possess all these qualities, and great care is necessary when selecting staff for foreign postings. Factors influencing the choice of individuals for expatriate jobs might include:

(a) *Individual characteristics*: qualifications and experience, track record, perspectives, adaptability and attitude, family situation (and whether the candidate's family genuinely wants the person to work abroad), language and area expertise, career plans and personal preferences.

(b) *The host country environment*: local business norms and cultures, degree of employee participation in management decisions, calibre of the foreign subsidiary's employees, how easily a foreigner will be able to 'blend in' with the local environment.

(c) *Company-specific factors*: technical sophistication of the business, nature of the industry, status of international (as opposed to headquarters's country) operations, organisational culture.

5. Free movement of workers

The Treaty of Rome does *not* establish an absolute right to freedom of migration for EU citizens, but does guarantee freedom of movement for 'workers' and their families. This is supposed to enable labour to move from high unemployment areas to places where there are labour shortages. Three Directives passed in 1990 extend the right of freedom of movement to (i) persons of independent means, (ii) retired people, and (iii) students undertaking courses in other EU countries. In all areas the individuals involved *must not be economically dependent on the social security system of the host nation*. Hence it is definitely not the situation that a long-term unemployed person can choose to reside in whichever country offers the highest rate of social security benefit. Rather, workers are free to move to another member country in order to accept offers of employment, and thereafter to remain in that country to continue employment.

A 'worker', according to the European Court of Justice, is 'someone who performs services for another during a certain period of time and under the direction of another in return for remuneration' (*Lawrie* v. *Blum* 1987). Part-time as well as full-time work falls within the definition. Self-employed persons are also guaranteed freedom of movement, provided they are economically active. The period allowed a person to look for work in another country has not been specified in any Directive or Regulation, but was set at a minimum of three months by the ECJ in a case heard in 1982 – subject to the individual being able to support him or her self without recourse to public assistance. A number of countries (including the UK) allow six months for job hunting. Once a person has found a job he or she has the right of residence, unless the job is given up voluntarily. Residence permits are issued for renewable five-year periods. When the worker retires he or she has the right to remain in the host country provided the person has reached the normal age of retirement for that nation and has lived there for at least three years, the last one of which must have been spent in employment. If a worker is incapacitated by an industrial disease or accident that entitles the person to a pension, then the right of residency applies regardless of the duration of previous residence. Persons incapacitated by causes other than employment are entitled to remain if they have two years' previous residence.

All residency rights apply to workers' dependants and family members, i.e.:

- the spouse and descendants under the age of 21 or descendants over 21 who are dependants; *or*
- dependant parents and grandparents of the worker and spouse.

The family must receive equivalent treatment *vis-à-vis* education, welfare, access to public housing, etc., as natives of the host country. Family rights end when (i) the worker loses his or her residence rights, or (ii) a person ceases to be a family member (e.g. on divorce or on the marriage of a child). At the time of writing it is unclear whether co-habitees qualify as 'spouses' in all EU countries. A worker's death does not deprive his or her family of the right to residence provided the family has lived in the country for at least two years or the worker died from an industrial disease or accident. Social security contributions paid by a worker during employment in one country must be taken into account when calculating benefits receivable in another.

Article 48 of the Treaty of Rome makes it unlawful to discriminate against job applications on the grounds of an EU applicant's nationality, *except* for public sector employment. However, public sector employers are required to justify such discrimination, and if a person from another EU country is given a public sector job then he or she must thereafter be treated in the same manner as local nationals.

RECRUITMENT AND TERMINATION

6. Cross-border recruitment

Free mobility of labour makes possible the recruitment of workers from other EU countries, particularly of workers possessing skills and competencies not available locally. This has the following consequences:

(a) Personnel managers require knowledge of recruitment practices in various EU countries and need to be familiar with:

(*i*) pan-European job advertising media capable of reaching good quality foreign EU workers
(*ii*) levels of pay and conditions of service necessary to attract high calibre Continental applicants
(*iii*) foreign EU educational and other qualifications.

(b) Possibilities for training staff via courses held in other EU countries, especially for training in European business practices, European transport and distribution systems, negotiation and tendering procedures in various EU states, etc. (Dany and Torchy 1994).

(c) EU-wide headhunting.

Cross-border recruitment can occur through placing job advertisements in foreign newspapers or trade magazines, personal recommendations from foreign business contacts (such as suppliers, customers or banks), extension of a firm's 'milk-round' to include Continental educational institutions, and by taking foreign EU students for sandwich-courses or other work-experience placements.

Laws on recruitment vary from state to state. In France and Belgium for instance it is illegal to use job vacancy press advertisements for implicit corporate image advertising (describing jobs that in reality do not exist). Additionally, French job advertisements cannot lawfully specify an upper age limit for applicants for the vacant post. Small fines may be imposed on advertisers ignoring this legislation. Application forms for French jobs cannot lawfully include questions concerning union membership, religion, politics, or family situation. German firms' selection methods must be approved by their works councils (*see* Chapter 10) and are subject to much Federal legislation. Applicants are legally entitled to privacy, the right to be treated with dignity, payment of interview expenses, and not to be asked 'improper' questions. The latter include questions concerning the candidate's politics or family situation. Italian job advertisements have to comply with the state Workers' Statute, which forbids mention of political views, union membership, racial or religious criteria. In Spain, a law of 1982 guarantees job applicants freedom from invasion of privacy. Also the Spanish state employment service is supposed to vet all job advertisements appearing in the press in order to weed out any that are sexually discriminatory, although this rarely happens in practice. In Belgium a legally binding national collective agreement between unions and employers' associations entitles job applicants to total privacy during the recruitment process. Questions concerning marriage or family plans are unlawful. The agreement requires employers to return to unsuccessful candidates all documents accompanying an application.

The Posted Worker Proposal

A 1995 Draft Directive on the temporary posting of workers seeks to prescribe which country's employment protection rules shall apply to workers temporarily posted from their home base to another EU nation, e.g. from a country with extensive employment protection to one with only the basic rules required by agreed EU Directives. The purpose of the proposal is to prevent the high levels of employment protection currently in force in northern Europe (excluding the UK) from being undermined via the widespread use of sub-contracted labour recruited in nations with poor employment conditions. Under the Draft Directive any employee posted to a foreign country for more than three months is entitled to the protection of all the employment laws of the *host* rather than his or her home country. Hence the posted worker must be given at least the legal minimum wage of the host nation and observe that country's laws on working hours, notice periods, sick leave, etc.

7. Termination of employment and other national differences

Every EU country imposes on employers statutory notice periods that have to be given to employees. These differ widely from state to state. Additionally, every country except Greece operates a system to enable statutory appeal against dismissal. Again there are large divergences in the compensation for unfair dismissal available in the various countries. Belgium, Denmark and Greece draw an important statutory distinction between white collar (salaried) and blue collar (manual) employees. Under Belgium's 1978 Contracts of Employment Act, for example, a worker's status as white or blue collar affects (a) his or her probationary and notice periods and (b) when notice of termination begins to take effect (the Monday following notification of dismissal for manual workers, the *month* following notification for white collar staff). Denmark also has distinct legislation for specific employee groups which determines sick pay entitlements and notice periods. In Greece, blue collar workers cannot lawfully be instructed to undertake clerical work.

Other national differences

All countries except Denmark and the UK have a statutory provision for paid leave for compassionate purposes (bereavement, marriage, sudden illness of a close relative, etc). The concept of the career break is legally recognised in some states, e.g. for parenting or to undertake a training or educational course, the period involved depending on the country concerned. Employers in these states are legally obliged to give career break sabbaticals to workers, though not necessarily to provide payment while the person is away. Spain provides employees with the highest number of annual public holidays. Denmark and France guarantee workers the longest statutory periods for holidays.

Greece is the only EU country that does not allow firms to place contractual restrictions on employees' capacities (i) to exploit inventions made during their course of employment, (ii) to set up in competition with the previously employing organisation, and (iii) to pass on confidential information. However, the extents of the constraints and penalties for non-observance vary among countries. In Belgium, for example, non-competition clauses are only valid for workers earning more than a certain threshold. Danish workers may compete with ex-employers after one year has elapsed since leaving their firms, and may disclose trade secrets after three years (unless special clauses are included in their contracts). German firms' restrictive covenants may not last for more than two years following termination, and the workers accepting them have to be compensated to the value of at least half their last year's earnings. Italy allows the imposition of restrictions for three years in the case of manual workers and five years for managerial employees. In Portugal the period is three years for both categories.

8. Parental leave

The term 'parental leave' is used to describe leave taken by women *after* the expiry of maternity leave and which is unpaid (or paid at a very low rate) and carries the right to re-engagement in a similar position in the former employing firm. Statutory provision for parental leave varies widely across the European Union. In Ireland there is no statutory right to parental leave whatsoever. Thereafter there are large differences in conditions and benefits, ranging from:

- Zero length of service requirements in five EU countries, four weeks' service in Germany, six months in three nations, and one year in the remaining half dozen.
- Leave durations of three months (in Greece) to three years (in France, Germany, Norway and Spain).
- No financial payment in four countries, a flat rate monthly sum in five others, through varying percentages of previous earnings elsewhere.

Nine EU nations give people returning from parental leave the legal right to insist that they be employed part time.

The issue of parental leave is important because of the huge increase in the number of working women in EU countries that has occurred over the last couple of decades, in combination with the rise of single-person households.

Advantages claimed for the practice of granting employees parental leave are as follows:

(a) Employment and family responsibilities may be reconciled.

(b) Equal opportunities for women are promoted (through enabling women to remain in the labour force).

(c) Women are encouraged to have more children. This is a critical factor in countries where the birth rate is in sharp decline.

(d) Unemployment is reduced as fresh workers are engaged to cover for people who are away on leave.

(e) Firms retain trained and competent staff for longer periods.

(f) Mothers have more time to spend with their families. Equal sharing of family responsibilities between men and women is facilitated, as women are relieved of the (stressful) burden of having to return quickly to a job while caring for an infant at the same time.

(g) The state formally recognises the social importance of parenting.

Criticisms of statutory parental leave are that:

(a) It is more efficient to allow market forces to determine whether parental leave is necessary. If firms really require the long-term services of the women involved they will be prepared to pay the appropriate rate to retain them.

(b) Employers' wage bills are higher than otherwise would be the case, possibly helping to make European firms uncompetitive in world markets.

(c) The long-term absence of key employees can severely disrupt an organisation's work.

(d) Having to find replacements for people away on parental leave is troublesome and expensive. Replacements have to be inducted and trained, only to be dismissed on the return of the absent worker.

Paternity leave

Seven EU countries give fathers the statutory right to a few days' paid leave at the times their children are born. The period involved varies from two days in Spain to ten days in Sweden. Additionally eleven EU states allow fathers to take, by law, a longer period of unpaid leave for parenting purposes, provided the mother waives her entitlement to all or part of her statutory parental leave. The shortest duration of this kind of paternity leave applies in Denmark (ten weeks); the longest in France, Austria and Germany (two to three years); six months is the commonest period. In 1994 the UK government vetoed an EU Draft Directive on parental leave that would have given all employees the right to at least three months' unpaid leave (whether working full time or part time) following the birth or adoption of a child. At the time of writing the other 14 EU member states are devising plans for introducing a revised form of the Draft Directive under the Maastricht Protocol.

Benefits resulting from the practice of granting paternity leave are as follows:

- Employees are helped to reconcile their work and family responsibilities.
- Gender equal opportunities are facilitated: women are allowed greater flexibility in their working lives and hence can better pursue and develop their own careers.
- Beneficiaries are likely to be more loyal to the firm.
- Companies can plan ahead to avoid possible disruptions caused by men taking time off work (through formal leave or deliberate absenteeism) when a child is being born.

The disadvantages include:

- The final costs imposed on employers
- Reductions in productivity caused by the use of inexperienced temporary replacement workers
- Adverse effects on individual career development.

EQUAL OPPORTUNITIES

9. Equal opportunities in employment

An equal opportunity employment situation exists when there is no unfair discrimination against either of the sexes or against any ethnic or legally constituted social group in terms of access to jobs, terms and conditions of employment, promotion, training, remuneration, or termination of employment. Today, many organisations have 'equal opportunities policies' in which they formally state their commitment to equal opportunity ideals. The advantages to having such a policy are that:

- Top management is seen to endorse equal opportunity measures hence creating an example to be followed at lower levels.
- As part of its policy the firm might critically examine the sex and ethnic compositions of all its departments, divisions, occupational categories and levels of worker, exposing any unfair employment practices currently operating.
- The best candidates for jobs will (or should) be recruited or promoted regardless of their sex or ethnic origin.
- Discontent among existing minority group employees may be avoided.

Problems attached to equal opportunity policies are:

(a) Organisations sometimes publish extensive equal opportunity policy documents in order to placate existing minority group workers and/or external bodies (local authorities, government, purchasing agencies, etc.) but in fact have no commitment to equal opportunities whatsoever. They have no procedures for *implementing* their equal opportunity policy demands. This creates disillusion and cynicism among all concerned.

(b) Recruitment costs increase substantially. Job advertisements have to be placed (expensively) in magazines and newspapers read by each of the sexes and by various ethnic minorities. All applications have to be examined carefully from an equal-opportunities viewpoint, interview panels need to be larger, more candidates must be interviewed and more time has to be spent in interviewing.

(c) An organisation might apply an equal opportunities policy to operatives and low-grade managers, but not to middle managers or senior executives. Hence the representation of minority groups collapses at higher levels, so that corporate strategy cannot be influenced by individuals from minority groups.

10. Equal rights for men and women

Article 119 of the Treaty of Rome demanded equal pay for equal work completed by men and women, and this (in principle, at least) is mandatory in all member countries. The Council of Ministers has also directed that there shall be equal pension rights and social security benefits for men and women. This has been interpreted by the European Court of Justice to mean equal retirement ages for men and women. Article 119 encompasses wages, fringe benefits, payments in kind, access to pension schemes, etc. Equal work means work of equal value (not just people engaged in identical duties) and the onus is on the employer to prove that any discrepancy between male and female rates of pay is not due to sex discrimination.

UK legislation extends to race as well as gender equal opportunities. This is not the case in all EU states (see below). In the UK, the Sex Discrimination Acts of 1975 and 1986 and the Race Relations Act 1976 make it illegal to discriminate in all aspects of employment, e.g. job advertising, selection, terms of employment, promotion, training, dismissal and retirement. Discrimination means the less favourable treatment of a person by reason of sex, colour, race or ethnic or national origin. Employers are liable if their subordinates discriminate unlawfully. Indirect discrimination is also unlawful, i.e. applying a condition or requirement which, although applied to both sexes or to all racial groups, is such that a considerably smaller proportion of one sex or of one racial group can comply with it, unless the employer can show the condition to be justified. An example would be a requirement for applicants for a senior clerical post to be at least six feet tall. The Sex Discrimination Act also covers unfair discrimination against people who are married.

Belgian victims of unfair sex discrimination can seek compensation (of up to six months' pay or the actual value of damages suffered) from a Labour Court. Criminal penalties ranging from small fines to one month's imprisonment are also available. The same applies to unfair race discrimination. Additionally, French firms employing more than 50 workers must prepare and submit to union representatives and the Labour Inspectorate an annual report on the degree of equality of men and women within the enterprise. Job applicants in Germany rejected on the grounds of sex may claim four months' pay for the work they would have done had their application been successful. The same applies for internal promotion.

In Greece, a person who suffers from an act of sex discrimination must apply to the civil courts for damages, although small fines can also be imposed by the Ministry of Labour. Irish victims can claim up to 104 weeks' pay, and courts may impose daily fines for as long as discriminatory practices continue.

The EU Code of Practice on the Prevention of Sexual Harassment at Work 1992

This is a broadly based set of recommendations that advises employers to produce a policy statement on the subject of sexual harassment, to establish complaints procedures and to communicate these to employees. Persistent offenders should be subject to the firm's internal disciplinary procedures and the necessary sanctions applied. However there is no requirement for EU member countries to introduce legislation on this matter, although several actually have.

Race discrimination

Ten EU countries have laws that prohibit race discrimination in employment (Britain, Finland, France, Germany, Ireland, Italy, Netherlands, Portugal, Spain and Sweden). Finland and Spain restrict protection to persons *already* in employment, while Irish legislation only applies to dismissals. In the other countries the law extends to recruitment processes as well as treatment within employment. 'Race' can refer to ethnic origin, nationality or skin colour. Six of the nine have anti-race discrimination provisions written into their constitutions (France, Germany, Italy, Netherlands, Portugal and Spain); the other three rely on *ad hoc* legislation. Note, however, that all EU nations apart from Ireland have ratified the 1965 United Nations International Convention on the Elimination of All Forms of Racial Discrimination, which requires governments to undertake to prohibit and eliminate racial discrimination in all its forms and to guarantee the right to everybody to equality before the law in relation to conditions of employment, free choice of employment, fair treatment at work, equal pay for equal work, etc. EU countries other than Ireland, Luxembourg and the United Kingdom, moreover, have signed the 1958 International Labour Organisation Convention on Discrimination in Respect of Employment and Occupation, which imposes on governments the obligation to 'declare and pursue a national policy designed to promote equality of opportunity in respect of employment and occupation with a view to eliminating discrimination.' Acceptance of such Conventions puts pressures on national governments to legislate in order to meet agreed international standards, but does not guarantee that they will do so.

To date, EU institutions have expressed concern about racism, although no substantial legislation has emerged. At the time of writing, however, a proposed Draft Directive on the matter is under discussion, which if adopted would effectively outlaw all forms of racial discrimination. The United Kingdom government has announced its intention to veto the proposal. Presumably the intended Draft Directive could then be implemented under the Maastricht Protocol. At present the only protection available via EU law is on the grounds of *nationality* rather than race or colour, since discrimination related to nationality is prohibited by Article 7 of the Treaty of Rome. Thus, for example, a black or Asian UK citizen seeking a job in an EU country outside the UK is not protected against discrimination on the basis of colour (as opposed to nationality). This lack of concern with race discrimination is in sharp contrast with the comprehensive EU legislation against sex discrimination that has been in place since 1975.

Age discrimination

Specific problems confronted by older workers include:

- early loss of employment because of age
- difficulties in finding fresh employment
- targeting of older people in company downsizing exercises
- what are in effect compulsory early retirement schemes
- exclusion from government retraining programmes and, where such programmes exist, the training materials used to reskill older workers being based (unsuitably) on those applied to the training of very young people
- loss of statutory protection against unfair dismissal once an employee has reached a certain age.

No EU country has constitutional provisions barring age discrimination, although Belgium, Italy, the Netherlands, Portugal and Spain have constitutional clauses from which the impropriety of age discrimination may be inferred. Italy's constitution, for example, states that all citizens must be treated equally regardless of 'personal and social conditions'. France and Sweden ban the use of maximum age limits in job advertisements, while decisions of the Irish Labour Court have held that specification of maximum ages can amount to indirect sex discrimination. Germany, Finland and Sweden have *ad hoc* laws that outlaw age discrimination *within* employment. In Ireland and Italy it is illegal to dismiss an employee on the grounds of age. Austria and France have laws that make it inconvenient and costly (though not illegal) to dismiss older workers, while in Sweden the minimum period of notice to be given to employees is age rather than service-related.

HEALTH AND SAFETY AT WORK

11. EU interventions

The number of EU Directives concerning health and safety is increasing rapidly, partly since EU health and safety Directives may be approved by a majority (rather than unanimous) vote of EU members. Already there exist important Directives on visual display units (*see* below), eye protection, the manual lifting of heavy loads, protective equipment, and other aspects of workplace safety. More are expected soon, possibly increasing the complexity of bureaucratic rules and the costs to employers of complying with health and safety laws.

The Framework Directive

In addition to *specific* Directives on health and safety, the Union enacted in 1989 a Framework Directive which contained a statement of *general principles* concerning the protection of employees' health and safety at work. It obliged employers to take 'appropriate measures' to satisfy these principles, according to detailed rules imposed by national authorities. Under the Framework Directive, employers must ensure the prevention of occupational risks, eliminate dangers, inform and consult with workers, and invite the 'balanced participation' of employee representatives when dealing with health and safety matters. The British government considers the UK Health and Safety at Work, etc. Act 1974 to meet the essential requirements of the Framework Directive.

The European Agency for Health and Safety at Work

This was set up in Bilbao in Spain in 1995. Its aims are to assess the impact of proposed EU legislation on industrial health and safety and then to advise the European Commission on these matters; to establish networks for the exchange of information about health and safety at work among EU member countries; and to conduct research and publish the results.

12. Management of health and safety

Several EU Regulations on the management of health and safety at work came into force in 1993, requiring employers to undertake 'risk assessment exercises' intended to identify potential dangers to the health and safety of employees or anyone else likely to be affected by the firm's operations. The Management of Health and Safety at Work Regulations 1992 in particular required that the risk assessment be completed by competent people (who may be outside consultants) and that, for firms with five or more workers, a permanent record of the exercise be maintained. In addition the firm is obliged to:

- Devise and implement specific procedures for dealing with emergencies.
- Draw up a plan for putting into effect preventative and protective measures.
- Train employees in safety matters and ensure that workers are capable of avoiding risks. Employees (including temporary workers) must be informed of risks in *language they can understand*.
- Take into account working conditions and local workplace hazards when selecting equipment.
- Identify unavoidable risks in relation to handling operations, having regard to the shape, size and weight of the load and the ergonomic characteristics of the workplace (humidity, space available, etc.).

Other major Regulations in the package were as follows:

(a) *The Provision and Use of Work Equipment Regulations 1992.* Under these regulations 'work equipment' is defined to include everything from hand tools to complete factories or refineries, while 'use' means every aspect of equipment operation, servicing and cleaning. Employers are obliged to make sure that equipment is suitable for its intended use and that it is only used for appropriate purposes. When selecting equipment, employers must take into account working conditions and the hazards of the workplace. Proper training and information relating to the equipment must be given to workers.

(b) *The Manual Handling Operations Regulations 1992.* These require employers to identify unavoidable handling risks in terms of the shape, size and weight of the load, the handler's posture while performing operations, and the ergonomic characteristics of the workplace (space available, humidity, etc.). By law, hazardous manual handling operations must be avoided wherever possible.

(c) *The Workplace (Health, Safety and Welfare) Regulations 1992, and Personal Protective Equipment at Work Regulations 1992.* The purpose of these two sets of Regulations was to tidy up and consolidate a large number of existing pieces of legislation currently spread over several different statutes. They concern such matters as the working environment (lighting, ventilation, room space per worker and so on), facilities (toilets, rest areas, drinking water, etc.), removal of waste materials, cleaning and maintenance of protective clothing and equipment, and the design and approval of new personal protective equipment.

Directive on visual display units 1990

This specifies minimum health and safety requirements for work with display screen equipment. Under the Directive, employers must:

- Analyse display screen workstations to identify potential hazards and take measures to remedy any health and safety problem discovered.
- Train employees in the proper use of display screen equipment, inform workers of relevant facts, and consult employee representatives on VDU matters.
- Plan VDU operators' daily schedules in order to interrupt long periods of screen work and to create changes of activity.

- Ensure that workstations satisfy the technical requirements of the Directive in relation to screen sizes and luminosity, keyboard design, working environment, etc.
- Provide employees with eye and eyesight tests prior to their commencing VDU work and at regular intervals thereafter. Firms must supply special spectacles if employees' normal spectacles are not suitable for display screen jobs.

EMPLOYMENT PROTECTION

EU interventions in the field of employment protection extend to working hours, nightwork, part-time working, the protection of pregnant employees, and workers' rights in relation to mass redundancies and the insolvency or transfer of ownership of undertakings.

13. Directive on the protection of pregnant employees 1992

Under this Directive, all pregnant workers are protected against dismissal on the grounds of pregnancy (regardless of length of service) and maintain all their contractual employment rights during maternity leave (of which a minimum of 14 weeks must be granted) and associated absences. State financial support is payable during maternity leave. Further entitlements are that:

(a) A pregnant worker may refuse to work at night if a doctor certifies that night working could endanger the woman's health. An alternative day job must be offered for a 16-week period, of which eight weeks must be prior to the expected date of birth of the child.

(b) The employer must assess the risks of particular jobs to the health of pregnant workers and inform the person of any potential hazards. Working conditions must be adjusted to protect the woman's health and safety. The exposure of pregnant employees to certain specified harmful substances and processes is illegal.

(c) Pregnant women may take paid time off to attend ante-natal examinations during working hours.

14. Directive on mass redundancies 1975

This requires companies to give prior notification of group redundancies scheduled for implementation over a period of 30 days or less. Additionally, consultation with employee representatives concerning the mechanics of imposing large-scale redundancies and on measures for avoiding them (e.g. through natural wastage or redeployment) is required.

15. Directive on safeguarding employees' rights following the transfer of ownership of undertakings 1977

The purpose of this Directive is to protect employees' rights and to compel management to inform and consult with employee representatives on the transfer of the ownership of a business. General information about the transfer must be disclosed, plus specific facts regarding its effects (redundancies for example) on particular groups of workers. Information must be transmitted early enough to permit proper discussions with employee representatives. Employees' terms and conditions of service cannot be altered at the time of transfer, and workers may only be declared redundant if this can be objectively justified at the moment the business changes hands. If redundancies are necessary, the new owner *automatically* assumes full responsibility for making statutory redundancy payments to the people involved.

16. Directive on the protection of employees following an employer's insolvency 1990

This obliges the state to pay to workers dismissed in consequence of an employing firm's insolvency all outstanding maternity pay, holiday pay for up to six weeks accumulated over the previous twelve months, up to eight weeks' arrears of wages, amounts due as compensation for redundancy or unfair dismissal, and pay for employees' statutory minimum periods of notice.

17. The Working Time Directive 1994

This entitles employees to a daily rest of eleven consecutive hours in any 24 hour period; to rest breaks during any working day longer than six consecutive hours; and a weekly rest period of 24 consecutive hours. The maximum working week is restricted to 48 hours, although member states have the right to opt out from this provision until the year 2006 *provided* employees are legally permitted to refuse to work more than 48 hours without jeopardising their employment. Full-time employees can take three weeks' paid leave annually (four weeks after 1999). Under the Directive, night workers may not work more than eight hours in any 24-hour period. They can also demand a free initial health assessment plus regular medical checkups thereafter. If night working causes an employee to experience health problems then he or she should (wherever possible) be transferred to day work.

Objections to the Directive have included the following:

(a) Rest breaks within a shift might be unworkable in continuous process operations where plant cannot be left unattended.

(b) Opportunities for overtime could be an important incentive necessary to induce employees to accept night-shift working.

(c) Overtime night-shift working is a convenient means whereby firms facing labour shortages can satisfy short-term increases in the demands for their products.

Note: The Working Time Directive was challenged by the UK in the European Court of Justice in 1994, on the basis that it is (allegedly) unnecessary and not relevant to the control of health and safety at work.

National restrictions on working time

Night work is strictly controlled in a number of EU states. Greek night workers must be paid at least time and a quarter of normal rates; double time at weekends. Spain and Portugal also have a statutory minimum rate of 125 per cent for night work. Spain bans night work for anyone under the age of 18. The Netherlands prohibits night work entirely unless the firm involved obtains a special licence from the Dutch Ministry of Labour. In Belgium night work has to be voluntary, approved by employee representatives, and only undertaken by permanent full-time workers. Pregnant workers have the legal right to be temporarily transferred from night to day working. Overtime is also subject to legislation in many countries. Additionally some EU nations set down minimum wage premiums for overtime working. French, Greek, German and Irish workers are entitled to at least time and a quarter for overtime; Portuguese employees have to be paid at least time and a half for the first hour of extra working and time and three-quarters from then on. Until 1994, all overtime worked in Spain attracted a 75 per cent statutory bonus. Since 1994 overtime rates have been subject to negotiation between managements and workers, but typically involve a 75 per cent premium.

The Directive on the protection of young people 1996

This establishes a minimum working age of 15 years (except in special circumstances) and requires that working conditions for employees aged between 15 and 18 be adapted to protect their physical, moral and social development. Persons under 18 are prohibited from undertaking certain types of work, and risk assessments must be completed before young people commence employment. Also they must not work for more than eight hours a day or 40 hours weekly; night work is heavily restricted. 'Working children' (i.e. school students under 15 years of age who are undergoing work experience or training) must be given 14 hours continuous rest in any 24-hour period. Other young workers under 18 must have at least 12 hours continuous rest daily. All young people are entitled to two consecutive days' rest each week. A half hour break must be given after four and a half hours' work. The UK has secured an opt-out from the Directive's provisions on the length of the maximum working week until the year 2000.

PART-TIME EMPLOYEES

18. Part-time and casual working

Part-time and temporary working has increased significantly in Western Europe over the past decade, with almost 15 per cent of employees currently on part-time and 10 per cent on temporary contracts. Part-time work is concentrated among females, with nearly 30 per cent of EU women employees lying in this category (5 per cent for men). In the Netherlands about 60 per cent of women work part time; for Britain and Denmark the figure is around 43 per cent. The lowest percentages are in Italy, Portugal and Greece (10 per cent) and in Spain and Luxembourg (14 per cent).

Spain and Portugal have the highest proportions of their workforces on temporary contracts (22 and 19 per cent respectively). Luxembourg and Belgium have the lowest (4 per cent and 5 per cent). Women are more likely to be working on a temporary contract in all EU countries except Greece. More than half of all EU temporary workers are under 25 years of age, although temporary working among older age groups is common in certain countries (notably Britain, Greece and Italy).

A number of EU countries provide statutory protection to those who work part time and/or are on temporary contracts. Also there are (quite severe) statutory restrictions on the circumstances in which temporary labour may be used by firms in certain nations. Belgian part-timers, for example, must be provided with work lasting at least one third the hours of a full-time employee and have at least three consecutive hours of work at a stretch. Importantly, employers are legally obliged to pay part-time workers pro rata to full-time employees. French part-timers have exactly the same legal rights as regards working conditions, protection against unfair dismissal, etc., as full-time employees. Also, French law strictly regulates the use of temporary contracts, which must specify details of the employee who is temporarily replaced (if appropriate) and the expected duration of the assignment (which may not exceed 18 months in normal circumstances). The law restricts temporary employment to seasonal work, *ad hoc* projects, unexpected increases in workload, and filling in for sick workers. Firms imposing redundancies cannot hire temporaries for six months after the redundancies have been implemented. A 15 per cent end-of-contract bonus must be paid to compensate a temporary worker for the eventual loss of his or her job. Essentially similar provisions apply in Germany and Portugal.

Comprehensive employment protection legislation in Germany has prevented the widespread use of casual labour that has happened in some other countries. The legislation inhibits management's ability to discard labour as demand reduces, but does compel businesses to devise long-term human resource plans – arguably to the benefit of the employing organisation. A 1987 court case (*Bilka Kaufhaus* v. *Weber von Hartz*) ruled that occupational pension schemes which exclude part-timers are unlawful because they discriminate indirectly against women (who form the bulk of the part-time labour force). This principle has been extended to other German court cases which have determined that *any* employment provisions that exclude part-timers are illegal unless they can be justified by objective factors. The same qualifying periods for access to benefits, legal protection, etc., must be applied to part-time and to full-time employees.

Italian part-timers and temporary workers must be given pay and benefits pro rata to those who work full time. In Spain a part-timer is not legally entitled to pro rata pay but does have the same statutory employment protection rights as a full-time employee.

19. HRM implications of the use of casual and part-time workers

Extensive use of part-time and/or casual workers creates a schism between, on the one hand, 'core' workers who are full-time permanent employees and, on the other hand, 'peripheral' workers who are hired as and when required on short-term and/or part-time contracts. Peripherals exercise little discretion over how they perform their duties. They might include job sharers, agency employees, homeworkers, and self-employed contractors as well as casuals and part-timers.

Special problems apply to the management of flexible workforces, possibly including:

- poor communications with and among peripherals
- deciding how to appraise the performances of casual and part-time workers
- securing adequate representation of peripheral employees in management/union negotiations, on health and safety committees, etc.
- low morale among peripherals, who do not feel they really 'belong' to the organisation
- preventing permanent full-time workers resenting the presence of peripherals, whom they might regard as a threat to their jobs.

In countries where there is minimal legal protection for part-time and casual workers (*see* above), a small number of companies have attempted to address such problems through such measures as:

- incorporating grievance procedures, right of appeal against dismissal, etc., into peripherals' contracts of employment
- paying peripheral workers to attend training courses and general discussions about the firm's objectives
- offering guarantees of re-entry to a job after a break in continuity of service
- making peripherals responsible for the quality of their outputs, and generally broadening the variety of tasks they undertake
- offering working conditions comparable to those of permanent core workers, including full recognition to peripheral employees' contributions.

20. Draft Directives on part-time and casual work

In 1990 the European Commission produced three Draft Directives on part-time and casual workers. The third of these concerned minimum health and safety requirements and was adopted in 1992. However, the first and second (which respectively demand working conditions and employment protection equal to those offered to full-time employees) have proven controversial and have yet to be adopted. Together the two Draft Directives provide for:

- the right of part-timers to claim unfair dismissal on the same basis as full-time workers

- proportional entitlement to paid holidays, sick pay, redundancy and retirement benefits
- equal rights in relation to health and safety at work
- equal access to occupational pension schemes
- making it unlawful to discriminate unfairly against part-timers when selecting employees for promotion
- equal access to social services
- equal access to vocational training
- wages for part-timers that are strictly proportional to wage levels paid to full-time workers doing the same work.

The proposals apply to all part-timers working at least eight hours a week. An employer intending to use part-time (or temporary) workers would have to inform employee representatives about this in good time. Employers would also be required to advise part-time (and temporary) workers of any permanent full-time vacancies that arose. Temporary and fixed-contract workers would become entitled to social security benefits identical to those of permanent employees. Individuals engaged under temporary contracts would have to be informed of the reasons for their being employed on temporary rather than permanent contracts. Additionally, the client companies of employment agencies would be made liable for the pay and National Insurance contributions of temporary agency workers following an employment agency's collapse. All EU health and safety legislation would apply equally to full-time, part-time and temporary workers.

If adopted, the Draft Directives would greatly increase the cost of employing part-time staff in countries where part-timers do not already receive these benefits.

Objections to the Draft Directives

Opponents of the Commission's proposals argue that they will:

- Interfere with market forces and create unemployment through reducing the number of firms willing to engage part-time or casual employees.
- Reduce the international competitiveness of EU industry. Wage costs will increase dramatically in certain countries, including the UK. In particular the Directive would oblige employers to pay National Insurance for all workers employed more than eight hours a week, including those earning less than the current NI threshold.

EMPLOYEE RELATIONS

21. Nature of employee relations

Employee relations is a subject that covers 'industrial' relations, employee participation in management decisions, communications, plus policies for improving co-operation between management and workers, the control of employee grievances and the minimisation of conflict.

Industrial relations

Industrial relations (IR) may be regarded as all the rules, practices and conventions governing interactions between managements and their workforces, normally involving collective employee representation and bargaining. The rules of IR define procedures for settling wages and conditions of work, for resolving disputes and dealing with disciplinary processes. Rules may be written or verbally agreed; internally formulated or externally imposed, e.g. through government legislation.

22. National differences

The employee relations system of each EU country is the outcome of complex and specific historical, cultural, political, economic and sometimes religious factors. Not surprisingly, therefore, many significant differences in employee relations laws and practices exist among members states. Major disparities occur in relation to the extent and nature of worker representation in management decisions, the role of trade unions, methods for resolving disputes, and the legal framework for collective bargaining. The main difference between employee relations systems in Britain and in other West European countries is that, whereas in the UK collective agreements are binding 'in honour only', in most EU nations they are *legally binding* so that workers or employers who break a collective agreement can be sued for damages by the other side. There are many other significant disparities in employee relations laws and practices among European states, particularly in relation to the extent and nature of worker representation in management decisions, the role of trade unions, and methods for resolving disputes. Note moreover that not only might collective agreements be legally binding in continental EU states, it could also be the case that national collective agreements automatically extend to and legally bind other firms and workers who were not party to the agreement. Thus an agreement could cover the bulk of the workforce even though trade union membership is minimal in the industry or country concerned.

23. Trade unions

The intensity of trade union membership varies enormously among EU states. It is highest (at around 70–80% of the employed workforce) in Belgium and Denmark, lowest in Spain and France. In general it is true to say that unionisation is today far less important in West European countries than in the past, except for Denmark and Sweden, where union membership has risen in recent years. (Note, however, that Scandinavian unions are involved in the distribution of social security benefits, so that workers in these countries have a powerful incentive to join trade unions.) Aggregate union membership has declined especially sharply in Ireland and the UK.

Undoubtedly, high unemployment and recessions in EU states have weakened unions. In addition there seems to have been a fundamental change in social attitudes towards the role of trade unions throughout the EU. Most EU countries have a government-funded industrial relations conciliation system, and there exists a wide range of restrictions on the right to strike. Compulsory arbitration and cooling-off periods apply in some countries. Secret ballots might also be needed prior to a strike. Lockouts and/or the dismissal of strikers may or may not be lawful.

The right to strike is written into the constitutions of twelve of the EU states (Ireland, the UK and Denmark being the exceptions). However, steady long-term decline in the number of days lost through industrial action (although figures can fluctuate sharply from year to year) has occurred in all EU countries, due partly no doubt to the higher levels of unemployment experienced through-out the Union over the last two decades. In most years labour disputes account for less than one per cent of all time lost to European industry. Sickness and accidents are responsible for a quarter of all time off; maternity leave and bad weather account for 3.5% each. Germany has the lowest number of days lost per 1000 through strikes (ignoring the public sector strikes occurring in 1992). Ireland has been the European Union's most strike-prone country in recent years. Tripartite industrial relations bodies exist in the majority of EU nations. 'Tripartism' means the bringing together of the government, major national trade union organisations and employers' associations in order to establish mutually acceptable frameworks for the conduct of wage and other negotiations, possibly to conclude collective agreements applicable to a wide range of major industries, and to resolve national labour disputes. In Belgium, the Netherlands, and Portugal, tripartite bodies have a statutory position.

TRAINING AND DEVELOPMENT

24. General and vocational education

Young people in the European Union are increasingly well-educated. According to Eurostat (the statistical service of the European Union) about a quarter of the EU's population is now in full-time education, a figure comparable to that of Japan and the USA. Students, moreover are spending more years at school and college: today a quarter of European students remain in education after the age of 19. The representation of females in higher education has risen sharply over the last 20 years, and is roughly on a par with males in most Union states.

Education and training systems in the European Union are characterised by their diversity. Major differences in national approaches include the following:

- the status afforded to vocational education and training (VET) in a nation's overall education system
- quality assurance procedures for attesting individual competence
- the financing of training
- workplace relationships between those who have experienced VET and those with other types of educational qualifications
- whether basic general education is broadly based or specialised.

A further important difference in national approaches concerns the role of vocational education *within* the basic school system. In some EU countries a vocational qualification obtained at school can serve as a means for entry to higher education on exactly the same basis as an 'academic' school-leaving certificate. Also, vocational education begins at a much earlier age in some countries than elsewhere. Note how certain nations maintain the tradition whereby any student in possession of basic matriculation qualifications has the legal *right* to enter higher education (subject of course to space availability in various institutions), whereas selection by colleges is practised in other states. The former approach results in large classes and high failure and drop-out rates, which are accepted as normal and inevitable consequences of the system.

25. Need for VET

Europe's workforce is aging rapidly. A consequence of this (according to estimates prepared by the European Commission) is that as older workers retire the size of the EU's total labour force will be shrinking by around one million per annum by the year 2005. At the same time, the bulk of the Union's workforce will be between 45 and 64 years of age, a cohort that has received minimal industrial training and will have experienced long bouts of (demotivating) unemployment. Lack of skill, moreover, leads to lack of self-confidence when confronted with new technologies. Equally, however, Commission forecasts predict that four in ten European workers will require university entrance level qualifications by the end of the century. This will badly affect employment prospects in countries which have not bothered to invest in the education of their young people. Possible consequences of the impending situation include:

- greatly increased training efforts by companies
- large-scale migrations of skilled labour across national frontiers
- higher levels of participation in the labour force by (educated) women and ethnic minority workers
- widespread use of loyalty bonuses to discourage skilled employees from changing their employer
- further pressures to use robotics and other fully automated production methods.

EU initiatives

The European Commission wishes to establish a common vocational training policy, applicable within all EU nations. To date, the Commission's activities have focused on three main areas:

1. Provision of training grants to individual countries via the European Social Fund. Also, a number of student exchange programmes have been implemented.
2. Establishment of agencies and databases to facilitate the development of vocational training.
3. Attempts to secure the mutual recognition of professional qualification. This is being done through the introduction of Higher Education Diplomas (*see* below).

26. Higher education diplomas (HEDs)

These are professional qualifications obtained after at least three years' study and recognised in all EU countries. Their purpose is to facilitate the mobility of professionally-qualified workers within the Union. In the past, member states restricted the right of entry to certain professions (e.g. accountancy, law, medicine) to persons who studied and qualified within their own national territories. HEDs, however, should enable these restrictions to be lifted. The training, examination and other requirements for specific professions are being harmonised across member states, and anyone possessing the appropriate HED will be free to practise his or her profession in any EU country (although some 'topping-up' of qualifications may be required in certain specific circumstances). Accordingly, professionally-qualified people will be able to offer their services on a European scale, possibly resulting in:

- greater competitiveness among professionals, and an increased supply of professionals in job markets offering the highest reward
- recruiting companies advertising for professionally qualified staff throughout the Union
- rapid transmission among professionals in different countries of new ideas and working methods.

Moreover, a number of Directives are in force which compel member states to recognise Certificates of Experience relating to experience obtained in a particular industry in another member state and issued by the authorities of that country.

27. European management training

Effective management training *necessarily* builds upon the basic education received by managers at school and college. Hence, the sounder the educational infrastructure within a country the firmer the foundation on which good quality management training may be constructed. Thereafter, the quality and extent of a country's management education typically depends on a mixture of state intervention and private provision by large corporations (it has always been the case in all EU countries that big and well-established companies undertake a disproportionately high proportion of management training).

Management training affects how managers define problems, choose strategies and determine the range of options to be considered when formulating policies. It influences the organisational structure of enterprises (number of levels of authority, delegation patterns, ratios of supervisors to operatives, control systems, etc.); and the attitudes, creativities, industriousness and capacities of individual executives. In turn these factors determine productivity levels within businesses and hence the economic performances of nations. A highly significant fact is that within a few years time the majority of European managers will be employed by firms engaged in the provision of services rather than the manufacture of products. It is essential therefore that the management theories that underlie training reflect this and not be based entirely on the experiences of manufacturing enterprises.

EDUCATION AND TRAINING IN FRANCE, GERMANY AND THE UNITED KINGDOM

Useful insights into the natures of and differences between national education and training systems in various EU countries can be obtained from a brief examination of the arrangements existing in France, Germany and the UK.

28. France

Secondary education begins at age eleven, on a comprehensive basis. The only private schools are religious and not a significant influence within the system. At the age of 14, about 15 per cent of pupils transfer to technical school, being joined at age 15 by a further 25 per cent of their cohort. The first set of transferees normally obtain a skilled worker certificate; the second a technical baccalauréat. Courses are full time and school based, although industry is requested to advise on the curriculum.

Those who do not enter the vocational stream at 15 study for a further two years in order to obtain a general education certificate (BEPC). Successful completion of a third year gives the student a baccalauréat and hence the automatic right to enter university. The baccalauréat subject combination based on mathematics and science (BacC) has great prestige, and is often sought by students intending to pursue careers not remotely related to science or mathematics.

At university, students can take a two-year diploma, followed if they wish by a third-year 'licence' (bachelor's degree) and perhaps a fourth-year maitrise (master's degree). Sandwich courses containing three to five month industrial placements are common. In addition to the universities, France has nearly 200 grandes écoles, which take about ten per cent of all entrants to higher education. Competition for places in the grandes écoles is fierce and involves extensive testing of candidates (in contrast to the universities, which are obliged to offer places to anyone possessing the baccalauréat). An estimated 75 per cent of senior executives in large French companies have a grandes écoles qualification, and there is much social contact between these individuals and civil servants and public sector managers with a similar educational backgrounds.

Criticisms of the French system

The French educational system places a great deal of emphasis on formal intellect and academic qualifications. And since there is a long tradition in France of graduates from elite grandes écoles going into industrial management the system has led perhaps to a French management style that is logical, intellectual, and lacking in intuition. Manifestations of this are evident in the sophisticated planning mechanisms common in large French organisations, a high level of abstraction, and careful attention to organisation.

Alleged deficiencies in the French system are that:

- Its inherent elitism excludes many talented people outside the orthodox hierarchy, especially those from working class backgrounds.

- Selection of entrants to management on the basis of high-level academic achievement can cause company administrations to lack common sense and to lose touch with the objective needs of the market.
- It encourages back-scratching, nepotism and old boy networks.
- The heavy concentration on mathematics distorts the entire education system.
- It produces 'jacks-of-all-trades' without specialist qualifications.
- There is insufficient emphasis on marketing and selling, especially international marketing.

Management training

French business was transformed in the 1960s and 1970s, with rapid economic growth and a general restructuring of firms away from traditional small- to medium-sized family enterprises and towards larger corporations. The removal of protectionist trade barriers, state investment in education and training and the general deregulation of business brought about by the country's membership of the (then) EEC encouraged these larger firms to adopt outward-looking internationalist perspectives. Annual growth rates approached six per cent on average during the 1960s, and exports became an important part of French gross national product. Labour productivity, living standards and educational levels rose to become among the highest in the world.

This expansion led to an upsurge of interest in management training and development, which itself has been encouraged by a law that requires companies to devote 1.5 per cent of the value of their payrolls to training or to forfeit this money to the government. Part of the levy must be used to finance training leave (*see* below), and some for the training of young workers. The levy requirement is reduced to 0.15 per cent of the wage bill for firms employing fewer than ten workers. Tax credits are available for companies that spend more than the statutory minimum on training.

The same law compels firms to publish their training and staff development plans and to grant paid leave (up to a certain limit) to employees wishing to undertake approved courses in further education. Training plans have to specify how the firm proposes spending its training budget and must be submitted for consideration by the company's works council. The actual training can be undertaken in-house or via external bodies. In-house training is most popular, leading to criticisms that the levy has encouraged training that is too narrow and firm specific. It has also been argued that the levy encourages companies *not* to provide training on a voluntary basis. External courses financed by the levy are provided by Chambers of Commerce (to which a part of the training levy is recycled for this purpose), and by private consultants and industry trade associations. These courses often last for several weeks.

Any employee with at least two years' service in an industry and six months with a particular company within it can apply to take a year off work (or 1200 hours part time) on 80 per cent of salary for approved training. The firm recovers its outlay from a central government fund. Workers under 26 years of age with no previous training and three months service with a firm are eligible for 200 hours of training per annum. Employers can refuse requests for training leave if the absences created would account for more than one per cent of total working hours.

Apprenticeships are available, but are few and far between and have much less status than in Germany. They usually last for two years and focus primarily on lower-level technical training.

29. Germany

The destruction of Germany's industrial capacity during the Second World War enabled the country to re-equip with up-to-date technology and to refocus its production towards high-quality advanced technology products specifically designed for international (rather than domestic) markets. This was made possible by the existence of a technically skilled industrial workforce, general consensus between management and labour on the need for improved methods, and government commitment to low inflation and the creation of a stable economic environment. Germany today can boast a first-class public education and vocational training system, a strong R&D orientation within its leading firms, and a commitment to developing human resources within industry unparalleled in the European Union.

German school students cover an extremely broad basic curriculum. They may leave school at age 15, but if they do so must then undertake part-time vocational education until they are at least 18. There are three types of school, catering for academic, intermediate and lower-ability students respectively. A few comprehensive schools operate, mostly in the Berlin area. About a quarter of German 19-year-olds take the Abitur examination, success in which gives the right to attend university. Note however that there are several other routes into German higher education. Student numbers in HE have more than doubled since 1975. Student loans are available; otherwise state support for university students is minimal.

A confusion arises in Germany in that whereas the basic undergraduate qualification is called the Diplom, the Diplom from a technical institute (Fachhochschulen – as opposed to the higher-ranking 'technical high schools' or 'technical universities') does not of itself give admission to postgraduate study. Graduates from Fachhochschulen are supposed to state their qualification as being DIPL(FH), whereas university graduates write Diplom, or sometimes DIPL(U) or (if they are from a technical school or technical university) DIPL(TH) or DIPL(TU). Fachhochschule courses are shorter than university programmes, and much more vocationally oriented. The most popular subjects are mechanical and production engineering, business economics, computing and information technology, and public administration. Sandwich courses are common. The majority of (West) German managers have received a polytechnic or university education, completing their studies at about 27 years of age.

Germans are interested in education generally, and the concept of 'lifelong education' has much currency (up to a quarter of all German adults are estimated to participate in continuing education annually). An interesting feature of the German approach is that it does not apply the same distinctions between arts and sciences that characterise educational divisions in some other countries.

313

Applied technology ('technik') embraces a number of subjects that elsewhere would be viewed as 'theoretical'. 'Technik' is *everything* concerned with manufacture, and technical competence is greatly admired in this nation.

The apprenticeship system

Apprenticeships are available in a wide range of occupations, and a large number of senior German managers have served an apprenticeship at some time during their careers (older people with academic backgrounds sometimes complete apprenticeships in order to obtain an additional and marketable qualification). The full German apprenticeship lasts three years; or two years for semi-skilled work. It comprises practical on-job experience plus day release study. Importantly, technical apprenticeships teach *management and administrative* skills (especially planning and cost accounting) as well as purely technical competencies.

The three-year apprenticeship combines in-company training with general education undertaken in a vocational school (Berufsschulen). Most apprentices are from general and intermediate schools, with a minority (five to ten per cent) from Gymnasia (Grammar Schools). Entrants from the latter will have completed 13 years of basic education, compared with ten and eight years for people from intermediate and general schools respectively. In-company apprenticeship training (which occurs in about half a million firms) is inspected and accredited by Germany's Chambers of Commerce, which register apprentices and conduct examinations. Vocational schools are financed and run by local government. Drop-out rates are low (less than ten per cent) and nine out of ten students pass the examinations.

Each year in excess of half a million apprentices embark on a three-year training programme. Many of the trainees will not be subsequently employed by their training companies. One important consequence of the availability of high-calibre apprenticeships in Germany is that many young people (up to 15 per cent of all school leavers possessing university entrance qualifications in some years) choose not to attend university right away but rather to complete a three-year industrial apprenticeship as their initial post-school qualification. A feature of the system is the low wage paid to apprentices while they are undergoing training (but also producing output), which in part compensates companies for their expenditures on apprentice training.

Apprentices might spend short periods with other firms as part of their programme. Examinations cover both theoretical and practical aspects of the apprentice's work and both must be passed in order to receive a complete certificate (Facharbeiterbrief). The latter is a valuable possession, acting as a passport to well paid work and responsible positions. Also the fact that the German system is standardised means that all employers know *precisely* what a person with a Facharbeiterbrief is able to do, creating thereby a national market for people with these qualifications. Two years after the Facharbeiterbrief has been acquired, a worker can undertake further (examined and certified) courses lasting 2–3 years in order to become a Meister and qualify for higher-level technical occupations. Administrative and organisational skills are taught in the Meister programme. In practice few people sit for higher qualifications until they are about 30 years of age. Possession of higher vocational qualifications can act as a passport to a managerial job.

Vocational education generally

Germany has a long tradition of technical education, stretching back to the medieval guild system. Many vocational education and training (VET) options are available to young (and not so young) people and a variety of vocational schools cater for basic intermediate and higher-level vocational studies. Importantly, there is a *legal obligation* on German employers (a) to release young workers for technical education, and (b) to grant up to one week's training leave per year to any employee demanding the facility. Also there is legislation guaranteeing equality of financial support for students in vocational and 'academic' education.

Vocational schools and colleges are financed by the local governments of the German regions (Laender). On-the-job training is organised jointly by employers and appraised by local Chambers of Commerce and Industry. The implementation of training programmes within a company is subject to control and discussion by its works council. Recipients of vocational education are highly regarded in German society; there does not exist the perception that vocational subjects are somehow inferior to non-vocational studies (an affliction prevalent in certain other EU countries). VET is standardised and formal, with attention being paid to theoretical as well as practical aspects. There is a structured hierarchy of vocational qualifications, with advanced work building on lower-level competencies (as opposed to teaching vocational skills as self-contained units). High-level vocational education is available in universities, technical universities, and technical institutes.

Management training

German managers are noted for their immobility between companies. Internal promotion is the norm and few executives change employers more than a couple of times during their careers. Headhunting is discouraged by the German authorities, although it is not explicitly unlawful.

Not surprisingly, therefore, most management training and development is conducted in-house, although external courses are sometimes used by smaller companies. Programmes tend to be company or industry specific, with more general aspects of management (decision making, employee selection and appraisal, time management, human relations, etc.) being dealt with in higher-level management courses. In-company foreign language courses are common. It is unusual for courses to last longer than a couple of weeks. All German companies have to belong to Chambers of Commerce, which use part of the membership fees they receive to provide management training courses. Chambers of Commerce sometimes possess their own training centres. Also, employers' associations and local government education authorities of certain Laender have established 'management academies' that provide in-house company-specific management development programmes. Courses given by these academies cover such topics as sales management, presentation techniques, and human and industrial relations.

315

On average a third of executive board members in German public companies (AGs) have doctorates; 50 per cent for the country's top 100 businesses.

30. United Kingdom

According to a number of surveys, British companies spend far less on training than French and German firms. Four in five UK manual and three in five non-manual employees have received no training whatsoever since leaving school. High-level vocational training in Britain, moreover, has suffered badly through the decline in the country's manufacturing base, and especially during the deep recession of the early 1980s and 1990s. Today, very few genuine apprenticeship schemes operate within British companies.

UK vocational training is fragmented and, many argue, unable to meet the demands of rapid technological change. Major problems have included the lack of meaningful standardised certification in many occupational areas, absence of liaison and co-ordination among training providers, and the short periods that individuals spend on courses. The British approach leaves industrial training to market forces, without any legal requirements compelling companies to train their employees. British vocational training tends to be firm or industry specific, hence tying the individual to a particular firm or occupation. The British system has also been criticised for focusing on skills, occupations and industries without a future and for being inflexible and generally resistant to change. Weaknesses in the system prompted the British government to introduce in the late 1980s a new framework for vocational education based on National Vocational Qualifications (NVQs), intended to rationalise and consolidate the system, determine national standards of occupational competence, and validate vocational qualifications.

General education

The UK system is largely comprehensive, although the private sector (accounting for about ten per cent of all school students) is extremely influential and provides a disproportionately high proportion of entrants to higher education. British universities and other higher education institutions attract large numbers of overseas students, including a rapidly increasing intake from other EU countries. Foreign students are attracted to the UK by (i) the desire to improve their English (the universal language of business and technology) while acquiring useful skills, (ii) the wide range of courses available in British institutions, and (iii) low fees in comparison with other EU nations. At lower levels however the British educational system has experienced a number of serious problems, including:

(a) A smaller proportion of students entering higher education than in leading competitor nations. Note however that the student drop-out rate is much lower in the UK than in many other European countries.

(b) Lower levels of achievement, on average, in mathematics and science than in other major industrial countries (especially Germany, France, Japan and the USA).

(c) Severe teacher shortages in critical subject areas, notably mathematics and science.

(d) Weaknesses in basic literacy and numeracy among a substantial number of school-leavers. Tests conducted on entrants to the UK Youth Training Scheme (a government programme set up to provide vocational training and work experience for unemployed young people) in the late 1980s revealed that a quarter of trainees had difficulty with elementary arithmetic and nearly a fifth were persistently unable to spell.

Management education

British approaches to management have their philosophical origins in United States business practices, and involve a heavy emphasis on the interpersonal skills aspects of company administration. Short courses are popular, and a number of very large UK companies have their own management training centres. It is probably the case, however, that managers in smaller enterprises receive fewer days of training annually than their counterparts in France or Germany.

Business studies is an extremely popular subject in British universities and colleges, and large numbers of students prepare for accountancy and other professional qualifications on a part-time basis. Training for the professions has a long and prestigious history in this country, and large numbers of young people take this particular route to a management career. The popularity of professional qualifications is due perhaps to:

- their practical orientation
- the ability of a professionally qualified person to make an immediate contribution to the work of a firm, without need for extensive further training
- the fact that individuals 'learn while they earn', hence ensuring that they have relevant work experience by the time they qualify
- their widespread recognition among employers, making a professional qualification an 'entry ticket' to well paid and interesting jobs.

Arguably, too high a premium has in the past been placed on 'gifted amateurism' and the ability to muddle through in chaotic situations. Competition arising from the country's involvement with the Single Market is changing this, however, and the country's increasing dependence on free EU trade is making it potentially adaptive and receptive to new ideas. Note for example the ease with which Japanese companies have been able to inject new business cultures and working methods into their UK operations.

THE EUROPEAN SOCIAL CHARTER

31. Social cohesion

Articles 117–122 of the Treaty of Rome committed the EEC to policies of improving the working and living conditions of all its citizens and to providing equality of opportunity to workers. In 1974 the Council of Ministers adopted its first Social Action Programme intended to achieve full employment, better living and working conditions, and increased participation of employees in management decision making (Rhodes 1992; Gold 1993).

The European Social Fund (ESF)

This was established under Article 123 of the Treaty of Rome with the aims of improving employment opportunities for EEC workers (especially through increasing their geographical and occupational mobility) and raising living standards within the Community as a whole. Initially there were substantial restrictions on how ESF money could be applied. Hence new rules were introduced in 1971 whereby the Fund could be used:

    (*i*) to respond to short-term changes in the Community's employment situation; and

    (*ii*) to help eliminate long-term structural unemployment, particularly in economically underdeveloped regions and areas affected by the decline of a principal industry.

The rules were further amended in 1977 to enable the Fund to concentrate its resources in countries with the worst unemployment problems, and to create jobs for young persons under 25 years of age and additional jobs which fulfil a public need. A number of priorities have been specified, as follows:

(a) Occupational training, especially in new technologies.

(b) Provision of incentives to employers to create new jobs.

(c) Assisting women to return to work after a long break.

(d) Helping young people who left school without acquiring the basic knowledge necessary to undertake vocational training.

Between 25 and 50 per cent of the value of national public expenditure committed to relevant projects is available from ESF sources.

The Social Charter

In 1989 the European Commission formally stated its belief that the completion of the Single Market could only succeed if there was 'social cohesion' (i.e. the bringing together of management and labour and the implementation of measures intended to improve employment and social conditions), and a general acceptance of the consequences of the free movement of people, goods, capital and services by *both* sides of industry (Wise and Gibb 1993). Accordingly it presented to the European Council in October of that year a *Community Charter of Fundamental Social Rights* colloquially known as the European Social Charter.

Origins of the Social Charter

The Charter originated during the 1987 Belgian Presidency of the EU's Council of Ministers. It was put forward as a suggested device for ensuring that basic employment rights would not be eroded following the intense business competition expected to occur in consequence of the completion of the single internal market. Further objectives were to encourage EU governments to harmonise national employment laws and practices and to confirm the EU's commitment to an active social policy. The Social Charter was intended as a grand gesture towards the EU's labour force, representing an unequivocal statement that *people matter* as well as business competition and that the interests of employees are just as important as those of firms.

There was of course an element of political self-interest in the EU's advocacy of the Social Charter, since to the extent that workers feel threatened by free trade and the intensification of business competition they might turn against the Single Market, with damaging political effects. The first draft of the Charter was published by the European Commission in May 1989 with the intention that each member state would implement its requirements at the national (rather than EU) level. Action would not be taken by the EU (via Directives, Regulations, etc.) provided the Charter's basic objectives could be effectively attained by member states or bodies within them.

32. Contents of the Social Charter

The basic rights to be established by the Charter were as follows:

(a) Fair remuneration. This would involve the specification of rules for establishing a fair wage.

(b) Health, protection and safety at the workplace.

(c) Access to vocational training throughout a person's working life, including the right to retraining.

(d) Freedom of association and collective bargaining, i.e. to belong or not belong to a trade union and for unions to have the right to bargain with employing firms.

(e) Integration into working life of disabled people – the provision of training for the disabled, accessibility to work premises, availability of special transport, and explicit consideration of disabled people during the ergonomic design of equipment.

(f) Information, consultation and worker participation in company decision-making, especially in enterprises that operate in more than one EU country.

(g) Freedom of occupation, residence and movement of workers, including equal treatment as regards local taxes and social security entitlements.

(h) Improvement in living and working conditions. This embraces equality of treatment for part-time and temporary workers, controls on night working, and requirements for weekly rest periods and paid holidays.

(i) Social protection, including adequate unemployment and other social security benefits.

(j) Equal treatment of men and women.

(k) Protection of young people, with a minimum working age of 15 years (16 for full-time employment) and a ban on night work for those under 18.

(l) Reasonable living standards for senior citizens, with a specified minimum income underwritten by the state.

Discussions and bargaining followed publication of the May Draft and a number of points were clarified. For example, it was established that Irish trade unions would still be able to offer no-strike deals to foreign companies investing in the Irish Republic, while Portuguese subcontract workers would be exempt from local social security payments while working in other EU states. At the same time, however, negotiations resulted in some ambiguities creeping into the Charter, notably that:

- The requirement that an equitable wage (i.e. a wage sufficient to provide employees with a 'decent standard of living') be established 'by law' was replaced by the requirement that equitable wages be set 'in accordance with arrangements applying in each country'.
- The insistence that each country have laws guaranteeing a worker's right to strike (and hence not face dismissal) was superseded by a right to strike, subject to 'obligations arising under national regulations'.
- Certain issues were classified as 'health and safety' matters (and thus subject to majority rather than unanimous voting so that the UK cannot exercise a veto). But where do 'health and safety' questions end and employment protection issues begin?

The final version was completed in October 1989, was signed in October 1989 by all countries except the UK, and is supported by the European Parliament.

33. The Maastricht Protocol

It is important to note that under the Single European Act 1987 (which amended the Treaty of Rome so as to facilitate the rapid completion of the Single Market), any proposal regarding employee rights and interests and/or the free movement of people requires unanimous agreement among member nations before it becomes legally binding. Accordingly, acceptance of the Social Charter is *voluntary* and may not be imposed on an EU state against its wishes. Accordingly the UK exercised its veto against the implementation of the Social Charter at the 1991 Maastricht summit, thus preventing the Social Charter from passing into EU law. In response the other eleven EU states resolved to adopt key elements of the Charter independently of the EU via a separate Maastricht Protocol that did not involve Britain.

34. The case for the Social Charter

Advocates of the Social Charter claim that it will:

- Create a social partnership between the two sides of industry and will improve social cohesion within the EU, hence raising living standards and the skill levels of workers and greatly contributing to increased productivity.

- Pull together into a unified whole a variety of currently fragmented employment and social policies.
- Have the force of law so that workers will be *guaranteed* certain minimum standards. Note that the Charter insists that signatories commit themselves to 'mobilise all resources necessary' to implement its provisions.
- Ensure a 'level playing field' where employment standards are concerned, with all firms in all EU countries knowing precisely the minimum terms and conditions to be offered to workers. In the absence of harmonised minimum conditions, firms with permanent establishments both in countries applying the Charter and in countries not applying the Charter will need to operate two-tier personnel policies and procedures, leading perhaps to bitter resentments among their lower paid and otherwise disadvantaged employees.

It is important to realise, moreover, that many continental EU trade unions have political links with the centre right rather than (as in France and Britain) the left, notably with Christian Democratic parties. Hence, there is no political mileage to be had from Christian Democrats criticising trade unions, or even the basic principle of social cohesion. Another factor encouraging widespread acceptance of the idea of the Social Charter is the fear expressed by the richer, industrially efficient high-technology countries that without the pan-EU application of minimum social and employment conditions, 'social dumping' is likely.

35. Social dumping

Concerns have been expressed (especially by the German trade unions and the European Trade Union Confederation (ETUC)) that the current situation makes possible the unfair undercutting of the price of labour by low-wage countries. Absence of a minimum wage, lack of employment protection for part-time and casual labour, no maximum working week and the widespread denial of Social Charter benefits enable employers to reduce wage and other employment costs and hence charge lower prices for their outputs.

Social dumping allows firms in certain countries to compete not in terms of the quality of their products, customer care and after-service facilities, etc., but through lowering terms and conditions of employment – possibly including health and safety standards. Also, businesses might set up or relocate their operations in countries with the lowest standards of employment protection, hence creating unemployment, reducing economic growth, and exerting downward pressure on pay and conditions in other nations. This is seen as a violation of Single Market principles and has led to calls for retaliatory actions, e.g. by having the European Commission critically examine the legality of domestic rules on business competition *as a whole* within these countries (merger, takeover and tied distribution arrangements for example).

The huge disparity in the treatment and employment conditions of part-time and casual workers in various EU states has attracted particular criticism. In some nations (e.g. France and Germany), part-timers must by law receive pay and benefits strictly pro rata to full-time workers. Elsewhere there is minimal legal protection, leading to allegations that employers in the latter nations enjoy a significant cost advantage (e.g. by not having to pay social security and occupational pension contributions and not having to provide access to training for part-time employees) compared to employers in other states.

Whether social dumping will in fact lead to the countries involved having a competitive advantage is questionable, since a low-wage low-productivity labour-intensive economy is only suitable for the production of certain items. In the long term it could lack the high technology skills, education and training systems and the dynamics needed for sustainable growth. Also, industrial relations problems may be more severe in low-wage countries.

36. Arguments against the Social Charter

The fundamental objection to the Social Charter is the proposition that unregulated labour markets allocate resources in the most efficient manner possible, boost the competitiveness of businesses, create jobs and attract international investment.

Note moreover that the employee benefits envisaged by the Charter – pro rata pay and equal access to superannuation schemes for part-time workers, protections for the casually employed, a minimum wage, legal rights to vocational training, compulsory employee participation in management decisions, etc. – have *already* been implemented in several industrially advanced continental states. Hence, no *additional* costs will be incurred when these provisions become law. Not surprisingly, therefore, the strongest supporters of the Charter are the EU countries with the most advanced employment protection and social protection legislation, as firms in these nations have nothing to lose through the Charter's introduction. At the same time, these countries have been the most economically successful. Introduction of the Social Charter in other states at high cost to businesses would give firms in the successful and advanced nations a *further* competitive advantage since (unlike firms in rival countries) they will not have to raise their prices.

Other objections to the Social Charter have included the following:

(a) Matters pertaining to consultation, employee representation, etc., are perhaps best resolved through *voluntary* bargaining between employers and trade unions.

(b) Cost increases in certain EU businesses necessitated by the implementation of the Charter could cause them to be uncompetitive compared to companies in Pacific Rim countries and the USA.

(c) As laws on social protection are harmonised there could be a tendency to 'harmonise upwards' towards even higher (and more expensive) common standards thus imposing unbearable additional costs on poorer EU countries.

(d) Application of some of the Charter's provisions would necessitate the creation of large bureaucracies within government departments and much administrative inconvenience within firms.

37. The Social Action Programmes 1992 and 1995

An Action Programme comprising ten Draft Directives on health and safety, seven Draft Directives on employment protection, five EU Recommendations, five statutory instruments, three Decisions of the European Court of Justice and three EU Regulations was proposed in 1992 by the European Commission in order to implement the Charter. Moreover, the Commission has stated its desire to achieve the following:

(a) An extension of the social dialogue between management and labour at both the pan-EU and industry sector levels.

(b) Encouragement of tripartism (*see* **23**) within EU member states. The eleven parties to the Maastricht Protocol agreed in 1991 that any proposal relating to social policy be referred to each nation's central trade union and employers' association for a consultation period of nine months. If consensus on this matter is not forthcoming among the Protocol eleven the European Commission will proceed to draft its own Directive.

(c) Initiation of research intended to identify the possibility for and obstacles to EU (rather than national) level employee relations, including collective bargaining.

The Social Action Programme 1995

Arguably the Social Action Programme announced in 1995 marked a retrenchment of EU social policy, necessitated perhaps by changes in economic conditions. The Programme itself outlined the European Commission's intended work in the social and employment field until 1998 and included the following provisions:

(a) Prioritisation of job creation as the number one goal.

(b) Linkage of social policy to the international competitiveness of EU industry and other economic dimensions.

(c) Extension of EU social policy beyond the world of work.

(d) An increase in the amount of research into social issues sponsored by the European Commission.

(e) Consideration of the possibility of enlarging the European Social Charter to cover a wider range of individual rights and responsibilities.

(f) Introduction of a Draft Directive on the portability of occupational pension rights within the EU.

In addition to the above, the Programme had a section headed 'potential legislative proposals' concerning matters about which consultations were to be initiated with a view to proposing further EU legislation. Subjects listed in this section included part-time work, individual dismissals, the right to payment on public holidays, and parental leave (*see* **8**).

Progress test 16

1. Define human resources management.

2. What is a Euro-executive?

3. List the main problems associated with the management of expatriate staff.

4. What criteria should be used when selecting staff for foreign postings?

5. The Treaty of Rome guarantees freedom of movement for workers. What does this mean in practical terms?

6. What are the implications for personnel management of the free movement of labour within the EU?

7. Give five examples of national differences in personnel management practice.

8. State the purpose of Article 119 of the Treaty of Rome.

9. List the main requirements of the EU Directive on visual display units.

10. The European Union has imposed Directives relating to employment protection in a number of fields. What are these fields?

11. What is the purpose of the Framework Directive on health and safety at work?

12. List the major objectives that have been voiced against the working time Directive 1994.

13. What are the implications for human resources management of the widespread use of casual and part-time employees?

14. Define the term 'employee relations'.

15. Which EU countries have the highest levels of trade union membership?

16. What is a Higher Education Diploma?

17. What were the purposes of the EU's first Social Action Programme?

18. List the main headings under which the European Social Fund is permitted to spend money.

19. What is meant by the term 'social cohesion'?

20. Explain the meaning of the term 'social dumping'.

REFERENCES AND BIBLIOGRAPHY

Abell, M. (ed) (1991), *European Franchising: Law and Practice*, Waterlow.

Agrawal, M. (1995), 'Review of a 40-year Debate in International Advertising: Practitioner and Academician Perspectives on the Standardisation / Adaptation Issue, *International Marketing Review*, 12(1), 26–48.

Alexander, D. (1993), 'A European True and Fair View', *European Accounting Review*, 2, (1), 59–80.

Anderson, O. (1993), 'On the Internationalisation Process of Firms', *Journal of International Business Studies*, Vol.24(2).

Andersen, S.S. and Eliassen, K.A. (1993), *Making Policy in Europe*, Sage.

Anholt, S. (1993), 'Adapting Advertising Copy Across Frontiers', *Admap*, Vol.28(10).

Ansoff, H.I. (1957), 'Strategies for Diversification', *Harvard Business Review*, Sept–Oct.

Archer, C. (1994), *Organizing Europe: The Institutions of Integration*, Edward Arnold.

Ash, N. (1990), 'The Privatization Dilemma', *Euromoney*, September.

Aylen, J. (1987), 'Privatization in Developing Countries', *Lloyds Bank Review*, Issue 163.

August, R. (1993), *International Business Law*, Prentice-Hall.

Baalbaki, I.B. and Malhotra, N.K. (1993), 'Marketing Management Bases for International Market Segmentation', *International Marketing Review*, Vol.10(1).

Van Bael, I. (1990), *Anti-Dumping and Other Trade Protection Laws of the EEC*, 2nd edition, CCH Publishing.

Baines, A. (1995), *Handbook of International Direct Marketing*, Kogan Page.

Balling, M. (1993), *Financial Management in the New Europe*, Basil Blackwell.

Barrell, R. (1990), 'European Currency Union and the EMS', *NIESR Review*, May.

Bartels, R. (1968), 'Are Domestic and International Marketing Dissimilar?', *Journal of Marketing*, Vol.32.

Bean, C. (1992), 'Economic and Monetary Union in Europe', *Journal of Economic Perspectives*, 6(4), 31–52.

Belkaoui, A. (1990), *Judgement in International Accounting: A Theory of Cognition, Cultures, Language and Contracts*, Quorum Publishers.

Bennett, R. (1996), 'Doing Business in a Single European Currency', *International Small Business Journal*, 14(2), 1–7.

Black, J.S. and Gregersen, H.B. (1991), 'The Other Half of the Picture. Antecedents of Spouse Cross-Cultural Adjustment', *Journal of International Business Studies*, 15(3), 19–23.

Boatright, J.R. (1993), *Ethics and the Conduct of Business*, Prentice-Hall.

Baddewyn, J. (1983), 'Foreign and Domestic Divestment and Investment Decisions', *Journal of International Business Studies*, 14(3), 23–35.

Bonaccorsi, A. (1992), 'The Relationship Between Firm Size and Export Intensity', *Journal of International Business Studies*, 23(4), 605–635.

Borden, N.H. (1965), 'The Concept of the Marketing Mix', *Science in Marketing*, (ed), G. Schwartz, Wiley.

Boyacigiller, N. (1991), 'The Role of Expatriates in the Management of Interdependence, Complexity and Risk in Multinational Corporations', *Journal of International Business Studies*, October.

Brewster, C. (1991), *Management of Expatriates*, 2nd edition, Kogan Page.

Brewster, C. (1994), European Human Resource Management versus the American Concept', in Kirkbride, P.S. (ed), *Human Resource Management in Europe*, Routledge.

Brewster, C. and Bournois, F. (1991), 'Human Resource Management: A European Perspective', *Personnel Review*, 20(6), 4–11.

Brewster, C. and Hegewisch, A. (eds), (1994), 'Policy and Practice in European Human Resource Management', *Price Waterhouse/Cranfield Survey*, Routledge.

Bridgeford, J. and Sterling, S. (1994), *Employee Relations in Europe*, Blackwell.

Britton, A. and Mayes, D. (1992), *Achieving Monetary Union in Europe*, Sage.

Brown, L. (1994), *Competitive Marketing Strategy for Europe: Developing, Maintaining and Defending Competitive Advantage*, Macmillan.

Buckley, P.J. and Casson, M. (1976), *The Future of the Multinational Enterprise*, Macmillan.

Buckley, P.J., Pass, C. and Prescott, K. (1989), 'Measures of International Competitiveness: A Critical Survey', *Journal of Marketing Management*, Vol.4(2).

Burt, S. (1989), *Trends and Management Issues in European Retailing*, MCB University Press.

Calof, J.L. and Bearush, P.W. (1995), 'Adapting to Foreign Markets: Explaining Internationalisation', *International Business Review*, 4(2), 115–132.

Carusgil, T., Yavas, U. and Bykowicz, S. (1992), 'Preparing Executives for Overseas Assignments', *Management Decision*, 30, MCB University Press.

Cheng, J.L. (1993), 'The Management of Multinational R&D: A Neglected Topic in International Business Research', *Journal of International Business Studies*, 24(1), 4–24.

Cho, K.R. (1988), 'Issues of Compensation in International Technology Licensing', *Management International Review*, 28(2), 70–79.

Christou, R. (1990), *International Agency, Distribution and Licensing Agreements*, 2nd edition, Longman.

Cobham, D. (1991), 'European Monetary Integration: A Survey of Recent Literature', *Journal of Common Market Studies*, 29(4), 363–83.

Commission of the European Communities [CEC], (1990a), 'Industrial Policy in an Open and Competitive Environment: Guidelines for a Community Approach', *COM* (90) 556, in *Bulletin of the European Communities: European Industrial Policy for the 1990s*, Supplement 3/91, Luxembourg.

Commission of the European Communities [CEC], (1990b), 'Enterprise Policy: A New Dimension for Small and Medium-sized Enterprises', *COM* (90) 328.

Commission of the European Communities [CEC], (1991), 'One Market, One Money', *European Economy*, 44, Commission of the European Communities, Brussels.

Commission of the European Communities [CEC], (1992a), *Easier Cross-Border Payment*, Commission of the European Communities, Brussels.

Commission of the European Communities [CEC], (1992b), *Twenty-First Report on Competition Policy*, Office for Official Publications of the European Community, Luxembourg.

Commission of the European Communities [CEC], (1993a), *Accounting Standards Setting in the EC Member States*, Office for Official Publications of the European Communities, Luxembourg.

Commission of the European Communities [CEC], (1993b), 'The European Community as a World Trade Partner', *European Economy*, No.52.

Commission of the European Communities [CEC], (1996), *Panorama of EU Industries 1995/96*, CEC, Luxembourg.

Corbett, R. (1993), *The Treaty of Maastricht From Conception to Ratification*, Longman.

Cordell, V.V. and Wogtada, N. (1991), 'Modelling Determinants of Cross-Boarder Trade in Counterfeit Goods', *Journal of Global Marketing*, Vol.4(3).

Crawford, M. (ed) (1993), *One Money for Europe*, Macmillan.

Crouch, C. (1993), *Industrial Relations and European State Traditions*, Clarendon.

Dany, F. and Torchy, V. (1994), 'Recruitment and Selection in Europe: Policies, Practices and Methods', in Brewster, C. and Hegewisch, A., *Policy and Practice in European Human Resource Management*, The Price Waterhouse/Cranfield Survey, Routledge.

Day, E., Fox, R.J. and Huszagh, S.M. (1988), 'Segmenting the Global Market', *International Marketing Review*, 5(3), 14–27.

Delors, J. (1989), *Report on Economic and Monetary Union in the European Community*, CEC, Committee for the Study of Economic and Monetary Union, Brussels.

Desta, S. (1985), 'Assessing Political Risk in Less Developed Countries', *Journal of Business Strategy*, 5(5), 40–53.

Devereux, M. and Pearson, M. (1989), *Corporate Tax Harmonisation and Economic Efficiency*, Institute of Fiscal Studies.

Dinan, D. (1994), *Ever Closer Union? An Introduction to the European Community*, Macmillan.

Dore, I.I. (1993), *The UNCITRAL Framework for Arbitration in Contemporary Perspective*, Graham and Trotman.

Dunning, J.H. (1981), *International Production and the Multinational Enterprise*, Allen and Unwin.

Dunning, J.H. (1988), 'The Eclectic Paradigm of International Trade: A Restatement and Some Possible Extensions', *Journal of International Business Studies*, Spring.

Dunning, J.H. (1992), 'The Global Economy, Domestic Governance Strategies and Transnational Corporations: Interactions and Policy Implications', *Transnational Corporations*, 1(3), 7–45.

Economist Intelligence Unit (1994), *Predicting European Banking and Capital Markets*, EIU.

Eichengreen, B. (1991), *Is Europe an Optimum Currency Area?*, National Bureau of Economic Research, Cambridge, Mass.

Eichengreen, B. (1993), 'European Monetary Union', *Journal of Economic Literature*, 31(3), 1321–57.

Emerson, M. and Huhne, C. (1991), *The ECU Report*, Pan.

European Industrial Relations Review [EIRR], (1994a), 'Farewell European Works Councils?', *EIRR*, 242, March.

European Industrial Relations Review [EIRR], (1994b), 'European Works Councils – The Action Begins', *EIRR*, 250, November, pp.14–17.

Eurostat (1995), *Data for Short Term Economic Analysis*, Statistical Office of the European Communities, Luxembourg.

Fagan, M.L. (1991), 'A Guide to Global Sourcing', *Journal of Business Strategy*, April 1991, 21–30.

Fagre, N. and Wells, L.T. (1982), 'Bargaining Power of Multinationals and Host Governments', *Journal of International Business Studies*, 8(2), 9–23.

Featherstone, K. and Ginberg, R. (1993), *The United States and the European Community in the 1990s: Partners in Transition*, Macmillan.

Ferner, A. and Hyman, R. (eds) (1992), *Industrial Relations in the New Europe*, Blackwell.

Ferraro, G.P. (1990), *The Cultural Dimension of International Business*, Prentice-Hall.

Fleming, J.M. (1971), 'On Exchange Rate Unification', *Economic Journal*, Vol.81, 467–488.

Francis, J. (1991), 'The Effects of Cultural Adaptation on International Business Negotiations', *Journal of International Business Studies*, 22(3), 421–422.

Frederick, W.C. (1991), 'Moral Authority of Transnational Corporate Codes', *Journal of Business Ethics*, March 1991, 166–176.

Frydman, R. and Rapaczynski, A. (1993), 'Privatisation in Eastern Europe', *Finance and Development*, June 1993, 12–15.

Gammie, M. (1992), *The Ruding Committee Report: An Initial Response*, Institute for Fiscal Studies.

Gates, S.R. and Engelhoff, W.G. (1986), 'Centralisation in Headquarters – Subsidiary Relationships', *Journal of International Business Studies*, Summer, 1986.

Geroski, P. (1989), 'European Industrial Policy and Industrial Policy in Europe', *Oxford Review of Economic Policy*, 5(0.2), 20–36.

Giles, M. (1986), 'Coping with the New Protectionism', *International Management*, 41(9), 20–26.

Gold, M. (1993), *The Social Dimension: Employment Policy in the European Community*, Macmillan.

Goshal, S. and Nohria, N. (1993), 'Organisational Forms for Multinational Corporations', *Sloan Management Review*, Winter, 1993, 23–35.

Grahl, J. and Teague, P. (1991), 'Industrial Relations Trajectories and European Human Resource Management', in Brewster, C. and Tyson, S. (eds), *International Comparisons in Human Resource Management*, Pitman.

Greenwood, J. *et al.* (eds) (1992), *Organized Interests and the European Community*, Sage.

Grilli, E. (1993), *The European Community and the Developing Countries*, Cambridge University Press.

Gros, D. and Thygesen, M. (1992), *European Monetary Integration: From the European Monetary System to European Monetary Union*, Longman.

Grubel, H.G. (1970), 'The Theory of Optimum Currency Areas', *Canadian Journal of Economics*, 53(2), 318–324.

Guild, I. (1985), *Forfaiting: An Alternative Approach to Export Trade Financing*, Woodhead-Faulkner.

Haack, W.G.C.M. (1972), 'The Economic Effects of Britain's Entry into the Common Market', *Journal of Common Market Studies*, 11(2), December.

Hamill, J. (1992), 'Cross-Border Mergers, Acquisitions and Alliances in Europe', in S. Young and J. Hamill (eds), *Europe and the Multinationals: Issue and Responses for the 1990s*, Edward Elgar.

Hamilton, C. and Winter, L.A. (1992), 'Opening Up International Trade in Eastern Europe', *Economic Policy*, 14(1), 77–116.

Harrell, G.D. and Kiefer, R.O. (1993), 'Multinational Market Portfolios in Global Strategy', *International Marketing Review*, 10(1), 60–73.

Harvey, M.G. and Lusch, R.F. (1995), 'A Systematic Assessment of Potential International Strategic Alliance Partners', *International Business Review*, 4(2), 195–212.

Hawk, B. (ed), (1991), *International Mergers and Joint Ventures*, Chancery Law Publishing.

Hawkins, D.T. (1993), *Business of Factoring: A Guide to Factoring and Invoice Discounting*, McGraw-Hill.

Hartmann, F.H. (1983), *The Relations of Nations*, 6th edition, Macmillan.

Hegarty, J. (1993), 'Accounting Integration in Europe – Still on Track?', *Journal of Accountancy*, 17(1), 92–5.

Hegewisch, A. (1993), 'The Decentralisation of Pay Bargaining: European Comparisons', in Hegewisch, A. and Brewster, C. (eds), *European Developments in Human Resource Management*, Kogan Page.

Helm, D. (1993), 'The European Internal Market: The Next Steps', *Oxford Review of Economic Policy*, 9(1), 1–14.

Hofstede, G. (1980), *Culture's Consequences: International Differences in Work Related Values*, Sage.

Hofstede, G. (1991), *Cultures and Organisations*, McGraw-Hill.

Hollinshead, G. and Leat, M. (1995), *Human Resource Management: An International and Comparative Perspective*, Pitman.

Hollis Europe, *The Directory of European Public Relations and PR Networks 1995–96*, 5th edition, Hollis, 1995.

Van Hulle, K. (1993), 'Harmonization of Accounting Standards in the EC. Is it the Beginning or the End?', *European Accounting Review*, 2(3), 387–96.

Hymer, S.H. (1976), *The International Operations of National Firms: A Study of Direct Investment*, MIT Press, Cambridge, Mass.

Incomes Data Services (1995), *Contracts and Terms and Conditions of Employment*, Institute of Personnel and Development.

Jackson, J.H. (1990), *Restructuring the GATT System*, Pinter.

Jacquemin, A. (1993), 'The International Dimension of European Competition Policy', *Journal of Common Market Studies*, 31(1), 91–101.

Jacquemin, A. and Wright, D. (1993), 'Corporate Strategies and European Challenges Post-1992', *Journal of Common Market Studies*, 31(4), 525–37.

James, C.D. (1987), *Tariff and Non-Tariff Barriers to Trade*, Department of Trade and Industry.

Jeffcote, B. (1993), *The Developing European Corporate Tax System*, Macmillan.

Johansson, J.K. and Thorelli, H.B. (1985), 'International Product Positioning', *Journal of International Business Studies*, 16(3), 57–75.

Johnson, H.G. (1963), 'Equilibrium Under Fixed Exchange Rates', *American Economic Review*, Vol.53, 112–116, (Papers and Proceedings).

Julius, D.A. (1990), *Global Companies and Public Policy: The Growing Challenge of Foreign Investment*, Pinter, for The Royal Institute of International Affairs.

Justicia, I. (1994), 'European Late Payments Survey', *Euro-Information*, December 1994, 75/94/EN, Commission of the European Communities.

Kay, N. (1993), 'Mergers, Acquisitions and the Completion of the Internal Market', in K.S. Hughes (ed), *European Competitiveness*, Cambridge University.

O'Keefe, D. and Twomey, P.M. (eds), (1994), *Legal Issues of the Maastricht Treaty*, Chancery.

Khan, M.S. (1988), 'Islamic Interest Free Banking', *IMF Fund Papers*, March 1988.

Kirkbride, P.S. (ed), (1994), *Human Resource Management in Europe: Perspectives for the 1990s*, Routledge.

Kotabe, M. (1989), 'Creating Countertrade Opportunities in Financially Distressed Developing Countries', *International Marketing Review*, 6(5), 36–49.

Kotabe, M. (1993), 'Patterns and Technological Implications of Global Sourcing Strategies', *Journal of International Marketing*, 11(1), 26–43.

Kotler, P. (1984), 'Rethinking the Marketing Concept', in *American Marketing Association News*, Vol.18, 1984.

Krugman, P. (1979), 'A Model of Innovation, Technology Transfer and the World Distribution of Income', *Journal of Political Economy*, 87(1), 253–266.

Kwon, Y.C. and Konopa, L.J. (1993), 'Impact of Host Country Market Characteristics on the Choice of Foreign Market Entry Mode', *International Marketing Review*, Vol.10(2).

Lamming, R. (1993), *Beyond Partnership: Strategies for Innovation and Lean Supply Relationships*, Prentice-Hall.

Lasok, D. and Bridge, J.W. (1991), *Law and Institutions of the European Communities*, 5th edition, Butterworths.

Lawrence, P. (1993), 'Human Resource Management in Germany', in Tyson, S., *et al.*, *Human Resource Management in Europe, Strategic Issues and Cases*, Kogan Page.

Leeds, C., Kirkbride, P.S. and Durcan, J. (1994), 'The Cultural Context of Europe: A Tentative Mapping', in Kirkbride, P.S., *Human Resource Management in Europe: Perspectives of the 1990s*, Routledge.

Lefferink, J.D. (ed), (1993), *European Integration and Environmental Policy*, Belhaven.

Levitt, T. (1983), 'The Globalisation of Markets', *Harvard Business Review*, Vol.61, May/June.

Litka, M. (1991), *International Dimension of the Legal Environment of Business*, PWS Kent, Boston.

Littler, D. and Schlieper, K. (1995), 'The Development of the Eurobrand', *International Marketing Review*, 12(2), 22–37.

Lodge, J. (ed), (1994), *The European Community and the Challenge of the Future*, 2nd edition, Pinter Publishers.

Lorange, P. and Roos, J. (1992), *Strategic Alliances: Formation, Implementation and Evolution*, Blackwell.

McCarthy, E.J. (1981), *Basic Marketing: A Managerial Approach*, Irwin.

McEnery, J. and Desharnais, G. (1990), 'Culture Shock', *Training and Development Journal*, April 1990.

McKinnon, R. (1977), 'The Euro-Currency Markets', *Essays in International Finance*, No.125, Princeton University, December 1977.

Magnifico, G. (1973), *European Monetary Unification*, Macmillan.

Maresceau, M. (ed), (1993), *The European Community's Commercial Policy After 1992*, Dordrecht: Martinus Nijhoff.

Maronick, T.J. (1988), 'European Patent Laws and Decisions: Implications for Multinational Marketing Strategy', *International Marketing Review*, 5(2), 20–30.

Maskers, K.E. (1993), 'Intellectual Property Right and the Uruguay Round', *Economic Review*, Spring 1993, 11–26.

Matsumoto, K. and Finlayson, G. (1990), 'Dumping and Anti-dumping: Growing Problems in World Trade', *Journal of World Trade*, Vol.24(4).

Mayes, D. (ed), (1993), *The External Implications of European Integration*, Harvester-Wheatsheaf.

Mazey, S. and Richardson, J. (1993), *Lobbying in the European Community*, Oxford University Press.

Mendelsohn, M. (1993), *Franchising in Europe*, Cassell.

Mendelsohn, M. and Harris, B. (1991), *Franchising and the Block Exemption Regulation*, Longman.

Millet, T. (1990), *The Court of First Instance of the European Communities*, Butterworths.

Mole, J. (1990), *Mind Your Manners: Managing Culture Clash in the Single European Market*, Industrial Society.

Monnet, J. (1978), *Memoirs*, Collins.

Moynihan, M. (1993), 'How MNCs Ease Expatriates' Return to Home Countries', *Business International*, February 1993.

Mundell, R.A. (1961), 'A Theory of Optimum Currency Areas', *American Economic Review*, 51(4), 657–664.

Murdock, G.P. (1945), 'The Common Denominator of Cultures', in R. Linton (ed), *The Science of Man*, Columbia University Press.

Neven, D. Nuttall, R. and Seabright, P. (1993), *Merger in Daylight: The Economics and Politics of European Merger Control*, Centre for Economic Policy Research.

Nicolaides, P. (1989), 'Economic Aspects of Services: Implications for a GATT Agreement', *Journal of World Trade*, 23(1), 125–136.

Nicoll, W. and Salmon, T.C. (1994), *Understanding the New European Community*, 2nd edition, Harvester-Wheatsheaf.

Nugent, N. (1994), *The Government and Politics of the European Union*, 3rd edition, Macmillan.

Ohlin, B. (1933), *Interregional and International Trade*, Harvard University Press.

Ohmae, K. (1985), *Triad Power, The Coming Shape of Global Competition*, The Free Press.

Ouchi, W.G. (1981), *Theory Z: How American Business Can Meet the Japanese Challenge*, Addison-Wesley.

Page, S. (1991), *The GATT Uruguay Round: Effects on Developing Countries*, Overseas Development Institute.

Papadopoulos, N. and Heslop, L. (eds), (1992), *Product Country Images: Impact and Role in International Marketing*, Irwin.

Peterson, J. (1992), 'Technology Policy in Europe: Explaining the Framework Programme and Eureka in Theory and Practice', *Journal of Common Market Studies*, 24(3), 269–90.

Pitt-Watson, D. and Frazer, S. (1991), 'Eastern Europe: Commercial Opportunity or Illusion?', *Long Range Planning*, 24(5), 19–24.

Poirson, P. (1993), 'Human Resource Management in France', in Tyson, S., *et al.* (eds), *Human Resource Management in Europe*, Kogan Page.

Poorsoltan, K. (1993), 'The US and Mexico Debate Free Trade', *Contemporary Review*, Vol.263, October 1993.

Porter, M. (1980), *Competitive Strategy*, The Free Press.

Porter, M. (1990), *The Competitive Advantages of Nations*, Macmillan.

Pucik, V. (1984), 'The International Management of Human Resources' in Fombrun, C.J., Tichy, N.M. and Devanna, M.A. (eds), *Strategic Human Resources Management*, Wiley.

Randlesome, C., Brierly, W., Burton, K., Gordon, C. and King, P. (1990), *Business Cultures in Europe*, Heinemann.

Rhodes, M. (1991), 'The Social Dimension of the Single European Market', *European Journal of Political Research*, 19(1), 245–80.

Rhodes, M. (1992), 'The Future of the Social Dimension', *Journal of Common Market Studies*, 30(1), 27–35.

Robson, P. and Wooton, I. (1993), 'The Transnational Enterprise and Regional Economic Integration', *Journal of Common Market Studies*, 31(1), 71–90.

Roney, A. (1993), *The European Community Factbook*, 3rd edition, Kogan Page.

Roessler, F. (1985), 'The Scope, Limits and Function of the GATT Legal System', *The World Economy*, 8(4), 287–298.

Rothery, B. (1992), *BS7750: The International Environment Standard*, Gower.

Royal Mail International (1994), *Marketing Without Frontiers*, 2nd edition, RMI.

Ruding, O. (1992), *Ruding Report (Committee on the Taxation of Enterprises Within the EC)*, Luxembourg, Office for Official Publications of the European Communities.

Samiee, S. and Roth, K. (1992), 'The Influence of Global Marketing', *Journal of Marketing*, Vol.56, April 1992.

Sbragia, A. (ed), (1993), *Euro-Politics: Institutions and Policymaking in the New European Community*, The Brookings Institution.

Schwartz, G. and Lopes, P.S. (1993), 'Privatisation: Expectations, Trade-Offs and Results', *Finance and Development*, June 1993, 15–21.

Seringhaus, F.H. (1986), 'The Impact of Government Export Marketing Assistance', *International Marketing Review*, 3(2), 37–56.

Sharp, M. and Pavitt, K. (1993), 'Technology Policy in the 1990s: Old Trends and New Realities', *Journal of Common Market Studies*, 31(2), 129–51.

Simpson, J.R. (1991), 'Rules of Origin in Transition', *Law and Policy in International Business*, 22(4), 665–672.

Singleton, S. (1995), 'Franchising', *Europe Bulletin*, Issue 29, July.

Starr, P. (1989), 'The Meaning of Privatization', in *Privatization and the Welfare State* (eds Kamerman, S.B. and Khan, A.), Princeton University Press.

Stalk, G. (1990), *Competing Against Time: How Time-Based Competition is Reshaping Global Markets*, Collier Macmillan.

Streeton, P. (1992), 'Interdependence and Integration of the World Economy The Rule of States and Firms', *Transnational Corporations*, 1(3), 125–36.

Subhash, C.J. and Tucker, L.R. (1995), 'The Influence of Culture on Strategic Constructs in the Process of Globalisation', *International Business Review*, 4(1), 19–38.

Swamidass, P.M. (1993), 'Import Sourcing Dynamics: An Integrated Perspective', *Journal of International Business Studies*, 24(4), 93–114.

Teague, P. (1993), 'Between Convergence and Divergence: Possibilities for a European Community System of Labour Market Regulation', *International Labour Review*, 123(3), 391–406.

Terpstra, V. (1987), 'The Evolution of International Marketing', *International Marketing Review*, Summer, 1987.

Thorelli, H.B. (1966), 'The Multinational Corporation as a Change Agent', *Southern Journal of Business*, July, 1966, 5–11.

Tillotson, J. (1993), *European Community law: Text, Cases and Materials*, Cavendish Publishing.

Tixier, M. (1994), 'Management and Communication Styles in Europe: Can They Be Compared and Matched?', *Employee Relations Journal*, 16(1), 8–26.

de la Torre, J. and Neckar, D.H. (1988), 'Forecasting Political Risk for International Operations', *International Journal of Forecasting*, 4(1), 221–230.

Tsoukalis, L. (1993), *The New European Economy: The Politics and Economics of Integration*, Oxford University Press.

US International Trade Commission (1993), *Potential Impact on the US Economy of the North American Free Trade Agreement*, US Congress, 1993.

Usunier, J.C. (1993), *International Marketing: A Cultural Approach*, Prentice-Hall.

Verzariu, P. (1985), *Countertrade, Barter Offsets*, McGraw-Hill.

Walsh, V. (1992), *Winning by Design: Technology, Product Design and International Competitiveness*, Blackwell Business.

Watkins, K. (1992), *Fixing the Rules: North-South Issues in International Trade and the GATT Uruguay Round*, Institute for International Relations, London, 1992.

Weigand, R.E. (1991), 'Parallel Import Channels', *Colombia Journal of World Business*, Spring, 1991.

Weiss, K. and Grippo, L.E. (1992), 'Look Carefully Before you Leap into that Overseas Assignment', *Journal of European Business*, June, 1992.

Welch, L.S. (1992), 'Developments in International Franchising', *Journal of Global Marketing*, 6(2), 81–96.

Welch, L.S. and Pacifico, A. (1990), 'Management Contracts: A Role in Internationalisation', 7(4), 64–74.

Wells, L.T. (ed), (1972), *The Product Life Cycle and International Trade*, Harvard University Press.

Wells, L.T. (1980), 'A Product Lifecycle for International Trade', in *International Marketing Strategy*, eds, H. Thorelli and H. Becker, Pergamon, New York.

Welt, L. (1990), *Trade Without Money: Barter and Countertrade*, Harcourt Brace Jovanovich, New York, 1990.

Whitelock, J.M. (1987), 'Global Marketing and the Case for International Product Standardisation', *European Journal of Marketing*, 23(7), 60–7.

Whittaker, S. and Roney, A. (1993), *Guidance on the Commercial Agents Regulations*, London Chamber of Commerce and Industry.

Wills, J. Jacobs, L. and Palia, A. (1986), 'Countertrade', *International Marketing Review*, Vol.3(2).

Wise, M. and Gibb, R. (1993), *Single Market to Social Europe: The European Community in the 1990s*, Longman.

Wortzel, L.H. (1990), 'Global Strategies: Standardization Versus Flexibility', in *Global Strategic Management: The Essentials*, 2nd edition (eds, Wortzel, H.V. and Wortzel, L.H.), Wiley.

Wyatt, D. and Dashwood, A. (1993), *European Community Law*, Sweet and Maxwell.

Young, S., Hamill, J., Wheeler, C. and Davies, J.R. (1989), *International Market Entry and Development*, Prentice-Hall.

INDEX